# Praise for
## A BRIEF HISTOR
# CHINA

"…a powerful, engaging and balanced account of the vast span of China's history… The reader can approach this book with confidence and—thanks to its well-chosen reading recommendations—use it as a springboard for deeper engagement with China, its culture and its people."

— **Ellis Tinios**, Honorary Lecturer in East Asian History, University of Leeds

"Clements' spare prose, bad-boy wit and encyclopedic knowledge of Asian facts, gossip and trivia put paid to any misgivings about uttering 'history' and 'page-turner' in the same breath. This succinct chronicle of China's rise to global power is essential reading for businessmen, politicians and creatives."

— **J. Christopher Westland**, Author of *Red Wired: China's Internet Revolution* and Overseas Chair Professor of Thousand-Talents Plan Scholar, Beihang University

"*A Brief History of China* is a pacy romp through China's long and layered history that successfully walks the tightrope of the scholarly and the entertaining. In brisk, engaging prose, Clements covers this book's vast territory with authority."

— **Pallavi Aiyar**, Author of *Smoke and Mirrors: An Experience of China*

"Clements tackles more than 5,000 years of Chinese history in an agile but comprehensible narrative of the Heavenly Kingdom. Useful for the general reader, the book has special value for the business person looking to understand the single largest commercial market in the world."

— **Alfonso Asensio**, Author of *World Wide Data* and *Chief Kickboxing Officer*

"Clements brings to light the voices of the hidden and the marginalized, through snapshots of real people, and readings between the lines of poetry, historical records, and contemporary literature. He pays particular attention to women, uncovering their often-buried impact on China's past, and…takes China's history back to its diverse human core, immersing booklovers in a vast cast of characters and a gripping narrative, effortlessly easy to enjoy."

— **Roxy Simons**, *AllTheAnime.com*

"Where was this book a decade ago, when I landed in China and needed a crash course on the country and the culture? With humor, respect, and a deft hand, Clements simplifies the complicated politics of 5,000 years of history and makes it accessible. He highlights and humanizes the most formative events and the people involved, so as not to overwhelm readers, and gives us insight into how events that happened long ago still resonate today."

— **Alicia Noel**, Founder & CEO, Cultivati, Inc.

# A BRIEF HISTORY OF
# CHINA

**DYNASTY, REVOLUTION AND TRANSFORMATION:**
**FROM THE MIDDLE KINGDOM TO THE PEOPLE'S REPUBLIC**

Jonathan Clements

TUTTLE Publishing

Tokyo | Rutland, Vermont | Singapore

## "Books to Span the East and West"

**Tuttle Publishing** was founded in 1832 in the small New England town of Rutland, Vermont [USA]. Our core values remain as strong today as they were then—to publish best-in-class books which bring people together one page at a time. In 1948, we established a publishing office in Japan—and Tuttle is now a leader in publishing English-language books about the arts, languages and cultures of Asia. The world has become a much smaller place today and Asia's economic and cultural influence has grown. Yet the need for meaningful dialogue and information about this diverse region has never been greater. Over the past seven decades, Tuttle has published thousands of books on subjects ranging from martial arts and paper crafts to language learning and literature—and our talented authors, illustrators, designers and photographers have won many prestigious awards. We welcome you to explore the wealth of information available on Asia at www.tuttlepublishing.com.

Published by Tuttle Publishing, an imprint of Periplus Editions (HK) Ltd.

www.tuttlepublishing.com

Copyright © 2019 by Jonathan Clements

Library of Congress Cataloging in Publication Data in process

ISBN 978-0-8048-5005-6

25 24 23 22
10 9 8 7 6 5 4 3 2    2205TP
Printed in Singapore

TUTTLE PUBLISHING® is a registered trademark of Tuttle Publishing, a division of Periplus Editions (HK) Ltd.

Distributed by:

**North America, Latin America & Europe**
Tuttle Publishing
364 Innovation Drive, North Clarendon VT
05759 9436, USA
Tel: 1(802) 773 8930
Fax: 1(802) 773 6993
info@tuttlepublishing.com
www.tuttlepublishing.com

**Asia Pacific**
Berkeley Books Pte Ltd
3 Kallang Sector #04-01
Singapore 349278
Tel: (65) 6741 2178
Fax: (65) 6741 2179
inquiries@periplus.com.sg
www.tuttlepublishing.com

**Japan**
Tuttle Publishing
Yaekari Building 3rd Floor
5-4-12 Osaki Shinagawa-ku
Tokyo 141 0032 Japan
Tel: 81 (3) 5437 0171
Fax: 81 (3) 5437 0755
sales@tuttle.co.jp
www.tuttle.co.jp

# CONTENTS

# Province Map

# Physical Map

KAZAKHSTAN

ALTAI
MOUNTAINS

KYRGYZSTAN

TIAN SHAN
RANGE

TAJIKISTAN

TARIM
BASIN

PAKISTAN

KUNLAN
MOUNTAINS

TIBETAN
PLATEAU

HIMALAYA MOUNTAINS

NEPAL

▲
Mt Everest
8848m

BHUTAN

INDIA

INDIA

BANGLADESH

MYANMAR

QIO
L
RAN

Mekong River

RUSSIA

MONGOLIA

GOBI
DESERT

LESSER
KHINGAN
RANGE

MANCHURIAN
PLAIN

CHANGBAI
RANGE

D.P.R.
KOREA

TAIHANG
MOUNTAINS

LOESS
PLATEAU

Yellow River

REP. OF
KOREA

Yellow
Sea

JAPAN

NORTH
CHINA
PLAIN

Yangtze River

SICHUAN
PLAIN

East
China
Sea

tze River

YUNNAN-
GUIZHOU
PLATEAU

SOUTHERN
HILLS

Xi River

VIETNAM

South
China
Sea

PHILIPPINES

110°E

120°E

130°E

50°N

40°N

30°N

20°N

# Dynasties of China

| | |
|---|---|
| Xia | c. 2100 BCE |
| Shang | c. 1600–1027 BCE |
| Zhou | 1027–256 BCE |
| Western Zhou | 1027–771 BCE |
| Eastern Zhou | 771–256 BCE |
| Spring and Autumn Period | 722–481 BCE |
| Warring States Period | 481–221 BCE |
| Qin | 221–206 BCE |
| Han | 206 BCE–220 CE |
| Former Han | 206 BCE–8 CE |
| Xin Interregnum | 8–23 |
| Later Han | 23–220 |
| Three Kingdoms | 220–280 |
| Western Jin | 265–317 |
| Southern and Northern Dynasties | 317–589 |
| Sui | 589–618 |
| Tang | 618–907 |
| Five Dynasties | 907–960 |
| Song | 960–1279 |
| Northern Song | 960–1126 |
| Southern Song | 1126–1279 |
| Yuan | 1271–1368 |
| Ming | 1368–1644 |
| Qing | 1644–1912 |

# Notes on Names

N ames are the nemesis of any popular account of Chinese history. Kong Qiu was known to his disciples as Master Kong—Kong Fuzi. Two thousand years later, this was garbled into Latin by Jesuit missionaries as Confucius. A brief history of China, such as this, can save dozens of pages by simply calling him Confucius, and trying not to get bogged down in the many similar crises of nomenclature that afflict almost every Chinese figure in some way. There are too many monosyllables, too many associations—the general reader cannot be expected to know her Chu (area south of the Yangtze) from her Shu (ancient Sichuan), and must remain ever watchful so as not to forget that Emperor Wu of the Han Dynasty (Han Wudi) is not the same as Emperor Wu of the Liang Dynasty (Liang Wudi).

Nomenclature can often reflect cultural assumptions—writers often mention the Northern and Southern Dynasties, but this echoes the rhythm of English speech. In Chinese, they are called the Southern and Northern Dynasties, reflecting not only the fact that south comes at the top of ancient Chinese maps, but that the chroniclers of later dynasties put the Han-centered, culturally "Chinese" south first.

When it comes to cities, I usually use the modern name—Beijing, Shanghai, Guangzhou—not one of the dozens of period-specific names. Even Beijing has had a dozen different names over the course of its history—I usually refer to it as Beijing ("Northern Capital"), even during those periods where the capital was elsewhere. When it was the capital of the Northern Wei, Datong was called Pingcheng, but this is of no use to you in a book that leaves the Northern Wei behind after only a few pages. I make a special exception for Chang-an (Xi'an), as it so often is mentioned by its archaic name in texts of the imperial era.

Chinese figures have nicknames and courtesy names, *nommes de guerre*, pseudonyms, and pen-names. Laozi was a title, not a name, of a man whose given name was thought to be Li Er. Sun Zi was "Master Sun"—

his real name may have been Sun Wu, although it seems that that, too, was more of a title. There are over twenty variant spellings of the name of the monk Xuanzang, although many books, including several of my own, use his nickname Tripitaka, the Sanskrit term for the Buddhist canon.

Chinese nomenclature often anachronistically uses the highest title achieved by an individual in their lifetime; occasionally, posterity even uses posthumous titles reflecting a promotion brought about by a successful descendant, or a demotion by a vindictive enemy. Yang Yuhuan, the beauty blamed for the fall of the Xuanzong Emperor, is universally referred to as Yang *Guifei*—Yang *the Precious Consort*, although many foreign authors assume that Guifei was her given name. Emperor Xuánzong (r. 713–756) and Emperor Xuānzong (r. 846–859) have different names in Chinese, but they look the same without the diacritic marks that have been scrubbed from this general account. Accordingly the latter is distinguished in my text from his great (x4) grandfather as being "Xuanzong II," not a form of address that a Chinese reader would recognize or condone.

I've clung to the more Mongol-friendly spelling of Khubilai for the ruler of China also sometimes written as Kublai, Qubilai, and in poetic form, Kubla. He's also known as Hubilai in Chinese, Fubirai in Japanese and Hot-Tat-Liet in Vietnamese, so life could have been much more difficult for all of us. Zheng Chenggong is usually known as Coxinga or Koxinga in English sources, but these reflect the Hokkien pronunciation of his title, the Knight of the National Surname, which in Mandarin is Guoxingye. I refer to him as Koxinga in my text, as that is the spelling that has achieved widespread usage in modern Taiwan, although my own book on the subject, *Coxinga and the Fall of the Ming Dynasty*, reflects English orthography more common in the 20th century. Sun Yat-sen was an alias for a man known in Chinese as Sun Zhongshan. Jiang Jieshi is better known abroad by the Cantonese pronunciation of his name, Chiang Kai-shek. Chairman Mao Zedong, as he is named with the 1950s Pinyin Romanization system, was known in English throughout most of his life as Mao Tse-tung, using the older Wade-Giles system.

And then there are the Emperors, beginning with the First Emperor (Shi Huangdi), named as such in this book for his combination of the terms *huang* and *di*, both of which are also sometimes translated by other authors as "emperor." I have translated those precursors variously as "sovereign" and "king," otherwise the empire of the "first" emperor only arises after a millennium of lesser "emperors" ruling regions more like kingdoms. As for what they were called, many of emperors are known to posterity not by their given name—which was taboo after their coronation in any context, even if it happened to have been the name of a famous mountain or river!—but by their reign title or temple name. So Liu Bang is usually known in Chinese by the imperial title he would eventually claim, Han Gaozu, even though it would be an anachronism in this book to call him that for much of the events described. The girl nicknamed Wu Meiniang (Fair Flirty Wu) by her first husband, would be known as Wu Hou (Empress Wu) while married to her second, and ultimately crowned as the first and only ruler of the short-lived "[Later] Zhou Dynasty." She is usually referred to in Chinese as Wu Zetian (Wu the Equal of Heaven), and in English as Empress Wu, although if we really want to split hairs, English does not distinguish between a female imperial consort and a female sovereign ruler, so some historians insist that it is more accurate to call her *Emperor* Wu.

And I probably shouldn't bring this up, lest I scare you off, but most of the above pronunciations are wrong. Or rather, they use the modern transcription of words that have transformed over the centuries. Many ancient poems don't rhyme any more in modern Mandarin, having been garbled down the centuries. Much of the tonal component of Chinese, in fact, is a remnant of missing archaic phonemes, much as the English word *what* becomes a second-tone glottal-stopped *wó* in my native Essex. The Old Chinese *khla* (chariot) is now *che*; the modern *mi* (honey) was once *mit*. *Sichya*, which once meant lion, is now pronounced *shizi*. *He* and *Jiang*, two modern words for river in Mandarin, sounded more like *Gai* and *Krong* in Old Chinese, the latter echoed in the *khlong* of modern Thai. Much as the best way to hear the English of the Dark Ages now requires a trip to Iceland, if you want to know what Chinese really sounded like in the Tang dynasty, you're better off eavesdropping on the streets of Guangzhou in the far south, or taking in a Sichuan opera. The Nan-yue people of southern China's frontier in the Han dynasty sounded more like Nam-viet at that time, and retained the phonemes in their local speech. Two millennia later, they would transpose the same characters to name their territory Vietnam. Throughout this book I use the modern Mandarin pronunciations, because without them you would never be able to look up any of the nouns elsewhere, but it was sorely tempting to refer to the State of Chu not by that name at all, but to use its pronunciation in 400 BCE, which was liable to have been something more like *Tshra*.

I have juggled hundreds of such issues in the background to spare you such endless qualifications and footnotes. Wonderful though it would be for us to talk about the resistance to the first Dzin emperor by the rebels of Tshra, nobody else would understand us, except perhaps Axel Schuessler, author of the *Etymological Dictionary of Old Chinese*.

# Preface

"Let the past serve the present." The word for history in Chinese, *lishi*, combines two terms from the high priesthood of the ancient Shang people: one meant to calculate or set things in series, the other used to mean an astrologer, one who watched the skies in search of omens and used them to predict the future.

History in the West is an enquiry. It is a constant, evolving quest to work out *what has happened here*, incorporating new findings and ideas. In China, it can often seem more like the reins or muzzle on a struggling beast, as new riders try to break it to their will. Vengeful enemies erase their rivals' names from the record. Entire cultures are written off as "barbarians"—their music and poetry unrecorded, their customs ignored—then co-opted into Chinese history almost overnight. Among modern China's 55 ethnic minorities (and indeed, within the genetic composition of the Han Chinese themselves) are the remnants of invading tribes that stayed and went native. Others are pushed far away from their place of origin, banished from their homelands by wars and struggles remembered now only as legends. Peasant rebellions, once written off as acts of treachery against the emperor, attained a new cachet in the Communist era as forerunners of class struggle.

Modern technology expands our ability to interpret the evidence that has survived. Computer simulations can recreate the appearance of the night sky once seen by a Bronze Age king. Digital photography collates and tags the facial features of every Terracotta Warrior. Simple word-processing software can search through the texts of the entire classical canon, transforming our understanding of problematic passages in ancient texts.

Those same technologies, which have so greatly expanded our understanding, can also be used to suppress it. The Great Firewall of China blocks local scholars from accessing many foreign publications on the Internet. Meanwhile, entire articles have been redacted from the online editions of Chinese journals if they no longer reflect the favored reality.

Skeptics of whatever the current consensus might be are pilloried in modern China as "historical nihilists"—the implication being that there is only one, approved narrative of history, and that anyone who questions it is sowing confusion and dissent. But this is merely the most modern manifestation of a tradition that has tampered with the evidence for centuries. The chronicles of many dynasties were usually set down by their successors, pushing historians and scribes to explain the failures of the last regime by concocting tall tales of hubris and repression, and divine portents of justifiable resistance.

Even proper nouns can be hard to pin down. Scribes were not allowed to use an emperor's true name in documents, causing a whole slew of places and people to be assigned new identifiers after any coronation. It was considered presumptuous to address a lady by her name, causing thousands of women in Chinese history to be known only by a vague descriptor or the names of their fathers. Noble titles are conferred not only on aristocrats, but also on their ancestors, leading to "emperors" who died before their grandson ever founded the dynasty, while men who died in disgrace are rehabilitated and posthumously ennobled or promoted. I have done my best to deal with these issues behind the scenes, keeping the main text as concise as possible—for some of the headaches facing an author in matters Chinese, see the Notes on Names.

Books are burned; traitors' families are annihilated through nine degrees; entire lost races are remembered only by the names used for them by their enemies; one religion piously vandalizes the relics of another; bronzes are melted down and recycled; temples drown beneath the waters of a modern reservoir. And yet, Chinese history is full of modern disclosures and surprises—Cave #17, the sealed "Library" in Dunhuang, was found stacked to the roof with lost Silk Road texts. Farmers sinking a well in drought-stricken Lintong uncovered the 7,000-strong Terracotta Army. Builders putting an annex on a hospital in Mawangdui, Changsha, smashed their way into an ancient noble's tomb, stacked with copies of books long thought lost. Truly vast resources and archives are available to the modern scholar—the chronicles of entire dynasties, love songs about people who have been dead for three thousand years…if we are daunted at the prospect of summarizing Chinese history in a single book, it is often not because of what has been lost, but the overwhelming amount that still remains.

Modern China contains 33 provinces, municipalities and special administrative areas, every one of them the size of a US state or European country. Its northernmost regions are level with the shores of Hudson Bay; its newly constructed airbases on the Spratly Islands are at the same latitude as Guatemala. Its footprint in historical time is similarly expansive, stretching back for 5,000 years. So I have had to be brutal for the sake of space and sanity, concentrating on specific moments of transformation that help to illustrate the progress of Chinese history. To get through five millennia in a book of this size, we must proceed on fast-forward, stopping only for a few scattered moments of slow-motion or freeze-frame.

Prehistory, as told through archaeology and myths, forms the basis of the first chapter, from the first hominids to the toppling of the Shang dynasty in 1046 BCE. Ensuing sections keep to the traditional, dynasty-based divisions of Chinese history, building in each case on the traditional narrative in Chinese chronicles. These include the *Spring and Autumn Annals*, attributed to Confucius (see Notes on Names), and *The Grand Scribe's Records*, which sift through Chinese history from the dawn of time to the early Han dynasty when Sima Qian compiled them. Most subsequent eras have at least one official dynastic history, usually assembled by those that came after them, often with axes to grind or something to prove. We must read between the lines of these bold, stark statements of fact, in search of people whose voices have been stifled, or events that have been misread. For this, I have often leaned on songs and poetry, anecdotes from each age, and occasional moments since immortalized in plays, stories and museum narratives.

As with my *A Brief History of Japan*, I have incorporated trends in modern scholarship, although this is not an academic book. Invisible to ancient chroniclers but increasingly obvious to modern historians, is the role played by climate and environmental change. We have learned to read between the lines of the surviving annals, to understand that when one entry records a bad harvest or a cold winter, followed by a "barbarian attack," on the borders, that both cultures were liable to be hurting, although we often only have documentary evidence from one.

The precise effects of climate fluctuations are difficult to determine— not all of China is affected by the same conditions at the same time. Cold weather can kill crops, but it can also cause the desertification that pushes the nomads off the arid steppes. Warm weather can create flourishing "biological" bounty, increasing not only the agricultural productivity of the farmers, but also the livestock and hence the wealth of nomad groups. In both cases, this might keep them happy and peaceful, or it might make them rich enough to fund a war. Modern climatologists point to more nuanced data, such as a still-prosperous core region having to deal with a revolt linked to famine on the frontier, as happened in 755 CE during the Tang dynasty. On that occasion, the trouble on the border was a harbinger of oncoming climate change—decreasing agricultural productivity in the Tang heartland itself from the 820s, capped by extreme droughts in the 840s. Sometimes, such evidence matches political problems so exactly that humanity can seem little more than puppets overwhelmed by the weather. But while climate data certainly offers compelling explanations for periods of unrest, it is never the whole story—sometimes historical events are shaped by how a culture copes, rather than how it fails to.

Another modern trend is the increased attention paid to women in history. Both chivalry and chauvinism have pushed Chinese women to the margins, not only in China, but also abroad, where patriarchal assumptions steered history into long lists of great men who did great things. The most famous women in Chinese history have often been the most *infamous*—blamed for the machinations of their fathers and brothers. Like a song stuck on Repeat, dynastic history is packed with court scandals that mask, to a greater or lesser extent, the power struggles of the "affines"— relatives by marriage. Redrawing family trees from the perspective not of the emperors, but of their wives and mothers, highlights entirely different dominant families, enduring in the shadows through multiple regime changes, like the Dugu sisters who became empresses in three different dynasties. Sometimes they are also reflections of an invisible culture clash, as successive generations of Han historians sputter and fume about the more powerful role that womenfolk were permitted in public life when parts of China were under nomad-derived rule.

It is common, of course, for old-fashioned history to concentrate on the rich and the powerful, as these are the people who get written about in chronicles, and who patronized the artists and artisans who created objects for the material record. They are also the people with whom the modern reader most wants to identify. You can have the life you have now, more or less, in times gone by, but living as you do would make you one of the rare creatures of privilege at the top of ancient society. Without machines, you would have to rely on human labor. For your laundry to be done and your food to reach your table, to keep the house clean and your kids busy, you would need the services of twenty or thirty servants and slaves. The energy coiled in a single barrel of today's oil is equivalent to ten years of hard labor. If you are not going to chop that firewood or clear that farmland, someone must do it for you, and that requires wealth and power. In the back-stabbing struggles of Chinese antiquity, we see the desperation of people not all that different from you and me, trying to hang onto their comfortable life, to keep a roof over their head and the wolf from the door.

It is common for history to tell the story of the winning side. The Chinese people share common prehistoric ancestors, but recurring genetic markers show that the Han ethnic group have undertaken a gradual migration southwards, mixing with the locals as they go. The history of China is usually presented through the eyes of the Han (90% of the population today, as they were two thousand years ago in the Han dynasty), and not the many races they defeated, supplanted or assimilated. But there have long been attempts by Chinese scholars to redress this bias—even the original *Grand Scribe's Records* included a novella-length chapter on the history of the Xiongnu nomads.

Parts of China have been under what the Han once called barbarian rule for more than half of the last two thousand years, but it is the Han record that we usually read. New arrivals often played along with this discrimination, discarding their original surnames and scrubbing any foreign habits from their lives. The historian must peer closely at the record to see glimpses of China's cosmopolitan, multi-ethnic past—the blue-eyed girls who danced in the taverns of Chang-an; the Silk Road traders whose Chinese names suggest they came from what is now Uzbekistan; the entire cities of Indian Buddhists that once dotted the green mountain slopes on the north side of the Taklamakan desert. China's ethnic diversity does not merely extend to the 100 million people who form its contemporary minorities, but in the contribution of numerous forgotten cultures to the Han population's self-image.

The Han worldview was centered first on the Yellow River, and had expanded by the time of the First Emperor to include the River Yangtze, Sichuan, South China and the northwest. But that is barely half of what constitutes modern China. The Han defined themselves by staying put.

They raised crops and built cities, the very definition of "civilization." The nomad peoples—including, at various times, the Xiongnu, the Tujue (Turks), the Xianbei, Tuoba, Tabgatch and Khitans (all proto-Mongols), the Uyghurs, the Jurchens (Manchu), and most famously, the Mongols themselves—sought a different form of sustainability, far more suited to the poorer soils of the north and west. They measured their wealth in herds of cattle, sheep and horses—livestock nourished by the grasslands, and maintained by periodic, seasonal mobility. The nomads moved in vast wagon trains, rumbling across the steppes between pastures, often in an agreed rotation, north in the summer, south in the winter, periodically orbiting close to Han civilization where the two very different cultures could exchange goods—silks for furs, or cooking pots for horses.

It is crucial, not only for an understanding of Chinese history, but also of Chinese society, to recognize that in modern parlance, these nomads would eventually be deemed just as "Chinese" as the Han people, even though their culture was radically different. This is certainly not how the Han saw it at the time—they drew a direct link between their culture and the Mandate of Heaven. In order to be accepted as Chinese, you needed to accept the sovereignty of China's ruler, and with it the rituals, obligations and assumptions that came with it, in everything from language to table manners. Ancient rulers of China did not so much have borders as diminishing influence on the areas around them. Their closest subjects were truly Chinese. In the outlying regions, there were vassal peoples who occasionally paid tribute, recognizing the authority of the sovereign, and aping some of its ceremonies in the hope of one day being accepted. Beyond them were increasingly hopeless barbarian peoples, who only vaguely appreciated the wonders that lay back in the Chinese heartland. Eventually, the power of Chinese culture faded into static, in remote kingdoms that had never even heard of the man who was the ruler of All Under Heaven.

The nomad peoples, however, were often close *enough*. Geographically, there are parts of the pre-modern Chinese world that could not sustain an agricultural lifestyle and parts that could not sustain the nomads. But there is also a broad zone of territory that could sustain either, thousands of square kilometers, cutting from the northeast to the Tibetan plateau. It is here that we will see much of the tensions of Chinese history played out, as nomads and farmers jockey for control. In the 1,112 years between the

Qin dynasty and the end of the Tang dynasty, for example, the span of Chapters Three to Five in this book, the Chinese fought 367 wars with various nomad groups. One might even suggest that when the Chinese capital moves west, as it did in the Zhou, Han, Sui and Tang dynasties, that this was a sign of prosperity in the core Yellow River civilization, and that when it moved east, as it *also* did in the Zhou, Han, Sui and Tang dynasties, this was a sign of a weakened core and strengthened nomad periphery. Understand that the Han Chinese have spent thousands of years facing a shadow self to the north and west, and so much of Chinese history makes more sense.

Although the idea has fallen out of favor, much writing on Chinese history in previous generations has assumed that Han culture is so unassailably superior that even when it has been conquered, it ultimately wins over its new masters. Nomads are mobile when their only wealth is measured in herds. As they become more "cultured," they gain more material goods and more to lose. They lose their full, seasonal mobility, and start to shuttle between walled forts where they can keep their luxuries. Eventually, they lock down into citadels supported by outlying suburbs of artisans and servants, and their nomad heritage becomes solely cultural or military—a trip to the ancestral steppes in the summer, or a pronounced love of hunting. Tough, invincible horse-lords seize power over the farmers, only to fall under the spell of their agricultural bounty and urban entertainments. Their sons are raised in palaces, married to Chinese ladies, and aspire to be lords of the manor. Today, a more refined appreciation tells us that even the Han people's sense of their own "Chineseness" has constantly evolved, appropriating new materials, technologies and ideas from other cultures. It is difficult to imagine Chinese food without chili or dumplings, Chinese religious life without Buddhism, or political life without Communism, but these are all foreign imports. Ancient Chinese kings once regarded Sichuan and Shanghai as foreign lands, and Guangzhou (Canton) as a distant place of exile.

Times change. Twenty-five years ago, Hong Kong was a British colony. Fifty years ago, nobody had heard of the Terracotta Army. A hundred years ago, respected scholars were ready to call the ancient Shang dynasty a mere legend... which is where we begin.

# Point of Departure:
# The Wastes of Yin

B eijing, 1899 CE—Wang Yirong was ill. His joints ached. His head hurt. He felt nauseous and shivered in bed, sweating through his hemp clothes. There was no chance he would be reporting for work at Directorate of Education any time soon. His wife sent a servant out to the market to bring back some medicine.

It was summer, and the ruts in the streets had baked solid into uneven dips and humps. The boy took a shortcut through a maze of *hutong* alleyways, dodging around porters and carts. Even when the courtyard gates were open, he rarely caught a glimpse of life inside, for the interiors were shielded by decorated curtain walls just inside the doors. He passed children's voices reciting key passages from the work of Confucius, and hawkers at the street corners selling hawthorns on sticks and scallion pancakes.

Near the rose-colored walls of the Forbidden City, the private district of the Emperor himself, he had to take a detour for several blocks. The Foreign Legation Quarter was an alien citadel in the middle of Beijing, a long city block protected by the steep *glacis* slope that surrounded it; its walls giving way to the shallow waters of the Imperial Canal. The boy saw pennants fluttering in the breeze above the rooftops—the flags of Britain and Russia, the United States of America, France, Italy, Germany and Japan. Modern soldiers marched on the parade ground, shouting in unison, while turbaned Sikh watchmen checked all visitors on the entrance roads.

There were, he had been told, pharmacies for the foreigners inside the Legation Quarter, selling Western medicines, but they were off-limits to the Chinese, as were the books in strange languages and the exotic foods on sale in the foreigners' ghetto.

No, the boy had his mission, and it was to buy a traditional Chinese remedy to help his master. Outside the city gate, at Caishikou, he entered the Darentang pharmacy and lurked, fidgeting, while the shopkeeper handed a neatly wrapped package to hunched old lady. Then he loudly demanded sweet wormwood to make into a tincture.

The shopkeeper laughed. They were out of sweet wormwood—everybody had malaria this season. But he could sell him some dragon bones—the remains of ancient leviathans, some so old that they had practically turned to stone within the earth. Ground up and served in the right broth, they were supposed to be good for malaria.

The boy took what he could get and darted back across town to Wang's house. His master, however, was out of bed. His friend Liu E had come to visit, and true to the rules of Confucian propriety, Wang had struggled out of bed to receive him. They were having a halting conversation about nothing, sitting on either side of a half-empty pot of slowly cooling green tea while Wang sniffed and coughed, and clutched his robe about him.

Gingerly, the boy showed the small pack of dragon bones to his clammy-faced master, and struggled with the strings that bound it. Wang fumbled in irritation at the packaging, and stared in surprise at the items revealed—flat, delicate fragments of bone and shell, etched with spidery squiggles. These were not fossils from the cliffs of Zhoukoudian to the southwest. They were something else—cattle shoulder blades and, yes, what seemed to be the flat underside of a turtle's shell. The writing was illegible, but Liu E realized he had seen something like before, on ancient bronzes. Could it be that it was not some forgotten language, but Chinese itself?

There was a character that looked like a little man, but so did *ren*, the Chinese word for person. Could it be that a picture of an eye actually meant *eye*? That the scribble that looked like a chariot from above actually meant *chariot*? Liu E began to investigate further, unaware of the immensity of the looming discovery.

It would take years to unravel. The following summer, China was plunged into a crisis, the Boxer Uprising, in which a faction within the Manchu ruling class secretly encouraged rebel cultists to rise up against the foreign invaders. The Legation Quarter was plunged into a 55-day siege, lifted only by the arrival of a multinational relief force. The Manchu masters fled to the west of the country, briefly abandoning their capital and their subjects. Wang Yirong, who had been pressed into leading a squad of Chinese soldiers, drank poison with his wife and daughter-in-law on the day the foreign troops arrived.

Liu E inherited Wang's dragon bones, on which the pair of them had been working for some months. In 1903, he published a book of rubbings from all the examples he could find, creating a new fad that even drew in foreign researchers. He managed to divine the meanings of 34 of the simpler or more obvious symbols, but other soon joined in the puzzle-solving. In 1906, Frank Chalfant's book *Early Chinese Writing* coined the term "oracle bones" as a more exact description, since it was widely understood that they were nothing to do with dragons, but instead had been used by ancient soothsayers, who would write questions and potential answers, and then heat them in a fire and interpret the cracks.

That didn't mean that anyone could yet understand the questions or the answers, but piece by piece, scholars were guessing at the meanings of the characters. They did, indeed, appear to be a form of ancient Chinese.

The main source turned out to be Anyang, a city 460 kilometers (285.8 miles) to the south of Beijing, long known as a source of ancient bronzes. It was not until 1928 that an archaeological dig got underway in the Wastes of Yin, a patch of scrubland on the outskirts of town, that was found to cover the ruins of dozens of buildings fashioned from pounded earth, tombs of ancient nobles surrounded by grave goods and sacrificial victims, and huge pits of discarded oracle bones, smashed into thousands of fragments.

Now scholars had many more materials to work with. The meanings of the inscriptions began to coalesce. As the jigsaw-pieces of the shattered materials were reassembled, they revealed the concerns of an ancient kingdom. The contents of the Wastes of Yin would eventually disclose some 30,000 different characters, although many of these are variant forms of a basic set of about 4,000. The word "chariot," for example, seems to be written slightly differently every time it appears, as if the priests had not yet worked out precisely how to describe such a new-fangled contraption. Today, we are able to decipher about 1,760 of the words on Yin oracle bones, which ask questions about the health of aristocrats; about the birth of the child of a lady general; attempts to predict the weather. *Will there be good hunting tomorrow? Which angry god is causing the king's toothache? Would thirty human sacrifices and five sheep appease him?*

The Wastes of Yin have revealed to us almost a thousand place-names from this kingdom, but most significantly, they also contained the names of several kings—Wuding, Zujia, Geng-ding, and others.

For years, Chinese scholars had debated the earliest passages of the ancient books of history. Plainly, many elements were legends and myth, gods falling from the sky in an iron ship, or using magic powers to tame flood waters. Ancient, legendary demigods and divine emperors were probably little more than fairy stories, too far removed from historical reality to be worth bothering with. There was no real evidence to be found, for example, of the prehistoric Xia dynasty, which was mentioned in the two-thousand-year-old *Grand Scribe's Records*. As late as 1930, some in the Chinese academic community also doubted the existence of the Shang dynasty, which had supposedly collapsed sometime around 1000 BCE.

But the names on the oracle bones matched the names on the Shang records. Anyang had been the last of several Shang capitals, and the discarded bones amounted to a ton of metadata about its last nine kings—the eclipses they had observed, the tribes they went to war against and even their health concerns. Since 1930, which is to say, within living memory, the verifiable history of China has had some 600 years added to it, with murky times of legend suddenly verified by archaeological evidence. Now that scholars could read the inscriptions on the bones, they could read them on ancient bronzes, which were found to refer to the same kings.

The Doubting Antiquity movement of early 20th-century Chinese scholars, which pushed for a healthy degree of skepticism about the claims made in ancient chronicles, gave way in the 1990s to the Believing Antiquity movement, which acknowledged that a whole bunch of outrageous assertions, unlikely tales and even supposed textual forgeries had been confirmed by modern archaeology. Even the traditional cures, or some of them, at least, turned out to be true. In 2015, the 84-year-old pharmacologist Tu Youyou became the first Chinese woman to receive the Nobel Prize for Medicine for isolating artemisinin, a powerful suppressant of malarial parasites. She got the idea from reading a book that was sixteen centuries old, which spoke of the curative properties of *Artemisia annua*—sweet wormwood.

But let's take a moment, here, to talk about history. Not everything about the story of the oracle bones is entirely true. Incredibly, the bits that seem improbable are the most genuine. The archaeological dig in the Wastes of Yin did indeed uncover relics of the lost Shang dynasty, and the names on the oracle bones, once translated, did match the king-lists from the *Grand Scribe's Records*. Paradoxically, it's the more modern part of the story that has been called into question.

There was no Darentang pharmacy in Beijing in 1899. The story of Wang Yirong's malaria only arose thirty years after his death—a tall tale to add a bit of drama. Liu E's quest to understand his "dragon bones" was much more everyday some chats with antique dealers, and picking through Wang's possessions after his death. Liu E did inherit Wang's oracle bones, and did publish a set of rubbings. The Wastes of Yin did transform our understanding of ancient China, not for the last time in the 20th century, but they were a happy accident. Sometimes the archaeological evidence supports what we think we know about the past; sometimes it just throws everything into question. I choose to begin this book with the story of Wang Yirong's servant-boy in 1899 because it is both true and apocryphal. We can be sure, from the evidence of Shang oracle bones and the testimony of the ancient *Bamboo Annals*, that the first rumblings of rebellion against the Shang dynasty happened around the same time as a total lunar eclipse in 1059 BCE, when the Moon turned blood-red. But that Beijing servant boy I described on the first page might never have existed.

# CHAPTER 1

# TO SERVE THE GODS WITH JADE: PREHISTORIC AND MYTHICAL CHINA

Despite the cold winter, she had been sweating when she died, coughing black spit that smelled of old fires. Her man wept, holding her as life drained away, the lice on her head tickling against his beard, until his relatives gently pulled him free, whispering words of condolence. *She was so young*, he sobbed. He spoke about her as if she were a girl, but she had seen more than forty summers. *Wrap her well*, he mumbled. *Don't let her get cold.* He was ushered from the tent, inconsolable, and the old woman got to work. Outside, they heard him howling.

They left her in the clothes she had been wearing—ankle-high leather buskins, and her long, patched goatskin skirt, the fur-side inward against the winter. They pinned her woolen wrap in place, fuzzy on the outside with extra loops of thread designed to catch more heat. They tied her into her felt woolen rain hood with the plaited red and blue cords she liked, the two long goose feathers she always wore, sticking from the top.

The men dug a pit in the hard ground by the lake that no longer had any fish in it, and laid her gently inside, her auburn hair flicking in the wind around the edges of her hood. They placed her wheat-winnowing basket on her chest, and by her side, they placed the tough comb she had used to pat down the threads when she wove.

They stood around the pit, the winter wind whipping aside their coats to show flashes of red and blue. Men and women alike had braided hair—the elders gray, the younger clans-people a mix of browns and reds, sometimes even a shock of blond.

It was cold, but it was parched. Time went on for the mourners, but for her, in her dry, dry pit, it no longer had meaning. The stars wheeled and turned above, the waters of the dead lake ebbed further away, never to return. The crops withered and the trees died. Her children drifted away, back to the west towards the larger oases; or north back towards the grasslands beyond the mountains they called Heaven; or south, to the two great rivers that crashed into the desert to dwindle and die, where you could find green pebbles in the water.

The years turned into centuries. There was no sign of what had been her home or her grave. The place where her village had once thrived was now nothing but sand, shimmering in the heat from white salt flats. Sometimes, there would be a ghost of the lake where her ancestors had once fished—spring rains might briefly run into the sand and form some shallow puddle where some of its deepest trenches once were, only to steam back into the sky by the height of summer.

People came from the north on horses. We don't know what she had called her home, but the newcomers called it Kröran. People came from the east, to buy the green pebbles, and called the place Loulan. But not even the newcomers stayed forever. Loulan, or places near it, was settled and abandoned on multiple occasions, seized by a squadron of horsemen and briefly settled by convicts given a second chance, only to be abandoned once more in a black, whirling storm of sand.

The place where she had once gathered barley by the lake became known as *Taklamakan*, the Place of Ruins.

$$\circ - \circ - \circ - \circ - \circ$$

In 1980 CE, a Chinese archaeological expedition struggled through the sands on the northern edge of Lop Nor, the salt flats of the Tarim Basin, close to the forbidden desert in western China where the People's Republic tested its atomic weapons. There, beside the trickle of the Iron Plate River, beneath the striking, hump-like *yardang* rock-formations called the Dragon City, they found her, desiccated by the desert heat, mummified. They carried her delicate body from the grave, and kept it safe by putting it in one of their tents. Mu Shunying, the only woman archaeologist in the expedition, was obliged to sleep each night beside the ancient corpse that would come to be known as the Beauty of Loulan.

Carbon-dating placed her time of death as roughly 1800 BCE. Chemistry established that her blood type was O. Facial reconstruction gave her features that, coincidentally or otherwise, strongly resembled those of the "Afghan Girl" who had graced the cover of *National Geographic* in 1985. Analysis of her clothes and grave goods suggests her ancestors had, indeed, come from somewhere over the Pamir mountains, from what is now Afghanistan. She probably represented the easternmost edge of the Tocharian culture, an Indo-European ethnic group that had ebbed back towards the west in ancient times, pushed out by new arrivals like the Wusun from the grasslands.

The Beauty of Loulan helps us paint a picture of a very different China, contemporary with the rise of the "black-headed peoples" that would be united by the First Emperor, before the establishment of the borders of the empire of the Han. She lived among the chain of desert oases that would eventually be known as the Silk Road, a thin, fragile route that occasionally connected east and west, allowing people and ideas to travel.

The Tocharians are long-gone, although some of their words may survive in Chinese, truncated with glottal stops and elisions. *Mjit*, for honey, entered Old Chinese as *mit*. *Sisäk*, for lion, arriving in Old Chinese as *si-chya*. Most shockingly for some scholars, *kukäl*, for wheel or chariot, migrating into Old Chinese as *khla*—see Notes on Names. The idea is controversial because of what it suggests for the rest of Chinese history— that the culture that thrived on the banks of the Yellow River could itself have been periodically implanted or supplanted by new arrivals from the west. In fact, most of the names for the parts of an ancient Chinese chariot seem to derive from non-native words. Meanwhile, China's oldest-dated bronze artifacts, not to mention the first noodles and later evidence of the first iron objects, are found not in the heartland of its civilization, but scattered along the Gansu Corridor that leads out to the plains and deserts of Central Asia.

Not for nothing, the origin-myth of Hou Ji, (Lord Cereal) legendary founder of the Xia dynasty, bears a strong relationship to the founder myths of nomad peoples. He is born when his mother steps into a footprint left by the Sky God, leading a charmed childhood in which he is saved from danger by numerous animal helpers. As a grown man, he experiments with growing crops, including beans, rice, hemp and millet, and it is in his honor that the ancient Chinese would hold a festival every spring, in which they drank fermented millet booze and barbecued a sheep.

The Beauty of Loulan died at the edge of the desert known as the Sea of Death or the Place of Ruins, which now forms part of modern China's largest province, the Xinjiang Uyghur Autonomous Region. It stretches west all the way to Kashgar, from which perilous mountain passes could take daring travellers through to what is now Pakistan, India, Afghanistan and beyond. Oases cling to the edges, some merely small villages around a well, others much larger. The biggest, at 50,000 square kilometers (19,305.1 square miles), is the Turfan Depression, a vast island of green amid the sand. To the south, the Tibetan plateau and the Roof of the World—the Himalayas. To the north, past the Tianshan (Heaven Mountains), the plains of the Ili river that lead out to Lake Balkhash and the Russian steppes. For some, but not all, of the distant prehistoric ancestors of the Chinese, this would have been the route they took to the east. Others walked around the coastline from southeast Asia, heading inland as the Ice Age ended and the waters flooded the coast to a distance of between 200 and 1,000 kilometers (124.3 and 621.4 miles).

China has been home to hominids for at least a million years—Peking Man, who lived some 700,000 years ago, was uncovered in 1921 at Dragon Bone Hill in Zhoukoudian, in what is now the Beijing suburbs. As the name implies, the site had long been mined for its fossils, which were used in Chinese traditional medicine. Excavations revealed a cave that had been home for multiple generations of human-like inhabitants from some 700,000 years ago. They left piles of bones charred by cooking fires, and hominid skulls smashed at the base to get at the tasty brains within.

But the remains of *Homo erectus pekinensis* are merely the most famous, and controversially cannot be subjected to modern analysis, because they disappeared during the Second World War. It is only logical that earlier, older remains lurk somewhere to the south, and modern archaeology periodically rings with new alarums as diggers find new sites— the 1.9-million-year-old ape-like remains found at Longgupo in Sichuan; the 2.25 million-year-old flint tools, believed to have been used by *Homo erectus*, found at Renzidong in Anhui. The Nihewan basin in Hebei, first excavated in 1923, was found in 2015 to have a two million-year-old "playground" of what appeared to be flint toys. Such discoveries play havoc with the traditional "Out of Africa" interpretation of the spread humanity, suggesting multiple waves or even reversals. 97.4% of modern Chinese DNA tracks back to African ancestry, which suggests that many of these sites may have hosted species or sub-species that failed to survive. In prehistoric times, China may have been discovered and settled by multiple groups of hominids, only a fraction of whom made it through harsh changes in climate and environment enough to pass their genes down to modern times.

130,000 years ago, something broke Maba Man's head. The cracked skull was found in a cave in Guangdong in 1958, and subjected to CT scans that revealed it to have suffered a severe blunt force trauma. He had been struck, probably with a club (although possibly by a deer's antler), and his skull was never quite the same again. But the regrowth of bone around the wound showed that he was not killed. Someone nursed him back to health, and he lived perhaps for years afterwards, before dying of other causes. This has made Maba Man an oddly contested find, seen by some as an example of early hominid-on-hominid violence, and by others as a striking example of early compassion and care.

Many prehistoric sites may be lost to us. Some scholars have offered the "bamboo hypothesis," suggesting that the presence in China of this versatile material meant that much of the Chinese "Stone Age" gave way to wooden tools that have long rotted away, leaving less evidence for archaeologists to examine. Many sites were probably drowned by the rising seas after the Ice Age. Still more may await discovery in China's deserts, which were more suited for human habitation in prehistoric times than they are today.

The land that would become home to the "ten thousand tribes" of prehistoric China comprised rich forests and grasslands, scattered with many lakes and streams, home to elephants, rhinoceroses, monkeys and peacocks. Alligators peeked from the rivers, and jackals shrieked from the hilltops, although such exotic creatures faded from the northern part of the country—hunted to extinction or driven southwards by the change in their habitat, until they were eventually found only in the jungles far to the south.

Of all the rivers, most of which flowed from west to east, the land was and still is dominated by two giants. The Chinese language has multiple words for river, but two were associated specifically with the main watercourses. *He* originally meant *The River* to the people in the north as they looked out over the muddy waters that flowed through their domain, heavy with loess silt from the hinterland—the Yellow River.

Its nickname, China's Sorrow, derives from its unpredictability. Dams of ice could form in its upper reaches near Mongolia, holding back huge volumes of water, only to suddenly break and send surges down towards the unsuspecting farmlands of central China. The muddiest river in the world, its waters created rich prospects for agriculture, but also made it unpredictable. As it flowed lazily through what is now the Chinese heartland, the Yellow River shed sediment by the ton on its own bed and banks, causing it to occasionally and catastrophically change course. Sometimes, it flowed north of the Shandong peninsula, into the Gulf of Bohai. Sometimes it flowed south, into the Yellow Sea. Roughly once a century, this bountiful river could burst its levees or suddenly veer off course like an angry dragon, drowning multitudes and leaving the survivors without food or homes. The futile, vainglorious attempt of human beings to control, or at the very least appease the Yellow River has formed the basis of much early Chinese religion and state organization. Ancient Chinese looked up at the Milky Way in the night sky, and believed it to be the farthest reaches of the same waters.

Further to the south, another waterway was also simply called *The River* by the people who lived near it. In languages that were not incorporated into the Chinese orbit until the closing days of the Warring States era, this word was *Jiang*—see Notes on Names. Today it is known in Chinese as *Changjiang*, the "Long River," although different parts of it have other names: the Tearful River at its headwaters in Tibet, the Golden Sands River as it passes through the tribal enclaves of Yunnan, and as it approaches the sea near what is now Shanghai, the name that it is known by in English, the Yangtze. At many times in Chinese history it has formed a major geographical boundary, often marking the high-water mark of barbarian invasions from the north. At the time of Marco Polo, when South China was only recently conquered by the Mongols, he wrote of the lands south of the Yangtze as if they were a separate kingdom. It is south of the Yangtze that the traveller from the north runs into "dialects" of Chinese that are really *topolects*—local languages that a Mandarin speaker struggles to understand. These include Shanghainese, which retains words from the ancient, non-Chinese kingdoms of Wu and Yue, and Cantonese, which echoes the way Chinese sounded in the medieval Tang dynasty—as close to Mandarin as English is to Dutch. Even today, it marks an important boundary within China's climate—houses south of the Yangtze rarely have central heating, on the understanding that the warm south does not require it.

The blue line on the map is misleading—at 6,380 km, the Yangtze is not merely the longest river in Asia and the third-longest in the world. It is also navigable for some 1,600 kilometers (994.2 miles) inland, through lower reaches linking freshwater lakes, all the way up to the fertile Sichuan ("Four Rivers") Basin. The Yangtze has always been less of a river and more of an inland sea for the Chinese, the center of a thriving trade and transport network.

China's other rivers, often linked north-south by canals, were similarly vital to the pre-modern economy. "Prior to the construction of railroads in the 19th century," notes Mark Edward Lewis in *The Early Chinese Empires*, "carrying grain more than a hundred miles by pack animal cost more than producing the grain itself." Water transport was the only way to move the commodities of pre-modern China—grain, rice, salt, lumber—in significant quantities. The rivers and canals were vital in making a land the size and scale of pre-modern China even possible. Lewis's simple statement is, for me, one of the most essential phrases for understanding the pre-modern world—we can see its shadow over many inexplicable decisions, such as the sudden move of an imperial capital, or the approval of vast expense for canal construction, even the location of borders or the path of military campaigns.

The landscape changes again to the south and west, towards Yunnan ("South of the Clouds"), a maze of mountains and valleys that climbs ever higher back into Tibet. Incorporated into the Chinese world by the Mongol invaders of the 13th century, but often shunned by Han administrators who would rather leave its thin air and tangled jungles to the natives, Yunnan remains one of the most visibly diverse provinces in China, home to 25 of the country's official minorities, and teeming with peoples who have close cultural ties to Vietnam, Myanmar and Thailand. Many parts of Yunnan were left to local princelings until early modern times—it remains a place of exoticism to the Chinese, but not as exotic as Tibet (in Chinese, the Xizang Autonomous Region). A rich prize in the Great Game between the British and Russian Empires, the Buddhist theocracy of Tibet long enjoyed a reputation as a place of magic and mystery, even after it was first incorporated into Chinese territory, again by the Mongols. Chiefly to hold off the British and Russians, China claimed Tibet in 1722 CE, and has maintained suzerainty over that country ever since.

The Autonomous Region of Tibet, like Xinjiang to its north, and Yunnan and Guangxi to its east, is part of the People's Republic of China, but also an enclave of non-Han cultures. So, too, is Inner Mongolia, China's longest province, which stretches all the way across the northwest, as is Manchuria, the northeastern homeland of the tribe that conquered China in 1644 CE. Now split into three provinces, Manchuria is now usually referred to simply as "the Northeast" (*Dongbei*), in order to relate it directly to the Han center.

There are other regions, of course. Hainan Island looks like a little dot on the map, but is really a province the size of Belgium. It, too, has its aboriginal population, as does Taiwan, an island only incorporated within imperial China in the 17th century when the Manchus needed to wipe out the resistance movement based there. Today, Taiwan is home to a different kind of dissenter, the inheritors of the Republic of China, ousted from the mainland by the Communist revolution. Other areas of studied difference include the tiny coastal enclaves of Hong Kong and Macau, "Special Administrative Regions" that were once stolen from China by British and Portuguese imperialists, peacefully handed back at the close of the 20th century, reunited but conspicuously different, afforded certain concessions until the 2040s.

Stretching down towards the Philippines, we find China's latest area of territorial interest—the shoals and rocks of the South China Sea, used as fishing grounds and anchorages for centuries by fisherman from the mountainous marine region of Fujian. Today they are a political hot potato, with increased strategic value, not only for defense, but for oil and gas resources. Neighboring states, such as Vietnam and the Philippines, beg to differ, protesting that many of these islands are not islands at all, and have had to be augmented by tons of Chinese concrete and landfill before they even qualify to be territory to claim. But as of today, you can stand in the blazing sun on a deserted South China Sea atoll barely big enough for the airbase it hosts, and know that China stretches away from you for thousands of miles, all the way to the heights of the Himalayas, the desert of Xinjiang, the steppes of Inner Mongolia and the sub-arctic forests of Manchuria.

China's history is as wide-ranging as its geography and it began with hominids wandering a domain that supported them all year. Early humans did not randomly forage for food. The lucky ones would find themselves in a sustainable environment that only required limited, seasonal migration, locking them into annual rotations between several familiar locations. Some might have even embarked upon a form of primitive agriculture, attempting to manage and encourage the growth of crops in the Stone Age.

When global temperatures dipped in the Younger Dryas Period (c. 11000 BCE–9700 BCE), food became harder to acquire. This sudden, sustained cooling is attributed with initiating a Neolithic Revolution, as early humans struggled to cope. Some concentrated harder on rearing crops, others tried to plan for lean months by storing food, leading to innovations in pottery and preservation. When the cool period passed, while it is possible that some communities returned to their old ways, others were now used to an agricultural lifestyle.

One stone in particular was of great importance in Neolithic China—jade. Originally mined in the Yangtze delta and parts of Manchuria and Mongolia (although those caches were exhausted by the late Bronze Age), it was regarded not only as precious, but as sacred and spiritual, forming a central component of ancient religious ceremonies. The word, in fact, for ritual in Chinese originally developed from an image of "to serve the gods with jade." Round jade discs, representing Heaven, and square tubes representing Earth, are found at many religious sites and tombs. The ancient Chinese believed that jade somehow amplified communication with the spirits, and preserved one's soul after death.

Jade was difficult to work before the advent of metal tools, and a concentration of jade items in the archaeological record suggests a society advanced enough to support its quarrying, polishing and ceremonial use. Ancient histories speak of the first legendary Sage King uniting "the ten thousand states that used jade and silk," suggesting many scattered clans. There is a cluster of jade artifacts found in archaeological sites along the midpoint of the Yellow River, marking the location of what is traditionally thought of as the origins of Chinese culture—the people thought to have been the ancestors of the first legendary Sage Kings, and the first Chinese dynasties. But two other clusters of jade point to other societies that coexisted with these proto-Chinese—one on the Liao River in the northeast, corresponding with the Yi people of antiquity, and another in the lower Yangtze, former homeland of the Miao-Man people.

The Yellow River region might claim to be the setting for China's early legends, but archaeology points to multiple alternatives which either contributed innovations or flourished independently. Many of these sites are outside the prehistoric "Chinese" core, on and around the lower reaches of the Yangtze. Kuahuqiao, for example, near modern Hangzhou, has given its name to the culture of several nearby sites, that in 6500 BCE were clusters of wattle-and-daub huts by a lake. The locals made pots, lived on a varied diet of fish, fruits and seeds, and cultivated rice. As for meat, their kitchen middens hosted the discarded bones of alligators, rhinoceroses, and wild boar, among more everyday hunting prey. Unfortunately, many relics of the Kuahuqiao culture have been destroyed in recent times by local villagers digging up the layers of clay where the old lake once was. But enough evidence remains to tell us that their rice was grown in wetland fields, the water kept in place by berms of earth, and fertilized with human waste. Later pot shards are encrusted with barnacles, suggesting that the site was abandoned when rising sea levels ruined the rice fields and washed out the villages.

In north China, foxtail and broomcorn millet were domesticated by 8000 BCE, providing a firm basis for further population growth as the temperature rose. It continued to go up, in fact, until it plateaued from 6000–4000 BCE in the Holocene climatic optimum. Chinese history, or at least its early myths, only begins as this warm period came to an end.

The rain changed. Between 7000 BCE and 3000 BCE, the path of the East Asian monsoon frontal dropped a thousand kilometers (621.4 miles) from a high mark just north of modern Beijing, to a low point near modern Hangzhou. This inevitably caused a southward migration by people who had lost their means of support, creating a conflict zone that would push south for millennia.

Around 3000 BCE, the original settlers of Tibet were swamped by a large-scale migration from what is now central China. Civilization was retreating from the north, giving up on homelands that had sustained communities for centuries. Those that stayed behind adapted with radical changes to their lifestyle. Similarly, archaeologists in Mongolia have uncovered the ruins of a hundred walled towns amid what were once agricultural fields. This lost civilization worshipped at stone altars and carried

C-shaped jade effigies of dragons. But its world was wiped out by a drop in temperature. By 1500 BCE the farmers were gone, the colder, drier plains transforming into grasslands more suitable for pastoral nomads.

That same dip in temperatures that depopulated the farms of Mongolia is sure to have had other effects to the south. Genetically, we can still see the aftermath in the prevalence of a Han mutation, M122-C. This gene exists throughout the modern population, but a greater mitochondrial variance in the south implies a sustained, long-term migration of Han men southwards over the centuries, interbreeding with non-Han women.

We are still in the realm of prehistory—this period is only documented in Chinese myths and legends. Fuxi and Nüwa the dragon-tailed brother and sister gods of Heaven and Earth, married one another and fashioned the first humans from clay. Fuxi taught the humans how to hunt and fish and herd animals. Shennong, the "God-Farmer," was his ox-headed successor, who taught humanity how to till fields and sow crops, and personally experimented with edible foods. He gave his life for his subject, dying after eating a poisonous yellow flower, but revered in the afterlife as the Medicine King.

After these godlike beings, the list of Chinese rulers begins to become more human, dropping elements of animal totems and divine powers. The Yellow Sovereign, believed to have reigned sometime around 2600 BCE, is credited with inventing the boat, the calendar the cooking fire and pottery. Sima Qian, author of the *Grand Scribe's Records* around 100 BCE, believed that the Yellow Sovereign had been a real figure, and that by collating scattered legends about him, he was reconstructing some semblance of his historical existence, not necessarily as an inventor and innovator, but as a tribal overlord who conquered two rival clans, that of the Flame Sovereign and Txiv Yawg. The latter is still worshipped among the Hmong people of South China and Vietnam, where his name means Grandfather-Ruler. In Chinese, however, it is written *Chi You*, "Jests Much"—echoes here of an ancient conflict that pushed some rivals southwards, and assimilated others within a new confederation.

"The farmer god taught us how to sow millet," goes a song of the Kam people, who now dwell in Guizhou far to the south, "but the [Yellow Sovereign] showed us how to use tools."

There has been much speculation about the Yellow Sovereign. Controversial claims have been made for him as the god-ancestor or real-life leader. Others have suggested that he is simply a river-god, the personification of the Yellow River that formed the basis of his worshippers' culture. Unfortunately, stories about him were already impossibly garbled by the time Sima Qian tried his early attempt at textual archaeology—he may not even have been "Yellow" at all, but some other variant on the word *huang*, redacted because of its similarity to a later ruler's name. Modern scholars believe that Sima Qian was struggling to make sense of a far earlier collection of legends, itself a patchy attempt to historicize the tales of the Shang people by the people who had overthrown them. There is certainly enough room in the Chinese legends to suggest that each of these figures represents a forgotten tribe or clan, co-opted within an ever-growing confederation centered on the Yellow River, their disparate animal totems slowly combining to form a fantasy creature—the dragon.

The prospect that there were discernible elements of a culture we might call "Chinese," before any of the historical dynasties, has turned the Yellow Sovereign into an important cultural icon, the mythical ancestor of all Chinese people, and the progenitor of all Chinese races. He became a touchstone of Chinese-ness in the early 20th century, when he was proclaimed to be the ancestor of all five colors on the flag of the new Chinese Republic—the Han, Mongols, Hui (Muslims), Tibetans and the Manchus. This has since been fudged further, to describe him as the ancestor of all China's ethnic groups. Attempts were made in the early twentieth century to establish the Yellow Sovereign's legendary birth as the starting point for a Chinese calendar, which would make 2019 CE, the year of this book's publication, the year 4716. His chief wife, meanwhile, was credited with the discovery of silk, a wondrous textile woven from the cocoon fibers of a humble worm. The Yellow Sovereign was succeeded by his grandson, his great-grandson, and two of his great-great grandsons, the latter of whom is remembered as the first great Sage King, Yao.

Yao represents the slow fading of myths into human history. He still retains certain supernatural elements, and is credited with a lifespan of 119 years, which gave him plenty of time to observe the heavens and create the beginnings of astronomy. Legends have him commanding minions not only to catalogue the movements of the stars and planets, creating a reliable calendar for planning agricultural activity, but also dispatching observers far to the south to take readings about the length of shadows. More famously and critically, he is remembered for abdicating his throne after seven decades, and handing it over not to any of his nine sons, but to a commoner that he deemed more suitable. Later Chinese philosophers, many of whom were appointees fighting nepotism at every level of government, would cite Yao's act as an example of his great virtue, arguing that the perfect leader promoted the most able man. The story, however, is rather suspicious, coming as it does after tales of a terrible flood, and ending with Yao deciding, apparently on a whim, to let both his daughters marry the new candidate.

Shun, the second of the three great Sage Kings, was a model much cited in China's imperial era. Humble and diligent, he continued to work with his hands while also somehow running a country, and fended off numerous assassination attempts by his jealous family. He ruled at Yao's side for thirty years, then as sole king for another fifty, travelling every five years among his provinces in order to personally officiate at ceremonies to bolster the authority of local satraps. He is credited with suspending the most brutal punishments of execution and mutilation, which suggests a program of resettling convicts in borderlands to aid in the development of the nation. Several of his legendary ministers crop up in later histories as the ancestors of major clans and dynasties, and on his death, like his predecessor, he pointedly ceded the throne to someone who was not his son.

A thousand years separate the lifespan of Yu, the third great Sage King, from the earliest surviving Chinese inscriptions. Another thousand years separate those inscriptions from the *Bamboo Annals* and the *Grand Scribe's Records* that attempt to make sense of the legends. The archaeological record suggests that stories of Yu the Great allude to a natural disaster on the Yellow River, which suffered catastrophic flooding around 1920 BCE. A landslide far upriver in Qinghai blocked the river for several months, forming a large, temporary lake. When it eventually breached its natural dam, the flood downstream has been estimated at up to 38 meters (124.7 feet) above the river's modern level. This would make it the world's worst river flood in the last 10,000 years, liable to have had after-effects for a generation. Yu was renowned for taming the waters of the river, not by building dams as his own father had tried, but by dredging the river bed and installing outlets where excess waters could be productively diverted into fields.

Yu, however, was where it all started to go wrong. That, at least, is how the Confucian scholars would see it when they eventually wrote these legends down. After several generations of rulers handing administration over the best man for the job, Yu decided to buck the trend and leave his throne to his son. The days of enlightened meritocracy were over, and by establishing heredity as the new marker for kingship, Yu had inadvertently started the first dynasty.

The Xia dynasty, as it has been termed, has left no written records, leaving all subsequent discussion to rest on legends and sparse archaeological evidence. It remains a subject of colorful and wide-ranging debate. Some scholars are prepared to claim that the whole thing is a fake, dreamed up by the later Shang dynasty to fake a precedent for their own rise to power, or even the Zhou dynasty that came after them, to justify and normalize their hubris in overthrowing the Shang! At the opposite extreme, there are scholars prepared to argue that with a little creative fudging, the legends of the Xia kings can be made to match the eclipses, conjunctions and other astronomical events that we know to have occurred.

Assuming that fictions elide at some point into fact, and that the *Grand Scribe's Records* grasps at least part of the truth, the Xia dynasty would have lasted from around 2100 BCE to 1600 BCE, somewhere in the central plain along the Yellow River. Several archaeological sites along the Yellow River have been pitched as the likely homeland of the Xia, but without any confirmation, they just as easily might be one of thousands of other clans dwelling in the area, rather than the one that is remembered as the progenitor of China's core culture. One such site is a pile of rocks by the river in Luoyang, marked with a modern sign that proclaims it to be the ruins of the first Xia palace—I stumbled across it in 2014 while my son played on a dilapidated bouncy castle nearby. Erlitou, not far from Luoyang, has also been mooted as a likely Xia site, based in part on its grave goods, which imply a stratified society rich in ritual objects, in which a distinct elite appeared to claim the privilege of communicating with gods and ancestors. Digs at Erlitou have unearthed evidence of burnt bones and cast bronze, suggesting that its occupants may have pursued similar rituals and metalwork to those that have been more readily confirmed in the heritage of later dynasties. But then again, so have digs at Erligang, further downriver near modern Zhengzhou, likely to have been an earlier capital of the Shang. Notably, Zhengzhou is the point furthest downstream that the premodern Yellow River could be trusted to hold its course. East of Zhengzhou, the Yellow River has chosen nine different paths to the sea in the last four thousand years, placing any culture in that area at risk. It's possible that the origins of the Xia dynasty could be sited at Zhengzhou for the simple reason that nobody was left alive downriver after Yu's Great Flood.

But as archaeologists compete over funding and provincial tourist offices seek the social capital of being the "birthplace of Chinese culture," everybody is jumping on the bandwagon. There were, it seems, many cultures dotted all over what is now China, although the evidence from innovations in pottery and bronze seem to suggest an increasingly greater concentration of those cultures along the Yellow River.

After millennia of flints, bone tools and crude pots, the archaeological record in places like Erlitou and Erligang shows a sudden leap in intricacy and material culture. Carved ivory, hammered gold, patterned pottery and finely-worked jade, however, are overshadowed by the incredible advance in bronze casting. Great cauldrons and tripods, standing on plump, tapering legs, resemble udders or jodhpurs. Wine cups stand on three spindly legs, with a long lip or spout to make it easier to for a slave to feed sips to a master. Decorations swirl in "thunder-patterns" around the rims, while other pots are covered in lumpy studs. Still more seem to bear stylized animal faces, the eyes stretching into an encircling mask.

Such items are likely to have belonged to what later peoples would call the Xia dynasty, although without written evidence—an inscription on a cauldron, for example, naming one of the kings—they are still merely examples of multiple cultures dotted around China. But on the understanding that much of what the *Grand Scribe's Records* said about the Xia's successors turned out to be true, it's worth a paragraph or two to summarize the stories of their 17 legendary kings.

Stories of the Xia dynasty, set down centuries later, feature much touring of the realm, much fighting of resisting locals, and occasional "celebrations of music," suggesting a mobile war-band demanding tribute from settled subject populations, and reinforcing its power with increasingly elaborate ceremonies. There are also telltale signs of conflict within the Xia dynasty itself—a struggle at the top for the chance to enjoy the meager luxuries of being Bronze Age aristocracy, being the head of "six hosts" that can be called up for punitive actions and raids on the neighbors.

"You who obey my orders," reads the speech of one Xia king, "shall be rewarded before my ancestors; and you who disobey my orders, shall be put to death before the altar of the spirits of the land, and I will also put to death your children."

Yu the Great's grandson was overthrown in a palace coup, ousted by his five brothers, who justified their behavior with claims that he had neglected his obligations to his ancestors and to his subjects, as if the state was being driven "like six horses with rotting reins." Subsequent rulers also seemed to enjoy only the shakiest of holds on their people, with several forced to fight for their position, and even fleeing, only to return with barbarian allies. Periodic complaints directed about them seem to focus on drunkenness, licentiousness, and attention paid to the wrong sort of gods. These factors all seem to be related—a later king would admonish his subjects that alcohol was only to be consumed as part of religious ceremonies, lest "Heaven send down its terrors." Rulers were divinely granted the right to rituals involving the preparation of meat and the consumption of intoxicants, cloaked in ceremonies to gods believed to have the power to sway fate.

Jie, the last king of the Xia dynasty, is remembered as a cruel despot, regularly ditching his wives in favor of new models, drunken to extremes, apt to taunt his subjects to the edge of their patience, only to execute them when they protested. He was demanding of his vassals, and waged war against anyone who did not send him tribute. The end of his reign was heralded by a series of dire portents, including a line of five stars in the sky, an earthquake and terrible rains. More specific weather data alludes to a summer cool enough that there was morning frost in July. If true, it is liable that many of the misdeeds recorded in the name of Jie were reactions to a struggle over resources caused by a sudden drop in temperatures. The *Bamboo Annals*, an extant ancient book, mentions "In the night, the stars fell like rain. The ground shook, [two rivers] became dry." The king made, "for the first time man-drawn carriages," implying a shortage of draft animals, and dug a canal to the river in winter, when no sane person would have attempted to work unless they were desperate to relieve unirrigated fields. There were "three suns in the sky"—a sun-dog effect, whereby the image of the sun is duplicated by being reflected in aerial ice crystals. If the weather were that cold, it should come as no surprise that the crops failed.

Scholars are still debating whether this is artistic license or evidence of a global volcanic winter, possibly caused by the eruption of Santorini in the Mediterranean around 1600 BCE, that same cataclysmic event that gave rise in Europe to legends of the fall of Atlantis. Whatever later scribes may have claimed about Jie's bad behavior, "omens" throughout his reign do seem like symptoms of weather troubles that undermined his power, until he was overthrown by rebellious vassals in a battle "amid great thunder and rain." The clan that toppled him was the Shang, a chariot-riding people whose previous appearance in the dynastic references show them taking military action on behalf of the Xia—they were proactive warriors whose punitive expeditions and wars of conquest elsewhere eventually united a coalition against the nominal ruler.

The last ruler of the Xia died in exile, and was supplanted by the Shang dynasty, whose first king's reign continued to endure climatic ill effects— the chronicles praise him for bringing an end to three successive years of drought by "praying in the mulberry forest," but do not mention that his kingly thoughts and prayers failed to end three previous droughts also mentioned. The chronicles of the Shang are sparse and often gloss over entire reigns in a mere sentence, but we are on surer ground historically, thanks to the concordance of the written documents with the epigraphs on bronzes and oracle bones, and the archaeological evidence at the last Shang capital, in Anyang.

The Shang kings seem little different from their predecessors, at least on the surface, riding in chariots (after around 1300 BCE), drinking booze of fermented millet and enjoying the fruits of hunting. Their malnourished subjects, however, still toiled in the Stone Age—there are no bronze tools in evidence, which implies that the metal was only used for the elite's religious or transport purposes, and that the common people still made do with flint and wood.

We still have the words of the hymns believed to have been sung by the Shang people at their great rituals. Intended both as songs of praise but as guides to religious etiquette, they contain accounts of their own protocols—although they finish with hymns in praise of the gods and ancestors, they begin with several verses that function like a checklist of the ceremony about to begin. The drums are put in place, and their beats summon the spirits. The descendants call upon their ancestors to arrive, the sound of flutes and stone chimes adding to the noise, until "bells and drums fill the air / and the dancers seem in flight / our visitors appear."

The modern reader is apt to see this as symbolic, although the chances are high that the Shang kings put on a show of really seeing them. Fortified by intoxicants or some other form of induced trance, China's early kings were given to shamanic visions—the words in Chinese for both "madness" and "disheveled" contain the symbol for "king."

Rulers of the Shang prayed to their founding ancestors' spirits for good harvest. Other hymns turn into recitations of lists of rulers, beginning with the divine siring of their first king, born of a princess and a bird, down to the great conquerors who warranted tribute from "the nine realms":

> Tributes great and small
> From lower states far and near
> Blessings received from Heaven
> Without his supplication
> Neither harsh nor soft to his subjects
> Kind in his dominion
> Recipient of one hundred blessings.

The Shang priesthood included those who prayed or recited the rituals, and those whose job it was to interpret the oracle bones, carefully wording the questions etched in the shoulder-blade or turtle plastron, and then interpreting the pathways made by the heat-cracks. There were also astrologers charged with keeping track of time and portents in the sky. Such men were called *shi*, the meaning of which would evolve over the next thousand years until it came to mean "historian." The final category of Shang priests were the butchers, whose role in such ceremonies is barely mentioned in the lyrics. It is, instead, the archaeological record that adds an extra dimension to these pious hymns—as the chanters spoke of kindness and blessings, their colleagues in the sacrificial faction would be spilling blood by the gallon.

The Shang were bloodthirsty—their kings expressed their authority through a tripartite expression of violence. Hunting and warfare were extensions of the third and most integral form of ritual violence, the sacrifices that tied the other pursuits together, followed by prescribed methods of dismemberment and display. Many of the comments on the oracle bones refer to sacrifices as attempts to cure illness or assuage the anger of the gods. Some turn into ghoulish decision trees, as the priests try one thing and then another, each of them causing harm to some poor creature at the sharp end of temple matters—should the sheep be bled to death or boiled in a cauldron? If we burn a man at the stake, will it bring rain? One Shang ritual, designed to appease the spirits of the winds, involved dismembering a dog. Buildings required the literal support of the dead, buried in their walls—there are over a hundred dog skeletons built into the surviving foundations of the Shang capital. An annual ceremony to appease the river god required ritual "marriage" of the river to a specially selected virgin, who was drowned as the big finish.

Of the thirty-seven different kinds of sacrificial ceremony found on the oracle bones, many seemed to involve partial destruction of bodies, carcasses, food or treasures—burning them seems to have been seen as a means of releasing their essence for the gods or ancestral spirits. This spelled disaster for a lot of dogs, as these animals were seen as guides, and hence would be thrown into the inventory as some sort of insurance policy.

Funerals were the worst. The tombs of the Shang aristocracy are piled high with the dead—sacrificed slaves or prisoners of war beheaded at the graveside, animals as food, steeds and companions in the afterlife. But a Shang funeral was a dangerous occasion even for the upper classes, who might find themselves called upon to prove their loyalty or friendship by joining their lord or lady in death. Concubines appear to have been sacrificed whole, strangled or buried alive rather than beheaded, in order to keep their bodies intact in the afterlife.

This carnage escalated as the Shang state both expanded and faced increasing problems both inside and outside its borders. Some 13,000 human sacrifices are scattered around the Shang capital for the reigns of its last nine emperors—an average of 33 victims a year, slain in cemeteries to open channels of communication with the ancestor-gods, or ritually sacrificed to "purify" princesses and dukes troubled by ailments or worries.

In the last days before the fall of the Shang regime, its kings mounted major rituals 360 times a year, with attendant musicians, dancers and priestly choruses, along with the screams of some animal or prisoner in front of the bronze altar-cauldron. However, the nature of the questions on the oracle bones transforms in the later years of the Shang. For a time after the introduction of the more symmetrical turtle plastron, the nature of the oracle questions becomes similarly dual in nature—yes/no or true/false answers. But the wording of the questions also changes, becoming less timorous and more hectoring. It was as if the later kings of the Shang, and the priesthood that served them, were no longer asking Heaven for approvals of explanations, but applying for concessions to which they felt entitled. Their wording implied they already knew the answer and were merely going through the motions, turning the role of the Shang diviners from oracles seeking truth to something more like spiritual accountants, ticking off a series of necessary calculations on behalf of smoothly running harvest or weather systems.

A supreme being, *Shangdi* the "lord above" was an unknowable deity, with whom only the king stood a chance of communicating. The motivations of nature spirits was also difficult to grasp, although appeasing them was a process that the priests claim to have worked out through a process of sacrificial trial and error. The spirits of the ancestors, however, were accessible to someone who knew the right rituals and payments, and could be prevailed upon to intercede from the afterlife. The natural accretion of prayers "answered" ensured that the older an ancestor was, the more likely he or she was liable to be credited with great powers. Often, according to the oracle bones, such ancestors were malicious or irascible, quick to take offence or to send bad omens as signs of their disapproval.

Although this description applies to the beliefs of a people from almost four thousand years in the past, they bear a remarkable similarity to the concerns of Chinese folk religion in the centuries that followed. Only the ruler was qualified to even approach the highest gods; nature was unfathomable, but possibly appeasable, and the ancestors continued to exert influence, even to the extent of continuing vendettas from the afterlife.

The Shang, their legends and their kingly lists, have forever steered our understanding of what ancient China was like. There are off-hand comments in surviving songs and legends of barbarian tribes on the periphery—of captured slaves of the Qiang (proto-Tibetans) and horsemen of the Rong (proto-Xiongnu), among many others—but the archaeological record suggests many forgotten cultures that either died out, were wiped out, or thoroughly assimilated within the early Chinese world. In the 1980s at Sanxingdui in Sichuan, for example, archaeologists uncovered a realm characterized by the wide, alien, elongated eyes of its bronze statuary, the strange design of its forked ceremonial swords and priestly staves covered in delicate gold leaf; the intricate bronze birds that decorated its huge bronze decorative "trees" like floor-to-ceiling chandeliers; wide bronze "masks" thought to represent the spirits of the ancestors. There, is, however, no writing to provide any clues to what it all means. Perhaps the images of birds and fish represent two different tribes, united under a powerful ruler.

The artifacts of the Sanxingdui culture are hauntingly beautiful, but we know little about the culture that produced them. They probably represent the civilization mentioned in ancient Chinese histories as the people of Shu, but there is currently no way to say for sure. Ancient accounts mention that the people of Shu worshipped tigers, and there are three real tiger teeth among the materials, drilled with holes to wear as necklaces.

Almost everything we know about them comes from the Sanxingdui site itself, and was mainly unearthed from two giant sacrificial pits. Someone—we don't know who—smashed up the beautiful Sanxingdui statues around 1150 BCE and tore down the delicate bronze tree sculptures, piling up all the fineries in a pit with dead animals, sea shells from the distant coast, jade and elephant tusks. Then they set fire to it—what we have today has been reconstructed from the charred, half-melted remains.

If you thought this was the sign of violent regime change, you would not be the first to propose that some unknown invader rolled into the nameless state, carted away its people as slaves and destroyed all visible elements of its culture. But it is difficult to imagine a conqueror destroying items of value—the ivories and jade were surely priceless; the sea shells were liable to have been used as a form of primitive money. Moreover, there were no human skeletons in the sacrificial pit, which would be odd if it were spiteful destruction by an enemy. This suggests that the destruction was caused by the people of Sanxingdui themselves, in an attempt to buy divine approval after some terrible natural disaster—a crop failure or earthquake signifying the displeasure of Heaven. Such finds are part of the joy and frustration of Chinese archaeology: shadows of entire civilizations now lost forever, forgotten cul-de-sacs from the onward march of Chinese history. It is the Shang people, not the people of Sanxingdui, whose story comes down to us.

The last of the Shang kings was called Dixin, although the word that is used for him in many historical records means "crupper"—the part of a saddle that is looped around the horse's tail, and is most likely to get covered in waste.

We only have the word of the dynasty that supplanted King Crupper. They claim that they had ample reason to overthrow him. There were intimations, in his younger days that he was brusque and arrogant, and legends that he had managed to insult the gods through his impious behavior, once even joking in a temple that the statue of the goddess Nüwa was so beautiful, he wished he could have sex with her.

He had enjoyed a long reign, and was enjoying his old age. He liked his drink, his food, and his women, and best of all among the women, he liked Daji. Said to have been one of the most beautiful ladies in Chinese history, she had entirely bewitched the King, to the extent that later legends would claim she was an evil spirit, sent by Nüwa to avenge his temple insult. The king would entertain Daji with lavish orgies and banquets. He indulged her cruel love of the sound of others in pain, and her evil medical experiments, which included cutting out the heart of one of his chief ministers. He even assented to the *paolao*, a torture device in which a naked victim was made to dance atop a heated cauldron, only to inevitably tumble into the burning charcoal beneath.

The great challenge to the Shang was mounted by another tribe in the area, the Zhou, former nomads who had been a vassal people of the Shang for several centuries, prized for their skills with horses and chariots. Whatever language they had spoken when they first arrived, they were thoroughly assimilated—they spoke Chinese and worshipped with the rituals and ceremonies of the Shang. We still have their songs and epics, which tell of a great migration in 1325 BCE, as the tribe left their native plains behind and moved into what is now Shaanxi, living "in huts and caves, for they had no houses." Their great ancestor rode out with his wife "at his right"—implying that they were in a chariot—and reached the foot of a mountain near the banks of the Wei River.

> The Zhou plain stretched away
> With sour reeds and sweet violets
> Divining by the tortoise shell
> It said to stop and dwell
> To build homes without delay.

The Zhou people made straight walls using taut string as guide-lines, and bound frames, into which they rammed buckets upon buckets of earth. Their cries drowned out the drums that timed their pounding, as they set up city gates and palace doors, and then an altar.

The land was already occupied. Local "barbarians" protested and were put to flight, initiating a series of raids and conflicts that would see the Zhou further extend their territory by assimilating others. A war in 1135

BCE saw the victorious Zhou moving their capital to the location recently occupied by their conquered enemy. They appear to have been powerful allies for the Shang ruler, becoming increasingly assertive as their own power rose and the Shang kings' faded. By the 1050s BCE, the Zhou elders were ready to trust in omens and portents that claimed the Shang era was over. Later legends, however, offer a far more scandalous motivation, suggesting that the Zhou acted in revenge for the death of their leader's heir, who had been executed on trumped-up charges of attempted rape and kingly slander, after he had rejected the sexual advances of the insatiable Daji. As an indicator of the degree to which the Shang dynasty had devolved by now, the same legend has King Dixin ordering the dead youth minced and baked into cakes, which his father was then obliged to eat.

The father died before he could avenge the insult, but his second son took on the task, uniting a coalition of several hundred disgruntled clans, and leading a grand campaign against the Shang. In order to attract a little symbolic magic, he had carved a stone memorial to his father, proclaiming the dead man to have been a king, and carried it in a chariot in the midst of his army.

The *Book of Documents*, used throughout the following centuries in teaching state officials, claims to have preserved the details of the leader's stirring speech to the rebels, a pole-axe in one hand, a troop commander's flag in the other, as he addressed an assembly of ministers, captains, legion commanders and centurions, and representatives of 800 other states.

He began with a saying that was ancient even then: "The hen does not crow at daybreak." There was man's work, and there was woman's work, and the King was allowing himself to be swayed by the words of a woman. He was ignoring the ancestral sacrifices and pandering to the needs of barbarians, refugees, immigrants and criminals. He had even neglected the ancestors' songs, which was to say, he was failing to carry out the right rituals and hymns to gain the approval and cooperation of otherworldly spirits.

Although the King was the high priest of humanity, it was time to overthrow him. The King, however, did not even leave his palace, but sent an army to stop the rebels, which clashed with them at Muye (the Shepherd's Wilderness), about 30 kilometers (23.6 miles) outside Anyang. But the troops' hearts were not in it. They "inverted their spears," signifying surrender, in one version of the story; in another, they fought hard, and were massacred until there was enough blood on the ground "to float a log."

The rebels poured into the inner compound of the Shang. Realizing all was lost, the last king of the Shang donned his "jade suit"—thought to be a shamanic robe covered in amulets and pendants—and set fire to his own palace. Mirroring the destructive sacrifices that characterized the offering-pits of Sanxingdui, he destroyed his home and himself in some final attempt to reach for spiritual escape. The rebel leader fired three arrows from his chariot into the smoldering body of the dead king, and then, for good measure, he climbed down and hacked off the corpse's head.

"Crupper," he announced, "last descendant of the Yin, forsook his ancestors' bright virtue, defied the deities, did not offer sacrifices, and in his arrogance, was cruel to the hundred surnames of the city of Shang. Let this be known to the gods above."

It was a lofty claim about the King's unfitness to rule, and his own fitness to replace him.

"I have been charged to change the great mandate," he announced, bowing twice to heaven, "to replace the dynasty and to receive the bright Mandate from Heaven."

This is the first time that the concept of a Mandate from Heaven turns up in Chinese history. The rebel leader, shortly to be crowned as first King of the Zhou dynasty, might have overthrown a hated despot, but he had also started an unending cycle of regime changes. It was now official—kings ruled at Heaven's sufferance. Kings had a duty to perform the right rituals and sacred ceremonies. If they failed in their duties, Heaven reserved the right to revoke its mandate, and to appoint a replacement. It would take eight hundred years, but even the luster of the Zhou would eventually fade to nothing.

# CHAPTER 2

# ALL UNDER HEAVEN: FROM THE BRONZE AGE TO THE RISE OF QIN

T here were six lines of temple dancers, marching in procession, carrying the black banners of Qin. The musicians struck bronze chimes, while the soldiers, their armor laced in black, pounded the skins of the great war-drums, shining with fresh sacrificial blood. Many of the Duke's forty sons marched in the procession, barefoot, in coarse hemp robes, holding stone plaques depicting his ancestors, along with princely guests from a dozen states, and twelve solemn ambassadors from the Rong barbarians, bearing animal totems that looked from a distance like a forest of antlers, fox-tails and cow-horns. A chariot rumbled along amid the walking mourners, pulled by four black horses, bearing a bronze drum—a gift from the King of Zhou himself.

Ying Renhao, who would now be known eternally as Duke Mu ("the Solemn"), had reigned for 38 years. He had taken his once-derided domain to new heights, instrumental in wars over the troubled rival state of Jin, ever-ready with barges of grain for allies in times of famine.

The women did not get too near. They waited in their mourning sackcloth dresses on a bluff scattered with thorn bushes, overlooking the open grave. Jianbi stood among them, who once as a little girl had joined her mother and brothers in the king's throne room, standing barefoot on a pile of kindling and pleading for the life of her uncle. A rival duke, the man had repaid Qin's help in time of famine by mounting an attack on the country. Duke Mu had captured him and ordered the temple swept clean,

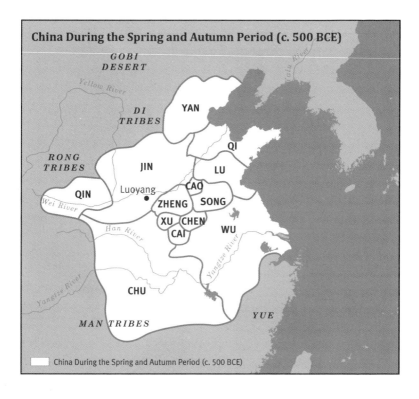

China During the Spring and Autumn Period (c. 500 BCE)

ready for a sacrifice. Only the tearful intercession of his own flesh and blood had saved the man's life.

There was a moment of shrill shrieking from the ceremony below—a serving girl had briefly wrestled free, begging for mercy, and suddenly silenced.

Jianbi thought on one of the funny stories about her father—the time his piebald horse had shaken off the traces from the chariot and run into the forests. By the time Duke Mu found it, the unfortunate animal had been butchered by mountain savages. Three hundred of them were gorging on it like jackals, and looked up to see the Duke, alone but for his charioteer and crossbowman.

"*You can't just eat that horse,*" he had said, as the savages reached for their daggers. "*You need to wash it down with wine.*" And he'd offered them a drink.

How the court laughed at that one. Such bravery in the face of overwhelming odds, and he dispelled the tension with a joke.

Far below, the music swelled, the pipes reaching higher, more discordant notes, drowning out the screaming of the horses and the struggles of the slaves. Bodies were tumbling into the pit, gouts of blood spraying in the air, rendering the edge of the tomb slippery. Etched ceremonial axes, their edges dulled by multiple uses, dropped into the dark after them, as the executioners took up new tools. It would take a lot to get through all 177 victims, but those were the rules. Status in death must reflect status in life, even if it meant throwing away good horses and strangling a dozen chamber-maids.

Three men stood by the grave, not dressed in hempen mourning, but in their best finery. The great and noble scions of Ziche, ready to follow their lord in death.

Jianbi squinted in the sunlight, unsure of what she saw. Could it be that Ziche Yanxi was trembling... actually weeping as he waited for the executioner's axe?

Was he not glad to do this final service for his lord?

Jianbi guessed not.

A yellow bird, its plumage marked only by a black, mask-like stripe across its eyes, twittered on a thorn bush, pecking experimentally at one of the berries.

Jianbi glared at it. This was a terrible waste. Her father's legacy should be a strong state and a bright future. But in death, he was failing his descendants. He was taking his best warriors with him to the grave. He was destroying his own legacy. Qin would probably never win another war again.

$$\circledcirc - \circledcirc - \circledcirc - \circledcirc - \circledcirc$$

Chinese imperial dynasties would come and go for 2,900 years after the Shang, and the historical record would all too often echo that same story, with tales of corrupt and cruel despots, a checklist of rumors about their misdeeds, and the arrival of some bright new hero compelled by Heaven to do the right thing and take over. But in invoking divine approval, the founder of the Zhou dynasty had created a new order. Rulers now needed to rule in the correct manner, or they, too, might lose Heaven's favor.

This was no invasion from afar. The procession from the Xia dynasty, to the Shang dynasty, to the Zhou dynasty seems to have been a simple swapping of hegemony between three groups that co-existed in central China. Similar jostling for power may have been underway between other tribes in other parts of China, but the narrative we have is of who communed with Heaven in the Yellow River area, and so this is the story we have of early "Chinese" history.

One only has to look at the vast pantheon of Chinese traditional religion to see the vestiges of many other cultures. There is more than one river god, more than one father of agriculture or weaver goddess—many different societies have rolled into one and continued to expand. The southern state of Chu, for example, had the fire god Zhurong, invoked in ceramics and bronze-casting. The Baiyue of the south had the storm goddess Longmu, the Mother of Dragons, who could be called upon to urge her four serpent stepchildren to bring rain. We have many similar legends about the distant corners of China, in the *Classic of Mountains and Seas*, but because it was not written down until many centuries later, we can never be sure how many of the stories genuinely date from antiquity. Instead, the only real evidence we have is from archaeology—such as cowry shells, brought from the sea coast many hundreds of kilometers away, and hence implying forgotten connections.

It is difficult to imagine people enthusiastically volunteering for the tin- and copper-mining jobs that fed the kilns of the Bronze Age. The ancient Chinese dynasties were slave societies, with a small aristocracy lording it over deferent farmers and helpless serfs. Outsiders were divided into arbitrary, catch-all classifications that have echoed throughout Chinese history—the barbarian *Di* to the north, the *Man* to the south, the *Yi* to the east, and the *Rong* to the west.

Wars with the barbarians kept a constant supply of human sacrifices and slave labor, sufficient to dig the raw materials out of the earth that would create the Zhou dynasty's eerie bronzeware, decorated with cubist *taotie* animal masks and swirls of *leiwen* "thunder-patterns," their dimpled chimes and ceremonial jade axes. The king of the Zhou bestowed entire peoples on his favorite sons and underlings, passing on the sovereignty of some fifty or so conquered states and vassals. Sometimes, these communities were moved elsewhere—in a vestige of the nomad days, entire tribes were ordered to pack up and relocate to new areas, where they might spend several hard years clearing new farmland and ramming the earth walls of a new citadel.

For divination, the Zhou acquired a new innovation that was more efficient and less messy than etching questions on turtle shells. The yes/no responses of the Shang oracle bones were replaced by a nuanced set of up to 64 possible replies, obtained by casting yarrow stalks to generate a series of random numbers. This was good news for turtles, but bad news for archaeologists, since there was no longer any material evidence of most of the questions asked. We do, however, still have the 64 possible replies, in the form of the *Zhou Changes* (*Zhou Yi*), better known today by its later name—*The Book of Changes* (*Yi Jing*). The book compiles and offers vague poetic interpretations of each answer, and its possible permutations, and would become the default method of Chinese fortune-telling for more than two thousand years.

But it was the chariot that was the true icon of the Zhou. Scholars are still unable to agree about its true usage. Was it itself a weapon of war, the tank of the ancient battlefield, or was it more of a symbol of status, a general's utility vehicle that allowed him to dart around the edges of the battlefield? Certainly, the lords of the Zhou were too important to walk, even if they were accompanied by foot-soldiers and spearmen. If you were anyone in the Zhou world, you had a three-man chariot—driver, swordsman and archer, united as a single military unit.

The Zhou had been just one of many tribes—we talk of them uniting 800 states, but we might easily have called them 800 villages, and there were hundreds more beyond the relatively limited compass of the Yellow River. But their rise to power came at a time when technology would allow for greater expansion and integration than had previously been possible. As the generations passed, the King's domain in Luoyang remained the same as it had done in ancient times—you could cross it on horseback in a day. But the outlying dukedoms, where authority was delegated to his sons and grandsons, had vast potential for expansion. Metal tools allowed for the clearing of forests; slave battalions provided the manpower to tamp down earthen flood-works and walls. Wars and diplomatic arrangements on the frontiers brought new peoples into their sphere of influence, many of whom were soon assimilated within a new vassal dukedom. Whereas the Shang had claimed allegiance and loyalty to the spirit of their own ancestors, the Zhou presented themselves in a broader fashion, as the pious servants of Heaven itself—they had, after all, introduced the topic of the Mandate of Heaven, so they were now bound to stick to it.

But all was not well under Heaven. Although the "Zhou dynasty" is remembered as the longest in Chinese history, spanning some eight centuries, it stumbled after its first 300 years, and never quite recovered. In a recurring trope, women got the blame, although it would be fairer to suggest that women were merely the public face of palace intrigues by their male relatives.

Technology was changing, and with it customs. The old aristocracy all but wiped itself out on numerous battlefields as the rival dukedoms began to turn upon each other in the rivalry for power. As the Zhou polity expanded beyond the original limits of the Yellow River flood plains, the terrain became unsuitable for chariots. New conquests began to favor armies of foot-soldiers, in turn fostering a military culture that began to rely on sheer weight of numbers, conscripts drawn from the common people. The old norm, a warrior elite that could not even acquire its weapons without being born into wealth, gave way to a mass of soldiery, with a promotional path based on achievements, not birth. At some point, in some unrecorded battle of the Zhou period, an aristocratic charioteer found himself facing a squad of foot-soldiers armed with crossbows, and the old era of champions fighting in single combat was over for good. Thereafter, a chariot was merely the command vehicle for a century of foot-soldiers, and the nature of battle changed.

So, too, did the court. As the aristocracy competed for power and influence, poisoning, bribing and back-stabbing, the smarter dukes began to realize that the best guarantee of loyal ministers was in a meritocracy like that to be found in the military. Instead of surrounding themselves with resentful minor nobility and vengeful cousins, they offered their patronage to common men of demonstrable talents. This, in turn, helped foster an intellectual revolution, as men from all over the known world tried to present themselves as worthy consultants on matters of state management, construction, politics and diplomacy. And, of course, that all-important question—how to keep Heaven happy and not lose its mandate?

There were omens, although it is all too easy to be wise after the fact. An earthquake in 780 BCE, wrote later chroniclers, should have been a clue. *The Book of Songs* (*Shi Jing*) an anthology of verse from the Zhou era, celebrates the bountiful harvests and healthy livestock of the previous king, but suddenly turns to ballads about untimely rains, wronged heroes, and this catalogue of disasters:

In the tenth month, the Moon crossed in front of the Sun…
  Both Sun and Moon diminished
the people plunged into disaster and melancholy…. Rumbles of
  thunder and lightning
no peace nor rest
the hundred rivers boil and leap
mountains and houses collapse
ridges turn to valleys and valleys to peaks. Woeful men of this
  day…

A list follows of the songwriter's chief suspects for Heaven's displeasure, ministers and magistrates and a captain of the guards, but: "All flatter the fair lady Bao." Seven named men are mismanaging the state, but the morose but beautiful Baosi, who shook the ruler's world in a wholly different way in the year after the earthquake, is the one who gets the blame. It would be enough, for most such stories, to say that she was a pretty girl who turned his head, but Chinese chronicles insist that she was a foundling child, born of a cursed mother, sired by a lizard that was itself born from the vapors of an exorcism, itself designed to deal with an infection of antique dragon saliva, released into the palace when a former king had opened a forbidden casket. With such a pedigree, it is unsurprising that Baosi should have been a striking beauty—even her name implies that she is a manifestation of an ancient curse, bringing the spirit of the conquered Bao tribespeople back to haunt the Zhou dynasty.

Baosi, which is to say, whatever clan or family supported her from the shadows, soon ousted the ruler's original wife and heir. Her new-born son was declared as the new crown prince, while the Zhou king tried desperately to make her smile. A hundred measures of gold were offered to anyone who could manage it, and when there were no takers, the King resorted to massive stunt. He ordered the lighting of the beacon-fires that summoned military aid from surrounding vassals, and Baosi laughed as entire armies rushed to defend the capital against a non-existent enemy.

"White Flowers," also in *The Book of Songs*, is a ballad about the queen that Baosi supplanted, as she idles away in a country retreat, seething that her husband has cast her aside. It is a masterpiece of jilted sentiment—she can't look out at the river flooding the fields, or logs being put on the stove, without her thoughts inevitably wandering back to her lord and his new mistress.

> The bell rings inside the palace
> I can hear it far away
> I think of him fondly
> But remember his harsh words.

> The heron is at the weir
> While the crane is in the trees
> She has what she wants
> While my heart reaps only bitterness.

If people can hear the bell outside the palace, they have certainly heard of her shame and exile. The heron can feed in the rich waters by the dam, but it has scared the crane away into the forest, where there are no fish. Every stanza is an artful observation of rural life, inevitably reinforcing her sense of abandonment and betrayal. This woman scorned, however, was not the only victim. Her son had been disinherited, depriving her father, the Marquis of Shen, from much of his influence at the court. The angry Marquis solicited the aid of the Rong nomads to the west, marching on the capital to avenge his daughter's honor. Guardsmen lit the beacons to warn the palace, but in ancient China's variant of the "never cry wolf" folktale, allies had become so tired of the Baosi-appeasing games that they failed to show up.

The Rong sacked the capital in 771 BCE, killing the King and Baosi's eight-year-old son, and carting away many of the palace treasures. The original heir was crowned as the new ruler, but after two years reigning over the ruins, with increasingly pushy Rong "allies" close at hand, his ministers got his assent to move the Zhou capital downriver.

"Boundless blue Heaven, who has brought our ruin?" asks *The Book of Songs*, unsure itself whether Baosi really deserved all the blame for what was truly a complex coup. The once-proud Zhou people fled 400 kilometers (248.5 miles) east to a new home—771 BCE marks the division between the Western Zhou, based near what is now Xi'an, and the rump regime of the Eastern Zhou, near what is now Luoyang. No matter how you tried to spin it, a supposedly infallible, inviolable king had allowed himself to be swayed by temptation, and plunged his state into turmoil.

The Zhou dynasty had been fatally weakened, and with it the authority of its kings, and the force of its traditions and rituals.

*The Book of Songs* contains wonderful glimpses of life in the Zhou state. Its lyrics speak of hunting for rabbits, chasing girls, happy wedding blessings, a lovelorn maiden sighing by a stream. There is a song about an old widower who misses his wife; the complaint of a wife abandoned by her husband; a soldier unhappy at his posting to the borderlands. A fuming girl waits at the spot agreed upon for a lover's tryst, convinced that her boyfriend is off with someone else. A wife pushes her husband out of bed at dawn to go hunting, assuring him that she will be pleased if he comes home with something to cook for dinner.

Some of the songs are credited to known historical figures, not necessarily as the original authors, but as the inspiration. An aristocratic mother frets over her two sons floating off in a river boat. A duchess mourns her fate, married to a man she does not desire.

*The Book of Songs* formed part of the Chinese curriculum for centuries. If you knew all 305, you would have a fair grounding in many of the rituals of the Zhou capital, even if you had never been there. You would know the lives and deeds of dozens of aristocratic celebrities, many of them parables with a lesson to teach. And you would catch a glimpse of yearning and heartbreak, misfortune and elation.

Notably, *The Book of Songs* gives voice to the concerns of Chinese women, who are often side-lined in the official chronicles. State records might occasionally offer pious words about a king's mother, effusive praise about a beautiful princess, or angry epithets directed at a kingdom-wrecking hussy, but chroniclers' were more concerned with matters of politics and diplomacy. It's *The Book of Songs* that points us at generations of forgotten lives, many elements of which ring true, even today—shy girls, bawdy girls, blushing brides, the happy home-maker and the wronged rape victim.

Many chapters collate songs from specific states, delivering doses of local color and gossip. In what is supposedly the first love song recorded in China, we hear a set of archaic rural allusions that would probably not win a lady over in the present day:

> Her hands like reaching reeds
> Her skin as smooth as lard

Her neck, white and slender like a tree maggot
Teeth like melon seeds.
Head like a dragonfly, brows like a moth
The dimples on her smile
And her cool, dark eyes.

At least she had a nice smile. This somewhat stumbling early love poem, hardly China's best, was written in praise of Duchess Zhuang Jiang of Wei, c. 750 BCE. Another song, "Swallows, Swallows," revisits the same woman decades later, childless and widowed, weeping as she waves off her best friend, a concubine of her husband who is now released from service.

Swallows, swallows in flight
Their darting wings
As she returns to her home
I follow her to the distant wilds
Until she dwindles beyond view
And my tears fall like rain.

Several other songs chronicle the life and family of the legendarily pretty Wen Jiang (d. 673 BCE), who was packed off to marry the Duke of Lu in 709. She bore him a son three years later, who would grow up to be celebrated as the greatest archer in the world in a breathless ditty—fair and grand and tall, and with such a high forehead and sparkling eyes. He fires four arrows and never misses. And he can dance. What a guy!

But while Wen Jiang's son would go on to be the next Duke of Lu, she herself found a different kind of fame when she journeyed back to her homeland with her husband in 694, and there openly rekindled an incestuous affair with her half-brother, now the Duke of Qi. There were plenty of songs about *that*, including a tongue-in-cheek wedding ballad that feigns confusion at why the brother's farewell is so clingy, and, under the pretext of land management, asks the bridegroom if his fields have already been ploughed. "Shouldn't you tell your parents?" it asks facetiously, referring to the background of his new bride.

Once the incestuous lovers were back together, another song from Qi compared her cuckolded husband to a trap that couldn't catch fish.

The worn basket at the weir
The fish swim freely
She comes home to Qi
Capricious like a cloud.

The worn basket at the weir
The bream and tench swim freely
She comes home to Qi
Inconstant as the rain

The worn basket at the weir
The fish in disarray
She comes home to Qi
As changeable as the waters.

The unfortunate duke was soon murdered at the brother's orders, and Wen Jiang stayed in her homeland thereafter. Her archer son, however, ruled Lu for thirty years, inadvisably marrying the daughter of the man who had arranged his father's murder, a woman who turned out to be oddly like his mother in many ways, although that is a story for another time. But compare this colorful commentary to the dispassionate entry in the *Spring and Autumn Annals* of the state of Lu, which simply reads: "The duke permitted his duchess, *née* Jiang to go subsequently to the state of Qi. In the summer, during the fourth month, on the [day of the Fire Rat], the Duke departed life in the state of Qi."

The centuries that followed saw numerous feints and slights against the failing Zhou kings. They huddled in the relatively small Royal Domain in Luoyang, while the estates of their dukes and vassals grew increasingly large. The mood of the time was also changing, and nowhere was that more obvious than in a conflict in 638 BCE that pitted old-school nobility against the new order.

The small state of Song was an enclave of the old ways, ruled by the descendants of the old Shang dynasty. It had been an act of mercy on the part of the Zhou dynasty, designed to show that the new kings were magnanimous in victory, but inevitably the dukes of Song became a breeding ground for revolution. They clung, rather quaintly to many of the old ways—such as passing on the dukedom not to the eldest son, but to the eldest brother. Duke Xiang (d. 637 BCE) was an aging nobleman who had fatally backed the wrong side in one of the many conflicts. He found his tiny state facing a massive onslaught from the huge state of Chu, rushing to the aid of an ally on his borders. As the Chu soldiers struggled to ford a river, it was the perfect time to attack them, but Duke Xiang refused to take advantage of their exposed situation. Instead, he waited patiently while they crossed the river, and gave them as much time as they wanted to get their ranks back together and prepare for battle. His enemies having been graciously permitted to prepare for battle, they then charged and annihilated his forces. Fatally injured, Duke Xiang still tried to point out he was doing the right thing:

> The noble man does not inflict a second wound. He does not capture those with gray hair. In days of old, soldiers on the march did not block those in transit. Though I am but the heir to a ruined state, I will not sound the attack drums while they are still preparing.

Duke Xiang's futile sense of righteousness would become a cruel joke throughout Chinese history among no-nonsense military men. "We are not Duke Xiang of Song," said Chairman Mao more than two thousand years later, "and have no use for his idiotic virtue and morality."

Times were changing. The sight of the diminishing temporal power, not merely of the Shang nobles, but also their successors in the Zhou dynasty created a suspicion that the Mandate of Heaven was similarly waning. And if the Zhou were doing something wrong, then it was anyone's guess what rituals and customs were lacking.

One of the most cutting lyrics in *The Book of Songs* is a protest about the practice of human sacrifice. It derives its name, "Yellow Bird" from the oriole sacred to the Yellow Sovereign, which has bright yellow feathers with black stripe on its head. The Yellow Bird is observed, on a nearby branch, as servants of a duke are executed at his graveside.

> This man… could hold his own against a hundred enemies
> But standing by the pit, he trembles in fear
> That blue presence, Heaven above, slaughters our best men
> If we could ransom him, his life would be worth a hundred.

The song can be dated precisely to 621 BCE and the funeral of Duke Mu of the western state of Qin, buried with 177 human sacrifices, including three of his most prized and loyal officers, dispatched merely to keep him company in the afterlife. The Qin people were doing their best to be as cultured as possible, observing Zhou ceremonial customs for the previous fifty years, but they had never been that keen on human sacrifice, and the funeral of Duke Mu just seemed wasteful to them.

The people of Qin were regarded by the more central states as an undisciplined rabble. They had only been accepted into the realm of civilized men in the 8th century BCE, when as vassals they had lent military aid to the unsteady regime of the Eastern Zhou. By forming a buffer state between the Zhou people and the Rong barbarians, the people of Qin were grudgingly accorded the status of a dukedom. However, in the Zhou core states, the reign of the late Duke Mu was regarded as a high point that the state was unlikely to regain. The author of the *Zuo Commentary* on the *Spring and Autumn Annals* would write that the execution of the Duke's best men at his graveside was sure to spell disaster for the state's future expansion—not only identifying the funeral as an epochal event, but also dating the authorship of the *Zuo Commentary* to sometime before Qin's rapid and unexpected resurgence. He, like the people of the Zhou core states may not have noticed or appreciated that the people of Qin were winning the war against the Rong, and hence extending their state far beyond its original borders. While the border walls of Qin looked unchanged to the Chinese neighbors, it would soon expand far out to the south and west, dwarfing all but the largest of the core states.

Apart from the controversial "Yellow Bird" protest song, most of the handful of Qin ballads in *The Book of Songs* should exhibit a common theme of hunting and warfare. Even their love songs favored the experience of a girl ogling a noble charioteer, or a loyal wife missing her soldier husband. The Qin people were very good at war, and they had been honing their abilities on the frontier, far away from the core states that they would soon turn upon.

One by one, the smaller dukedoms winked out of existence, assimilated by larger powers. The latter part of the Zhou dynasty, from the relocation of the capital in 771 BCE to the abdication of its last king in 256 BCE, is split into two periods. The Spring and Autumn era (771 BCE–451 BCE) derives its name from the title of the main source for its events, the *Spring and Autumn Annals* of the state of Lu. It is followed by the self-explanatory Warring States era (to 221 BCE), in which the former dukedoms fight to become the new ruler of "All under Heaven."

Philosophers asked what had gone wrong. Neither of the two most famous intellectuals of the later Zhou period saw themselves as the instigators of a school of thought. Both were trying in their own way to summarize what was already known. Although both were probably real historical figures, much of what has been written about them in the intervening centuries has the taint of myth-making, such that we cannot even be sure if they genuinely wrote the works that now bear their names. That, however, does not really matter. Postmodern critics may pick at the veracity of Laozi's *Book of the Path and Power* (*Dao De Jing*), but for two thousand years he was regarded as its author, and consequently as the founder of the religion that would come to be known as Daoism.

Laozi is said to have served in the early 6th century BCE as a scribe or librarian at the Zhou capital. His book was supposedly written after he quit the capital to seek a peaceful retirement, shortly before he rode off towards the west, past the last watchtower that faced the desert.

Daoism is a rural, parochial religion. It fixates on a worldview of the village farmer or forester, content with a simple country life. It has no interest in wars or cities, politics or wealth—such things do not concern the Daoist, who prefers to concentrate his mind and achieve one-ness with the universe—"The Way," or the *Dao*. Daoism may have once been a collation of folk beliefs and ancient religion, but also became a safe-haven for many of the beliefs and ideas that later, agnostic philosophers wrote off as superstitions—divination, magic and myth. It also preserves the ancient Chinese understanding of the cosmos—a constant search for harmony between dark, female essence and light, male essence, or *yin* and *yang*. The Daoist universe is comprised of five mutable elements, wood, fire, metal, water and earth, themselves liable to have been derived from the observable planets, and from an agrarian description of the cycles of the seasons.

If you had to ask, you would never know. Or as the first line of the *Dao De Jing* puts it: "The Way that can be spoken of is not the Way." The true Daoist pursued, as far as possible, *wu-wei*, a philosophy of inaction, steering out of trouble, trying not involve himself in the material world. In generations to come, this would be variously interpreted by pro-Daoist ministers, either as an appeasement policy in foreign affairs, or as a suggestion that the best of rulers should stay out of everyday politics and leave it to his trusty officials. After all, coveting power and possessions only led to sorrow. Daoism's enduring symbol, flashed by many a statue today, is for the hands to point above at Heaven, and below at the Earth, recognizing that man sits between them. Daoists priests hail one another with clasped hands in which the thumbs form a spiral—an evocation of the swirling sign of *yin* and *yang*.

The Daoist quest for perfection was a personal, inner-directed quest, far from the troubled of the world. The successful Daoist, having eaten the right foods and ingested the right potions, calming his spirit and achieving a blissful harmony with the universe, would become an immortal. This gentle fading into the natural world, a reflection of a life well lived and a peaceful old age, was often misinterpreted by aristocrats as some sort of alchemical secret of eternal life. Many are the Daoist priests in the historical record, harried by aging despots used to getting their way, demanding fast-track answers about how to beat death.

Daoism was a repository for myriad gods and demigods, local folk heroes and nature spirits, many of which had been marginalized by the establishment of Zhou power. Its legendary founder, Laozi, was a former official in retreat from the material world, famously said to have hectored a younger, up-and-coming scholar about his needless concentration on protocol. That man was Kong Qiu, known in the west as Confucius (551 BCE–479 BCE), obsessed, with almost comedic passion, with doing the right thing.

Confucius was perplexed by the difference between the ancient legends and the miseries of contemporary life. He conceded that there could be some propaganda, lies, and the jealousies of "petty men," or that some texts might be corrupt or incomplete. But however you explained it, something had gone wrong. The perfect ancestors of ancient legend, with their centuries-long lifespans and incredible powers over beasts, elements and spirits, were nowhere to be seen. Confucius bluntly considered only the material evidence around him—a likely source of his disdain for divination in all forms, and his refusal to engage on matters of the afterlife. He wondered what it was that had caused the Shang dynasty to lose the Mandate of Heaven, and although he never quite expressed it in such direct terms, what was causing the evident decline of the Zhou.

All other answers, he thought, would stem from that. Clearly, there were rules of propriety that people needed to stick to, and some of them had been forgotten, so that modern men didn't even know that they were breaking the law. But if we were able to recreate the perfect religious ceremony, the perfect ritual, the perfect music, manners and modes of living, then the state that followed those lines would itself become perfect. There would be no more wars, because even barbarians on the border would flock to imitate and join the ideal state. There would be no crime, because would-be criminals would not arise. Harmony was not something that you lounged into, like a Daoist, it was something that you made yourself, through education and right-thinking.

Confucius envisaged a rigid social order of respect and obligation, in which everyone knew their place. Children should obey their parents; women should obey men. Good relations within the family should be repeated in the outside world—rulers should behave as rulers; ministers and ministers; fathers as fathers and sons as sons. Humanity, for Confucius could not merely be fixed; it could be improved. The closer a society came to perfect behavior, the easier life would become. The conditions that created unrest, or criminality, or unhappiness, would be removed. People could make their own luck, preparing against misfortune by keeping granaries of emergency food, and by correctly maintaining earthworks and flood measures. State administration would make it easier for a ruler to rule if his ministers were proactive.

Even in his own time, Confucius was often ridiculed. If the story of his youthful encounter with the aging Laozi is true, the author of the *Dao De Jing* scolded him for being obsessed with rules and etiquette. Incumbent officials regarded him as naïve and unrealistic, and he spent much of his later years as a wandering exile, travelling from state to state as a celebrity consultant, offering his services to local potentates and invariably annoying their ministers. The words that begin his collected sayings, *The Analects*, are often cited in welcome by Chinese hosts, but might equally have been a pointed, passive-aggressive comment from an unwelcome visitor:

> Confucius said: "It is a pleasure to learn, and to put your learning to good use. It is delight to receive friends from afar. It is a quality of the true of heart that they do not care they are not famous."

Confucius saw himself as the interpreter of ancient traditions, not as the inventor of a new one. If he did not himself compile *The Book of Songs*, he certainly used it in his lessons. His recommended curriculum also included *The Book of Rites*, which outlined the customs, ceremonies and manners of both the Zhou and their predecessors, and *The Book of Documents*, which collated writings and speeches of prominent Zhou rulers—including the "Mandate of Heaven" address given by the Zhou leader on the morning of the Battle of Muye. He was also obliged to lecture on *The Book of Changes*, although Confucius appears to have been a reluctant teacher. Extant accounts show him poring over its passages in search of wisdom, but also refusing to use it for its intended purpose of divination. He never spoke, claimed *The Analects*, on matters of "extraordinary phenomena, amazing feats of strength, disorder or the spirit world." He also supposedly compiled the *Spring and Autumn Annals*, a year-by-year chronicle of important happenings in his native state of Lu.

The *Spring and Autumn Annals* ends with a portentous event—the sighting of a *qilin* "unicorn" in the state of Lu. The strange beast was reported to the aged Confucius, who interpreted it as a sign that the time of troubles was over, and that a new Sage King would soon arise. He wept, supposedly from happiness, crying "For whom have you come? For whom have you come?" He went to his grave in 479 BCE, believing that all his teachings were soon to be put to use in the hands of a great statesman who would end all the world's troubles.

Instead, the conflict between the states escalated to an all-time high, focused on the struggling kingdom of Jin, which imploded in civil war and was split into three smaller states by the aristocratic families that were stripping its assets. The collapse of Jin, a slow agonizing death by siege and starvation during the 450s, marks the end of the Spring and Autumn period, and the beginning of the even more hard-fought Warring States period.

It was a time of increased boldness. Over the next 150 years, the various dukes stopped even pretending to acknowledge the authority of the Zhou dynasty, instead proclaiming themselves kings in their own right. The names of these petty kingdoms have resonated throughout Chinese history—sometimes disappearing for centuries before recurring once more as the names of provinces, ducal domains and new dynasties. The state of Jin, for example, might have died in the 5th century BCE, but it would be appropriated by no less than six aspiring dynasties over the next millennium, and endures today both as a modern prefecture and the official abbreviation for a Chinese province.

The increasingly larger kingdoms argued over an initially unspoken question—if the Zhou had lost the Mandate of Heaven, then who had the right to claim it? Nobody dared call themselves the new chosen one—that might invite its own disasters. Instead, the various leaders argued over who would be the *Ba* or Hegemon—the chairman of a council of nobles. This nebulous position was held, or at least claimed, by several leaders over the years. At least two of them implied that they were thinking of restoring the bloodlines of the lost Shang kings. Several were scandalously not even "civilized," including the rulers of Wu and Yue, both in the Yangtze river delta, Chu, which was south of the Yangtze, and Qin, to the west.

It was, some claimed, a sign of the times that such societies even thought they had a chance. In one infamous incident, the king of Chu wrote to the Zhou ruler, inquiring about the weight of his nine sacred bronze cauldrons. Nobody would need to know such a statistic unless they were planning on taking them somewhere else, turning the question into a calculated insult.

The constant struggle turned people mean. That, at least, was how a Confucian might have explained the mood of the times, as states became increasingly brutal and conniving in their activities. Some were merely applying the message of military treatises like *Sun Tzu's Art of War*, and particularly its thirteenth chapter, pursuing espionage and intrigues at all costs in order to avoid the even greater costs of open conflict. Others openly questioned the validity of statecraft typified by Confucius and instead proposing a tougher regime based on the strict enforcement of laws and punishments—Legalism.

Although he was by no means the first Legalist, Shang Yang (c. 390–338 BCE) would become the most famous, because he got to put his ideas to work in an entire state. Lord Shang was born from minor nobility in a minor state, but sought employment elsewhere. Unlike Confucius, who rarely found himself in a position to put his ideas into direct practice, Lord Shang found employment in the westernmost state of Qin. He arrived with a striking letter of recommendation from his homeland patron, advising the Duke of Qin to either hire him immediately, or put him to death to prevent him becoming the worst of all enemies.

Back in the day of Duke Mu, the man whose funeral inspired the song

"Yellow Bird," Qin had been one of the most powerful states in the known world. Now it had sunk back into obscurity, and its duke was ready to invite expatriates from all over China to come and make Qin great again. Lord Shang was right at the front of the queue, ready to offer his advice on a cool, calculating version of statecraft. There were, he said, thirteen vital statistics that every administrator needed to know, including headcounts of livestock, able-bodied men and women, grain stores and animal fodder. With a certain, dictatorial air, Lord Shang distinguished sneeringly between "those who made a living by talking" and "useful people," apparently counting himself among the latter.

Lord Shang contrasted these important statistics (numbers that an administration could work with) with the parasites that drained the energy of a state: a checklist of Confucian textbooks, virtues and assumptions. These wasteful pursuits included "rites and music, *The Book of Songs* and *The Book of Documents*, self-cultivation and goodness, filial piety and fraternal obligations, honesty and sincerity, integrity and inflexibility, charity and righteousness, disrespect towards the military and objection to war." For Lord Shang, political factions were a distraction; the best of leaders played along with ceremonies and protocol only when it suited them, otherwise they were locked into the tracks of the past. There was no point being polite to one's foes like the foolish Duke Xiang, or being soft on crime like the timorous people of Confucius's homeland of Lu. That was the way of the loser and Lord Shang was only interested in winners. The way for Qin to win was to militarize the whole state, and to control the people with a ruthless system of rewards and punishments.

Qin was already markedly pragmatic. The state had banned human sacrifice in 384 BCE, supposedly because of a growth in humanitarian ideals, although a cynic might suggest that there was rarely anything philanthropic about Qin policies, and that it was far more likely to be a recognition that the labor of a living slave was worth more to the state than a rotting corpse. Lord Shang took such realism to new extremes, turning the whole state into a military enterprise. Conscripts swelled the armies, and the army's conquests brought in legions of slave labor to work on huge infrastructure projects—new roads, canals that also opened new farmlands, and plenty of wall-building, both as dams and as fortifications to hold back any warlike neighbors. State granaries stored food as insurance—although nothing could ever stop bad weather and poor harvests,

China was henceforth better prepared to endure tough times.

There were tax breaks for making babies, and penalties for remaining unmarried. The inhabitants of every "ten houses," which is to say, any village, were responsible for policing their own neighborhood. If a crime were committed and the neighbors did not report it, they would be cut in half at the waist.

The death penalty was extended to cover a whole bunch of relatively minor crimes, along with other punishments including exile and mutilation, and harsh, multi-generational penalties that would find a corrupt minister's grandchildren still paying his fines decades later. Poverty and vagrancy were themselves crimes, punished by enslavement in the government's work gangs. Slaves that were so badly mutilated that they could not work were assigned to the "hidden offices," crammed into alcoves to operate doors and fans.

Even the nobles were not exempt. Below the ruling family of the Qin state, nothing was hereditary. Nobody got a post just because his father held it. Soldiers in training received bonuses based on their ability to put arrows in a target. On the battlefield, aristocrats of Qin faced demotion if they did not win glory on the battlefield. That, after all, was what they were for. Bonuses were awarded for acts of bravery and heroism; there were penalties for retreating.

The Qin law was as uncompromising as its architect—read between the lines of *The Book of Lord Shang*, and there is a chillingly jocular tone, as if he expects the terrible severity of his laws to be an incentive and deterrent. "If I say that there are severe penalties that extend to the whole family," he wrote, "people will not dare to try, and as they dare not try, punishments will not be necessary."

If you were caught committing a petty crime, which was highly likely, because helping you get away with it would itself be an offense for your friends and family—you could buy your way out of trouble. If you could supply slaves to perform labor for the state on your behalf, or failing that, a suitably monetary donation that allowed the government to source some on your behalf, you could get away with it.

However, in matters of *serious* crime, nobody was safe. The ultimate test of Qin law came when Duke Xiao's own son committed an unspecified but severe crime. Nobody, Lord Shang had said, was above the law, although he could not really act directly against the heir to the dukedom.

Instead, the boy was made to watch as one of his tutors was mutilated and another was inked with tattoos marking him as a criminal.

"The next day," reports the *Grand Scribe's Records* laconically, "the men of Qin all hastened to obey the laws." Lord Shang had made his point, but he had also made a deadly enemy in the form of the duke's son and heir.

Lord Shang served for ten years as the leading minister of Qin, but he would not live to see his project reach fruition. He was the favorite of the Duke of Qin, but when the old man died, his thirteen-year-old successor spoke for an entire faction of embittered rivals who had been biding their time. The boy ordered Lord Shang's arrest for conspiracy and treason, and the Nine Familial Exterminations—the execution of nine levels of Lord Shang's relatives, children and grandchildren, cousins and in-laws. Lord Shang went on the run, only to be foiled by his own laws. He tried to stay at a roadside tavern, but the innkeeper refused to let him in unless he followed the letter of Qin law and presented his identification. He tried to seek political asylum across the border, but the neighboring kingdom was so afraid of Qin reprisals that they sent him back. The army caught up with Lord Shang, and he was sentenced to be pulled apart by chariots.

The boy who ordered his death would still not have his manhood ceremony for another seven years. He had grown up in Lord Shang's militarized state, and would ultimately proclaim himself to be its first King, in imitation of other coronations breaking out all over the vassal states of the Zhou dynasty. He would also temporarily drop out of the power politics of central China, choosing instead to conquer the Sichuan region to his southwest, doubling the size of his domain beyond the reach of his rivals. By the time he died in 311 BCE, Qin was at war in the very center of the Zhou world. His son would occupy the Zhou capital itself and, just to show that the people of Qin were still kind of punchy, die aged 23 after inadvisably attempting to lift one of the Zhou ruler's sacred palace cauldrons in a drunken bet. He dropped it in on his shin, and took a day to die.

The dead weight-lifter's half-brother was enthroned while still a teenager and ruled for 57 prosperous years, initially with his mother as regent. There are some truly baffling stories in the annals about Queen Dowager Xuan (338–265 BCE), who constituted an entire second front while her son was off fighting her homeland of Chu, south of the Yangtze. She pursued, seduced, and had two children with the leader of the barbarian Yiqu people, supposedly all part of an elaborate plan to lure the nomad chief to his death, and thereby winning the entire Ordos region for Qin. She lived into her early seventies, and famously mused on her death bed that she would like her current lover to accompany her to the grave, before changing her mind. She remembered, in the nick of time for some lucky man, that the people of Qin held no truck with thoughts of the afterlife. Tombs of the Warring States era show that her attitude was catching on all across China, with symbolic figurines in place of actual sacrifices among the grave-goods.

Qin inflicted severe damage on the state of Chu, south of the Yangtze, and spooked the remaining kingdoms enough for them to form numerous alliances against it. This only served to make the Warring States period even more confusing, with buffer states shored up in order to keep enemies apart, and skirmishes between countries that did not share a physical border, leading to collateral invasions and proxy wars.

Lord Shang's grand project, to create an institution and a monarch fit to rule All Under Heaven, was approaching fruition. After Queen Dowager Xuan's son died of old age, Qin saw a deeply suspect series of sudden royal funerals. The son and grandson both died within four years, leaving yet another thirteen-year-old boy on the throne in need of a regent.

Ying Zheng (259–210 BCE) was the culmination of the Legalist scheme, although he was also liable to have been intended as a puppet for other figures. Chief among the powers behind the throne was his mother Zhaoji, and her once and future lover, the merchant millionaire Lü Buwei, whom some writers assumed to have been the new king's true father.

Lü Buwei has been harshly treated by posterity, written off as an uncouth business tycoon with ideas above his station, obsessed with the art of the deal, funding the entourage of Ying Zheng's father in order to buy his way into political power. His biography in the *Grand Scribe's Records* features him cynically weighing the likely return on investment—tenfold on agricultural development, a hundredfold on trading in gemstones, but potentially infinite for a man who could somehow buy into a kingship. Soon serving as a leading minister to the boy-king, and, it was said, resuming his relationship with the young king's widowed mother, Lü Buwei also tried to purchase scholarly integrity, funding the multiple authorship of an ultimate almanac and encyclopedia. Likely to have formed, or at least reflected, the curriculum of the boy-king's studies, the *Annals of Lü Buwei* was heralded by its patron as the perfection of all knowledge, impossible to improve by the addition or subtraction of a single word. It was, however, something of a departure from Qin's Legalist policies. It told stories about the hated Confucius, and even repeated his observations that the greatest of rulers in antiquity had appointed the ablest man for the job, rather than relying on the succession.

If Lü Buwei was setting himself up to persuade the young king to relinquish his throne in favor of the man who had all the best words, he was fatally mistaken. The boy's own tutor, Li Si, was a fearsome Legalist cut from the same cloth as the late Lord Shang, and proved able in out-maneuvering the power-brokers who planned to have the young king killed and replaced by a more pliable brother. At least one (possibly several) palace coups were thwarted, leading to the official end of the regency amid a whirl of banishments and executions. As one of his first acts in power, Ying Zheng proposed a purge of all foreign influences from the state of Qin—a draconian measure to wipe out diversions from its militarist destiny, but also to remove dangerous intrigues by the last few enemy powers. Li Si, who was, like many of the king's servants, himself an expatriate, delivered an impassioned speech in defense of Warring States diversity.

The Qin court, he observed, drew on a rich community of immigrant advisers and concubines, and was adorned with artifacts from all over the known world. The king's jade was quarried from the Kunlun Mountains at the north edge of the Tibetan Plateau. His women painted their faces with cinnabar from Sichuan. He wore the Bright Moon Pearl from Hebei, and rode a horse given to him by the Rong nomads. He wore the Taia Sword, an antique blade that had once been wielded by the kings of Chu, south of the Yangtze. His standards had green peacock feathers from the far south; his drums were made of alligator skin. But these icons and artifacts were *no longer foreign*—they were now all part of Qin, an accretion of objects and materials that now helped define a newer, greater nation.

"Mount Tai does not deny a clod of earth," Li Si had said, referring to the sacred peak said to be closest to the gods, "and thus it is able to achieve its greatness."

Lü Buwei was exiled and soon died. Li Si became the new chief minister, and the armies of Qin continued to fight against the few surviving states. His enemies hatched a final plot to kill him before he could lay claim to All Under Heaven: a convoluted scheme to put a suicidal assassin in his throne room. The man in question was Jing Ke, a swordsman of ill repute, who arrived in Qin in 227 BCE and announced himself as an undercover emissary from the northern state of Yan.

As a symbol of his lord's integrity, he presented the king with the head of a fugitive Qin general in a box. The man had sought asylum in Yan, but here was proof that Yan wanted to appease Qin.

Jing Ke was beckoned onto the royal dais to show Ying Zheng the map he carried, which marked out great areas on the Yan borders that were to be ceded to Qin without a single arrow being fired. It was surely the grandest victory that Qin could hope for, the very pinnacle of the Art of War, the creation of a state so fearsome and powerful that rivals would surrender voluntarily before war had even been declared. But this was a moment that would be celebrated ever more in a Chinese proverb.

*"As the map unrolls, the dagger is revealed."*

It was the culmination of years of planning. It had costs dozens of lives, since even those only peripherally connected to it had been killed to maintain their silence. The traitor general had willingly given his life to buy Jing Ke access to the King. Jing Ke himself was on a suicide mission, sure that neither he nor his henchman would make it out alive. He had taken his payment in advance, living for several years at the height of luxury and excess, granted all the luxuries and women of Yan. The dissident kingdom had gambled all of its resources on this last-ditch attempt to stop the King of Qin before it was too late.

Jing Ke snatched up the poisoned dagger, and leapt.

# CHAPTER 3

# YEAR ZERO: THE EMPIRES OF QIN AND HAN

L iu Xijun was glad that she never knew her father, that traitor against the throne, that pervert who bedded his own sister; the murderer who would overturn a boat full of ladies, just to watch them drown. That, at least, was what she had been told about him. But his downfall had also been hers, when she was still an infant. Her mother, executed for witchcraft while she was still a child, dooming her to life in the palace little better than a slave's, and then the tap on the shoulder, the opportunity of a lifetime: the chance to be a princess once more, the chance to make a royal marriage, to serve Emperor Wudi by bringing in a rich dowry of strategic consequence, to live out her days as a ruler of men.

Her eyes sprang open. For a moment, she could believe she was in a richly appointed palace. A tumble of furs across the sleeping platform, still-warm stones holding back the dawn chill. Light streamed in through multiple pinpricks in the roof. The wall shook with a strong gust of wind. This was no palace, it was a yurt, a tent with wicker walls and knotted beams made from saxaul wood.

Lieqiaomi dozed beside her, his tanned chest a mess of faded tattoos. A white, frothy mess of sour horse's milk bubbled on his lips and stuck in his moustache and beard—*koumiss*, chosen tipple of the nomads. She gingerly squirmed out from beneath his arm, and gathered her robes about her. They smelled of smoke and milk, but she supposed, so did she.

The tent was full of snores and farts. A pile of Wusun tribesmen was

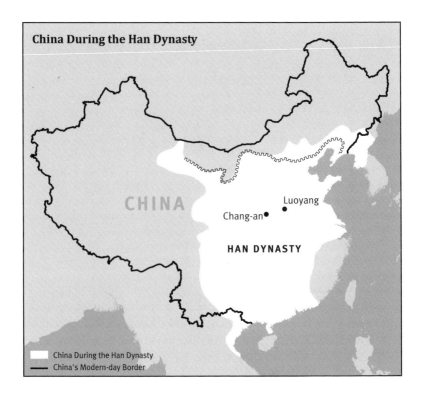

**China During the Han Dynasty**

CHINA

Luoyang

Chang-an

**HAN DYNASTY**

China During the Han Dynasty
China's Modern-day Border

to be found on the other side of the central screen, nestled against each other for warmth, empty *koumiss* gourds scattered around them, half-eaten dishes of jerky and scattered cheese.

She pulled aside the tent's front flap, stepping over the puddles of vomit she knew would be there—it was a capital offense to spew one's food or drink inside a tent, but "outside" began tantalizingly close. The tents around were already a bustle of activity, but only from the women and the slaves. Already there was the acrid tang of dung fires in the air.

Outside, the morning sun stung her eyes. The green hills in the distance were dotted with sheep and goats, and the grays and browns of horses. Most of the black ones were already back at the capital, of course, a hundred of them granted to the Chinese as part of her dowry. The grass was short, as far as she could see. It would not be long before they would have to move again.

A servant girl, scurrying past, turned and bowed without stopping.

Was she not now a princess of the Wusun? Was she not the Lady of the Right, a wife of the king? Lieqiaomi had favored her last night, and that would mean that the Lady of the Left, a towering, muscled nomad woman with a face like a demon, was sure to be a perfect bitch for the next week.

Servants were approaching, carrying dishes and boxes. With mounting horror, she realized that she would not get her tent back all day. If Lieqiaomi had spent the night, as he evidently had, then her yurt was the site of the Wusun court for the rest of the day. Unending hours of argumentative councils in a language she could barely speak; pointless displays of bravado and subjugation.

Something was tugging at her sleeve, weighing it down. She reached inside and found her prized bronze mirror, its shiny surface already dented from a couple of falls. She gazed briefly at her face, devoid of make-up. Someone had said something about tattoos last night. She didn't follow all the Wusun language, but it was apparently a big joke.

Not my face, she pleaded with the mirror. Not my face.

Something else. Crumpled white silk, once the lining of a robe. But it was flat and it held ink. She held it open and admired her handiwork—a letter to the Emperor Wudi, informing him of her ongoing mission in the distant west, waiting in her sleeve to be handed to the first squadron of Chinese soldiers that passed through on patrol. She had waited weeks, and still no-one had come. She had ample time to get the tone just right. She knew, somewhere deep down, that she was never going home, but she could at least shame him into sending her some luxuries.

> They married me off, to the other side of Heaven
> Far away to a strange country, to the king of the Wusun
> A tent is my home, its walls made of felt
> Raw meat is my food, and koumiss my drink.
> All day my heart aches with longing
> If only I were a brown goose that could fly away home.

$$\odot-\odot-\odot-\odot-\odot$$

The assassination attempt on the King of Qin did not work. Jing Ke chased Ying Zheng with his poison dagger around the pillars of the throne room in a fateful, fruitless scuffle, the King struggling to pull the oversized Taia blade from his belt. His physician threw his medicine bag at the would-be assassin, distracting Jing Ke for a vital moment. Ying Zheng finally unsheathed his sword and cut Jing Ke down, hacking at his body as it slumped against a pillar.

If anything, the botched mission presented Qin with a new excuse to stage a punitive invasion of the state that had tried to have him killed. Within a few years, the last kingdoms had fallen. With nobody to stand in his way, the King of Qin proclaimed himself to be the First Emperor, combining two old words for sovereign to make an ultra-ruler, greater than all the others.

The simplicity of the name was intended as a Year Zero—a removal of all previous precedents. There would, hoped the First Emperor, be no more need for complex lineages and ever-changing reign-names or temple names. There would simply be a First Emperor, followed by a Second Emperor, and then a Third, and so on, for ten thousand prosperous years.

The swords of the conquered kingdoms were melted down and refashioned into twelve colossal guardian statues, which would survive far longer than his empire—the last of them was not destroyed for 400 years. The language itself was also hammered into a new shape. Local accents and slang might have remained audible around the empire, but now there was a single, approved character for each written word. Weights and measures were standardized empire-wide, and a generation of slave laborers, the prisoners of the long war to unite the empire, were put to work on irrigation projects, road-building and defense. Most famously, they linked together several fortifications in the north, creating a single "Great Wall" to mark the frontiers of the Qin empire—the First Emperor was not the master of All Under Heaven after all, and there was still a nomad threat.

Qin had been ruthless in destroying the archives of conquered states, and had overbearing disdain for scholars who attempted to cite legendary parables or warnings. During his reign, the First Emperor initiated a nationwide purge of all books that were not directly concerned with matters medical, military, astronomical, or agricultural. Now there was a single empire, Qin wanted a single narrative of history, the removal of ancient king-lists and histories of noble houses. Nobody in the Qin court would be able to admonish him with tales him of how things were done in days of old, or cite authorities like Confucius. Many of the works written before the time of the First Emperor have only survived because they were buried in tombs before his accession.

Mercifully, it did not last. The First Emperor died in 210 BCE, possibly poisoned by one of the many immortality elixirs he was quaffing in a vain attempt to conquer death. Ironically, in the death of China's very first emperor, we see signs of the kind of court politics that would hound the imperial system for the next two thousand years. Very little is said in the ancient annals about the women of the First Emperor, although he undoubtedly had multiple concubines. It is not clear if he had an official "wife"—protocol may have demanded that no one woman was worthy of being favored above any other, in order to prevent any signs of favoritism towards the conquered states. When we read of the court factions that dueled over which of his sons would replace him, we may actually be reading of the affines, which is to say, relatives by marriage, as they push and shove to get their boy put on the throne. For generations to come, such influence was supposed to be curtailed by the use of a staff of palace eunuchs—castrated servants who could present no threat to the harem. In-laws hoping to push their family influence would hardly volunteer to be castrated themselves: it was a punishment reserved for rapists and other criminals, and in ancestry-obsessed China, an admission that the eunuch was the end of his line.

However, even eunuchs often still had family members to promote, positions to protect and favorites to play, as did the First Emperor's ministers. The great tragedy of the First Emperor's legacy was enacted by a eunuch called Zhao Gao, who had a personal vendetta to pursue against some of the First Emperor's most trusted military men, the Meng family. The records, as ever, are garbled, but it may well have been that one of the Meng family had sentenced Zhao Gao to castration in the first place, in punishment for an unnamed crime. Zhao Gao and the First Emperor's chief minister, Li Si, kept the Emperor's death quiet for as long as possible, while issuing edicts in his name to settle scores and remove opponents. As part of his vendetta, Zhao Gao arranged for the death of the First Emperor's eldest son along with the Meng family, coincidentally destroying the Qin dynasty's military capabilities in the north.

The First Emperor is remembered today for his lavish tomb outside modern Xi'an, the home of the fabled Terracotta Army, life-sized figures of more than 7,000 soldiers, each with individual features. The reason for such exactitude may lie in the Qin nation's love of money-making schemes, and the Qin people's disdain for human sacrifice. By Qin's own customs, a tomb needed to be a material reflection of a person's importance while alive, and since the First Emperor was, by definition, the most important person who had ever lived, he was sure to have a tomb to match. Qin laws being what they were, surely his honor guard would be afforded the opportunity to buy their way out of accompanying him in death? What better way to validate their contributions by commissioning life-like effigies of each and every one, to stand guard at his tomb for all eternity?

However, the tomb complex was never completed. Although the First Emperor was laid to rest in the great tomb mound (or a nearby jade mine, depending on which chronicler you believe) and many of the temple precincts were constructed, at least one of the great pits was left empty. Only a handful of swords have been found at the site itself, suggesting that the Terracotta Warriors stand empty-handed, relieved of their original weapons by rebels who needed the weapons to overthrow the Second Emperor.

The Second Emperor was the First Emperor's youngest son, persuaded by his puppet masters that he served the empire best by being neither seen nor heard. As a result, he was kept in the dark about his empire's decline until it was too late. His short reign is characterized in the *Grand Scribe's Records* as a set of calamities: vindictive putsches against his half-brothers and their families, the inadvisable raiding of provincial granaries to feed the capital, and the dogged pursuit of ongoing large-scale building projects, even as the empire slid into revolt. In an moment that has passed into Chinese legend, and a mocking parody of the writing reforms of the Qin empire, Zhao Gao tested the loyalty of the courtiers by telling the Second Emperor that a red deer (in Chinese, a *malu* or literally "horse-deer") was actually a horse. Only those who agreed with him or abstained were allowed to hold onto their lives; everyone who protested it was really a deer was executed. In Chinese, "*pointing at a horse and calling it a deer*" has become a proverbial analogy for deception.

The brief, single-generation dividend in infrastructure development, paid largely in slave labor, was all but used up. Although there were thousands of aristocratic hostages close to the Qin capital, there were sufficient discontents of all classes to start multiple revolts. One of the biggest began in what had formerly been the state of Chu, where two army officers, late for duty because of a rainstorm, rebelled against the death penalty they were sure to receive under Qin law. Figuring they had nothing to lose, they led their company of 900 men in a revolt. This swelled to thousands, although the untrained nature of the rebels was no match for the loyal Qin troops.

Chu soon became the site of a far more organized rebellion, when a local family tracked down a grandson of one of its last kings, and proclaimed the royal house to be restored. This resurgent state was merely the most prominent of several rebel standards, chiefly because two generals that fought in its name would eventually fight each other for supreme control. Xiang Yu was the son of the original kingmaker who proclaimed Chu to be back in business, a towering, ruthless military figure from an aristocratic family, who infamously ordered the burial alive of 200,000 surrendered Qin troops. The other was Liu Bang, a self-made man who had served Chu both as a kingdom and as a Qin province. Like the instigators of the first uprising, he was supposedly propelled into action by the threat of Qin punishments—escorting convict laborers to the site of Qin emperor's tomb, he had allowed several prisoners to escape. Realizing that his life would be forfeit, he released the rest and went on the run, finding himself as the leader of a rebel army, its ranks swelled by many of his own freed prisoners.

Xiang Yu and Liu Bang tore up the old Qin provinces in a series of victories against the luckless Qin army, which itself was lacking in support from the Second Emperor's collapsing regime. As they marched on the Qin capital, the eunuch Zhao Gao feared that he would be executed for incompetence, and preempted any punishments by staging a palace coup. The Second Emperor pleaded for his life in a diminishing set of bargains that poetically encapsulates the fall of Qin. At first, he begged to be given a command as a prince in the new order, or failing that, some noble title and an estate somewhere. His last recorded words have him begging to be allowed to live as a commoner with his wife and children. When even this was refused, he took his own life.

There was no Third Emperor of Qin. The Second Emperor's nephew was placed on the throne as a mere "king," reigning for 46 days. It was just long enough for him to personally murder the treacherous Zhao Gao and execute the eunuch's relatives. As the Chu army approached his city, he placed a rope around his own neck, and rode out to surrender to them in a white chariot pulled by white horses, as if heading for his own funeral.

The rebel King of Chu, who inconveniently died in 206 BCE, had promised the Qin heartland around modern Xi'an, as a kingdom to whoever occupied it first, leading to an increasingly bitter rivalry between the two generals. Liu Bang won the race, occupying the city and accepting the surrender of its ruler. He did so with relative compassion, ordering his men to keep the city intact and to spare its residents. Under the terms of his deal with the King of Chu, this made him the putative new ruler of the region, a fact that Xiang Yu, who had four times the manpower at his command, refused to accept.

He invited Liu Bang to what must have been one of the tensest banquets in Chinese history, the Feast at Hong Gate, the name of which remains a poetic synonym for a trap, in which the victim is "caught like a fish between knife and chopping board." A scheme to have Liu Bang murdered in a "sword-dance" gone awry was thwarted by his alert lieutenants. Liu Bang escaped on the pretext of going to the toilet, and was eventually fobbed off with the kingship of the region of Hanzhong, to the west, named for its proximity to the Han river. This is the point at which Liu Bang was proclaimed to be the "King of Han," which is why the year 206 BCE is usually backdated to mark the start of the Han dynasty, although his rule as emperor of all China would take several more years to establish.

The enmity between the two generals was soon rekindled, in a series of campaigns that saw them both warring against each other and against other states. Since Liu Bang was the lord of the Han river region, and Xiang Yu was a scion of the royal house of Chu, the final struggle for mastery of China became known as the Han-Chu Contention. It is symbolized, even today, in the central well of a Chinese *xiangqi* chessboard, marked as the "River of Chu and the Mountains of Han." Whoever wins the game gets to name the dynasty.

It could have all too easily ended very differently in 203 BCE, when the two generals hurled insults at each other from opposite sides of a river. The *Grand Scribe's Records* uses this occasion to list Xiang Yu's many faults, as Liu Bang comes up with a ten-point list of his worst sins, including his war-crime against the Qin soldiers, his destruction of the Qin capital (burning the library, and with it many of the sole surviving copies of pre-Qin books), and his vindictive decision to execute the First Emperor's grandson. Xiang Yu responded by ordering his archers to shoot Liu Bang, wounding the self-righteous general, but also rather making his point for him.

The two adversaries divided China between them in a short-lived truce, before it was settled for good in 202 BCE at the Battle of Gaixia, when Liu Bang and his allies advanced from multiple sides, and a dejected Xiang Yu, most of his forces dead, refused a ferry to safety and chose to make a last stand at the riverside against overwhelming odds. His morose supper on the eve of the battle, as he reflects on his changes in fortune, forms the setting for the Chinese opera *Farewell My Concubine* (*Bawang Bie Ji*), as his long-term mistress tries to cheer him up, before preparing for her own suicide.

Victorious at Gaixia, Liu Bang allowed himself to be proclaimed as the first Emperor of the Han dynasty. Already in his fifties, he would reign for only seven years before his death from an arrow wound sustained in a battle with yet another rebel princeling. However, his son would succeed him, and the Liu family would remain at least nominally the rulers of China for much of the next 400 years.

A climatologist can tell you that it is no coincidence that the Roman Empire and Han Empire should spring up at roughly the same time, and last for similar periods. Both benefited from the Roman climactic optimum, a relatively warm and stable period that lasted until 200 CE. Both foundered when they tried to stray too far from the agricultural core that enjoyed the most climatic benefits. Expansion in the Yellow River region placed increasing emphasis on the levees of the river—unmaintained, they could cause disastrous flooding, as they did in 14–17 CE. Harvests were just better in the early Han dynasty, and the desert did not come so close.

Until very recent times, when political correctness got the better of it, it was common to describe the Chinese people as "the Han," even though that term technically applies only to the 90% ethnic majority. This is all because of the Han dynasty, which was, literally, the definitive regime in Chinese history. Its borders encompassed one of the largest expansions of Chinese power for the next millennium, establishing our much of our modern concept of where China ends and the outside world begins. Everything within that world was now Chinese.

That was not, however, how things must have looked in the dynasty's early days, with the empire ruined by unrest that had lasted a generation, and a peasant's son elevated to the throne. Liu Bang was a no-nonsense ruler, who had to be prodded into conducting himself in a more suitably imperial fashion, and hectored over several years into appreciating the value of court ceremonial. It was his Confucian minister, Lu Jia (d. 170 BCE) who admonished him with words that would resonate throughout

Chinese imperial history, after Liu Bang rejected books and poetry, claiming that he did all his conquering from the back of a horse.

"Once my lord is done with the conquering," said Lu Jia, "does he also intend to rule from the back of a horse?" The reader of Chinese history sees this phrase turn up on many occasions in the centuries that follow, often spoken to braggart despots.

Startled by Lu Jia's comment, Liu Bang ordered him to assemble a report on what the Qin dynasty had done wrong, and how he might avoid their mistakes. But he was more concerned in his early days with dealing with a new problem that had been created by Qin "successes." A campaign in 215 BCE had pushed the Xiongnu nomads back across the Yellow River, north of the long bend that curves around their former pastures in the Ordos region. This victory caused internal strife among the Xiongnu, uniting them under a new overlord, Maodun (c. 234–174 BCE), who would return at the head of a newly militarized Xiongnu Empire of his own.

Hearing that his general in the north was being oddly conciliatory towards the Xiongnu, Liu Bang led a punitive military force against them in 200 BCE, discovering a little too late that he was dealing not with a few scattered horsemen, but with a confederation of tribes that matched his empire in size, spanning East Asia from what is now the Korean border to Lake Baikal and Lake Balkhash, incorporating all of what is now Inner and Outer Mongolia and much of northern Xinjiang. Hemmed in by the Xiongnu and fearing for his life, Liu Bang resorted to bribery, promising huge annual "gifts" of silk and grain, as well as an imperial princess as a wife for Maodun. This was the first of the deals under the "treaties of amity" (*heqin*), regarded by some Chinese as an embarrassing concession, paying what amounted to tribute to the Xiongnu in order to keep them from raiding the borders. Apologists for the policy, however, instead spun it as a long-term scheme, designed to tempt the Xiongnu with Chinese culture and luxuries, and to stealthily plant Chinese women as the mothers of future kings.

The Han Chinese came to see the Xiongnu as their dark half—a savage Other that lived an inversion of civilized life. Despite the dangers this presented to protocol, the *chanyu* overlord of the Xiongnu was regarded as a "brother" to the Chinese emperor, ruling over a topsy-turvy land that was China's literal opposite. In fact, the Chinese tried a little too hard to make the Xiongnu sound different, ignoring many points of agreement and similarity, and indeed the fact that many of the "Chinese" who fought the Xiongnu on the frontier were barely a generation away from being Xiongnu themselves. They claimed that the Xiongnu all wore furs and skins and lived in a frozen waste, they gave pride of place to the young rather than old, and practiced distasteful customs of marrying their dead brothers' wives. As if to prove this last point, at the death of Liu Bang, Maodun sent a marriage proposal to the widowed Empress Lü—an act regarded among the Xiongnu as the highest of compliments, and among the Chinese as the rudest of insults. He could have probably phrased it better, though, raunchily suggesting that they were a pair of singletons who could clinically console each other: "*I can use what I have to make up for what you lack.*"

Conflict with the Xiongnu was only over the zone where both cultures could subsist. Further north, the Xiongnu realm was written off by the Chinese as a dreadful wilderness of permanent winter. Conversely, the lands to the south of the Chinese core, below the Yangtze, were decried for being an awful tropical jungle, riddled with disease and predators. The air was so bad, claimed the Chinese, it forced poison into the lungs and created a race of impetuous hot-headed sorcerers, able to curse trees to wither, and to kill birds by merely spitting on them. Liu Bang was lucky he had made his home away from such miseries, between the extremes of terrible cold and dreadful heat—China once again presented as a pleasantly "middle" kingdom.

At the beginning of the Han dynasty, Chinese culture was still impressively diverse. Liu Bang had become the overlord of a patchwork realm that could have easily collapsed once more into the former Warring States; his China was still a riot of contending traditions. The *Grand Scribe's Records* reports an early religious ceremony at which Liu Bang, hedging his bets, let the priests and priestesses from all over his domain worship in whatever fashion seemed best to them. The shamans from south of the Yellow River made offerings to recognizable deities—Heaven, Earth, and the Waters [of the River]. The shamans from the north, closer to the steppes, had their own little pantheon, including the Five Lords (presumably the planets), the Lords of the East and the Clouds, and the First Cook (presumably a fire deity). Priests from further to the south, along the banks of the Yangtze, sacrificed to their ancestors, but also to beings such as the Controller of Lives and the Shimi Gruel God. River priests dealt directly with the Yellow River, while the "Nine Skies" priests performed a ritual of their own. Bringing up the rear, some shamans from the southern mountains, who had clearly not thought through the recent regime change, were still worshipping the recently overthrown Second Emperor of the Qin dynasty. These differing practices would last through several reigns, before Liu Bang's great-grandson, Emperor Wudi, began streamlining Chinese court ceremonies. The pantheon of Chinese traditional religion remains impressively varied, but many of these deities and spirits have shrunk into the shadows, of obscure regional festivals and catch-all saints' days. Almanacs remained fiendishly complex assemblies of portents and spirits, but day-to-day religious life was reduced to a far more limited set of gods.

Modern archaeology might have offered some dissenting opinions, but since very little survived the purges of the Qin dynasty, our understanding of what preceded it now relies heavily on books written in the Han era. Most of the works that do survive from before the Han dynasty, survive only in Han editions, reflecting the language and editorial whims of that later time. In compiling the first grand dictionary, the Han dynasty established the meaning and provenance of words themselves. The Han dynasty set the works of Confucius literally in stone after decades of mutation and interpolation, carving them onto slabs in approved editions, ready for eager scholars to take exact rubbings and locking them into the form that they retain today.

Sima Qian's *Grand Scribe's Records* collated and also redacted China's sense of its own history from the time of legends to his own era. The Ban family's *Book of Han* continued the story, and also the methodology of Sima's work, setting the precedent for the dynasties that followed—dour, detached biographies of each emperor, their best and worst ministers, their consorts and a few odd characters. The emphasis was always on learning from the past, on presenting a frank account of earlier times, so that the contemporary reader could avoid making the same mistakes. The result, however, would be to force much subsequent writing into a fixed pattern. A new dynasty arises, it flourishes and grows, but then its later members lose their way, ultimately ruin everything, and have the Mandate of Heaven revoked. Eventually they are supplanted by a new dynasty, and the pattern begins again, even if the new dynasty is initially comprised of foreign invaders, or takes several generations to get its act together. The historian and the reader get a recurring sense of *déjà vu* as each dynasty seems to follow the same narrative—it may be historically accurate, or we may be seeing chroniclers searching around in the evidence for scandals that match the template set by earlier dynasties.

The Han in their early, shaky years were keen to prove that they were entirely different from their Qin forerunners, leading to a concerted smear campaign. Much of the horror stories of the Qin dynasty and its fearsome First Emperor might easily be written off as tales designed to persuade the people of Han that life was so much different and better under the new dynasty, even though many of the laws, situations and practices remained in place. Opinions were divided between officials who accepted the Qin dynasty as the beginning of a new, imperial age, and older traditionalists who regarded it as an unacceptable perversion, to be corrected by a return to a federation of independent states.

The early Han dynasty was an uneasy compromise. The core area of central China, locked together with the First Emperor's infrastructure, was under direct imperial control. Outlying regions in the south and east, the last to be conquered by the Qin and the first to rebel against them, could not be administrated directly—lines of communications were too long. They required local administrators who could speak with the authority of the emperor, leading Liu Bang to set up 18 commands—districts ruled by his relatives or allies as subject kings (*wang*) or lesser nobility—from this point on in Chinese, the old word for king is often translated as "prince," on the understanding that such men lacked royal autonomy. They certainly were wealthy enough to deserve the title—it is the princes of the Han dynasty that found posthumous fame in our own era for being buried in priceless suits of jade. These are not the trinket-festooned costumes of archaic Shang rulers; these are like suits of jade armor, covering the body from head to toe, and invading its various orifices with jade covers and plugs, believed to be all the better to preserve it for the afterlife.

Unsurprisingly, these commands would gradually shift under central control over the decades to come. Equally unsurprisingly, their rulers often seemed to resent this, and several of the outlying regions would develop ideas above their station.

Not every part of the former Qin empire remained loyal. The far south, encompassing today's northern Vietnam, Guangdong and Guangxi, was an independent kingdom for a century. Cut off from the revolution and civil war that created the Han, it enjoyed a relatively peaceful transition, followed by an uneasy relationship with the Han emperors. Reflecting the dilemma over kingdoms or empire also underway in the north, one faction within what became known as the Nanyue kingdom (in Vietnamese, *Nam Viet*) supported reintegration with China; another, Nanyue's continued existence as an independent state. Han China's political dealings with Nanyue, meanwhile, were a reflection of how much power it was able to wield at any given time.

Nanyue's first king, Zhao Tuo, was the Qin general who had held the area under the First Emperor, enjoying a solid power base and an uncontested rule for decades, until his death at the ripe old age of 103. In the 180s BCE, Liu Bang's widow, Empress Lü, tried to lay down the law with Nanyue, imposing a trade embargo restricting the supply of horses and iron. This was intended to show Zhao Tuo that his little kingdom was nothing without the vital supplies from the north, but Zhao Tuo at first assumed that the pressure was coming from the Changsha command to his north, not the imperial capital. It was only when he heard that Empress Lü had executed his relatives in China and destroyed his family tomb that he angrily declared himself to be an emperor, mounting a direct challenge to the Han dynasty—it is for this reason that some Vietnamese sources call him the first historical emperor of Vietnam. Zhao Tuo's army marched on Changsha, seizing territory within the Han empire. Empress Lü's reinforcements, unused to the southern climate, were wiped out by disease, leading to a stalemate that endured until Empress Lü's death and a subsequent normalization of relations.

Zhao Tuo died in 137 BCE as a vassal king of China. His grandson, Zhao Mo, was soon embroiled in a war with a nearby kingdom, and forced to appeal to Han China for military aid. His own son was raised in the Han capital of Chang-an, and married to a Han woman, who would subsequently become the Queen Dowager with influence over her own son, the next king.

By the reign of Han Wudi (r. 140 BCE –87 BCE), the two factions within the Nanyue court had daggers drawn. The Chinese-born Queen Dowager and her son the king were ready to offer the full integration of Nanyue within the borders of the Han empire, and its effective reversion to provincial status. A local-born, pro-independence minister eventually had the Queen Dowager and her son killed, putting the king's half-brother on the throne. Han Wudi, never one to run away from a fight, sent an army south to clear up the mess, leading to the tardy incorporation of Nanyue into the empire around 98 BCE.

China in the early Han period had been subject to severe postwar austerity. Even Liu Bang, the founding emperor, noted the *Grand Scribe's Records*, could not always find matching horses to pull his carriage, and lesser military figures, amid a huge shortage of horses, had to settle for ox carts. It took decades to get things back on track, and Han Wudi's reputation as the dynasty's great military man, while deserved, rested on the achievements of his forefathers. If he embarked upon great, sweeping conquests on the frontier, he did so with monies that had been carefully amassed by his prudent father. Generationally, he was often dealing with the grandsons of the original princes of the periphery—not the original trusted officers and relatives, but local despots, often born into privilege, secure in their local power and unwilling to concede they were merely caretakers. He had the supreme confidence to keep on pushing, expanding China's borders all the way to what is now North Korea, and extending diplomatic and military tendrils far to the west. When the money inevitably ran out, his father's frugal nest-egg blown in decades of warfare, Wudi turned to new methods of revenue generation, declaring that the production of salt and iron were government monopolies, and continuing Liu Bang's *heqin* policy for winning over the nomads.

Maps of Han dynasty China retain the central core of antiquity, but with a long arm reaching up to the northwest. This is the Gansu Corridor, an arid stretch of land crammed in between mountain ranges and deserts, leading to the forbidden wastes of what the Han called the Western Regions—known today as Xinjiang. In a departure from the *heqin* policy of his ancestors, Wudi began offering women and gifts not to the Xiongnu, but to their enemies farther afield.

We have already encountered Liu Xijun (c. 123–101 BCE), Wudi's teenage grand-niece, one of many brides sent west to buy horses and goodwill among the nomads. Keen to establish strong links with the Wusun of the Ili Valley, Wudi promised their chief an imperial princess, scouring the outlying halls of his palace for a girl he could live without. Born through no fault of her own into the family of a disgraced princeling, Xijun bought honor for herself by agreeing to marry the Wusun leader.

Accompanied by an entourage of eunuchs and ladies in waiting, the princess travelled 5,000 kilometers (3,106.9 miles), up the Gansu Corridor, beyond the Jiayuguan gate in the Great Wall, skirting the edge of the Taklamakan desert until she reached the green Ili valleys. She became Lieqiaomi's Lady of the Right, although he seemed to spend far more time with his original wife, the Lady of the Left. The two did not get on, there was a huge language barrier, and Xijun wrote bitter reports home about the miseries of life on the wild frontier. She even wrote her feelings down in verse form, claims the *Book of Han*, in a poem that even made the Emperor in Chang-an feel sorry for her.

Liu Xijun died in her early twenties, leading the Wusun to ask for a replacement and Wudi to oblige with a second fallen woman: Liu Jieyou, whose rebel grandfather had once been accused of an affair with Liu Bang's concubine. Jieyou's tenure among the Wusun was far more successful, albeit not without its hiccups. She protested vehemently to the Emperor that her original husband was handing her off to his own grandson, a common practice among the Wusun, but incest in the eyes of Confucian propriety. But Jieyou stuck it out, eventually being "married" in some sense to three leaders of the Wusun, becoming the mother and regent of one of the subsequent kings, and cementing vital diplomatic deals between Chang-an and its nomad allies. On the death of her last husband, she petitioned to come home to Chang-an, where she enjoyed a welcome retirement, honored as a powerful influence on China's foreign relations. Her handmaiden, who also married a prominent Wusun, would become famed as China's first female ambassador to the Western Regions, which, during the reign of Wudi, amounted to 36 vassal kingdoms loyal to China, held in place with a combination of military might and feminine wiles.

The relationship of the Han dynasty with the Western Regions fluctuated throughout the centuries. China certainly involved itself directly in those kingdoms, such as Loulan on the frontier, the king of which was ousted in a China-sponsored coup in 77 BCE, and replaced with his own younger brother, who had been raised in the Chinese capital and was more sympathetic to the Emperor's requests.

The new king of Loulan, facing some surly resistance among his own people, soon put in a request for China to send military support. Reports were sent back to the heartland about Loulan's mediocre prospects for re-development or irrigation. As has been true throughout Chinese history, right up until the discovery of oil and gas reserves beneath the sands, much of the Western Regions were lacking in resources, unable to pay their own way, except as a path to somewhere else. Invariably, this led to disappointments in the Chinese heartland, as government scribes questioned why the emperor was pouring resources into oases that delivered nothing but reeds and rocks.

The Han dynasty's interest in the Western Regions was political and logistic. There were always problems on the borders with the Xiongnu horsemen, and the best way to hold them off was to create firm lines of demarcation. A long rammed-earth wall stretched out into the west, designed to make life as difficult as possible for the barbarian nomads. It didn't even need to be that high—a wall that came up to your chest would prove to be impassable for any tribesman leading a herd of hundreds of horses or cattle, particularly if there was a nearby watchtower that could signal his approach and send a squadron of soldiers out to scare him away. Beyond the wall, there were watchtowers on the road, and then open desert, but the Han dynasty's interest lay in the mountain slopes around the desert's edge, which were habitable. Oases and villages were dotted all the way across the north side of the desert, and some way along the south. There was trade to be had, on the south side with the peoples who mined jade in Hetian. In the north, the route afforded access to the Wusun tribe that had pushed the Tocharians out of the Ili Valley, and whose steeds were prized for their strength. But if you made it all the way along the top of the desert and through the pass at the end, you would reach the Ferghana Valley in what is now Uzbekistan, home to the greatest horses in the world.

It is the Ferghana horses that are celebrated in the most famous piece of Han statuary to survive to the present day—like many ancient figurines, it has been reproduced in giant form as a centerpiece for modern public spaces. Originally only 45 centimeters (17.7 inches) in length, the Flying Horse of Gansu is an exquisite bronze reputation of a horse galloping at full pelt, its hoof resting not on the ground, but on the back of a surprised-looking swallow, which has jerked its head around to stare in cartoonish amazement. It is a wonderful piece, beautiful in its elegance and simplicity. But it encompasses the wonder and excitement the Han Chinese felt at hearing stories of the "blood-sweating" horses of Ferghana.

The *Book of Han* records two different songs of praise of the Ferghana horses, one of which proclaims it to be a "friend to dragons" and notes its "sheen of scarlet sweat, froth of ochre." The parasite *Parafiliaria multipapillosa* caused mild hemorrhaging below the skin on the head and forequarters, causing the horses to seem to sweat blood. The second, longer song, describes both the horse and its journey to the presence of the Emperor Wudi:

> The Horse of Heaven comes, out of the far west
> Across the shifting sands of the nine barbarians
> The Horse of Heaven comes, through the Bubbling River
> Twice a tiger's strength, swift as a devil... The Horse of Heaven
>     comes, conjurer of dragons
> Cantering within Heaven's gates, he looks upon the Jade Terrace.

The Western Regions would long be a problematic area in Chinese politics. Throughout history, they have been an expensive region to defend, vital for trade in certain precious commodities, but unlikely to attract any willing colonists. Even the military men, settled there as sometime farmers with watchman duties, often comprised battalions of convicts, given the choice between service in the Western Regions or execution. Meanwhile, the Western Regions were so far from the Chinese center that Han money was of debatable value. What use was it to carry a heavy sack of coins 1,000 kilometers (621.4 miles) through the desert, only to hand it to a horse-trader or jade miner who had no use for it? Faced with a distance that took their servants to the very edge of the Chinese world, the Han dynasty found another way to pay them.

Silk was durable, washable, and did not break if you dropped it. It was of immediate, obvious value even to the barbarians of the periphery, who valued its lice-repelling qualities, its lightness and its decorative value. But even if they did not want to fashion it into clothes or curtains or tents, it still had a demonstrable value to anyone else they ran into. Accordingly, the Han dynasty sent tons upon tons of silk, entire wagon trains loaded with it, to the Western Regions every year, to be doled out to the border soldiers in lieu of money. This silk made its way to their barbarian allies and rivals, all of whom were equally at a loss to put all of it to use. Inevitably, it made its way further west, into the hands of peoples the Chinese had only vaguely heard of. It formed the eerie, rippling fabric of Parthian banners and finery for Indian priestesses. Eventually, it made its way to the Mediterranean, sometimes after a detour through Egypt to be embroidered, sold for a hundred times its original value, where a fad among young girls for "glass" dresses, the fabric so thin as to leave the wearer practically naked, scandalized the menfolk of the Roman Empire.

In 53 BCE, Wudi's great-great grandson, the Emperor Yuandi seized a new opportunity to deal with the Xiongnu, to the horror of many of his advisers. A succession war broke out among the Xiongnu themselves—while conflict now occurred far from the Chinese frontier, the constant fighting led to a stream of refugees and non-combatants, allowed to settle within China's borders. Five factions were fighting over who got to be the supreme leader of the Xiongnu. Huhanye, one of the leaders, lost a battle with his own half-brother, and made the fateful decision to seek the help of the Han emperor.

It was a deeply controversial move. Many of the Xiongnu elders regarded it as a betrayal of everything they stood for. A leader who bowed before the Chinese, they said, would lose all respect among the hundred tribes of the steppes. His chief adviser, however, commented that times were changing. Since the days of their great-grandfathers, the Han people had been in the ascendant. Many of the nomad peoples had already made peace with them—even the "Mad King" of the Wusun.

Huhanye's mind was made up. He sent his own son ahead to Chang-an, as a hostage, and ordered his people to pack up their tents and head towards the border. It would take them over a year, moving at the meandering pace of their slower livestock, dawdling on the pastures, but an entire nation was on the move. So, too, were their enemies—Huhanye's half-brother and sworn enemy was also heading towards the Han realm, and had also sent a son ahead as a hostage. Whoever struck the deal first could count on Chinese support to become the lord of lords on the open plains.

As Ban Gu, author of the *Book of Han*, was careful to note, rulers in ancient times had disregarded barbarians as a force of nature. They could no more conclude a treaty with them than they could with birds or beasts. They were feckless and unreliable, literally impossible to pin down—there was no Xiongnu fortress to attack or lands to seize. They did not even observe the Chinese calendar.

> When they come, we must be stern and watchful. When they go, we must be ready and on our guard. If they are swayed by our righteousness and wish to present tribute, then we should receive them as guests. But we must keep them under loose reins, not cutting contact, but let them take the blame if relations sour.

Such is Ban Gu's summary of the arguments at the Han court, where much of the debate was over what exactly the Sage Kings of legend had done about the barbarians beyond ignoring them. Wasn't marrying Chinese girls to the nomad kings already a step too far? The minister Xiao Wang-zhi, tutor to the Crown Prince, thought that it was asking for trouble to officially make the Xiongnu a subject people. Someday, he was sure, their heirs would "flee like birds and hide like rats," forgetting their obligations for tribute and protocol. It would be far better, he argued, to treat them as visiting emissaries from a foreign kingdom—to exchange valuable gifts that essentially paid them to go away.

Huhanye left the mass of his people at the frontier, and rode across three provinces with his immediate entourage. The Han made sure that they put on a show of strength, supplying two thousand horseman to ride escort in each region, and Emperor Xuandi made sure that an entourage of tens of thousands of assimilated barbarians was waiting respectfully, with him as he welcomed the nomad leader.

The Emperor welcomed Huhanye, conferring upon him a gold seal on a twisted ribbon that implied he was a vassal king of a foreign kingdom. Other gifts had similar symbolic value—a ceremonial chariot, fifteen horses, a bow with 48 arrows, clothes suitable for a Chinese courtier, heaps of gold ingots and copper coins. That money was sure to be spent in China, quite possibly on materials for his war against his half-brother. For financing ventures out on the steppes and in the desert, the Emperor gave him 8,000 rolls of silk and a truly vast quantity—6,000 *jin*, or 1.5 metric tons—of silk floss.

Huhanye asked to settle on the Chinese borders, volunteering to be a buffer zone against any further incursions by his half-brother. Xuandi promised to consider it, and for now sent him back to the frontier with a conspicuously powerful entourage of 16,000 cavalry.

Huhanye's rival Hutuwusi did not have quite so much luck. His emissaries also enjoyed exchanges of gifts with the Emperor, but not at the same level. He had been well and truly outmaneuvered, and sought to outflank Huhanye by striking out towards the west, towards the Wusun. The leader of the Wusun killed the Xiongnu envoys, plunging Hutuwusi into a new war in the west, and distracting him from the Chinese frontier. As for Huhanye, he moved north again within a decade, having exhausted the pastures and hunting in his new lands.

There are suggestions in the historical records that everyone was having problems, not just the Xiongnu. The court annals report plague in 48 BCE, followed by a flood, then famine in 47 BCE. In 46 BCE, the Han gave up on the southern island of Hainan, having lost several legions trying to put down local insurrections. In 44 BCE, budget cuts at the Han court reduced the daily meat allocations by 50%, and reduced the number of horses pulling even imperial carriages to the barest minimum. 43 BCE was "an exceptionally cool summer." An entry for 42 BCE off-handedly mentioned that the empire had been "plagued by a succession of crop failures over the past several years."

On his third visit to the Chinese capital, in 33 BCE, Huhanye had asked to become an imperial son-in-law. As if the gifts of silk and gold, brocades and tools were not enough, he wanted a Han princess in his bed as well. It was not the first time that a Xiongnu chieftain had demanded a Chinese woman, but Xuandi's son and heir, Yuandi, was not in the mood for giving up one of his concubines' daughters. Figuring that Huhanye was sure to be easily impressed by any girl showing up with a suitably glittering entourage, he decided to fob him off with the plainest girl in the palace.

Some sources say the girl in question actually volunteered. Her name was Wang Zhaojun, and she had been stuck at the palace for years without even meeting the emperor. Gathered up in one of the periodic sweeps of the Chinese provinces for suitably beautiful women, she had been sent to Chang-an as an imperial bride. Life in the palace, however, was not all it was said to be. Merely being one of the most beautiful women in China was not enough, because the competition was fierce. The Emperor was obliged to attend to his official wife, and the top-ranking concubines, and whatever favorites took his fancy. Dozens of the other palace women were little better than servants and chambermaids, meekly awaiting the day when the Emperor might catch a glimpse and ask for her to be brought to his bed.

On a dull night, the Emperor might sift through a selection of portraits made by the court painters. They were renowned for their ability to perfectly capture the image of their subject, which left Yuandi sure that if his heart was moved by a picture, he would like the real thing.

Wang Zhaojun's picture was never going to win her his attention. She looked plain and haughty, and had a "widow's tear" mole near her eye which was regarded as an ill omen. In fact, it was odd that she had even been brought to the palace—she was demonstrably the worst-looking girl there, and if she wanted to volunteer to be a barbarian's wife, then good riddance to her.

The Yuandi Emperor obviously had a lot on his mind. There were the usual natural disasters and salt taxes, and grain reports. There were plenty of women to distract him in the palace, and he had something of a penchant for watching wild animal fights. He was hence not of a mood to read between the lines of what he had just said out loud—that somehow an ugly girl had been admitted to the ranks of his palace attendants.

In fact, Wang Zhaojun was anything but ugly. A poet once wrote that she was so beautiful that the sight of her could make the birds drop out of the sky. She had no bad-omen moles or other marks, but she had made the fatal error of failing to bribe the palace artists to make her look good. Yuandi had not only failed to notice the most attractive woman in his palace for years, but had just agreed to send her away.

The extent of his error only became apparent when he tardily set eyes on her, at the audience to see her off for her life in exile as Huhanye's bride. His mistake was catastrophic enough to make it into the dynastic chronicle, the *Book of Han*, which did not usually have the space for such matters.

> Her beauty, dazzling in its radiance, lit up the entire palace hall.
> She glided into his presence with effortless elegance and grace,
> leaving all who saw her with a sense of profound admiration
> and awe.

The Emperor immediately tried to come up with a plan to go back on his word to Huhanye, but the ecstatic nomad prince had already ridden home, bragging of his good fortune, and promising to keep China safe from even worse nomads than his own: "I will be the border sentinel of Han... not for this lifetime, but forever and in perpetuity," he said. "Please withdraw your troops from the frontier."

Wang Zhaojun set off to her wedding to the leader of the Xiongnu, soon becoming a subject of multiple Chinese poems, ballads and plays about her noble sacrifice. Furious, Yuandi cast around for someone to blame, and ordered the execution of the court artists. He didn't withdraw his troops from the border, either, sending a messenger to Huhanye to claim that the Chinese garrisons also kept bad elements *from China* from entering into the realm of the Xiongnu, and stopped some of the Xiongnu's enemies from making larger-scale migrations. He added that the border fortifications—that big wall and the watchtowers and so on—had cost inestimable sums to construct, and were best still occupied to keep them maintained. While everything was cordial between the Xiongnu and the Han for now, it would be foolish to suggest things would stay that way forever.

And so it went for decade after decade, the Han on their farms and the Xiongnu on the steppe, rubbing up against each other in that fatally long zone that sustained both ways of life. The countries of the Western Regions, oasis city-states, desert jade mines and valleys of horse-breeders, were often political footballs between the two cultures, declaring allegiance to whomever presented the most immediate threat. Sometimes the desert cities would scorn Chinese tribute demands; sometimes they would go scurrying to Chang-an pleading for military aid against Xiongnu raiders who wanted even more.

By the first century CE, the Han Chinese strengthened their presence in the region with a discount effort, settling "military garrisons" of more ex-convicts on the frontier. General Ban Chao (32–102 CE) used these enclaves as bases from which to launch more ambitious operations, with a modest force. Reflecting a far greater appreciation of the region's limitations in sustaining a large army, Ban Chao's thirty-year "war with the Xiongnu" often utilized a posse of only a few hundred men. It did, however, keep lines of communication open between China and the passes to the west, and is one of the reasons why there is a statue of Ban Chao in the center of modern Kashgar, at the westernmost edge of China. We are oddly well-informed about this period in the west, in part at least, because Ban Chao's father, brother and sister were the co-authors of the *Book of Han*, and are likely to have derived the chapters in the dynastic history relating to the Western Regions directly from correspondence with their relative. It is from him, and the reports of the scouts he sent even further afield, that the Chinese chronicles derived much of their knowledge about the furthest edges of the world—such as the Land of the Angels (India), which was south through the mountain passes. A great ocean that led from Parthia to Egypt ("West of the Sea") that formed the exotic edge of another empire regarded as so like China that they paid it the compliment of calling it Greater Qin. "Their kings are not permanent," comments the *Book of Later Han* about Rome. "If there are unexpected calamities, such as unprecedented gales and storms, he is dismissed and replaced."

The sheer scale of Han lines of communications seems to have taken its toll, leading a certain world-weary tone to creep some of the dynasty's songs. Soldiers have always missed home, but there was a daunting vastness to the thousands of kilometers of desert that separated the farthest outposts from the capital. And it was all part of an elaborate operation to outflank an enemy that was sometimes invisible for years, then suddenly manifest in the thousands. A soldier could come home after ten years' service, only to discover his old hometown overrun with Xiongnu settlers anyway.

Surviving Han dynasty songs are far less enthusiastic about warfare than their equivalents in previous eras. The melancholy in songs of the Zhou and Qin era was reserved for homesickness and separation from loved ones. By the Han dynasty, songs about war had become far more graphic and mournful, including "We Fought South of the City Wall," which includes a visceral address from the dead:

> Tell the crows for us: "We were brave men
> But now we lie unburied in the wilds
> How can our rotting flesh evade you?"

In its reduction of Chinese soldiery to carrion picked over by scavengers, it is radically different from the glorifications of the past. Such comments reflect a growing distaste for warfare among the upper classes—whereas in the Zhou dynasty, hunting, sacrifice and war had been the central pillars of an aristocrat's duty, the Han nobleman would much rather farm out such jobs to others. Military conscription was officially abandoned in the first century CE, although try telling that to the men tilling thin soil in a desert oasis, who had been given the choice of that or death. The people of Han China increasingly relied upon barbarians to fight barbarians, offering status and rewards for one nomad chieftain if he would handle his cousins with extreme prejudice before they even made it to the frontier. Such deals kept the wagon-trains piled with silk heading west, while the central axis of China from Chang-an downriver to Luoyang, pulled in ever larger numbers of urban dwellers.

Thoughts turned to what it was that separated the fortunes of the Han empire from the short-lived Qin empire that had preceded it. Han historians settled upon Legalism as the Qin's ultimate mistake. The First Emperor's regime failed, they said, because it was too cruel—when in fact, it was far more likely to have been brought down by rebellious factions from the old states and noble houses that the First Emperor had tried to obliterate.

Lord Shang's authoritarian policies were seen as a poison at the heart of government—a political wrong turn that the Han people were swift to correct. Increasingly, as the dynasty grew and flourished, this came to mean an emphasis on the opposite of Legalism: Confucius. Although he was largely ignored in his lifetime, and his school struggled to find followers after his death, Confucius increasingly became regarded as the most important of philosophers, turning his teachings into an ever more influential state ideology. This not only included *The Analects*, a complete edition of which was recovered, intact, in 154 BCE, where one of his descendants had hidden it from the Qin book-burners, but also *The Spring and Autumn Annals*, which chronicled the history of the state of Lu from its beginnings up to his death. Han scholars came to believe that Confucius's wording was so exact, his choice of phrase so infallible, that every single character was perfectly placed. Entire commentaries and concordances were devoted to explaining odd turns of phrase and elements that might have otherwise been ignored as spelling mistakes or transcription errors. Confucius was faultless, and his veneration took on the aspects of a state cult. Of course, this was not merely because Confucianism seemed to offer some handy tips on government. There were political reasons, too, not the least that Confucius was regarded as the "uncrowned king" of antiquity, a sage emperor that the people had failed to recognize in his lifetime. Sima Qian, the author of the *Grand Scribe's Records*, would go so far as to include Confucius's biography among the lists of ancient monarchs, rather than merely among the era's prominent philosophers.

Since such storied messiahs were supposed to arise once every 500 years, enthusiasm for Confucianism reached fever pitch as the fifth centenary of his birth approached. Crown princes were inculcated with Confucian texts, in the hope that they would regard themselves as the long-awaited enlightened ruler. Behind the scenes, their wiliest ministers hoped that they would go all the way with the implications of the Confucian canon, appointing their ablest ministers to rule for them. One such minister took matters into his own hands, and briefly declared the Han dynasty over in 9 CE, seizing the throne from an infant emperor and proclaiming himself to be the foretold sage-emperor. The 45-year-old official Wang Mang was utterly convinced that he could restore the Golden Age of the height of the Zhou dynasty, although his brief interregnum was hounded by political troubles. His land reforms created widespread resentment, his new coins brought joy to nobody except future generations of numismatists, and he created problems not only on his borders, but among rioting farmers in the hinterland.

If anything, Wang Mang's short-lived 14-year Xin ("New") dynasty temporarily revitalized Han confidence. He was held responsible for almost everything that went wrong during his reign—predictably, a side-order of blame went to Zhao Feiyan ("Flying Swallow"), the legendarily slender low-born dancer who distracted the unfortunate infant emperor's father, and whose sister may well have killed him with an overdose of aphrodisiacs. So, as ever, women and an over-reaching official got the blame, while the resurgent Han rebels took the credit for restoring order. They did not, however, necessarily deal with any of the problems that were eating away at the foundations of the dynasty.

The capital was moved downriver from Chang-an to Luoyang, just as in the Zhou dynasty a millennium earlier. Families with powerful, local power bases were able to exert increasing degrees of influence over imperial decisions. Chang-an had always been, first and foremost, a military stronghold—commanding the plains of the Wei valley, and possible to hold from all sides. Luoyang, on the other hand, was strategically difficult to defend, but sat at the center of the broader Yellow River plain. It was hence a place that put a greater emphasis on "culture"—if the location of Chang-an helped foster a militaristic, Legalist attitude towards government and society, then Luoyang was its opposite, the ideal place for culture and Confucianism to thrive.

That was certainly how Ban Gu, the chief author of the *Book of Han*, saw things as he wrote the history of his age. The Eastern Han, built on the ruins of Qin, had continued to make the mistakes of the First Emperor and his brutal, Legalist regime. But he regarded the Western Han, built on the site that had once been the royal seat of the Zhou kings, as an altogether more cultured place, restoring the rituals of old, and the cycles of obligation and benevolence that Confucius had once called for.

Demographic records from the first century CE obscure a flight to the south, as increasingly strong Xiongnu incursions scared away Han Chinese settlers from the northwest, cramming them into the Yellow and Yangtze River regions. The Han Chinese were unwilling to resettle the depopulated regions, causing the emperors to allow Qiang (proto-Tibetan) and even other Xiongnu to move there. Many of those Xiongnu soon became indistinguishable from the Han, turning parts of the northwest into a conflict zone between assimilated "good" Xiongnu and untamed, "bad" Xiongnu. In an effort to contain the problem, the Han Chinese offered rewards to a rival tribe, the Xianbei, for every Xiongnu head taken. This certainly solved the problem for a while, until the source of revenue from dead Xiongnu dried up. The Xianbei became increasingly bold in their demands for different rewards, and soon the Chinese were obliged to pay them off much as they had done with the Xiongnu themselves.

Despite the supposedly Confucian leanings of the administration, the need to find someone to blame led to an overt belief in superstitions. From around 100 CE onwards, the default answer to any bad omens, or misfortunes was to assume that Heaven was criticizing the Emperor's officials. Nobody would dare suggest that Heaven was criticizing the Emperor himself, leading to a recurring fad for dismissing his three most important ministers every time there was an earthquake or some Fortean event. The emperor could appoint the most able chancellor or prime minister ever known, only to have to fire him after two weeks if someone saw a comet or a two-headed chicken. Power and authority inevitably devolved to the palace eunuchs, the only officials suitably long-serving and middle-ranking not to be removed at a moment's notice.

The most obvious sign of decline came in 110 CE, when the Han Chinese gave up on four entire provinces. The Western Regions were abandoned—Chinese settlers were ordered out, and their homesteads and crops burnt so as to leave nothing for the enemy. Closer to home, local governors found funding from the center almost non-existent. If a revolt broke out, such as in the southern provinces in 137 CE, then the emperor could not afford to fight back. Instead, he was more likely to ennoble the rebel leaders, making them the new governor and leaving local issues of famine relief or disaster prevention in their hands for as long as they could afford it.

Although a veneer remained of imperial unity, China was devolving back into separate states. Local rulers commanded respect and obedience, while imperial edicts were toothless. By 169 CE, the dynasty was in unstoppable decline, its authority challenged by repeated uprisings and breakaway regions. In the capital, an emperor died without proclaiming his heir, leaving the decision in the hands of his widow, a teenage girl.

Within days, a clique comprising her father, brother and two cousins had selected the new emperor, sight-unseen—an eleven-year-old distant cousin, who had grown up in obscurity hundreds of miles from the capital.

The 20-year-reign of Lingdi (r. 168–189 CE), crowned age twelve, began with his mother's vendetta against her late husband's nine concubines, and with the promotion of Dou Wu, his grandfather, to a supreme general's rank. It would proceed, as would so many reigns in declining regimes, with a bitter conflict between his mother's family and the eunuchs of the palace, who had already failed in their primary duty, to keep in-laws out of politics. However, running underneath the palace politics throughout Lingdi's reign was a far more insidious and damaging problem—disease. The *Book of Later Han* refers to no less than five outbreaks of an unspecified sickness in the years 171–185 requiring serious government intervention all over the empire. It is still impossible to tell what this disease was, but it is likely it was the same as the "Antonine plague" that ravaged the Roman Empire for roughly the same period. Rome's sickness was brought home from Baghdad by troops; China's taking a slower but equally sure route among the traders of the Western Regions. There is no description in Chinese sources, but the Greek doctor Galen recounted vomiting and diarrhea, black, dried blisters and fever analogous to either smallpox or measles. Death rates in China climbed as high as 30% in some areas, which only helped feed the growing sense that the Han emperors had lost the Mandate of Heaven.

By 178 CE, there were simply not enough qualified officials to go around, and imperial "reforms" offered all high offices to the highest bidder, creating an institutionalized corruption that only made things worse. The aristocrats in the capital knifed each other over who got to enjoy its luxuries, while uprisings and secessions continued on the frontier. In 188, Lingdi's court tacitly admitted its powerlessness, appointing regional trouble-shooters to exert direct control over troubled provinces—these appointees were given the innocuous-sounding name of "shepherds" (*mu*), but the creation of such a post amounted handing over power to local warlords.

Lingdi died in 189, and was predictably replaced by a thirteen-year-old son, soon deposed by a warlord called into the capital to eliminate his faction. His successor and brother would be held under house arrest by another regional warlord for two decades, until he abdicated in 220, his empire already a distant memory. But since the dynasty had already suffered a major setback with the interregnum caused by Wang Mang from 9–23 CE, there were plenty of people ready to believe that it could and would be restored. A notional restoration under another warlord, Liu Bei (see next chapter), stumbled along until 263, before it, too, collapsed. In 304, yet another "Han dynasty" rose and fell within 25 years in the north. It was founded by Liu Yuan, a Xiongnu warlord whose imperial-sounding surname derived from the fact that he was descended from a princess-bride, sent by the first Han emperor to marry one of his ancestors.

# CHAPTER 4

# SPACES BETWEEN: CHINA DIVIDED

*A* *ll life is suffering. Suffering is caused by desire. Suffering ceases with the end of desires. There is a path that leads from suffering.* What could be more Buddhist than a dynasty that would barely last a generation? Emperor Wu (464–549 CE), founder of the Liang dynasty, surely knew that his domain was rickety and unstable. He did not show it, throwing himself into creating the best possible place for the devout and the good. He wrote a poem about a candle, so fragile and so small, yet it sends out its "rippling rays," and illuminates the shadows, however briefly.

Confucius had once said that there could not be two suns in the sky, but there were now several men in China who called themselves emperors. A former general in the wars against the Northern Wei, and a former governor of a province, Emperor Wu had been born into a regime that itself had barely lasted fifty years. His own Liang dynasty was fated to sputter out only six years after his death, before a general would depose his grandson and proclaim *another* dynasty that would itself only last a generation.

But Emperor Wu clung on as best he could. His reign would be one of the longest of any imperial era, even if his state would barely outlast him. He initiated grand flood-work schemes to protect his farmers, and became an enthusiastic patron of the arts. He was haunted by dreams of his former empress, whom he believed to occasionally adopt a dragon's form and splash around in a well near the palace. He hectored his ministers over their lack of attention to census data from previous dynasties, which remained useful in his own era, and deserved better treatment than being abandoned in storehouses to be "pawed by dogs and nibbled by rats." And

China During the Southern and Northern Dynasties

Rouran nomads

States of the
Western Regions

Northern Dynasties

Tuyuhun Tribes

Qiang tribes

Southern Dynasties

☐ China During the Southern and Northern Dynasties
— China's Modern-day Border

he embarked upon a lifelong exploration of religious belief, which he himself summarized in a poem.

"In my youth," he wrote, "I emulated the Duke of Zhou and Confucius."
He avidly read the ancient classics, and idolized the uncle-regent of the
first Zhou king, and the great sage himself. In middle age, he turned to
Daoism, exercising a more hands-off approach on government, prizing
secret acts of goodness. As his hair turned gray, he found a new, foreign
philosophy that would stay with him for the rest of his life.

> In my old age I open the Buddhist scrolls
> they are like the moon shining forth amidst stars
> I begin to understand suffering and its accumulation; cause and
>    effect are finally illuminated.

Emperor Wu became a zealous convert to Buddhism, vastly increasing public funding for translation and cataloguing of sacred scrolls from India. Obscure sutras in Sanskrit were suddenly rendered comprehensible, and non-monks gained access to glosses, compendia and biographies of Buddhist celebrities. By 511, he had decided that loopholes allowing Buddhists to eat meat were dishonest, and that he would henceforth be a vegetarian. By 514, he had given up sexual intercourse. He started to lecture monks about their own lifestyles, telling them that fish was still meat, and that drinking alcohol was definitely wrong, no matter what certain abbots might allow. By 517, he had forbidden the use of animal sacrifices in all ceremonies, and even the imperial rituals now only offered fruit and vegetables to the ancestors and spirits.

Emperor Wu might have had a grasp of some of the less welcome teachings of the Buddha, but he was also interpreting the scriptures in a markedly imperial fashion. Just as previous emperors had been the interface between gods and men, Emperor Wu saw himself as a cut above even the priests in the temples, a *dharma* king and defender of the Buddhist faith. In 521, he founded an orphanage; in 529, when his capital was hit by a plague, he knelt before a statue of Buddha and begged to become a human sump for the ills of the world.

So, of *course* he wanted to meet Bodhidharma, that shaven-headed mystic from south India, said to be a hundred years old, who had walked across China, some said from the Western Regions, others up from the southern ports.

Bodhidharma was ushered into the throne room, a short, brown-skinned man, clad in simple robes, walking with a staff but not leaning on it. His eyes bulged noticeably, and when he spoke, his teeth looked broken and half-gone, but his age was indeterminate. Severe ascetics did terrible things to their bodies—fasting and pilgrimages, and the ravages of untold diseases could mean he was any age over forty.

It wasn't clear to Emperor Wu how long Bodhidharma had been in China. When he spoke, his Chinese was accented but clear, if a little blunt, as if he were not used to the niceties of polite conversation.

Emperor Wu asked about the *dharma*—the teachings of Buddha were so varied, the sutras sometimes so contradictory, he appreciated any chance to talk to a true Indian monk about what it all really meant. What was Bodhidharma here to teach?

"Nothing," said Bodhidharma. "The teachings are empty."

Emperor Wu asked the monk about merit. He was, after all, himself famously devout, and he had caused thousands of copies to be made of sacred books. He had personally arranged for the translation of previously unknown sutras. He had founded and funded monasteries, and he was curious as to how much merit that was worth.

Bodhidharma stared at him impassively.

"No merit at all," he said.

It was not an answer that Emperor Wu was expecting, but it had admittedly been a little selfish to make everything about his own charitable acts. Maybe he would get a better response from this man if he asked him something about scripture. There were, he knew, Four Noble Truths—related to the unquenchable desire for satisfaction, and the suffering created by craving; the craving that causes endless cycles of rebirth and death. But he was wondering: which was the greatest and most profound of the noble truths.

Bodhidharma stared back at the emperor like he was an unruly child.

"Nothing," he replied. "There's nothing noble about them, anyway."

Emperor Wu's face reddened. His courtiers did not meet his gaze.

"Who do you think you are…?" he growled.

"I have no idea," replied the monk.

Emperor Wu curtly dismissed him, and the brown-skinned man left.

"Who was that idiot…?" he muttered.

The courtiers waited in silence, and he stormed off to his chambers, where he read a sutra by candlelight and tried to get to sleep.

But he was still awake in the dead of night. He could not stop thinking about the monk's odd words.

Before dawn, he ordered his heralds to chase after Bodhidharma and bring him back, but he never saw him again.

$\odot-\odot-\odot-\odot-\odot$

The conquests of the First Emperor and the glory of the Han dynasty established the great dream of Chinese history and geography—a single political entity occupying the space that we understand as "China" today. This, however, has not always been true. In fact, although the First Emperor's domain is usually understood to be the norm to which China aspires, for half of the 2,200 years since the Qin dynasty, China has been either fragmented or ruled by foreign invaders.

The period from the fall of the Han dynasty in 220 CE to the rise of a new imperium in 581 CE lasted for longer than the story so far of the United States of America, and yet, because it does not feature any convenient unifying Emperor, is often glossed over in history books that favor the easy progression of dynasty to dynasty. A cynic might argue that it only really registers at all with the Chinese because its earliest period, which saw three despots fighting to be regarded as the new emperor, would become the subject of one of China's most famous novels, *The Romance of the Three Kingdoms*.

Cao Cao (155–220 CE) is the most well-known contender—a successful official and general with a knack for offending powerful local families in the dying days of the Han dynasty. His career peak was suppressing the Yellow Turban Rebellion, a millenarian Daoist cult that proclaimed "Blue Heaven's day had passed, and that Yellow Heaven soon would rise." The Yellow Turbans, however, were merely a symptom of widespread famine and floods in the agricultural north. Cao Cao was dragged out of retirement in the tussle over Emperor Lingdi's sons, which ended with Luoyang destroyed, the capital briefly moved back to Chang-an, and the last Han emperor, Lingdi's eight-year-old younger son Emperor Xiandi (r. 189–220), in Cao Cao's custody. Cao Cao might have successfully reconquered China in his young emperor's name, were it not for a disastrous defeat at the Battle of Chibi (the Red Cliffs) in 208. Shortly after Cao Cao's death in 220, his son Cao Pi ordered the hapless emperor to abdicate, and proclaimed himself the ruler of a new dynasty—the Cao Wei. However, Cao Pi's domain only encompassed China north of the Yangtze. The family of one Liu Bei, a distant descendant of an early Han emperor, vainly claimed to be continuing the Han dynasty in Sichuan and adjoining areas. Meanwhile, southeast China broke away to form its own independent state, Eastern Wu, ruled by the family of the warlord Sun Quan.

Although the three men all claimed to be emperors, this era is remembered as the Three *Kingdoms*. Cao Wei was eventually usurped by a new ruling family, shortly before a succession of barbarian incursions shoved the Han Chinese southwards and altered the demographics of the north.

The period is impossibly confusing, packed with immense cultural transformations and foreshadowing of later eras, but also a riot of kinglets, tin-pot emperors and dynastic squibs, some aspiring to reunite the lost empire, others striking out alone, with modest ambitions to be a mere city-state or small nation. A "brief" history of China only has space for the high-points, which is a disservice to them, since even a transient, forgotten spark like the aforementioned Emperor Wu's Southern Liang (502–557) lasted three times as long as the First Emperor's famous Qin dynasty.

Chinese historians look back on this period as the "Age of Disunion," but they do so with the surety that China would once be whole again. That was by no means how things looked for many of the people of the time, some of whom were content to dwell in peace in one of the Sixteen Kingdoms that came to make up China north of the Yangtze for over a century, or one of the Southern and Northern Dynasties into which China was divided in the 5th century—the north belonging to a series of regimes ruled by nomad-derived overlords; the south to dynasties that proclaimed their origin in Han stock. However, in both cases, we see an extreme hybridity—the "nomads" of the north adopted many Chinese ways, while the Han men and women over whom they ruled soon developed skills in archery and horsemanship. Meanwhile, the Han who moved to the south soon intermarried with locals, leading to new evolutions of culture and custom.

Mark Edward Lewis, in his definitive history of the period, summarizes the disparity between the regions as: "south China had a dynasty with no army, while north China had armies with no dynasty." There were plenty of kings and princelings prepared to preemptively proclaim themselves to be the new Emperor of All Under Heaven, but China would not be fully united again for four hundred years.

In climate terms, they were difficult times. Tree-ring data points to three "mega-droughts" in Central Asia, each lasting for several decades, around 360, 460 and 550 CE, and each sure to have pushed nomads both east and west, threatening the equilibrium of both Europe and China. From 400–570, China experienced a prolonged period of dry desertification, favoring nomads in the north and pushing farmers south. Towards the end of the period, a cluster of eruptions on a different continent (possibly beginning with Ilopango in El Salvador) prompted a worldwide "volcanic winter" after 536 CE, with attendant famines, crop failures, population movement and unrest, from which China only began to emerge in the 580s.

In the north, the constant arrival and occasional settlement of nomad peoples could sometimes prove to be a burden on resources for a hardpressed minor regime; equally, they be an immense benefit, revitalizing a struggling economy, bringing prosperity to formerly derelict areas, and offering military skills that could upgrade a small state into a far larger, more proactive one. Cavalry in this period became substantially heavier, thanks to the use of the stirrup to keep a horseman in his saddle. Stirrups have been found on tomb figurines dated as early as 322 CE, by which time they appear to have already become commonplace.

Those same nomad arrivals in the north prompted many of the Han Chinese to head south. They migrated south of the Yangtze in their thousands, swamping underpopulated provinces with their genes and culture. The region south of the Yangtze, previously dismissed for its hot-headed, sorcerous locals and its savage customs, was now the last redoubt of true Han culture in the eyes of its new occupants. Its mountains were unattractive enough to the nomads for them to leave alone. Over the next few centuries, the expanding population of Han Chinese would push local tribes like the Lisu, Kam and Baiyue into the uplands and hillsides, seizing the valleys and plains for themselves.

By the end of the period, south China had been transformed into a zone of agricultural plenty, its farming output vital for sustaining China's growing population. Meanwhile, the sense of displacement from home, and the belief that savage invaders were now squatting in the ruins of once-great capitals, propelled the Han Chinese into a powerful, enduring output of culture. Despite, or in fact because of their exile status, they clung to their traditions with a vengeance. We might reasonably call at least some of this a form of snobbery on the part of the south, although many of the poems and songs from the north do seem somewhat lacking in sophistication:

> I just bought a five-foot sword
> From the central pillar I hang it
> I stroke it three times a day—
> Better by far than a maid of fifteen.

While the ballads of the north got oddly excited about stroking their swords, songs of the south luxuriated in a rich ecology of allusions, a proscriptive list of do's and don'ts for genteel song-writing, increasingly strict rules on rhyming schemes and assonances, and an entire subgenre of literary theory. Even the nobility got involved—Cao Pi, first ruler of the short-lived kingdom of Wei, achieved lasting fame as a champion of literature as the truest and most precious form, not merely of renown, but of existence itself. Emperor Wu of the Liang, when not funding and encouraging the translation of Buddhist scriptures, was the center of a salon of poetic aspirations.

Some complained that the southern Chinese were trying so hard to be cultured that they were demolishing many of the traditions of old. The Hundred Entertainments of the Han dynasty—a panoply of circus routines, dances and conjuring tricks—began to develop a storied depth, reenacting moments from Buddhist iconography or incorporating folktales from the conquered southern tribes. In these performances, we see the first steps of Chinese drama away from shamanic rituals and simple songs towards true theater. As for the words, there were new rules of approved topics and even colors. The Chinese were so keen to prove their cultural superiority to their new neighbors—both north of the Yangtze and on the nearby mountain-tops—that they dug deep into a well of recursive, obscure classical references. Poetry became crammed with symbolism and call-backs to archaic kingdoms and historical figures, rendering much of it unintelligible to outsiders. Once regarded somewhat snootily as a mere clerk's skill, calligraphy itself became a gentlemanly pursuit, and Chinese characters were now works of art in themselves, with connoisseurs of the pressure of the brush on the page, and the sweep of a master's ink.

North of the Yangtze, things were very different. The most widespread form of writing was mass-produced, as converts to Buddhism sought religious merit by paying for the copying of scriptures. Woodblock printing ensured that entire sutras could be replicated in minutes, all the better to buy favor in the next life.

Tales of Buddha had first reached China during the Han dynasty after the regime's expansion into the Western Regions, which brought it into direct contact with Buddhist city-states, Indian traders and missionaries. One Han emperor had dreamt of a "golden man," leading to one of his followers to interpret it as a vision of a man in India who had "achieved the Dao," who could fly in the air, and whose body had the brilliance of the sun. These words already demonstrate one of the recurring problems that Buddhism would face in its first few centuries in China—the constant trend among the Chinese to translate it using local terms. Buddha was hence described as a man who had "achieved the Dao," like some immortal sorcerer. Early translations of Buddhist sutras recklessly substituted

Chinese terms that were only tenuously related, leading to several later waves of translation reformers—such as Buddhabhadra (359–429), Kumarajiva (344–413), and Bodhidharma (5th century, although stories about him seem to date from the early to mid-6th). Chinese Buddhism went through multiple schisms, as newly translated sutras completely reversed previous assumptions. Sometimes, the Chinese got it completely wrong, twisting certain phrases in translation to imply, for example, that wives should obey their husbands, as a Confucian might expect to hear. Sometimes, as in the case of the fighting Buddhist monks of the Shaolin temple near Luoyang, new revelations about old texts would maroon them in ideological islands, unable to reconcile their military training and meat-eating lifestyle with notions of a non-violent existence. Such cases could often lead to even more elaborate rationalizations and qualifications, creating complex hierarchies of karma and ethics. Or, in the case of the inscrutable Bodhidharma, a blanket rejection and reduction of the intricacies of Buddhism, in "a special transmission outside the scriptures," a wordless, instinctive "pointing at the soul of man." The iconoclastic variant brought to China by Bodhidharma would come to be known as *Chan*, or "meditative" Buddhism, although it is better known today by its pronunciation in Japanese: *Zen*.

There is some confusion over the location of the first Buddhist temple in China. This accolade is usually claimed by the White Horse Temple (Baima-si) near Luoyang, founded in 68 CE by monks from Afghanistan, invited to China by a curious Han emperor. But it is extremely unlikely that Buddhism would suddenly leapfrog 4,000 kilometers (2,485.5 miles) across the desert to the Chinese capital without leaving an impression en route. Buddhist temples and grottoes were sure to have been scattered all the way along the Silk Road, and hence "in China" some time before, although ironically, at the time that the Baima-si was built, the Western Regions had been abandoned to the Xiongnu, and would not be recaptured in the name of the Han dynasty for another decade. The Xiongnu, of course, and other nomads like them were also exposed to Buddhism in the Western Regions, and embraced it with equal if not greater enthusiasm than the Chinese. Much of the sudden, vibrant expansion of Buddhism in China during the Dark Ages can be attributed not only to its converts among the Han people, but also among the nomad tribes who would form several of the aristocracies in the north. It was, ironically, attacks on Bud-

**PEKING MAN** Bust of "Peking Man," *Homo erectus pekinensis*, based on remains found at Zhoukoudian, now in the suburbs of Beijing. *Photo: Kati Clements.*

**CONFUCIUS** Statue of Confucius (c. 551–479 BCE), China's most influential philosopher, from the Confucius Temple in Beijing. *Photo: Kati Clements.*

**LAOZI** Statue of Laozi, the founder of Daoism, riding an ox, at the Louguantai temple, Zhouzhi, Shaanxi, said to be the location where he wrote *The Book of the Path and Power (Dao De Jing). Photo: Kati Clements.*

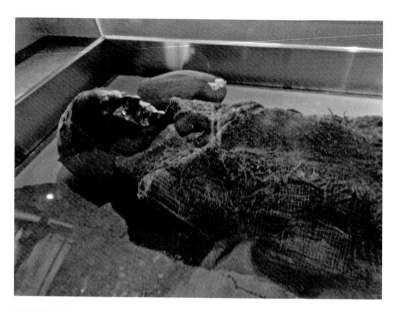

**THE BEAUTY OF LOULAN** Human remains, excavated by the Tieban River, near Lop Nur, Xinjiang in 1980, known as the Beauty of Loulan. Carbon-14 dating on the body places her death at roughly 3,800 years ago. Although little evidence remains in China of her Indo-European culture, she may have been part of a foreign group that introduced the words into Chinese for wheel, lion, and honey. *Photo: Alicia Noel.*

**SANXINGDUI** Bronze mask from Sanxingdui, Sichuan, one of the few extant artifacts of what may have been the culture referred to in ancient chronicles as the Shu people. Much of the most precious evidence at Sanxingdui comes from sacrificial pits, seemingly destroyed by the Shu people themselves in an attempt to placate angry gods of harvest or weather. *Photo: Kati Clements.*

**ORACLE BONE** This ox scapula from Anyang, Henan, has been etched with questions for the gods on behalf of the health of the Shang king Wuding, c. 1200 BCE. The discovery and deciphering of oracle bones in the early twentieth century transformed the Shang dynasty from a myth into verifiable history. *Photo: BabelStone.*

**TERRACOTTA WARRIORS** The First Emperor was buried with the 7,000-strong Terracotta Army, a collection of life-sized figures said to have been modeled on his real honor guard. It is possible that their diverse features were a form of likeness identification, to buy wealthy sponsors out of accompanying the Emperor into the afterlife for real. The Emperor's women were not so lucky, and were executed at his funeral. *Photo: Kati Clements.*

**ONE OF MANY**
Detail of one of the First Emperor's Terracotta Warriors. At the time of burial, they were decorated with vibrant paint that has faded over the centuries. *Photo: Kati Clements.*

**THE FIRST EMPEROR**
A modern artist's impression of the First Emperor of China (259–210 BCE) from the grounds of his mausoleum in Lintong, Shaanxi. *Photo: Kati Clements.*

**TRIPITAKA**
Painting of Tripitaka (c. 602–64), the Buddhist monk who travelled to India, with a towering backpack stacked with sacred scriptures.
*Photo: Alexcn/ Tokyo National Museum.*

**THE SILENT GIRL** (Above)
Bust of Lin Moniang (960–87),
the girl from Fujian known
after her death as Mazu, Goddess of the Sea, from the dock-
side at Tainan, Taiwan.
*Photo: Jonathan Clements.*

**THE GODDESS OF THE SEA**
(Top left) Effigy of Mazu, Goddess of the Sea, from the Zheng
family temple in Nagasaki,
Japan. Mazu worship spread
throughout Chinese maritime
communities who believed the
spirit of Lin Moniang would
protect them on the seas.
*Photo: Kati Clements.*

**THE VAIROCANA BUDDHA**
(Left) The Vairocana Buddha,
carved into the cliff wall at
the Longmen Grottoes,
Henan. Completed in 676 CE,
it is rumored to have the face
of Empress Wu, who donated
the money to carve it along
with her husband, the ailing
Gaozong Emperor.
*Photo: Kati Clements.*

**EMPRESS WU ZETIAN**
Portrait of Empress Wu, painted five centuries after her death in the Song-dynasty book *Some Ceremonial Pictures (Sanlitu)*, c. 1176. *Photo: Private Collection.*

**YANG GUIFEI** Modern statue of Yang Guifei (719–56) in Xi'an, Shaanxi. The "Precious Consort" charmed an Emperor and was regarded as one of the most beautiful women in Chinese history. She also took the blame for the decline of the Tang dynasty. *Photo: Kati Clements.*

**DRAGON TILES** Tiled wall decoration from the Manchus' Forbidden City in Beijing, depicting dragons rampant. *Photo: Kati Clements.*

**THE KNIGHT OF THE NATIONAL NAME**
Statue of Zheng Chenggong (1624–62), a.k.a. Koxinga, leader of the Ming resistance, in the Koxinga Shrine, Tainan, Taiwan. *Photo: Jonathan Clements.*

**THE EMPTY GRAVESTONE** The controversially blank memorial stone left at the tomb of Empress Wu by her children. Despite presiding over the height of the Tang dynasty, she was demonized for centuries by Chinese historians determined to discourage women from politics. It is only in recent times that she has come to be reconsidered as a feminist icon. *Photo: Kati Clements.*

**THE PEOPLE'S HERO** Yue Fei's mother tattoos his back with the words "Utmost Loyalty in the Service of the Nation." Formerly a national hero, he was downgraded to "people's" hero in 2002 because his enemies were now regarded as culturally Chinese. This painting, from the Long Corridor of the Summer Palace in Beijing, dates from centuries after his death. *Photo: Rolf Müller.*

**THE YUAN MING YUAN** The ruins of the Garden of Perfect Brightness (Yuan Ming Yuan) in Beijing, left as a reminder of the Opium Wars. Treasures looted from it show up all over the world, from California swimming pools to French hotel lobbies, although modern China's economic might has seen a vogue for repatriating stolen antiquities. *Photo: Kati Clements.*

**UYGHUR MOSQUE** Completed in 1778, the Emin Minaret in Turfan, Xinjiang, was built to honor the exploits of the Uyghur leader Emin Khoja, who helped the Manchus conquer the region. The near impossibility of separating Uyghur culture from Uyghur religion has been a constant issue in modern Chinese regional politics, which looks down on all "superstitions." *Photo: Frederik L. Schodt.*

**THE GREAT WALL** Of the many border fortifications that have separated China from the realm of the nomads, the "Great Wall" of the Ming dynasty is the most architecturally impressive. However, it proved useless against the Manchus, who were invited in by the general Wu Sangui in 1644. Ever

since, the "border" it marks has been hundreds of miles inside Chinese territory, which now incorporates the realm of the Manchu invaders. *Photo: Shutterstock © Zhu Difeng.*

**THE WOMAN WARRIOR OF MIRROR LAKE** (Left) Qiu Jin (1875–1907) a People's Heroine in the struggle against the Manchus, executed for plotting a revolution. *Photo: Gamaliel.*

**THE LAST EMPEROR** Aisin Gioro "Henry" Puyi, the Xuantong Emperor (r. 1908–12), better known as the Last Emperor, photographed here in 1934, during his brief period as the figurehead of the Japanese puppet state of Manchukuo. *Photo: Rekishi Shashin Kai.*

**THE PEOPLE'S HEROES**
Monuments in the People's Republic celebrated the masses, lionizing workers, soldiers and the common people such as these tableaux from the Monument to the People's Heroes in Tiananmen Square, Beijing. *Photo: Kati Clements.*

dhism by Chinese traditionalists that caused China's native religion, Daoism, to first be codified into a recognizable canon. *Essays on the Barbarians and the Chinese* (*Yi-Xia Lun*), written in 467, catalogues everything that was apparently wrong with Buddhism—including that it was an Indian religion which had no place in China, that its scriptures were infamously confused and contradictory, and that its priests unforgivably shaved their heads: an insult to the wholeness of the body inherited from one parents. In particular, the Buddhists lacked filiality—in concentrating on the perfection of the self, they allegedly ignored the societal obligations of the civilized world. Buddhist authors soon responded in kind, lampooning Daoism as unclear and ephemeral, and adding insult to injury by claiming that many recent Daoist texts had been inspired by or even plagiarized from Buddhist scriptures.

Although Daoists and Buddhists were often at odds, the former bragging that their beliefs were fully and truly all-Chinese, whereas Buddhism was a foreign latecomer, the two religions still cross-pollinated each other. The Chinese afterlife, only rarely discussed in anything but the vaguest of terms, gained an entire hierarchy of hells inspired by Buddhist iconography, as well as a set of paradises with more levels than a loyalty scheme. This, in turn, invested Buddhist priests with a new authority to deal with the dead, or at least to help smooth the passage of loved ones into a better world. Nobody could say for sure whether reincarnation or an afterlife waited after death, but just to be safe, it was worth paying a Buddhist priest to say some prayers. From this humble beginning, an entire religious industry began to escalate.

Daoism from the second century CE onwards had pushed a notion of "inherited burden" (*chengfu*), suggesting that the conditions of one's fate, including obligations, was derived from one's parents, or even from the deeds of the society into which one was born. Human beings were hounded throughout their life by the Three Corpses (*sanshi*) that worked to defeat, sicken and destroy life, and whose influence could be counteracted with prayer and recognition of sins. In other words, by the 400s, Daoism in China had developed a sense of karma by another name, as well as an increased concentration on the intercession of good and evil spirits and saints.

For some, Buddhism was a religion of the end of the world. Buddhism increasingly found roots even among the Chinese in the south, who saw in it a certain sympathy for the bitter upheavals they had endured in their flight from their homeland, and the possibility that such disruptions heralded a coming apocalypse and paradise. The *Lotus Sutra*, translated into Chinese five times after the fall of the Han dynasty, spoke in grave terms of a coming apocalypse, from which only the faithful would be saved:

> When the living witness the end of the age
> When all is consumed by the great fire
> This land of mine is safe and peaceful
> Ever filled with gods and men.

That, at least, was genuine. Other stories spreading during the period were purportedly Buddhist but related to no known sutra—Daoists may have had their own end-of-the-world scenario, garbled by new Buddhists into the story of Prince Moonlight, who foretold the coming of a great flood and a paradise awaiting the survivors.

Just as the Chinese in the south reimagined and refashioned their new home as something that was truly, indelibly Chinese, the worldview of the northern conquerors also expanded China's sense of itself. The Western Regions were once more part of the Chinese world, dotted with Buddhist cities all the way to the mountains. So, too were the northern steppes as far as Mongolia, and so, too, were the places that Buddhist missionaries travelled—Japan, in particular, transforming in this period from a mythical realm beyond the horizon to a verifiable place, from which a Queen Himiko sent an embassy to Luoyang in 238.

The Chinese who remained in the north came to develop an appreciation for newly imported foreign ways. Wheat had been around since ancient times, but writers of the Southern and Northern Dynasties pointed to a series of new uses and styles for cooking it—stretched into noodles or molded into parcels with tantalizing names: like the ring stick, piglet's ears and dog's tongue, as well as several untranslatable terms deriving from foreign recipes. The 3rd century poet Shu Xi (263–302), in his *Rhapsody on Pasta*, writes timelessly of steamers above cauldrons of boiling water, and eager customers "poised like tigers."

> People strolling by drool downwind
> Servant boys, chewing air, cast sidelong glances

[Porters] lick their lips
Those standing in attendance swallow drily
And then they dip them in black meat sauce.

One of the most successful northern dynasties was built on the ruins of two earlier regimes by Xianbei tribesmen. Former vassals of the Xiongnu, the Xianbei eventually pushed them out of China altogether—what happened to them thereafter is still unclear, but it remains possible that their distant descendants, after many decades of wandering, turned up in Europe as the Huns.

The Xianbei era is referred to today as the Northern Wei Dynasty (386–534), to distinguish it from several other Wei in Chinese history, including the Eastern and Western Wei into which it would eventually fragment. The Xianbei were known for their multi-branched "leaf" headdresses and their golden belt buckles, both of which would slowly fade from their fashions during their years ruling the Chinese. Other distinctly non-Chinese customs included the mandated men's hairstyle, a long braid, wound repeatedly around the head and covered with a cap—a useful style for anyone who habitually rode a horse, but alien to the average Chinese. Meanwhile, officials were not paid a salary, but were instead granted a number of specific households, which they were expected to oversee, and from whom they were expected to derive their own income.

Northern Wei empresses were not chosen for their looks or family connections, but supposedly after a bizarre talent contest in which they would have to prove their ability at casting a metal statue. Wet-nurses were accorded considerably more respect, and often named as Nurse Empress Dowagers if they survived to see their ward crowned as emperor. This was, in part, because any new emperors were usually orphans. In what appears to have been an effort to suppress the bloody conflict of many a dynastic succession, the mother of a newly appointed crown prince was expected to commit suicide, thereby recusing herself from any of the politics that might follow an emperor's death.

Even with the ongoing migration to the south, the Han population of China north of the Yangtze still amounted to up to 30 million people. The new Xianbei overlords amounted to barely a million in their heyday, relying for their long-term endurance on powerful connections with local families. In their early years, they continued to act with a nomadic disregard for permanent settlement, moving 100,000 fellow Xianbei to their new capital in Datong in 398, and ordering several mass movements of population in the fifty years that followed—often aimed at forcing peasants to occupy and farm land close to the capital, or forcibly moving artisans and craftsmen to Datong from the old heartland.

Southern Chinese were scandalized by the power and confidence enjoyed by northern women. "A woman's function in the household," fumes the educator Yan Zhitui, "should be limited to taking care of meals, clothes and the like." He repeatedly contrasts the traditions still observed south of the Yangtze with the social upheavals underway in the barbarian-riddled north, where women were apt to wear trousers, ride horses, and even leave the house without veils.

> In the customs of [the north], it's the women that head the family. They deal with outsiders, request interviews or receive guests. Their carriages fill the streets. You can see them at the government offices, flouncing around in their silks. They dicker over jobs for their boys, or put the case for their husbands. I suppose they get this from the Xianbei.... North of the [Yellow] River, it is the wife who deals with the majority of visitors... the husband is no longer in charge; they do not even use polite forms of address in speaking to one another.

In an admission that must have stung him, Yan goes on to admit that northern girls are all better at weaving, knitting, tailoring and embroidery, despite the airs and graces of the southern elites.

The most famous fictional woman of the Southern and Northern Dynasties was first revealed sitting at her loom in the opening lines to the song that bears her name. The regular, repetitive sound of the first line is revealed not to be the flicking of the shuttle or the switching of the frames—instead, she is pouting about the injustices of the world.

> *Ji... ji...* and back again, *ji... ji...*
> Mulan has her face to the door
> You can't hear the sweeping of the shuttle
> Only the daughter's sighs.

The *Ballad of Mulan* is a perfect integration of the cultures of north and south, playfully confronting the expectations of the old-style Han Chinese with the world of the northern immigrants. Its subject is introduced as a sulky teenager, getting on with her chores with comical reluctance, and batting away any attempts at parental enquiry. No, she isn't thinking about a boy. No! She isn't missing anyone!

It's only in the third verse that her story takes a sudden turn. Set up as a jaunty love song, it suddenly reveals its heroine as one of those northern girls we keep hearing about, ready to take the initiative and get stuff done. The khan of the Northern Wei (the song uses the nomad term for ruler, rather than emperor) has issued a draft notice, and every family must send an able-bodied son to fight. This call-up dates all the way back to the rule of Cao Cao, when the warlord tried to restart agriculture by settling soldiers and homeless peasants on abandoned land—some of it derelict, some confiscated from the Yellow Turbans. The plan was not dissimilar to similar military colonies established in the Han dynasty in the Western Regions, but now the policy was turned inwards, all along the lower Yellow River. Some military colonies were simply expected to pay a hefty tax—up to 60% if they rented government oxen—others paid lower amounts, but were obliged to provide a man of military age whenever called upon to do so.

But Mulan's father has no son; Mulan has no elder brother, and so she boldly declares that she will fight in his place, to fulfill her family's hereditary military obligation. The song talks us through a shopping trip to buy her gear, and her swift departure for the lands north of the Yellow River.

> Ten thousand leagues she goes on missions of war
> Across mountain passes as if in flight
> The early winds carry the rattle of metal
> Cold light shines on iron
> Generals die in a hundred battles
> The strong return after a decade.

Mulan stands before the "Son of Heaven" (confusing the terms for emperor and khan, very much in the spirit of the age) and refuses all awards and bonuses, asking instead only for a stout camel to take her home. She returns to a previously unmentioned elder sister who was not quite so butch, and a younger brother born during her absence. Her parents greet her, clutching at each other in glee and relief, and she rushes indoors to change.

> I shed my wartime gown
> And put on my old skirts
> At the window she fixes cloud-like hair
> At the mirror she dabs on yellow flower powder
> At the door, she greets her comrades
> Comrades all in shock
> Twelve years travel together
> And they did not know Mulan was a girl.

The song's final verse has a cartoonish flourish, focusing on two rabbits darting close by. Neither of them can tell if she is a girl, either. It is a far cry from the way that girls were treated in the south, where Yan Zhitui shook his head about the cavalier way in which many Chinese were prepared to disown their children. The birth of a girl, he argued in his *Admonitions for the Yan Clan*, was the will of Heaven, and should be welcomed, even if it meant that the family was fated to raise a hungry mouth that was destined merely to marry into another household. He quotes a Han dynasty official who once light-heartedly observed the cost of girls: "A house with five daughters attracts no burglars." But he goes on to report the chilling result of such an attitude, as found in the family of one of his distant relatives who had a lot of concubines:

> When one of them is going to give birth to a child, she will be kept under close watch by the janitor, who will peep in through her room window at the time of delivery. If the newborn is a daughter, the janitor will enter and snatch it away while the mother staggers behind screaming and wailing in a heart-breaking manner.

North and south gradually drifted together in attitudes and outlook. The alien qualities of the north would fade as the Xianbei aristocracy adopted Chinese ways. The Northern Wei also adopted Buddhism en masse, turning it from a foreign fad into a national obsession. Eventually, the Northern Wei moved into the old Han Chinese capital, giving up on rainswept military campaign further south and occupying Luoyang in 493. A hundred years earlier, there had only been a few dozen Buddhist temples in the ancient city of Luoyang. However, according to the historian Yang Xuanzhi:

> …when the Wei emperors accepted the Mandate of Heaven and chose the… area as the site of their capital, the Buddhist converts swiftly increased… Princes, dukes and ministers donated precious items like elephants or horses as generously as if they were slipping shoes from their feet. The people and great families parted with their treasures as easily as with forgotten trash. As a result, Buddhist temples were built side by side, and stupas rose up in row after row. People competed among themselves in making or copying the Buddha's image.

The evidence of their religious devotion is still to be seen today on the outskirts of their two capitals, Datong in Shanxi, and Luoyang in Henan. The Yungang (Cloud Harbor) and Longmen (Dragon Gate) grottoes are religious complexes carved out of the local rock, caves painted with images from Buddhist iconography, and statues whittled into the cliffs. Each one is a conspicuous demonstration of piety—from large statue groups designed to buy an emperor merit, to cave-shrines painted in memory of a departed loved one, to simple, finger-high statuettes commissioned by some forgotten merchant, grateful to have made it across the desert with his goods intact.

The move from Datong to Luoyang reflected increased sinicization among the aristocracy of the Northern Wei. Sitting at the edge of the Mongolian steppes, Datong was fine as a base for rulers with a foot in each society. But despite the Northern Wei's efforts to create a new capital by proclamation, it was ill-suited to support a large urban population. Firewood had to be sourced from dwindling forests; grain had to come by caravan. Many of those luxuries and treats that were supposed to denote Chinese civilization were hard to come by. A well-supplied pre-modern state demanded a capital that sat at the nexus of a river network—Luoyang was still in ruins, but there is a reason why it had been the capital for several earlier dynasties, and the Northern Wei eventually gave up and moved in.

The figure behind the move was the Northern Wei Emperor Xiaowen (467–499), as part of a major effort to make his dynasty more Chinese. His mother had been Chinese, and this may be where his apparent resentment of Xianbei customs came from. He had been crowned aged four, upon the abdication of his 17-year-old father. Court annals do not specifically say that his Chinese mother was obliged to commit suicide at this point, but she appears to have done so, amid much anger from the Chinese courtiers and to the horror of her young son.

His childhood and teenage years were dominated by the regency of his stepmother, but upon assuming power in his own right, he began a long-term campaign to purge the Xianbei of their tribal traditions. His policies accelerated in 495, banning Xianbei clothing and the use of the Xianbei language for all subjects under 30—effectively announcing that it would die out with the older generation. The following year, he ordered the Xianbei to drop their original surnames and adopt Chinese ones, setting an example himself by changing his own from Tuoba to Yuan. Most of the prominent Dugu clan were now called Liu, for example, and the Wuniuyu family were now known as Yu. In an enforced racial integration, the emperor also ordered his six brothers to take Chinese wives, demoting their original spouses to mere concubines.

Xiaowen was not good at setting an example in family matters. His stepmother, the Empress Dowager, had ensured that he was kept busy in bed with her nieces, in the hope that one of them would bear him an heir, and even if she were forced to commit suicide, the others were likely choices as stepmothers and power-brokers. However, his first two concubines became seriously ill, possibly with smallpox—one died and the other, Feng Run, was packed off to a nunnery. When she returned after her recovery, she discovered that her place had been usurped by a third sister, to whom she refused to yield in matters of palace protocol. Feng Run eventually caused her sister's downfall by spreading rumors that she was secretly flouting the directives to act in a more Chinese fashion. By this time, however, the emperor was away at war south of the Yellow River, and fearing that an affair with a courtier would be discovered, Feng Run engaged witches to put a curse on him to ensure that he died before he could come home and hear the charges. The emperor inconveniently made it home alive, and was sufficiently convinced of the story to disown her, observing to his courtiers that as a member of the Empress Dowager's clan, she was untouchable, but that he hoped she would one day do the decent thing and kill herself.

The couple continued to remain at odds, with Feng Run refusing to take orders from eunuch emissaries, and Emperor Xiaowen ordering his mother-in-law to whip her with a cane to teach her some manners. As he lay dying in 499, he ordered that she should accompany him to the grave, but she refused, claiming that it was a plot by his latest bedmate to get rid of her. Accordingly, Empress Feng Run was helped along by being force-fed poison peppers, and then buried with her estranged husband to keep up appearances.

The year 535 was bad all over the world. Scientists continue to debate the causes of the extreme weather events reported in multiple chronicles— a comet impact, a meteorite, but most likely a volcanic eruption that seeded the atmosphere with dust and created unprecedented bad weather. "The Sun gave forth its light without brightness," wrote the Byzantine historian Procopius, "like the moon during this whole year, and it seemed exceedingly like the Sun in eclipse." Similar conditions struck China, with temperatures so low that snow fell in August, leading in turn to food shortages, floods, and disease. Tensions within the ruling class resolved along cultural lines, with some demanding a return to the "original" nomad values and traditions, and others pushing for the Northern Wei to remain "Chinese." After several murderous scandals in the palace between the usual cliques of emperors, affines and officials, the Northern Wei split into two warring factions, each led by a puppet emperor that would soon abdicate in favor of a new dynasty founded by his generals. The east briefly flourished as the Northern Qi; the west as the Northern Zhou (557–581), which was victorious in the 570s and then initiated the long-awaited reconquest of the south.

The choice of name was a deliberate attempt to invoke the golden age of antiquity. The Buddhist translator Yang Xuanzhi visited Luoyang a decade after it fell to the Western Wei general Dugu Xin, and observed the historical irony—that he now knew precisely how the original Zhou people must have felt when they made the journey in reverse back in the Bronze Age.

The outer and inner city walls lay in ruins, palaces were toppled, temples and monasteries were in ashes... Walls were covered

> with wild vines, and streets were dotted with thorny bushes. Wild beasts lived under deserted stairways… while farmers… grew crops on the grounds where palace towers once stood. […] Within and without the capital city, there had been more than one thousand temples. Today they are mostly demolished; one cannot hear the tolling of bells at night.

The Northern Zhou presented themselves as a restoration of the original Zhou, as if the last thousand years had been a wrong turn, and the abandonment of Luoyang for Chang-an somehow recreated the proper order of things. They used a playbook that was often copied from the speeches and policies of the Bronze Age, dismissive of "new" additions like Buddhism. But it was not quite as old-school Chinese as it first appeared—its aristocracy also frowned on Daoist superstitions, which were themselves living fossils of the Zhou era. And there certainly was no return to the good old days of princely charioteers. Instead, the Northern Zhou fiercely inaugurated a scheme of tax breaks in return for military service, whipping up twenty-four legions of reserve infantry ready to fight not only in the battle with their Northern Qi cousins, but with winning back other areas of lost territory, including Gansu, Sichuan and with it, the upper reaches of the Yangtze.

Downriver, Emperor Wu's proud Southern Liang sank without him. Its capital (modern Nanjing) fell to a rebellion and then an invasion from a similarly short-lived upstart dynasty. It might have fallen to the Northern Zhou, were not that dynasty fatally delayed by the death of its penultimate ruler, and the succession of an infamously weird despot, Emperor Xuan (r. 578–579). Barely nineteen at the time of his accession, Emperor Xuan had supposedly led a Northern Zhou army against a Xianbei offshoot called the Tuyuhun in his mid-teens, but he had been merely a figurehead. Instead he misbehaved with his cronies, leading his imperial father to beat him up with a baton on his return. It was not the last time that the troubled teen suffered physical abuse, with his father repeatedly insisting that he was only keeping him on as his heir because his brother was even worse.

Emperor Xuan enjoyed a brief but dramatic reign. We might grant him that the trauma of losing a parent, however bad their relationship, and the very real threat of a palace coup by his uncles and cousins might have made his behavior somewhat erratic. Caressing the visible scars of his childhood punishments, he berated his father's corpse for taking too long to die. He reversed his father's ban on booze in the palace, quaffing wine from the sacred sacrificial vessels reserved for rituals. He also invited the late emperor's concubines into his own bed—incest under Confucian rules—and raped a cousin's wife after getting her drunk. The loudmouth, grasping quality of the Northern Zhou, desperately aspiring to mimic a long-gone Golden Age, found its peak in Emperor Xuan, who embarked upon ever more lurid and ostentatious displays of power, in an attempt to demonstrate that he was not only the emperor, but the greatest emperor ever.

He was soon no longer Emperor Xuan—he demanded to be addressed as "the Celestial Origin," and broke with all tradition by elevating five of his concubines simultaneously to the rank of Empress. Declaring himself above earthly matters, he "retired" barely into his twenties, leaving his empire in the care of his infant son. Whereas the rules of propriety demanded that an emperor have twelve rows of beads on his crown, the elevated Celestial Origin had twenty-four. This numerical symbol was duplicated in every aspect of his entourage, so that he now went everywhere accompanied by twice as many followers, standards and outriders as any previous ruler. He was, mercifully, seen less and less by the courtiers, since he was usually drunk with his women, and demanded that anyone approaching him undergo three days of fasting and a purification ritual usually reserved for communing with the gods. His father-in-law, Puliuru Jian (541–604) commented to a bereaved minister that this, too, would soon pass, since "the Celestial Origin" was deluded, and his face bore every indication that he was not long for this world. He died in 580, supposedly of a stroke, aged 21.

The inheritors of the Southern and Northern Dynasties were, fittingly, a hybrid of both. The Northern Zhou was itself usurped by Emperor Xuan's father-in-law, who killed off a bunch of rivals, had the child-emperor proclaim him to be the Duke of Sui, and then crowned himself as the first emperor of the new Sui dynasty (581–618), which would carry the military legacy of its predecessors to final victory. The short-lived Sui would conquer the south, declare China whole again once more, and then thrash itself to an early death in an ill-fated series of campaigns on the Korean frontier.

Despite his Xianbei surname, Puliuru was a Han Chinese of mixed heritage, triumphantly reclaiming his original surname of Yang. The bans were lifted on Buddhism and Daoism, and the Northern Zhou's archaic pretentions cast aside, along with a purge of 60 of the late child-emperor's cousins and uncles, just to make sure there would be no restoration. But if this might appear like the Han ethnicity of old, stepping out from behind the shadows, we should remember that north and south were now linked by centuries of inter-marriage, albeit divided by their different cultures.

According to the scholar-official Yan Zhitui (531–591), by the time China was reunified, the modes of speech between north and south had become distinctly diverged. People of all classes from the north spoke a Chinese peppered with archaisms, and slurred with a rustic burr. The upper classes in the south spoke a more refined and diligently soft-spoken Chinese, although the common southerner's speech was even worse than a northerner's, riddled with vulgarisms and non-Han slang. "I have demanded of my children," he writes, "correct pronunciation even in their early childhood... I dare not give a name to any home-made contrivance unless I have found a proper term already on record."

Meanwhile, despite a series of revolts that takes us from the end of the Northern Wei in 534, to the Western Wei, then to Northern Zhou, and then to the Sui in less than forty years, a single family dominated all this politicking from behind the scenes. The aforementioned general Dugu Xin, a man of Xianbei extraction, married his daughter and grand-daughter to the last two emperors of the Northern Zhou. Another of his daughters was married to the founder of the Sui dynasty, and the mother of its second emperor. His third daughter, however, was the mother of Li Yuan (566–618), the Duke of Tang, who would soon overthrow his Sui cousins, inherit the unified land they had died to create, and proclaim still another change in regime. But this one would last.

CHAPTER 5

# EMPIRE OF THE SILK ROAD: THE TANG DYNASTY

T he warm mist in the baths was scented with a pungent mix of ginseng and sandalwood. It was hard to see through all the steam, as servants upended new jugs of hot water into the vast, tiled pool. One of the women in the water squealed and giggled, her soaked silk tunic clinging to her body. The others laughed at her and splashed playfully in her direction.

Xuanzong waited calmly, but nobody noticed him.

The man in the bath was in his late forties, and hairy beyond belief, all but covered in a swarthy mat of black, bristly fur. His hair fell to his waist, and clumped into a thick, dark beard and moustache, without any evident sign of gray. He was covered in soap bean suds—an upturned dish had scattered pink soap-bean balls across the floor.

A squishing noise beneath his sandals told Xuanzong he had just stepped on one.

One of the women gasped at the sight of his shining yellow robes— only one man in the world was permitted to wear imperial yellow. Xuanzong stroked absently at the twin ends of his moustache, unreadable, inscrutable.

Suddenly, the room was very quiet. A couple of the outlying bathers took timid backward steps, their heads bowed in the beginnings of a curtsey. Their eyebrows might have been raised in surprise, but this was not possible. Their eyebrows had been shaved off, and the water had washed

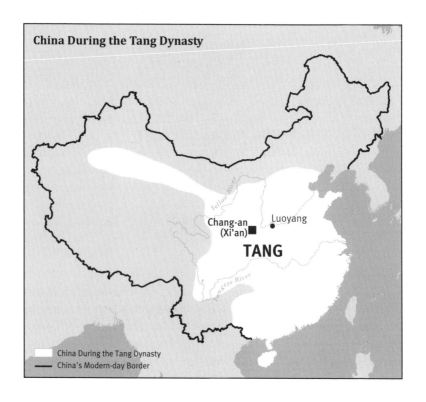

**China During the Tang Dynasty**

Yellow River

Chang-an
(Xi'an)■ ●Luoyang

**TANG**

Yangtze River

☐ China During the Tang Dynasty
— China's Modern-day Border

away the "moth-brow" dabs of cosmetics that usually replaced them.

Precious Consort Yang met Xuanzong's gaze, a sly smile on her lips.

"What…" began Xuanzong slowly, "in all under Heaven is going on here?"

"Can't you see?" she answered immediately, her single, confident voice filling the space where once there had been many. "I'm washing my little baby."

She patted the fat man's head tenderly.

Roxshan, for it was he, pulled his thumb out of his mouth with loud pop and jumped to his feet, causing a small tidal wave in the pool as the waters sloshed to accommodate the change. He was wearing a single, diaper-like loincloth around his privates.

"Mama!" he cried, and Xuanzong burst out laughing.

Within moments, the women began laughing along with him, their smiles pasted on, their glances meeting cautiously. But Xuanzong kept laughing, squelching across the tiles towards them, a beaming smile on his face.

"Such a commotion!" he said. "Over such a big baby."

"He's wearing the birthday diaper I bought him!" laughed Precious Consort Yang, snapping Roxshan's waistband with her fingers. It elicited a dramatic cry of pain from him, and more giggles from the girls.

"It won't be so much fun when you have to change him!" said Xuanzong, to a mixture of titters and groans from the concubines.

"I'm about done anyway," said Roxshan climbing up the steps out of the water. One of the Precious Consort's ladies in waiting tried to put a towel around his shoulders, but could not reach high enough. He took it from her and wrapped it around himself.

"I shall take my leave," he said, bowing to the Precious Consort.

"Until tomorrow, mother dearest," he said.

There was a sharp intake of breath from the youngest and newest serving girl.

"I am a barbarian," Roxshan explained. "We bow first to our mothers, and then..." He turned to the Emperor Xuanzong. "And *only* then, to our fathers!"

Xuanzong nodded back with a smile.

"It's a thing we do," he reassured the scandalized girl. "He means well."

The tall, bearded Turk towered above Xuanzong, who barely came up to his chest. He stood with his hands on his hips, rivulets of water still dripping from his heavily muscled arms, hit oversized pot belly glistening with the last of the suds.

Xuanzong, patted Roxshan's portly stomach with a gentle, wet slap.

"What lies beneath all that blubber of yours?" he mused.

"Oh, my Emperor," sighed Roxshan. "Nothing but a loyal heart."

Everybody laughed.

$\odot - \odot - \odot - \odot - \odot$

The period from 551–760, spanning the rise of the Sui dynasty to the peak of the Tang, was bolstered by a localized warm period and a gradual weakening of the summer monsoon. The desertification and reduced biological activity of the previous era was reversed in China's heartland. The early Tang dynasty is remembered as a time of plenty, but a climatologist might point out that this mixes up cause and effect—it was the time of plenty that came first, allowing the Tang dynasty a greater degree of expansion and success.

The Sui and Tang are often lumped together because one fed directly into the other—indeed, they were so closely related by marriage that a grandson of the last Sui ruler came within a hair's breadth of becoming the third Tang emperor.

The Sui dynasty retook the south by 590, with armies crossing the Yangtze at eight points, and an armada of five-story battleships sailing downriver from Sichuan. The new emperor subscribed to a new definition of "tradition," mapping many systems and institutions in imitation of the Han dynasty, and cancelling sinecure positions and unnecessary bureaucratic ranks that had accreted over centuries of politicking and nepotism. He also asserted a devout, personal Buddhist faith that he had suppressed during the Northern Zhou bans. While the political institutions of Sui China would have looked familiar to a Han dynasty subject, the inspiration for his religious outreach program—an empire-wide distribution of Buddhist relics—seemed drawn from the time of the Indian emperor Ashoka. In many parts of China, Buddhism had previously been a mere religious belief, unthreatening to the Daoist and Confucian elites. Now, the Buddhists *were* the elites, with better guarantees for returns on donations.

This was a gross misrepresentation of Buddhist ethics, but many were still confused by the mistranslations from the scriptures. Old soldiers like the Sui Emperor wanted to buy back their karma with grand gestures of benevolence and reconstruction. Great families pushed some of their sons and daughters to monasteries and nunneries, where some of them would manage family estates under the tax-free guise of "donations to the temple." Unexpectedly, Buddhism also offered a limited military dividend, since its adherents were less likely to shy away from battle on foreign fields out of a Daoist-derived desire for a burial in their home village. This, of course, was hardly much of a consolation, particularly when the Sui emperors embarked on a fruitless series of campaigns against the Koreans on their northeastern borders.

The Sui, however, would not be around to enjoy the fruits of their labors. A provincial governor faced demotion over his inability to control incursions by Turkish nomads. Throwing himself into a succession crisis, initially in support of one of the Sui claimants, he took Chang-an and was proclaimed Duke of Tang, before taking the throne for himself as Gaozu, first emperor of the Tang dynasty. Later chroniclers would suggest that Gaozu was more of a figurehead for a revolution engineered by his startlingly proactive children, including his second son, the future Emperor Taizong, and his daughter, the Princess Pingyang (598–623), who would raise "the Army of the Lady" in his name and assimilated several rebel divisions into her command. When she died, still in her twenties, she was controversially buried with full military honors befitting a male general.

Gaozu's reign did not last long. There was soon a conflict among his sons, erupting into a fight at the palace gate in which two of them were killed. The terrified father quickly assented to the last man standing becoming the new crown prince, and put up little resistance a few months later when the son suggested that he abdicate. Gaozu lived another decade in quiet seclusion, ever fearful of a knife in the dark, while the second Tang emperor, Taizong, is remembered as one of the greatest in Chinese history.

Taizong traced his ancestry back not only to the Han people, but to their bitter enemies, the Xiongnu. His mother and grandmother were Xianbei—perhaps explaining his sister Pingyang's military acumen. He thus had some 75% nomad ancestry, and yet is remembered as a "Chinese" emperor. Much of the peace and prosperity of the early Tang dynasty was brought about by Taizong's dual status—he was not only the emperor of China, but also recognized as the *Tenggeri Qaghan* (The Godlike Ruler) of the nomads. He had, in fact, used a division of nomad horsemen in his rebel army—it has been suggested that their support was conditional on Taizong installing Gaozu as emperor, rather than simply protecting the Sui dynasty from other rebels.

Much as the Han dynasty had reaped the benefits of the First Emperor's slave labor gangs and ethnic cleansing, the Tang dynasty got to take all the credit for the Sui emperors' big plans. Millions were poured into the construction of canals, including a vital connection that skirted the unnavigable waters of the Wei River to link Chang-an to the Yellow River, and the greatest of all, the justly titled Grand Canal. Linking several rivers in the south and a long passage northwards, the several disjointed pieces of the Grand Canal allowed ships to move between the Yangtze and Yellow River, and all the way north to what is now Beijing. This would become one of the most fruitful enterprises in Chinese history, even if it was first used for a waste of resources like supplying the front lines in the war on

Korea. When that bankrupted the Sui and their Tang cousins took over, the Grand Canal became a vital economic conduit for all of China, creating entirely new markets for what had once been landlocked local products. The rich farmlands could now supply food to the capital, but the Grand Canal also fostered trade between distant regions. It is, for example, in the Tang that we first see tea spreading beyond Sichuan and Yunnan, pottery shipped far from its place of creation, and with it, a new-found use for transporting fluid contents—sauces and liquor. It is also in the Tang dynasty that we see the first signs of regional specialization, as entire towns of silk-spinners accrete upstream from towns of silk weavers, themselves within a barge trip of a town of brocade makers, increasing the volume of production through a slow but recognizable division of labor, itself relying on the ease of bulk water transport. In connecting trades from disparate parts of China, the Grand Canal helped foster the erosion of local differences. By the end of the Tang dynasty delicacies prized in one part of China were sure to be consumed all over.

The environmental impact of such grand schemes was heavy around Chang-an. The sheer size of the city had long been a drain on the surrounding countryside, even more so when provisions were required for all the soldiers garrisoned to protect it. After the loss of the Tibetan horse trade, attempts to raise horses locally only served to deplete nearby grasslands. Evidence of dropping pollen counts shows that the treeline receded rapidly from the city limits. With an ever-increasing need for lumber and firewood, the government built a canal to more distant forests, only for them, too, to swiftly disappear. Sichuan, once heavily forested, lost most of its trees by the mid-Tang, leading farmers and soldiers (who were obliged to source their own materiel) to plant fast-growing alder trees that could yield reasonable lumber in only a few years.

Throughout the Tang dynasty, the imperial court would shuttle periodically between Luoyang and Chang-an. Sometimes, this was for tactical reasons in times of military danger; usually, however, it was simply an attempt to give each city time to recover from the damage done to its lumber and food supply by such a demanding upper class. Frederick Mote, in his *Imperial China*, even suggests that periodic switches in the capital were necessary "just to avoid starvation."

Foreign contacts helped create the Tang dynasty's famously cosmopolitan culture. Traders from beyond the empire, such as the Sogdian merchants, ran camel trains along the edges of the western desert, and formed entire enclaves within Chang-an. Their taverns were famed for their raucous dancing and exotic foods, while their religious beliefs were administered to by Nestorian Christian priests. Alopen, a Syrian monk, arrived in Chang-an in 635 and is recorded as administering to an immigrant flock. Some of their scriptures, the so-called *Jesus Sutras*, were uncovered in a desert ruin in the 20th century, and, much like early Buddhist writings in Chinese, reflect a hybrid form of Christian belief mapped onto Daoist terminology. Other foreigners tried a little harder to fit in, many of them adopting approved Chinese names that reflected their place of origin—*An*, for example, for men from Bukhara; *Kang* for men from Samarkand, or *Shi* for men from Tashkent.

Turkish trend-setters peppered the culture of Chang-an with new-fangled dances, foods and fashions. Persian indigo supplied the main ingredient in the blue kohl that darkened the eyes of Tang women; dabbed in spots high on the forehead, it was also used to create "moth brows" to replace shaved eyebrows—a poetic allusion to the facial features of Duchess Zhuang Jiang in the Bronze Age. Yellow lead or golden arsenic added an alien sheen to their faces. Such rich pigments did not merely turn the women of the Tang into glittering goddesses; they also brought rich and enduring alterations to Tang arts and crafts, creating new palettes of available color for carpets, tapestries and paintings.

Barely a month went by at the Tang court without some exotic embassy for foreign climes—Persian princes, or ambassadors from the Byzantine Emperor Constans II. At the height of the Silk Road, the most traded commodity from west to east was coral from the shores of the Red Sea, its reds and blues deemed of great value in Buddhist statues and mandalas. Glass beads also travelled west from the Mediterranean, along with several diplomatic missions vainly hoping to secure China's cooperation in containing the growing power of Islam. Fame of Taizong and his empire spread all the way to the Mediterranean, where the 7th-century writer Theophylactus Simocatta wrote of a land of special "Turks":

> The ruler of the land of the Taugas is called *Taissan*, which signifies, when translated, the Son of God… The nation practices idolatry, but they have just laws and their life is full of temperate wisdom. … The territory of Taugas, of which we are speak-

ing, is divided in two by a river, which in time past formed the boundary between two very great nations which were at war with one another. These nations were distinguished from one another by their dress, the one wearing clothes dyed black, the other red.

We can see in Simocatta's account a garbled but recognizable appraisal of China, not only as it was in the reign of Taizong/Taissan, but refracted through a Turk's-eye view of the divisions of the Southern and Northern dynasties. It is, in fact, fascinating to see just how *Turkish* Simocatta's understanding of China is—he is impressed by China's elephants, by its trade with India, and by its mastery of silkworms. When he describes Chang-an, the greatest city in the world, he calls it by its Turkish name, *Khubdan*, and wrongly presumes it was founded by Alexander the Great.

Simocatta has been pilloried by some scholars for his mistakes—Edward Gibbon lampooned his "want of judgment"—but more forgiving readers might be impressed at the accuracy of his description of China around 630, recognizably naming its sovereign and reasonably summarizing the divisions of the Southern and Northern dynasties. If Simocatta's account is garbled, this is surely because it came to him second- or third-hand, based on the reminiscences not of a native Chinese, but of a boggled visitor from Central Asia—the "Western Regions" that formed the far frontiers of Taizong's realm.

The Tang dynasty clung on to the Western regions for as long as it could, eliciting pledges of fealty from distant oases, and shoring up buffer states to keep the worst of the nomads at bay. The "loose rein" policy once pursued by the Han dynasty was now applied to entire protectorates, granted nominal court positions and silken gifts, for as long as they remained friendly to China. This was made considerably easier by Taizong's dual status—he did not have to lower China's status to commune with barbarians, as the Han emperors had been accused of doing. Instead, he was the imperial paragon of the Chinese, and the khan of khans of the nomads.

One of the most famous subjects of Taizong is a man who disobeyed his commands. The monk Tripitaka (602–664, see Notes on Names) might have easily pursued a career as a Confucian scholar or minister in less troubled times, but grew up during the upheavals of the fall of the Sui dynasty. Seclusion in a monastery may well have saved his life, and turned him into a devout Buddhist priest. A dream in 627 persuaded him to travel to the homeland of the Buddha, even though the Emperor Taizong's ongoing war with the Turks had led to a ban on all foreign travel. Disregarding the emperor's decree, Tripitaka somehow made it out past the last watchtower on the Great Wall, across the oasis states of the Western Regions all the way to Samarkand, and then south to India. His journey took a leisurely three years, and once in India, he stayed for over a decade, travelling between the local kingdoms, collecting sutras and relics.

He returned to Chang-an in 645, where he was welcomed by Taizong and heaped with honors. He refused posts in in Taizong's government, instead sequestering himself in several local monasteries for the next twenty years, where he devoted the rest of his life to making new, substantially better-informed translations of Buddhist scriptures. The most famous of his residences is a temple in what is now Xi'an, dominated by the Great Wild Goose Pagoda, a sturdy, tall ziggurat with walls as thick as bank vaults, designed to be a fire-, flood- and earthquake-proof repository for Tripitaka's scrolls. However, before he embarked upon his enduring religious legacy, he spent a year compiling a detailed report for Taizong of everything he had seen during his long travels. Taizong had only a passing interest in Buddhism—he claimed that his surname, Li, made him a direct descendant of the Daoist founder Li Er (Laozi), and hence spent more time pursuing that religious direction. But he wanted to pick Tripitaka's brains as much as possible about the world beyond the Great Wall.

"Wherever I went I made notes," Tripitaka writes, "and in mentioning what I saw and heard I recorded the aspirations for [Chinese] civilization. It is a fact that from here to where the sun sets, all have experienced [His Majesty's] beneficence, and where his influence reaches, all admire his perfect virtue."

Except the people who didn't. Tripitaka's *Great Tang Record of the Western Regions* is one of the few surviving sources for the city-states and kingdoms along the Tang Silk Road, many of which were only tenuously or theoretically connected to Taizong's empire, and some of which were wiped out by later wars and disasters. Tripitaka describes a rich string of Buddhist city-states, some of them with populations and priesthoods from India itself, their allegiance switching from nomad to Chinese depending on whichever army is closest. Modern statues of Tripitaka often show him with an oversized backpack loaded with scrolls, but although sometimes he appears to have been walking the road like a vagrant hitch-hiker, he reports multiple occasions when kings send him on his way with an escort, and loaded with precious goods for the next city-state over, using him as an impromptu emissary across the sands.

In Kucha, on the south flank of the Tianshan range, Tripitaka found a devout Buddhist state, its city gates flanked by towering statues 30 meters (98.4 feet) tall. The local ruler had red hair and blue eyes, suggesting a genetic connection to the ancient proto-Indo-Europeans who had once dwelt in the Tarim Basin.

> This country yielded millet, rice, grapes, pomegranates, and plenty of pears plums, peaches and apricots. It produced also gold, copper, iron, lead and tin: its climate was temperate and its people had honest ways; their writing was taken from that of India, but has been much altered; they had great skill with wind and stringed musical instruments.

A land with five thousand monks and veritably littered with shrines, Kucha was the site of lavish Buddhist carnivals, where icons of Buddhist saints were carried in processions through the streets.

Tripitaka's account also alludes to the great dangers facing anyone travelling in the region. Thousand-strong companies of Turkic nomads roam the foothills like mobile natural disasters, and are studiously avoided by caravans hoping to avoid entanglements or demands of "tribute." The oasis-countries of the Western Regions are separated by long tracts of hostile desert, or by dangerous mountain ranges—one in three of Tripitaka's experienced henchmen fail to survive the hazardous Bedel Pass. He reached the shores of Issyk-Kul in what is now Kyrgyzstan, the "warm lake" where the Turks liked to winter, and marveled at the waves that crashed on its shore, straight-facedly reporting that its waters held both fish and dragons.

He was received by the Turkish khan, a turbaned man in green satin, flanked by countless guardsmen, and dined in a gold-studded tent amid courtiers clad in rich and multi-colored silk brocades. "Regarding these circumstances of state," comments Tripitaka, who had only read the Han Chinese version of history, "although he was but the leader of a wandering horde, yet there was a certain dignified arrangement about his surroundings."

Fifteen years later, his homeward journey from India would take him across the south of the Tarim Basin, scooping up data on a different group of Chinese vassals. In Hetian, the home of much Chinese jade, he found a decidedly Indian city, the inhabitants of which claimed to be descended from ancient Indian exiles. He scratched his head at the site of a local cult that worshipped a plague of benign rats, "the size of hedgehogs," said to have eaten away the saddle fastenings of an invading Xiongnu horde. He noted the many ruins in the desert, where lost rivers and dried-up wells had caused multiple sites to be abandoned in ages past, recording one story about a dead river that had been brought to life again only after a human sacrifice to the *naga* river goddess. But for the substitution of the Buddhist *naga* for the word dragon—a common translation decision in sutras before his time—it is a tale strangely redolent of ancient Chinese myths.

Many centuries later, the archaeologist Aurel Stein would recall Tripitaka's comments himself, observing not only that the locals told the same stories, but that they maintained a certain "Sodom-and-Gomorrah" attitude towards such ancient tales—living in such an inhospitable environment, surrounded by ample evidence of lost cities from ages past, the religious piety of the Xinjiang region takes on a new aspect.

Tripitaka crossed the hostile Taklamakan desert, where "sands extended like a drifting flood," and human wanderers were obliged to fix their eyes on what were often the only landmarks in the distance—the bones of previous travellers. His official account stops in Loulan, the desert city at the edge of the Lop Nor salt pan, which he considered to be the edge of the known world. As his journey took him further to the east, he was back in Chinese territory, and considered there was no reason to record what would be familiar to Chinese readers.

Under Taizong's patronage, and under the patronage of his successors, Tripitaka spent 19 years translating his scriptures, revitalizing China's Buddhist community and becoming something of a religious celebrity. Taizong was easily mollified over his illegal departure from the country, considering the valuable intelligence he had brought back, which was of great use in Taizong's continued struggles over the Western Regions.

The historical record remembers Taizong as one of the greatest of Chinese emperors, although Taizong himself broke protocols by meddling in what his own chroniclers were writing about him. He was certainly a go-getting monarch, dispatching armies westwards, leading attacks himself on the Koreans who had bankrupted his Sui predecessors, but also working hard in the palace. Chroniclers depict Taizong not merely charging rival Turks on horseback, but leaping from bed at dawn in a chamber pasted from floor to ceiling with reminders and rosters, the names of ministers to be considered for appointments, and endless to-do lists on matters of everything from religious donations to tax reforms. Taizong was a genuinely active emperor, making his ministers work in shifts in order to maximize managing the empire, but his reduction of public works to save his subjects from compulsory labor projects was less about austerity, and more about his Sui predecessors having done all the heavy-lifting.

He was a powerful military leader, but also a smart diplomat. His decrees rapidly spread through his empire, thanks to a realm linked by 1,297 post stations at roughly ten-mile intervals. A decree issued in Chang-an or Luoyang was guaranteed to reach the furthest outpost of the empire within two weeks, delivered by riders or runners switching at every station, so that the message itself travelled at full speed. The system was conceived in imitation of something similar at the time of the First Emperor. Punishments for failure were severe—a whipping for delivery a day late; two years' hard labor for six days. If the message was a classified military matter on which lives depended, a tardy post rider could face execution.

At least for as long as Taizong was alive, there was no problem with barbarian invaders because the barbarians accepted him as one of them. He was also ready to listen to reason from his ministers—where lesser Emperors might have fired or punished people who remonstrated with him, Taizong was at least prepared to consider dissenting views. This led to occasionally irascible exchanges with some of his officials, but an administration that did not bleed away its ablest ministers over petty squabbles.

Beyond the Turks of Central Asia, Taizong's other foreign problem was a new-found mirror image, the just-proclaimed Tibetan Empire with whom he established a precarious but lasting peace. Just as the Tang dynasty had come to power in 618 within the Chinese heartland, troops acting in the name of the newly crowned Tibetan king Songtsen Gampo (r. 618–650) pushed out of their homeland in the Yarlung valley to create the new Tibetan Empire. This political entity would last roughly as long as the Tang dynasty itself and almost eclipse it in its later years, seizing not only the Western Regions (known in Tibetan, unsurprisingly, as the Northern Regions), but also Bangladesh, Yunnan and parts of Sichuan. Taizong let the Tibetans inflict damage on his Tuyuhun enemies in the Western Regions around 637, but refused the teenage Songtsen Gampo's demand for a princess-bride. After several skirmishes along the Chinese frontier in 638, the two new Emperors, neither of whom really wanted a war with each other when they had so many other people to fight, concluded a peace treaty that would last the rest of their lives. It was sealed with the dispatch of a Chinese princess-bride for Songtsen Gampo, who would join his other wife, a Nepalese, in promoting Buddhism at the Tibetan court.

At least before things turned sour in the eighth century, Tibet and China enjoyed a cordial and vibrant cultural exchange in the early Tang. Chinese historians refer to a "Tea-Horse Road" that linked Tibet with southwest China and the Indian Ocean coast, moving tea, ponies, and salt between three regions united by a common interest in Buddhism.

Chinese annals began to claim, rather patronizingly, that although the Tibetans derived from the savage Qiang people who had been enemies and slaves of the Chinese in the Bronze Age, their ruling class might be descended from Chinese nobles who had fled the collapse of the Southern and Northern Dynasties. With orientalist glee, the Tang annals describe the Tibetans as an illiterate race (they had adopted a Sanskrit-based script only under Songtsen Gampo), ministers from which carried a "golden arrow" as a symbol of office, and where justice was reminiscent of cruel antiquity. "Their punishments are most severe," observed one author. "And even for small crimes the eyes are scooped out and the nose cut off, or stripes inflicted with a leather whip."

Tibet in the Tang annals is presented, much as the steppes of the Xiongnu in ages past, as an awful, drab dead-end, where snow never entirely disappears, and even the height of summer is little warmer than a Chinese spring. The people sacrifice sheep, dogs and monkeys, first breaking their limbs, then ripping out their intestines, and although they have a few walled cities, many live in felt tents and follow their herds. "The rooms in which they sleep are filthily dirty, and they never comb their hair nor wash."

Tang annals scoffed that Tibetans didn't even have cups, having to hold wine in their hands, and with armies little more than bandit riders who had to scavenge their supplies by raiding. They are, however, presented as fierce and feral warriors, for whom death in battle is a preferable end, and whose kings were buried with half a dozen voluntary human sacrifices. At no point, it seems did the Tang annals notice that they were describing a culture very similar to the Shang dynasty.

Taizong died, barely into his fifties, exhausted by a lifetime of military campaigns and long hours of court administration. His son and heir, Gaozong (r. 649–683) lacked his vitality. Gaozong was the third of Taizong's three sons by his Empress, and the *fourth* choice as crown prince. His full brothers had proved to be unreliable schemers. A half-brother was regarded as an eminent prospect, but had been sired by Taizong on the daughter of the last Sui emperor, and so risked resurrecting the previous generation's intrigues.

Gaozong is portrayed in the chronicles as something of a milksop and a weakling, and most infamously, besotted with the lowly concubine tasked with changing the sheets on his dying father's bed. It was as forbidden as love could be—even Theophylactus Simocatta, writing 7,000 kilometers (4,349.6 miles) away, was aware what happened on the death of an Emperor:

> When the prince dies he is mourned by his women for the rest of their lives, with shaven heads and black raiment; and it is the law that they shall never quit the sepulchre.

When Taizong inevitably died, the palace women who had not borne him children were sent away to a Buddhist nunnery, but this one was soon smuggled back into the palace amid a whirl of mealy-mouthed accusations—suggesting that she had never been intimate with Taizong, that her shaven hair had magically grown back, and that she was of more use to the palace as a diversion for Gaozong than praying for his father's soul.

Her name was Wu Zhao (624–705); she is better known today as Empress Wu. Still in her twenties at the time of her recall to the palace, the charismatic Wu fast-tracked up the ranks of palace concubines, and after accusing Gaozong's chief wife of murdering her child, and another rival of witchcraft, ousted her more established competitors.

By the time she was 32, Wu had arranged for her own son by Gaozong to be named Crown Prince, and as the Emperor's health took a turn for the worst, exerted increasing authority over his decisions. By the time his epileptic "confusions" had given way to full-blown incapacitation, possibly by a series of strokes, the chroniclers report Gaozong sitting, silent, "with folded hands," while Wu appointed herself the sole interpreter of his commands.

If Gaozong's reign were a non-starter, it still enjoyed the pay-offs of Taizong's hard work. Militarily, the Tang Empire expanded at an impressive rate. Its armies leapfrogged across the oases of the Silk Road, establishing permanent garrisons in remote cities that kept the barbarian horsemen at bay. In the capital, ministers constantly debated whether it was worth all the trouble. In 642, the minister Chu Suiliang likened the Gansu corridor to a superfluous limb extending to the middle of nowhere. If the heartland was a figurative heart, than what was Gansu but an armpit in the desert? A generation later, the minister Di Renjie made a similar point, suggesting that it might be a smart strategic move for China to give up on the Western Regions completely, and reinvest in better defenses closer to home. If enemies from the West wanted to attack China, let them come, and let the heat and thirst work on the Emperor's behalf, creating a forbidden zone that would defeat all but the hardiest of armies before they even reached China.

He might have been right. Tang China's involvement in Central Asia left it exposed to an entirely new threat from further to the west, as Arab invaders swept across Persia. A daughter of Yazdegerd III, last Shah of Persia, had been one of Taizong's minor concubines. Shortly after Gaozong was enthroned, the Persian princess's brother Firuz arrived in China with thousands of refugees, fleeing the Islamic conquest of his homeland. Firuz was welcomed by Gaozong, and his people permitted to settle on the far edge of China, in numbers as high as 120,000. When the young prince grew to adulthood, he and his people formed a buffer state between China and Islam, supposedly in preparation for a reconquest, although that day never came. When he died, sometime around 700, he urged his people on his deathbed to set aside all hope of retaking their homeland. "Contribute your talents and devote them to the Empress. We are no longer Persian. We are Chinese."

Not all of the immigrants were settled at the edge of the desert. Those who could make a living trading silks and slaves soon migrated east to Chang-an, where local slang refused to admit the possibility of a "poor Persian." This, however, was economical with the truth—many Persian men formed the backbone of the early Tang's "Chinese" armies, while many of the Persian *women* who made it to Chang-an did so as slave girls and indentured labor. Poets of the mid-Tang sing the praises of wild dancing girls and fast women of the Chang-an taverns, but asides hint at the tawdry reality of human trafficking. Along the so-called "Silk Road" in the 7th century, as well as the corals and glass beads, one of the chief commodities travelling from west to east was Persian slaves. For generations to come, Persian heritage dissipated in the Chinese gene pool. It is most obvious today, of course, in China's far west, but many of Persian descent managed to intermarry into the elites of China. Several emperors had Persian concubines, and the descendants of Firuz himself married into the Chinese aristocracy. In the Tang dynasty and the fragmented period that followed it, Persian culture and community was a major contributor to the exoticism of the period.

There are intimations of this lavish era in the surroundings of the grave that Gaozong and Empress Wu share—a hollowed out mountain west of modern Xi'an, approached by a Spirit Road that contains such exotica as ostrich statues, thought to have been inspired by tribute gifts from Afghan allies. An array of 61 statues forms an honor guard of foreign princes and ambassadors. Beheaded by vandals at some unknown point, the statues once presented a symbolic image of Tang China's long reach—Persians and Turks, Koreans and Japanese, possibly even a Syrian or two, matching similar images to be found in nearby tombs. The double tomb of Gaozong and Wu itself, however, remains controversially unopened. Seemingly untroubled by robbers, it is liable to be the largest grave find in Chinese history, and may well be stacked to the brim with the largesse of Tang high-life—kingfisher-feather robes, the richest of silks, and treasures beyond imagination. It may, however, turn out to be the worst anti-climax in archaeological history—buried by a son whom she had previously forced to abdicate, Wu might equally have been laid to rest in an empty chamber.

The extent to which Empress Wu contributed to Gaozong's empire is difficult to determine because almost all the material written about her 50-year reign, as empress consort, empress dowager behind the thrones of her two sons, and ultimately empress regnant, was written by her enemies. For a long while, posterity regarded her era as a ghastly, barbaric lapse, not only putting a woman in charge, but allowing her to hold the door open for other women. Under Wu's regime, a series of reforms asserted, for the first time, that dualist philosophies of a male and female universe surely required these complementary opposites to be *equals*. The most infamous incident of this came at the sacred Mount Tai in 666, when Gaozong undertook to perform the greatest of all religious ceremonies.

Known as the *feng-shan*, the ritual had only been performed on a handful of occasions in Chinese history. It was intended as a statement of perfection—an audited report to Heaven that all was well in the world, and hence only performable in times of extreme prosperity and peace. Determined to show off his golden age (which, as you have probably already guessed, was largely his late father's achievement) Gaozong set off for Mount Tai to perform the ceremony, which was known to involve carving the emperor's report on slabs of jade, and burying them on the mountaintop.

That, at least, was part of the ritual. It had been so long since it was last performed, and was so rarely undertaken even then, that nobody was sure exactly what was involved. Although there are multiple mentions of it in Zhou chronicles, it had only been performed three times in the previous 600 years—once in the short-lived reign of the Qin emperor, and twice in the early Han dynasty. Think-tanks and commissions were kept busy for years arguing over the precise music, movements and order of business. If Confucius in ancient times had attempted to reconstruct the perfections of old, the *feng-shan* project was an order of magnitude above it all, and a wonderful contradiction—in announcing just how perfect everything was, the incumbent regime risked making a fool of itself by bungling the ceremony.

Discussions towards a *feng-shan* ceremony had been mooted in the days of Gaozong's Sui predecessors, and by his grandfather and father. Poring over decades-old reports on possible practice, Gaozong's own ministers gingerly reported that Confucius himself, the guru of ritual matters, had never once mentioned the *feng-shan* ceremonies in his *Book of Rites*. Was the Emperor even sure it was a thing?

The emperor wasn't. Gaozong was admirably timid about bragging about his successes, and postponed several possible *feng-shan* dates over bad harvests or unsuccessful military campaigns. But he kept returning to the matter, pressed on it repeatedly by Empress Wu. She nagged at him until he put the grand project into action—as ambitious an act for a Chinese emperor as a moon-shot. The imperial party travelled to Mount Tai on specially-built roads, across newly commissioned bridges. They underwent extensive ritual purification, and in an act of extreme effort for the crippled Gaozong, the emperor climbed the mountain unaided to make his report. It was only as the final rituals approached that Empress Wu pointed out that everything looked a bit *male*.

> In previous Supreme Sacrifices, the spirits that partook of the offerings were those of former empresses, but the ceremonial duties were performed by male ministers. In the humble opinion of your spouse, this would seem to be an error. Why would we expect the spirits of empresses to manifest before the presence of a male? It seems both improper, and contrary to the nature of the sacred ceremony.

At Wu's urging, the *feng-shan* ritual was hastily rearranged to incorporate male and female celebrants. True to the implied duality of yin and yang, Wu herself took an equal role in the imperial ceremony, with her hand-maidens and ladies-in-waiting drafted in as assistants. It was an act entirely in keeping with her hold on Gaozong, cited by both her supporters and detractors as the epitome of her era.

Wu's power would grow as Gaozong's health faltered. When he inevitably died, she continued to rule from behind the throne of her son Zhongzong. When he proved unhelpfully assertive, she ordered his abdication in favor of his younger brother Ruizong, another puppet. It was only in 690 that Wu stepped out of the shadows entirely, proclaiming herself to be a ruler in her own right, initiating fifteen years as China's only empress regnant.

For this, she was denounced for centuries. It is only in living memory that Wu has been reclaimed as a feminist icon and progressive thinker, but even then there are dissenters who will brook no kind word said about her. The respected historian Lin Yutang compared her to Stalin and Hitler, citing vindictive purges and ill-judged changes in policy. The historical record of her regime is either literally silent—her children infamously leaving the memorial stone at her grave entirely blank—or in the hands of conservative chroniclers determined to paint her as the ultimate bitch. Paramount among her supposed crimes is the proclamation of herself as a goddess made flesh, the fulfillment of a Buddhist prophecy that a woman ruler would herald the final incarnation of Buddha, and the announcement that she was the founding empress of a new "Zhou" dynasty.

One certainly gets a sense of imperious vainglory in the surviving quotes from Wu, although one might expect them in a woman who had advanced from chamber-maid to living goddess solely on her wits and sun-bright personality. The degree to which her short-lived Zhou dynasty was a genuine regime change or a tactical move designed to hold off affines, is unknowable. In old age, she conceded that Zhongzong, her predecessor and successor, would ascend the throne as a "Tang" emperor, implying that even she thought of her Zhou dynasty as some sort of temporary fix.

Wu was undoubtedly a creation of her time. The increased role of women in society and culture owed much to centuries of northern, nomad-derived influence, but also to the increased prosperity brought about by the Tang dynasty's climatic dividend. As for her acts as Empress, it is necessary to separate the disapproval of misogynist commentators from the realities of imperial life. There is, to be sure, very little that Empress Wu did that would not be regarded as entirely normal for a male emperor. Many of her alleged crimes are not mentioned even in anti-Wu propaganda of her own lifetime, although she was herself haunted by some of her more vicious acts, suffering throughout later life from nightmares about two women she had executed. This may have contributed in some fashion to her overblown devotion to Buddhism in later life, when she became an enthusiastic patron of the celebrity monk Tripitaka, and even once rashly promised him her third son as his acolyte—she eventually went back on the deal. Examples of her benevolence to Buddhist institutions can be found all over the countryside near her two capitals—a feathered cloak donated to the Famen Temple; a memorial stupa in her mother's name, still standing at the Shaolin Temple, and most impressively of all, the giant Vairocana Buddha at the Longmen Grottoes near Luoyang, dwarfing the lesser carvings left there in times past by the Northern Zhou. The Vairocana Buddha is the largest statue in all Longmen's centuries as a Buddhist pilgrimage site, carved in 676 after a direct donation from Wu herself, and rumored to have been given her facial features.

Allegedly, Wu let herself and her policies be swayed by a rakish Daoist drug-dealer and a sycophantic Buddhist priest, but she was by no means the first or last Chinese ruler whose head would be turned by a persuasive bed-mate. In her dotage, she kept a harem, the Office of the Crane—an entourage of 120 fiercely pretty boys, as if a similar number of concubines would not be regarded as somewhat understaffed for any male emperor. She played favorites with her ministers and courtiers—passive-aggressively flirtatious with her long-time adviser Di Renjie; passionately hot and then icily cold with the handsome Persian refugee prince Firuz—but this is hardly remarkable. Her seventh-century heyday was a brief flourishing of female power and concerns, and the women who grew up in it accepted such conditions as normal. Her speech-writer and leading minister, the former slave-girl Shangguan Wan'er was thought of as one of the greatest poets of the age. Her daughter, the Princess Taiping, regarded imperial rule as her own birth-right. Both would be slaughtered in the series of coups and counter-coups that broke out after Wu's death—barely a few phrases from Shangguan's ten volumes of collected works survive to this day.

The woman once referred to by an adoring Japanese visitor as "Granny Strong," and by a political opponent as a creature with "the heart of a serpent and the nature of a wolf... hated by men and gods alike" continued to excite strong opinions today. Modern retellings of her story mix elements of Cinderella and a serial-killer. In 2014, a television series based on her life was taken briefly off-air in China while editors were removed the historically accurate plunging necklines and scenes of kissing. Even in the 21st century, she was too hot for TV.

Wu's brief feminist utopia was over-written by what followed. Her grandson, Xuanzong (685–762) presided over a continued age of prosperity, but is remembered for losing it all for love. This, too, is unfair, but it allowed later generations of historians to avoid underlying issues in policy and strategy, and lay the blame for the decline of the Tang dynasty at the feet of a woman.

Xuanzong began as the lead actor in two bloody palace coups. He was instrumental in the restoration of his father, the Ruizong Emperor in 710 after the luckless Zhongzong, on the throne a second time, was allegedly poisoned by agents of his scheming Empress. He was similarly central to the thwarting of a new conspiracy in 713. In both cases, Chinese chroniclers present these attempted coups as the last gasps of Empress Wu's perverse age in which women held sway. Ruizong had had enough by this point, and conceded the throne to his son—Xuanzong's ensuing reign (r. 713–756) would be the longest of any Tang emperor, and for the first twenty years, proceeded without an obvious hitch.

With hindsight, we can see the problems slowly mounting. Even as Tang China contended with Tibet over the Western Regions, parts of their prize fell to a new, ideological invader: Islam. Increased border problems all over the empire led to a crowd-pleasing suspension of many conscript contracts, replaced with mercenary troops that were often barely a shade different from the "barbarians" they were fighting. What vigor Xuanzong may have had at the start of his reign was played out by 737, when he was left inconsolable by the death of his favorite concubine, Empress Wu's great-niece—there was definitely something special about those Wu girls. In his early fifties and facing the mother of all mid-life crises, he developed an unhealthy obsession with his daughter-in-law, Yang Yuhuan (719–756). Married to Xuanzong's son at fourteen, she was still not yet twenty when Xuanzong ordered her divorced, briefly declared a nun for appearance's sake, and then rebranded as his Precious Consort, Yang *Guifei*.

The more sympathetic accounts of this sordid incident attempt to excuse it with his bereavement, as if the son he cuckolded were not just as devastated. Chinese popular culture, especially the broad strokes of the tourist industry, likes to describe Xuanzong and Yang Guifei as "the Romeo and Juliet of Chinese history," as if there was anything romantic about a 52-year-old widower deciding to steal away his grieving son's teenage bride. For her part, Yang was said to be so beautiful that her face would put flowers to shame, although she is remembered by Chinese chroniclers more as a flighty bimbo, unaware of the immense power she wielded.

The relationship between Yang Guifei and her emperor was famously obsessive. Yang's hold over Xuanzong turned him practically monogamous—a dangerous decision in a court riddled with scheming affines. Xuanzong would not be the last middle-aged man in history to be bewitched by a girl young enough to be his daughter—they became avid fans of Sogdian dances and exotic booze, and their soirees would erupt in loud arguments that would occasionally see Yang Guifei banished or fleeing the palace, only for a tearful reconciliation and epic make-up sex. Xuanzong would indulge all her whims, and happily looked the other way when her desire for fresh lychees required the abuse of his vital post rider system, tying up days of imperial dispatches in order to get the treasured fruits to the capital from the south.

Li Bai (701–762), one of the greatest poets in Chinese history, was dragged into their orbit against his will. Drafted into a consultant position at Xuanzong's academy, Li Bai was summoned to the palace and made to produce verses on command praising Yang Guifei's beauty. Drunk (he was usually drunk), Li Bai came up with something that praised her garments flowing behind her like a cloud, the radiant bloom of her face, and the likelihood that she was some kind of apparition, usually only seen in the Crystal Palace of fairyland. Everybody liked that one, but Xuanzong badgered the barely conscious Li Bai for a repeat performance. A reluctant Li Bai made the Emperor's chief eunuch take off his shoes to help to him think, and then dashed off the most back-handed of compliments.

> Hers is the charm of the vanished fairy
> That broke the heart of the dreamer king…
> Pray, who in the palace of Han
> Could be likened unto her
> Save the lady Flying Swallow…

There are some who think that Li Bai's verse was perfectly benign. "Flying swallow" (*feiyan*), as the more well-read of the Tang court might have noticed, was a reference to Zhao Feiyan, the famously slender beauty of the Han dynasty. John Wu, in his *Four Seasons of Tang Poetry*, observes that Yang Yuhuan was as "overjoyed at the praise as a fat lady must be when made to believe she was as light as a 'flying swallow,'" although such a comment may read modern-day fat-shaming onto a woman who was thought beautiful *because* she was chubby. In fact, there is even a Chinese proverb, "plump [Yu]huan, slender Fei" (*Huan-fei Yan-shou*), that contrasts the two women as two co-existing paragons of beauty. What really caused problems for Li Bai was his likening of Yang Guifei to a woman who, while beautiful, was also a notorious kingdom-wrecker. The eunuch who had been humiliated by being made to remove Li Bai's shoes soon convinced Yang Guifei that the poem had been a high-handed insult, and she blocked Li Bai's further promotion at the capital.

Predictably, her powerful position in the palace opened the door for some her relatives, including her wastrel cousin Yang Guozhong, who had mismanaged his last appointment so badly that he left his post unable to afford the cost of returning home. The chronicles for the 740s are full of tales of political scandal and corruption, with Yang Guozhong as their undeniable star. He would fight for political appointments, clambering over better qualified men, only to get cold feet and delegate them to his cronies. An entire war against the southwestern state of Nanzhao was "overseen" by Yang the military governor from his lounge in Luoyang, while his appointee sacrificed 200,000 Chinese lives, including innocent locals forcibly conscripted to replace lost soldiers.

Meanwhile, both Yang Guifei and the Emperor Xuanzong became friendly with a giant Sogdian-Turk warrior known to the Chinese as An Lushan—the surname pointing to his Sogdian origins, while Lushan is liable to have been a Chinese attempt at Roxshan. Even across 1200 intervening years, Roxshan seems to have been one of the most charming men in Chinese history: ever ready to impress the court with some trinket or curiosity from the edges of the empire, always at hand at public occasions with tall stories of military daring and hard-won victories.

Not everybody was taken in. Court officials marked him as troublemaker and potential rebel. Some of his most famous victories were matters of pure luck, and his record was stained with plenty of occasions where his foolhardiness or provocative behavior had cost his troops dearly. Indeed, his first appearance at Xuanzong's court was as an officer facing the death sentence for insubordination—a sentence commuted by Xuanzong on the understanding that Roxshan was too good a soldier to waste. He was a hit with Lady Yang, who doted on him to the extent that she officially adopted him as her own son, an act leading to a bizarre palace skit in which Roxshan was paraded as a giant infant in a diaper. But Roxshan was already living on borrowed time. By 751, even as he was playing the fool by dressing up as a baby in the palace, he was already planning a revolution, not out of any desire to betray his imperial patron, but because he rightly feared that the knives would be out for him after Xuanzong's death. A large part of Roxshan's humor, it seemed, relied upon facetious bluster and making others the butt of his jokes, and the heir apparent was sure to avenge himself as soon as he was crowned. Roxshan hand-picked a personal honor guard of 8000 soldiers from the armies of defeated enemies, and honed them into a force that was loyal only to him.

His rebellion was a symptom of other problems. The Chinese heartland was enjoying a golden age of prosperity, but out on the borders, the Tang expansion had reached its peak. A climatic downturn was heading China's way, and it was affecting the outer frontiers first, before the still-prosperous capital was truly aware of it. The poet Li Bai wrote a pastiche of the

Han dynasty verse about "Fighting South of the City Walls," vastly expanding the distances of the battles—one is on the banks of a river in the far northwest, another is in the Pamir mountains near what is now Afghanistan; still another suggests troops washing their swords in a western sea.

> Three armies have grown gray and old
> Fighting ten thousand leagues away from home
> The Huns have no trade but battle and carnage
> They have no pastures or ploughlands
> Only wastes where white bones lie among yellow sands.

Li Bai, better known for his many elegies to wine and song, seems to simmer with resentment at his state's commitment to distant wars, coolly observing that the Qin dynasty built walls to stop this sort of thing, and that the Han dynasty had diligently manned them with watchtowers and beacon-fires. Li Bai saw the Tang dynasty's commitment to foreign conflicts as an unwelcome over-extension of China's sphere of interest.

In 751, Arab forces from the Abbasid Caliphate routed a Tang army at the Battle of Talas, forever shutting down China's hold on the lands west of Kashgar. The Chinese defeat was occasioned by the defection of their allies from Ferghana, one-time home of the "horses of Heaven," and Karluk mercenaries that switched side at a critical moment. Any chance of China regaining the upper hand was ruined by Roxshan's rebellion, which caused all China's armies in the west to be recalled to defend the center.

Roxshan's forces amassed in the northeast and swept up the Yellow River, taking both Luoyang and Chang-an. Xuanzong and his court were forced to flee westwards towards Sichuan, where they hoped to regroup with reinforcements coming home from the Western Regions. When food turned out to be in short supply at Mawei station, just 30 kilometers (18.6 miles) outside modern Xi'an, Yang Guozhong got the blame. He did, after all, hold up to forty government positions, none of which he seemed to be much good at, and some suspected that he was planning to hand Xuanzong over to Tibetan emissaries on the road to Sichuan. With tempers frayed and egos bruised, the troops mutinied, refusing to go on until the imperial party was flensed of the hated Yang family.

Xuanzong had gone from being the ruler of the civilized world, sunking of the height of the Tang dynasty, to being an old man nearing 70, feebly protesting as his chancellor was struck down, along with the chancellor's son and several cousins. The coup against the Yang family was complete, although one still remained. The soldiers came for Yang Guifei herself, and Xuanzong tearfully, impotently handed her over to his eunuch servant to be strangled.

The whole sorry affair would be celebrated by one of China's greatest poets, Bai Juyi, in his *Song of Everlasting Sorrow*:

> But one hundred li west of the capital gates
> The six divisions halted and left him with no choice
> Struggling, she of the moth eyebrows died among the horses
> Her ornate headdress fell to the ground, and none took it up
> the kingfisher, the gold sparrow and the jade hair clasp
> But his Majesty covered his face and said nothing.

It was the end of Xuanzong's reign. A broken man, he abdicated in Sichuan and left his son Suzong (r. 756 –762) to clear up the rebellion. Roxshan's forces were having trouble hanging onto the Chang-an region, and Roxshan himself would soon be murdered by his own son. But Suzong faced considerable resistance both from Roxshan's surviving divisions, and from Chinese rebels elsewhere, led by his own brother. In desperation, he wrote to the second Abbasid caliph, Al-Mansur, asking for help—eventually receiving 4,000 troops that would settle in China and form one of its earliest Muslim communities. But in order to secure the vital reinforcements to retake Chang-an, he formed an alliance with Bayanchur Khan, the leader of a confederation of nomad tribes called the United Peoples (*Uy-ghur*). As was traditional, they sealed the deal with a pair of princess-brides, a Chinese girl for the khan, and a Uyghur girl for the Emperor. Inheriting a domain roughly equivalent to the Xiongnu steppes of old, the Uyghurs were in the process of turning away from life on the steppes, with a new, permanent citadel in Mongolia that was fast becoming a city to rival China's best. But they retained plenty of horsemen, becoming a vital, if expensive, factor in the retaking of Chang-an and the suppression of the rebellion. Thereafter, the Uyghurs would become much like many a previous nomad ally in Chinese history, valued greatly for their aid in times of trouble, but fiendishly difficult to get rid of without extensive gifts of valuable silk.

The Chinese were right to be suspicious. Bayanchur's son and heir plotted to take China for himself, only to be overthrown before he could act by a pro-Tang faction led by his uncle. For the next 80 years, the Uyghurs would become a powerful ally to China's northwest, and together with their Sogdian allies, the *de facto* masters of the Western Regions that had formerly been Chinese territory.

Their empire would founder only a few decades ahead of the Tang itself, when they were pushed out of their heartland by new arrivals from the north, the Kyrgyz. The last remnants of the Uyghur empire fled south to Xinjiang, where they become farmers and herders, far removed from their old nomad selves. Those Xinjiang Uyghurs, however, were lucky ones. Many Uyghur refugees made the mistake of fleeing eastwards into China, where they found the late Tang deeply unwelcoming to their former allies. Regarding them as little more than marauders, the Tang sent armies to hunt them down, most notably in 843 at the mountain known thereafter as Sha-hu—"Kill the foreigners."

The term *hu*, barbarian, never referred solely to the Uyghurs. But it is one of several old terms for outlanders that one can find surviving in odd places in modern Chinese. Neither it nor any of the several other terms for barbarian are used to describe ethnic groups any more, although it persists in the names of many foodstuffs that were regarded in times past as "foreign" imports, such as pepper (*hujiao*), walnut, (*hutao*), coriander (*husui*) and carrot (*huluobo*). *Huqin*, a catch-all term for certain stringed instruments, points to the barbarian heritage of many parts of a Chinese orchestra. But it also persists in a third category of words—modern Chinese coinages for carelessness, drivel, unshaven, swarthy, bullshit and half-assed. Although the DNA of the *Hu* is firmly integrated into modern China, their linguistic heritage is often snide and belittling.

The later Tang dynasty turned mean. Roxshan's rebellion had already created an intense sense of anti-immigrant feeling, likely to have contributed to a massacre of Arab and Persian merchants in Yangzhou in 760. Chinese subjects with foreign blood did what they could to pass as locals—the Uyghurs within the empire adopted Chinese dress and customs, and many with foreign surnames swapped them for less conspicuous Chinese ones. However, the weather was turning ever colder and drier—the year 760 had been the last peak of the warm period that brought such prosperity to the early Tang, and China was just about to face a century of declining crop yields and frontier pressure. The Late Tang Weak Monsoon Period lessened rainfall for a century, reducing both immediate crop-watering and the flow into rivers from glaciers until 940. Local weather conditions, of course, were seen as a reflection of a decline in the Mandate of Heaven, further undermining the authority of the emperors. Weather conditions further afield, in Tibet or on the steppes, were of no concern to the Chinese until their aftermath unsettled foreign regimes and unleashed armies. Where the Tang had once been a welcoming, eclectic community, it increasingly shuttered itself away from the outside world, turning in stages on anything that seemed un-Chinese.

The emperor Wuzong (r. 840–846) was the epitome of his age, clinging zealously to Daoism as a native, entirely Chinese tradition, and clamping down hard on foreign rivals. With China almost bankrupted by the war against the Uyghurs, Wuzong turned on the Buddhist monasteries, which he regarded as tax-dodging institutions propagating unwelcome foreign ways. The monasteries, he thought, were not merely scandalously tax-exempt, but they lured in his subjects by the thousands, turning them from useful, tax-paying workers into idle priests and nuns.

Wuzong did not merely have it in for the Buddhists. The Christians from Syria and the Zoroastrians and Manicheans from Persia also came under fire, and were eventually deported. Thousands of Japanese and Korean monks, studying Buddhism in China, were sent back to their homelands, and the temples where these foreign religions had once been studied were looted for their wealth.

Nor did Wuzong stop with the dissolution of the monasteries. Even though he was only in his thirties, he became obsessed with Daoist immortality treatments, and contemptuous of Buddhism's aim for the erasure of the self. His decrees took on an increasingly swivel-eyed tone, including one that banned wheelbarrows on the grounds that the single wheel destroyed the traditional integrity of Chinese roads. Ironically, it was probably his beloved immortality potions that were both addling his brain and affecting his health—he died in 846, poisoned either by his elixirs, or more likely by eunuchs who decided enough was enough. Buddhism would spring back under his successor, but the other foreign religions, stripped of their immigrant representatives, were wiped out except in the port cities.

Sometimes, the global crisis allowed the Tang dynasty to feel it was on the up again. The emperor Xuanzong II (see Notes on Names) presided over an era in which China was seen to regain much of the territory previously lost to the Tibetan Empire. The Tibetans, however, were in the midst of a civil war that followed the death of their emperor Langdarma (r. 838–841). They, too, had turned on Buddhism in their midst; they, too, had been overwhelmed by Uyghur refugees; they, too, were facing agricultural decline. At a higher altitude, they were facing it a few years ahead of the Chinese themselves, who were soon beset with farmers' revolts at home.

In 878, the rebel general Huang Chao occupied Guangzhou in the south, where his soldiers trampled the mulberry groves used to feed the city's all-important silk worms. Chinese sources were less forthcoming about Huang's treatment of the city's immigrant population, although a letter survives from a Muslim resident outlining a massacre of the city's wealthy merchants in 879—Jews, Muslims, Persians and Christians, an entire immigrant community, slaughtered for the riches they were presumed to be hoarding.

Chang-an suffered badly in the conflict: occupied by Huang Chao in 881, only to be retaken in 882 by Tang forces whose Uyghur allies looted the city for themselves. Falling once more to Huang Chao soon afterwards, the city's battered inhabitants were subjected to purges and executions for being too welcoming to the enemy. A thousand locals a day were slaughtered for food—euphemistically described as "two-legged mutton." By the time the city was finally back in Tang hands, it was a ruin. The military governor, speaking in the name of the last Tang child-emperor whom he was soon to usurp, proclaimed the city a dead loss, and ordered it stripped for parts. Once the greatest city in the world, and the capital of China for over a thousand cumulative years, Chang-an was torn down—its wooden buildings dismantled and loaded onto barges, to be taken downriver to Luoyang. A small garrison lurked within a block barely a sixteenth of the size of the old city. For decades to come, the once-great city would be a wasteland dominated only by the stone towers of the abandoned Little Wild Goose Pagoda and Tripitaka's Great Wild Goose Pagoda, both monuments to the city's heyday, when it had been the center of a flourishing Buddhist world.

Chang-an would never be the capital of China again. Today, the Shaanxi History Museum in what is now Xi'an effectively comes to a halt in 905, waving away the ensuing millennium as a period of relative unimportance. An art installation in Xi'an's Da Ming Gong Palace Park mourns the end of its reign over all the cities in China, with a statue of a riderless horse, chewing sadly at the grass in a field scattered with discarded sandals and broken swords.

The cultural center of China had moved eastwards. Luoyang would occasionally serve as a subsidiary capital, but after the upheavals and fragmented mini-states that heralded the end of the Tang, the Chinese would establish a new capital further down the Yellow River at Kaifeng—more convenient for the Grand Canal that united north and south.

# CHAPTER 6

# TRIUMPH OF THE NOMADS: THE SONG AND YUAN DYNASTIES

S he was born in the year that the rains came back.

At first, they only knew about her on the island. Meizhou, the mountain in the sea, home to a thousand fishing families. None of them could read, but they all had stories to tell about Lin Moniang (960–87), Lin the Silent Girl. There was something of the shamaness about her. On the rare occasions she did speak, she had a habit of foretelling the future.

You could sometimes see her mending nets down on the shore, or caulking the boats with the other womenfolk, but the Silent Girl of the Lin family had chosen a new task for herself, and nobody stopped her. When the storms drove in from the black sea, driving sand into stinging clouds on the shore, darkening the skies, Lin Moniang would put on her bright red dress and climb up to the cliff top. She would stand in defiance, holding a lantern in the wind, transforming herself into a human lighthouse.

Her father and her brothers would always come home, no matter how great the swell, no matter how driving the rain, and Lin Moniang's fame grew. She remained unmarried, wed instead to the idea that she was a protector of the fishermen, sometimes entering a trance when a storm beset them out at sea. People talked about her over on the mainland, on the Putian coast, where looming cliffs stretched out like fingers into the sea, shielding deep, long bays where other fishing villages clung to the hillsides

China During the Song Dynasty

LIAO (KHITAN)

XIXIA
(TANGUTS)

GORYEO
KINGDOM

Yellow River

TIBETAN KINGDOM

SONG DYNASTY CHINA · Hangzhou

Yangtze River

Southern Song
1127-1279

DALI
KINGDOM

☐ China During the Song Dynasty
— China's Modern-day Border

like barnacles. Her birthday, on the 23rd day of the third lunar month, came to be celebrated with increasing opulence and visitors.

One day, her prayers didn't work. She counted back the fishing boats as the storm began to rise, but one of her brothers failed to show. She stood on the cliff top in the driving rain, her red silks slick and water-logged, but there was no sign of the ship. Hysterical and weeping, she went down to the shore and walked into the sea, until the red dress disappeared in the black water.

Her brother's ship returned, but Lin Moniang's body washed ashore at the place where they would build the first temple to her. The Daoists claimed that she was one of them, a star sent down from heaven to protect those in peril on the sea. The Buddhists said she was one of *them*—a devotee or perhaps even incarnation of the Goddess of Mercy. In a world teeming with gods, where every village had a snake spirit and a rainmaker, a hearth god and a trickster, it was likely that the Silent Girl would fade into the background noise of local folktales.

But the Putian coast became busier. Refugees from the north crowded the southern provinces. Sea trade and fisher-folk prospered in the decades that followed, and the legends of the Silent Girl did not go away. Worshippers began to pray to her for safe passage on the sea, calling her first Auntie Lin, then *Ama* (Granny), or the more respectful *Mazu-po* (Grand Maternal Ancestor). In doing so, they addressed the woman who had died without issue as if they were her descendants.

In 1122, a Chinese diplomat reported seeing the light of Mazu wreathing the mast of his ship as a storm faded. In search of heroes at a time when the military were failing the state, in 1156 the Song Emperor Gaozong took notice of the Mazu cult in the south, and conferred a new title on its figurehead: Lady of Numinous Grace. In 1192 his grandson upgraded her to Princess of Numinous Grace. In 1281, after the Mongol conquest of China, the new emperor Khubilai Khan felt he needed divine marine assistance after his fleet was wiped out in an attempted invasion of Japan. Keen to appease the red-clad woman whose effigy could be seen in thousands of sailors' temples, he renamed her the Illuminating Princess of Heaven Who Protects the Nation.

Her titles would continue to grow throughout the centuries, as emperors sought divine sanction for armadas and invasions. Today, there are 1,500 temples to her, scattered in over a dozen countries throughout the world, in every place Chinese sailors might be found, flanked by her demonic suitors, the Thousand-Mile Eye and the Wind-Following Ear. There are 20 temples alone on her native Meizhou island, 90 in Hong Kong. The temple to "Ama" in Macau is probably what gave that city its name. Her towering statues dominate the shorelines in Tainan and Tianjin. There are temples to her in Nagasaki and San Francisco, Melbourne and Bangkok.

Many of her worshippers disregard the ceremonies and protocols that come with her state promotions. Some might call her the Holy Princess of Clear Piety, Pure Faith and Helpful Response, or the Heavenly Princess Who Protects the Nation and Shelters the People, of Marvelous Numen, Brilliant Resonance, Magnanimous Kindness and Universal Salvation, but the legend goes that such convoluted titles only delay her blessings. She hears the honorifics, and rushes to get her hair ready, to put on the right robes, to honor her worshipper by dressing to meet the occasion. If you need a fast response from Mazu, if you want to get her help one-to-one in the middle of a storm, then a straightforward "Granny" will do.

⊙—⊙—⊙—⊙—⊙

The weather in China picked up around 960—a return of a stronger monsoon until 1250, and with it, better crops and a healthier population. Granaries could be stocked against minor fluctuations in the weather, creating a stable situation for a new dynasty to arise. However, this period of potential prosperity arrived at the same time as a series of fierce droughts to the north in Mongolia. Tree-ring data suggests long periods of extreme dryness on the steppes, spanning the years 900–1064, 1115–39 and 1180–90. These did not necessarily impact directly upon China, instead affecting it second-hand, as pressures from the Mongol steppe acted upon other nomads, and pushed them into China.

Barely fifty years into the political fragmentation that followed the collapse of the Tang, a general in a minor state centered on Kaifeng usurped the throne from a child-emperor. Over the next 19 years, he would reconquer most of the scattered pieces of the Tang era, proclaiming the Song dynasty, which would run, at least officially, from 960–1279. Historians, however, tend to divide it into two, the Northern Song (960–1126) when the capital was at Kaifeng, and the Southern Song (1127–1279) when the capital was moved to Hangzhou at the mouth of the river Yangtze. Northern China was lost to foreign incursions, first the Khitan nomads, and then their successors, the Jurchens.

The Song dynasty was, at least in part, created by the barbarian menace. It was fear of their invasion, falsified or otherwise, that propelled the first Song emperor to seize control of the upstart Later Zhou kingdom in a military coup. It was the threat of their return that kept the Northern Song mobilized throughout its early regime. Unable to commit enough troops to its northern borders, the Song began as it would continue, buying off the Khitan to the northeast and the Tanguts to the northwest with silver and silk.

After two generations of occasional skirmishes and multiple schemes to stab each other in the back, the Khitans and the Chinese signed the Treaty of Chanyuan in 1005. The border with the Khitans was fixed at roughly the latitude of modern Beijing, for which the Song would pay them 200,000 bolts of silk and 100,000 taels of silver (about four tons).

This price was later increased. Pointedly, the Song Chinese referred to this as a gift, while the Khitans called it "tribute." Regardless of how they spun it, it was an embarrassment for the Chinese to deal with barbarians as political equals.

And yet, perhaps it was the smartest decision that Chinese policy makers had made in centuries. Dieter Kuhn, the historian of the Song, suggests that this pay-off helped foster "one of the most humane, cultured and intellectual societies in Chinese history, perhaps in all of world history." Despite the vast expense in annual bribes to hold off would-be invaders, the cost of the Chanyuan Treaty was still palpably cheaper than mobilizing an army. Full-scale war was averted for decades, creating an uneasy truce along the new frontier, although espionage and dirty tricks continued. Adding insult to injury, the Khitans persuaded the neighboring Tangut kingdom in Gansu to try a similar tactic in 1044. Meanwhile, the Song intrigued with the Khitans' own enemies, the Jurchen tribes in Manchuria and Siberia, encouraging them to attack the Khitans from the other side.

While such politicking continued, Song China flourished. Scholars talk of a Tang-Song transformation, pointing to the immense difference between the China of the Silk Road era, and the China of what we might call the high Middle Ages. The Grand Canal, rather than the Silk Road, became the most important conduit of trade and commerce, focusing China on its own southern provinces. Zhang Ruyu, a Song-era author, went so far as to say that this was merely an acknowledgement of a reality that had been growing for centuries. Even back in the Tang dynasty, he wrote, when the capital was Chang-an, the Chinese state still relied "on revenue from the southeast for its income and expenditure, and there is virtually no revenue from other prefectures... there has never been a time when the fiscal revenue on which the state relies from the southeast has not been plentiful."

Arguably, the very prosperity of the Tang dynasty had ruined north China. Soil erosion became a serious issue along the Yellow River, with vast areas of forest chopped down for lumber and fuel. This crisis was at least mitigated in the south by the rise of coal as a fuel, which not only saved the treeline from further plundering, but enabled the firing of hotter kilns for better porcelain.

The printing industry pivoted in the Southern Song to replace many of the books presumed lost in the conquest of the north. Bargain editions of the classical canon formed a substantial part of publishing in the early

Southern Song, as teachers and their pupils strove to replace their libraries. As the Southern Song went on, those same publishers drifted into new areas, preserving some of the earliest plays, printing new treatises on gentlemanly pursuits, reprinting the most highly regarded works of Tang or Northern Song poetry and serving a new subgenre of history books that attempted to think through the state of affairs and how best to deal with it. Pocket books, for people who had been and suspected they would still be on the move, became a new format, along with valuable works that, in their efforts to preserve the knowledge of the lost north for the south, handily also preserved it for us. Some of these publications were cookbooks, including *The Chef's Manual, The Basic Needs of Rustic Living*, and *Madame Wu's Recipe Book*. These not only allow us to see the sort of things cooked in a Chinese home, but the kind of luxuries abandoned in the Kaifeng kitchens.

One influential book in the Song period was *The Ledger of Merit and Demerit of the Taiwei Immortal* (1171, *Taiwei Shunjun Gongguoge*), written by a Daoist priest who claimed to have received a revelation from the titular demigod. Saving someone from the death penalty was worth 100 points; saving the life of an enemy, eight points; breaking up a fight, one point per person dissuaded. Praising a good deed was worth a point, as was keeping quiet if you saw someone misbehaving. Demerits included a point lost for not recommending the right person for a job; six points for killing an animal for food, and three points for buying meat and eating it. Taking a step beyond the karmic calculations of the Buddhists, the *Ledger* suggested that the devout keep literal accounts of their good and bad deeds, all the better to steer themselves towards a better life, and, who knows, perhaps to improve the dynasty's overall luck.

Not all the Song exiles embraced their fugitive state. The poet Li Qingzhao (1084–1151), who lived a life that spanned the loss of Kaifeng and the exodus to Hangzhou, allegorized the thinning of Chinese culture as a slow, inevitable decline, like an aging beauty, clinging to her old regalia.

> A chill comes to pallet and pillow, damp with tracks of tears
> I rise to take off my gossamer dress and just happen to ask:
>   "How late is it now?"
> … The same weather as in times before, the same old dress—
>   only the feelings in the heart are not as they were before.

Wheat and wine were replaced as main staples by rice and tea, both of which could be grown in multiple annual crops in the verdant south, and shuttled north on the Grand Canal to feed urban populations. China's sense of its own geography began to change. In previous eras, the elite of China had been concentrated in a single metropolis (usually Chang-an, but occasionally Luoyang), while the rest of the population was distinctly second-class. Now, increasing mercantile wealth created several urban centers with just as many amenities as the capital, and just as high a standard of living. Yangzhou, Nanjing and Hangzhou, for example, all key sites along the Grand Canal, became thriving urban centers, as did southern sea ports like Quanzhou and Guangzhou. Zhang Ruyu regarded this as a simple economic reality.

> The state of affairs under Heaven is just like holding a pair of scales, and if one end is heavy, the other end will be light. Therefore, if the southeast becomes gradually more important, then the northwest becomes gradually less significant. During the Song, the southeast became increasingly important, while the northwest became increasingly insignificant.

It was, to be sure, a wonderfully pragmatic spin on the loss of half of China—Zhang's bluntly economic description of China suggests that the north was a waste of time and energy anyway, and that the south was well rid of it. For some in the Southern Song, this was indeed a way to get on with life. Periodically, however, regimes and subjects would awake once more to the fact that the old Chinese heartland had been lost.

The growth of inland shipping on the canals and rivers, and the steady rise of Indian, Arab and Malay merchant merchants in the southern ports, brought about another transformation in the Song dynasty. With the land routes to Central Asia cut off, but with new facilities for transporting large, bulky, breakable cargoes, China began exporting ceramics by sea, via India, to the Middle East. Song porcelain became a relatively common sight as far afield as Alexandria, Istanbul and Baghdad.

Early Song emperors favored a spare, monochrome sheen, rimmed with gold or silver to hide an unglazed edge where they were stacked in the kiln. After these northern kilns were lost to the invaders, the Southern Song rulers began buying from kilns that used an iron oxide in their glaze that created a greenish tint. These *ru* wares would also often have a crazed, cracked pattern in the surface, caused by a glaze that cooled faster than the body. Earlier dynasties might have regarded this as an imperfection, but in the Song it came to be regarded as a mark of quality. Simplicity remained the keynote of most Chinese designs in the period—increasing demand from the Middle East for patterned ceramics were regarded by the Chinese as gauche and uncultured, but did not stop them making such items to please that distant market.

The straitened conditions of the state created better potential for social mobility elsewhere. The court could not afford the same levels of entertainment as in previous centuries, although the merchant class, bloated with the proceeds from foreign trade and concentrated urbanization, had money to spend. This, in turn, allowed entertainers, once the privilege of the elite, to diversify into new venues. While we often lack information about anyone outside the nobility in earlier regimes, during the Song we have access to a growing repertoire of plays and songs about the life of the common people. Tea houses and restaurants became the place to catch singers and performers—acrobats, circus acts and conjurors. A thriving red light district sprang up in both Kaifeng and the Southern Song capital of Hangzhou, while China was scattered with itinerant theater troupes. An entire sub-genre of performance, the "one-donkey shows" began to arise, named not for their content, but for the fact that all the paraphernalia required could be strapped to a single beast of burden for transport between towns.

Chinese theater began to develop a canon of stock characters—fixed costumes and make-up for the bold warrior, the noble scholar and the delicate love interest. The orchestra appeared onstage, matching its music live to the speech and deeds of the actors (if you think Chinese bands often sound like they are playing catch-up, it's because they are). Performances start to coalesce into genres, with space for clowns, for a dance, for an acrobatic display, while types are distinguished by their distinctive facial make-up. "Lion dances," in which two acrobats hide inside a heavily stylized animal costume, arose all over the country

Another transformation came about through the administrative class. The old aristocracies faded, or rather were diluted by an ever-growing pool of educated literati. Previous centuries had been dominated by old money—by aristocratic families that somehow clung on to their positions as the affines and ministers of many a dynasty. It was in the Song dynasty that these old families finally lost their lands and their influence, to be replaced by new elites. Without family heirlooms to dwell on, they focused on their own achievements, with the typical Song scholar expected to be a master of painting, poetry and calligraphy. It is in the Song period that Chinese art develops its enduring fetish for imaginary vistas—an idealized, dreamscape of a lost China that may have never been in the first place, with lone, contemplative figures dwarfed by the looming mountains and waterfalls of a fantasy landscape.

The Song dynasty saw a huge expansion of the examination system designed to assess the suitability of young men for government posts. Exams were held at the local, provincial and national levels, testing candidate's ability to write essays, comment on passages from the Confucian classics, and compose poetry. The local exams—we might call them bachelor's degrees—created an entire class that was at least officially qualified for government service, although there were rarely enough posts to go around. They did, however, bring with them a certain social cachet, improving a young man's marriage prospects and the chances of his finding a job in the private sector. Merely being considered worthy of sitting the exams was an achievement in itself—teachers at some provincial schools boasted that they had sat the exams and *almost passed* several times.

At least in theory, the examination system created an egalitarian society where anyone, no matter how low-born, might hope one day to be an emperor's chief minister. In reality, since the exams relied on poetry and knowledge of the classics, one needed to be steeped in them to stand a chance of passing. You could, again in theory, buy such access, but the nature of the examinations privileged the culture of the already-rich who were born into it. You needed the *habitus* of growing up with the poems of Li Bai and Du Fu, and the assurance that came with having memorized the Confucian classics. Even if some farmer's son were somehow hot-housed into passing the examination, he would only come in at the bottom rung on the promotional ladder, in a tenth-rate clerical position loaded with menial work and overtime obligations. The sons of noblemen, the wealthy, and former officials would enter several ranks ahead of him, straight into fifth or sixth-rank posts, putting them years ahead from the start. Common men made good were publicly feted, but were rare outliers in a system that still cosseted and favored its privileged members. It did, however, create a growing population of intelligentsia, a thriving market for books and poetry, calligraphy ink and artists' brushes among those young men who sometimes spent years trying to pass the exam. It also created a common ground among men from all parts of the empire—for any official or businessman posted far from home to a strange province, his fellow men were sure to have studied the same poems and classics. Some even internalized the curriculum to such a degree that, upon graduation, they found the real world wanting. China was, after all, boasting of its inherent superiority while paying back-handed bribes to keep foreign invaders away.

Life for young women was not so hopeful. The Song dynasty saw the flourishing of a custom among the Han Chinese that literally hobbled centuries of women—foot-binding. Legendarily originating in a minor kinglet's desire to have his concubine dance with her feet tied into dainty points—not unlike those of a modern ballerina—foot-binding under the Song became a convoluted process by which little girls' toes were systematically broken, and bent back under their foot. The result, after years of painful intervention, would be a foot more like a horse's hoof, little more than four inches long, with a pronounced arch.

It was utterly pointless. As early as the 13th century, the scholar Che Ruoshui wrote: "Little girls as young as four or five years old, who have done nothing wrong, nevertheless are made to suffer unlimited pain to bind [their feet] small. I do not know what use this is."

The custom was primarily a Han affliction, and did not spread to most of the minorities. Feet so small that a woman could barely totter a small distance came to be regarded as a sign of wealth and good breeding among the Han, and soon became a matter of erotic speculation among Han men. For Han women, it destroyed their ability to function independently, and greatly reduced the mention of dancing as an activity in Chinese sources. It also added a whole raft of new ailments that might strike a woman with bound feed, including obesity, septicemia, chronic pain both from walking and from the rebreaking of partly healed bones, and the stench from necrotic tissue.

Meanwhile, in the north, the Khitans were becoming more Chinese. Even before they pushed the Song dynasty south and occupied Kaifeng, they were split by periodic squabbles over their heritage. Should they stay Khitans, lording it over the Han Chinese, or had they come to China in order to *aspire* to be Chinese? The widow of the first Khitan emperor was the epitome of this dilemma—she was determined not to allow her China-loving eldest son onto the throne, but even as she proclaimed her love of nomad culture, she refused to accompany her husband in death, as would have been traditional. Instead, she cut off her right hand and left it in his tomb; the eldest son ran for China, where he became the first of many Khitan defectors to collaborate on the Song dynasty's constant intrigues with their foes.

Chief among these enemies were the Jurchens, a name liable to have derived from their own term for "reindeer people." A confederation of tribes from north Manchuria and what is now southern Siberia, they were united under their own great leader in 1115, and began pushing at the frontier of the Khitans just as the Khitans had once pushed at the Chinese. Calling themselves the Jin (Golden) dynasty, they presented a mounting threat to the rulers of north China, which the rulers of south China were swift to exploit.

In a move that surely seemed dangerous even at the time, the Southern Song struck a deal by sending ship-borne envoys to the Jurchens in 1120, offering to split the Khitan realm with them if both nations embarked on a pincer assault. The Jurchen agreed to what became known as the Alliance Conducted by Sea, and turned out to be the more proactive and successful in the campaigns of 1121–3 that did, indeed, chase the Khitans out of China and briefly restore sixteen provinces to Chinese rule. Ironically, however, few of the people in those provinces seemed keen to embrace the Song—raised for generations to regard the Song as their enemies, and treated as collaborators and cowards by their new Song masters, few of them embraced their liberation with the enthusiasm that the southerners had expected.

Within a few years, the Jurchens had reoccupied the liberated regions, often with the enthusiastic support of the locals, and swept down to seize all of China north of the Huai river, midway between the Yellow River and the Yangtze. This included the Song capital of Kaifeng, which fell to the invaders in 1127.

The city was looted. Mass executions went on for days. Palace women, regardless of rank, were corralled in the laundry rooms and sold off as slaves. The emperor's daughter, whose husband was still alive, was handed over to a Jin warrior as a concubine. Others (but as many later Chinese commentators fumed, nowhere near enough to satisfy honor) committed suicide rather than endure it. The multi-faceted atrocities are known to Chinese historians as the Humiliation of Jingkang, a name derived from the reign period in which the events took place. Worst of all for the establishment, however, was not the rape of princesses and the plundering of palaces, but the fact that the conquering Jurchens had managed to capture two Chinese emperors alive.

The Huizong Emperor (r. 1100–26) would have been remembered as a painter and a poet, had he not mismanaged his foreign policy to the extent that he was obliged to flee his own capital. He did so during the Jurchen invasion, after first abdicating and dumping all the problems on his son, the Qinzong Emperor (r. 1126–7). Both were captured, ritually humiliated, downgraded to commoner status and marched to northeast China, where they were made to perform mourning rituals for the Jurchen ancestors.

The Jurchens hoped to use their captives as bargaining chips, only to be thwarted when Huizong's twenty-year-old ninth son, Gaozong (r. 1127–62) was crowned as the new emperor in Hangzhou by the Song court in exile. In retaliation, Gaozong's captive mother, who had previously been relatively protected as a concubine to a Jin general, was transferred to the military brothel run out of the laundry courtyard.

Hangzhou would remain the capital of the "Southern" Song for the next century, its suburbs swelled by refugees, its administration retooled to become the hub of a southward-facing China centered on the Yangtze. With southern rice paddies now able to turn over three crops a year, the influx of new people was not necessarily a burden on the rich south, creating instead a firm basis for trade and prosperity. South China, it seemed, could survive relatively well without the north, an unwelcome truth that haunted the Southern Song for the rest of its reign.

Despite the hacking of China in half at the waist, it seemed that many in the Southern Song were thriving. Wang Mai, a scandalized official, wrote that jade and gold, once solely the prerogative of the nobility, were now being flaunted on the clothes of merchants' wives. Merchants, supposedly, were beneath the notice of noble Confucian officials, and the Song dynasty saw repeated attempts by the rulers to restrict the conspicuous consumption of the lower classes.

These days the families of artisans and merchants trail white silks and brocade, and adorn themselves with jade and pearls. In nine cases out of ten, if one looks a person over from head to foot, one will find that he is breaking the law.

Costume jewelry, imitating the largesse of the aristocracy with tin and gold foil, was affordable even by farmers' wives and bar-girls. But this gaudy fashion paled into insignificance before the grand mercantile scandal of the day—the Chinese were trading with the enemy. Large quantities of the silver paid out in bribes to the Jurchens in the north soon trickled back to the south as payment for tea, spices and luxuries from the civilized south. Taking a leaf from reforms in the later Tang dynasty, the Song government did not clamp down on such trade, but let it flow, choosing instead to extract tax revenue on the cross-border exchange. Such pragmatism shocked the stricter Confucians—the philosopher Zhu Xi observed that the Jurchens were the archetypal enemy under the same sky, which the Chinese could not suffer to live "because they have murdered our fathers."

The early years of Song Gaozong's reign were characterized by skirmishes along his long border with the Jurchen-occupied lands. But as the years passed, he and his advisers in Hangzhou began to form an appeasement policy—perhaps out of a sense of political reality, but as many historians have alleged in the years since, possibly out of the fear that any substantial rapprochement with the north might lead to the return of the hostage emperors and the end of his own hold on power. It was this undercurrent at the Hangzhou court that would lead to one of Chinese history's great miscarriages of justice.

Despite its poor military showing, the Song dynasty produced one of China's greatest military heroes, the general Yue Fei (1103–42). Born in the northern lands that China would soon cede to the Khitans, Yue Fei derived his name from a large bird that supposedly perched on the eaves of the house in which he was born. Thinking it to be a legendary roc, sent by Heaven to protect the land even in times of dire peril, his parents called him Fei (Flight). He joined the Song military in 1122, and but for a couple of mandatory absences to mourn his parents' deaths, served for the rest of his life.

Yue Fei was well-versed in the Confucian classics, but also practically minded. He was notable among Song generals for insisting on military training for his men, even when there were no wars to fight—for this reason, possibly with justification, he is credited in the lore of several martial arts traditions as the inventor of certain fighting techniques. He was also welcoming towards other scholars, creating an odd culture of military entertainments in his camps, where fellow literati were called upon to sing or publicly tell stories of great warriors of the past. Yue Fei took such matters to heart, even to the extent of having a patriotic slogan tattooed across his back: *Jin Zhong Bao Guo* "Utmost Loyalty in Service of the Nation."

Yue Fei fought for the Song as it lost a series of battles against the Jurchen invaders, pushed back from Kaifeng and south of the Yangtze. When put in charge of an army of his own, he was able to launch a fierce and successful counterattack, progressing through the lost lands, and eventually preparing to lay siege to Kaifeng itself in 1142. It was during this time that he supposedly wrote *The River All in Red* (*Man Jiang Hong*), a fierce poem loaded with anti-nomad rhetoric from antiquity.

> My hair bristles beneath my helmet, I stand at the railing, the
>      pounding rain ceases
> My eyes lift to heaven and I roar my passion
> My thirty years of deeds now as dust, three thousand leagues
>      on the road, following the clouds and moon
> The youth's head grows white, wounded by regrets
> the Humiliation of Jingkang lingers like unmelted snow
> Is there no end to the suffering of the Emperor's children
> Let us ride our chariots through the Helan Pass
> And there feast on the flesh of the Foreigners
> Laughing shall we drink the blood of the Xiongnu
> Let us regain our lost mountains and rivers, to report to the
>      Emperor.

However, Yue Fei was remaining loyal to a *Northern* Song ideal of a unified China fighting the barbarians, calling them "Xiongnu" in an evocation of enmities past. The Southern Song had spent the previous decade reconciling itself to a situation in which north China was abandoned to its new masters. With Yue Fei poised ready to retake Kaifeng, his superiors in Hangzhou were confronted with the possibility that the two hostage emperors, held captive since 1127, might be within reach. Yue Fei was ordered to halt his advance and report back to the court—a command which came as a shock and surprise to both him and his gung-ho troops.

Back in Hangzhou, Yue Fei was held for two months' intense interrogation, by officials determined to pin some kind of crime on him. With increasing public demands for an explanation, his court enemies continued to press on the grounds that there "must be something"—*mo xu you*, their precise wording, has been a Chinese byword for trumped-up charges ever since. Executed for no good reason, Yue Fei would be posthumously pardoned by Gaozong's successor in 1162 and canonized as a national hero in 1179. His official biography, which made it into the chronicles of the Song dynasty, was written by his grandson in the 1180s, by which time tales about him were already growing steadily taller. Statues were commissioned for his tomb of the four conspirators who caused his death, kneeling in contrition. For centuries to come, these effigies would be cursed, spat on and urinated upon by numerous patriots—chronic vandalism repeated to such an extent that they have had to be replaced at least twice, and the versions that stand today are fenced-in replicas.

By the time of Yue Fei's shameful death, the stalemate between the Jurchens and the Chinese had left little difference between them. Both now implied they were the true inheritors of the Mandate of Heaven, mounting increasingly lavish religious ceremonies in attempts to prove their piety and suitability. Both ruled populations in conditions of relative prosperity, who yearned to be reunited with their fellows across the border. Both were about to have their dreams quashed by a new an unexpected enemy: the Mongols, who would bring unity at a dreadful cost.

The Mongols began and just another tribe in the steppes and forests of the north. Tang dynasty chronicles of the 700s record the *Mung-nguet* of the north, using the *Meng* character that is still used to classify them in modern Chinese. They seem to have wandered westwards over the next few centuries, out as far as Lake Baikal.

The meaning of the word Mongol, however, changes radically in the lifetime of their great leader Temujin (1162–1227), whose rise to power united multiple clans of the steppes, turning them from a rabble of horsemen on the edges of the Jurchen realm into an unstoppable, roaming nation. The Mongol word for both a court and a camp, deriving its name from the impression left in the grass by a tent, is *ordu*. From it, multiple European languages would derive the term "horde." The original Mongols swelled to include other tribes: the Merkits, Naimans and Tatars, the Uyghurs and Keraits, an ever-growing confederation that proclaimed Temujin in 1206 as the greatest of leaders, the *Genghis Khan*.

Temujin's rise to power ran alongside the third and last of the period's fierce mega-droughts, from 1180–90. Desperation and deprivation honed the nomad peoples into a tough, hardened army, and their unification came just as the weather turned ideal for horse-rearing. Climate-wise, the period of the Mongol expansion would be the warmest and wettest that the world had been for the previous 1,122 years. It created ideal conditions for feeding and raising horses—the chief contributor to the early phase of Mongol expansion was the ready availability of provisions beneath the horses' feet. Meanwhile, the nature of the Mongols' social order required constant expansion. For Temujin's people to stay united, they needed to keep pushing ever outwards to reward their cavalry and keep supplies coming in. Rather than look back, at fractures and enmities within his ranks, Temujin led his horsemen ever outward, out of the grasslands, towards the lands of the Tangut Empire, the Uyghurs, caliphates of Central Asia, and of course, China.

There is no denying Temujin's prowess in battle, charisma and administrative skill, within the terms of his native culture. His tough early life and proud Mongol traditions had created an uncompromising figure, determined to take whatever he wanted. When asked what was best in life, he infamously replied: "To cut my enemies to pieces, drive them before me, seize their possessions, witness the tears of those dear to them, and embrace their wives and daughters."

Temujin proudly accepted his role as the scourge of "civilization," in the sense that he regarded cities and farms as an unwelcome poison to be eradicated.

> Heaven is weary of the inordinate luxury of China. I remain in the wild region of the north; I return to simplicity and seek moderation once more. As for the garments that I wear and the meals that I eat, I have the same rags and the same food as cowherds and grooms, and I treat the soldiers as my brothers.

Some later writers have suggested that Mongol atrocities, which are many and varied in the historical record, were calculated attempts at terror, designed to cow conquered populations into cooperation, and to scare nearby townships into immediate surrender. However, while some of them certainly had that effect, Temujin's attitude seems to have been far more apocalyptic. He killed thousands because he regarded them as surplus to requirements. Intent on restoring the world to its original, blessed status as empty grassland, he just didn't see the point of all those people.

A fellow Mongol had observed that the Chinese were no fighters, and sure to be nothing but a burden. It was probably best, all things considered, to kill them all and turn Kaifeng back into pastures, so at least the horses would get some food. It was only the intercession of a Khitan defector, Yelu Chucai (1190–1244), which swayed Temujin, when he carefully pointed out that Temujin needed to think outside the box. There was more to China than ruined grassland. Civilization created new artifacts and wealth that were an entire order of magnitude above the cattle and horses that a Mongol prized. The Mongols, like many a nomad dynasty before them, could simply become the lords of the Chinese, and collect tribute from them—silver, silk and grain.

Temujin was persuaded. Instead of massacring all the people he found, Temujin allowed for Mongol garrisons to watch over them, with local control often left in the hand of a Mongol appointee. Such men, the *darugha-chi* (governors), were often Khitans or Uyghurs, as these races were early converts to the Mongol cause, but in later decades of the Mongol conquest, they would also include Tibetans, Persians, assimilated Chinese and, it is claimed, one famous Venetian.

The Jurchen Jin dynasty had an army of 600,000, but most of those soldiers were concentrated along the long, uneasy border with the Southern Song. As ever, the Mongols relied on defectors, breaching north China's defensive walls by striking a deal with a turncoat general, and advancing on Beijing. The city's walls, however, presented an impossible barrier to the horse-mounted archers of the Mongols, so it remained untaken while the Mongol horde pillaged the surrounding countryside. In 1214, Temujin was back with catapults built by foreign vassals, and the Jurchen emperor paid him off, as might a Chinese sovereign, with gold, silver and a princess-bride.

The Jurchens, however, were only trying to buy time, running south to Kaifeng, where they hoped to mount a better resistance. Temujin laid siege to Beijing a second time, destroying the city, massacring its inhabitants and carting off what treasures remained. But the Jurchen-ruled Chinese were not his sole concern in the period. The Tanguts of the Gansu corridor, whose empire had lent troops to the Mongols for the attack on China, refused to help him in an additional campaign against Eastern Iran. On the way home from Eastern Iran, the Mongols wiped out the last remnants of the Khitans in Central Asia, before marching in a force 180,000-strong on the Tanguts.

The Tangut Empire (in Chinese, the Xixia), which endured from 1038–1227, occupied a substantial chunk of what is now northwestern China. They were Buddhists who spoke a Tibeto-Burmese dialect, and we know very little about them. The word "Tangut" is based on the Mongol term for them—in their own language, they probably referred to themselves as the Great State of the White and High, but details are sparse because the Mongols killed them all. Incensed at their refusal to play along with the terms of their previous treaty, Temujin ordered the eradication of the Tangut state. When their ruler surrendered, he was executed, his family tombs desecrated and despoiled, and his subjects massacred.

At least part of the genocide enacted against the Tanguts may have been *because* Temujin died during the campaign. Asides in Mongol histories suggest that he "fell from his horse," although rumor has long had it that he was stabbed in the crotch by a Tangut girl he was trying to rape. Whatever the cause of his demise, the realm of the Tanguts was wiped off the map. Today, the site of their capital is known as Ningxia (literally, "the Tanguts quelled"), and is known as a Muslim region, because it was settled by descendants of the Uyghur soldiers who formed the frontline of Temujin's shock-troops. The Uyghurs and the Tanguts had been at odds with one another for decades, but it was the Uyghurs who had the final, devastating victory.

Later phases of the "Mongol" expansion similarly incorporated troops from conquered vassals. It was, for example, a mainly Korean and Han Chinese "Mongol" army that would eventually conquer the Southern Song in the name of Temujin's grandson. Conditions allowed the Mongols to keep expanding for three or four generations, by which time the outlying edges of their constant search for plunder and provisions were at opposite ends of Eurasia, and the spread of the core Mongol aristocracy was thin indeed.

Temujin fretted about the likelihood that civilization would win in the end. Around him he already saw Mongols wearing their jackets inside-out to show off the bright silk and gold-threads of the Chinese lining; Mongols wearing silk under their armor; Mongols developing a taste for grape wine and spirits, which in turn was turning them into alcoholics. A real man, fumed Temujin, shouldn't get drunk more than three times a month; several of his sons and many of his grandsons would drink themselves to death.

> After us, the people of our race will wear garments of gold; they
> will eat sweet, greasy food, ride splendid coursers, and hold in
> their arms the loveliest of women, and they will forget that they
> owe these things to us.

And yet, on his deathbed, Temujin would try to break one of the Mongols' strongest traditions. Bloody tanistry, in which brother would fight brother to determine who was the strongest, was practically encouraged on the steppes. Temujin ordered his sons not to follow the old way, but to keep the confederation together by agreeing peaceably on a single successor as Great Khan. They would, in fact, settle on his son Ögedei (r. 1229–41), although in generations to come, the old fraternal competitions would arise again, plunging many later rulers into civil wars with their relatives.

The persuasive Yelu Chucai would remain an influential figure in mitigating Mongol destructiveness, the ringleader of a group of officials that would impose taxes, reopen schools in Beijing, and create the workings of a Mongol-influenced but demonstrably Chinese state—ironically, most of them were of Khitan or Uyghur descent. "You can conquer a country on horseback," he said to Temujin's successor, Ögedei (r. 1229–41), "but you cannot rule it from horseback"—the words of Lu Jia, with even greater relevance 1,400 years after they were first spoken, warning that a conqueror should understand that he, too, was about to be changed by his conquest. Yelu Chucai dissuaded Ögedei from the planned mass population movement of Chinese to the west and Uyghurs to the east, which would have destroyed both cultures, and interceded on many occasions on behalf of those who would have otherwise been victims of the Mongols. A chilling aside in Chinese chronicles has Ögedei teasing Yelu with the words: "*Are you going to weep for the people again?*" Plainly, Yelu's career was a lifelong exercise in brinkmanship and tragedy.

Historians are apt to concentrate on moments of crisis and transformation—the great battles and regime-toppling natural disasters, but we should occasionally remember that for long periods, and for large sectors of the population, life went on regardless. In Liuzi village, north of the Huai river in Anhui, archaeologists have uncovered a forgotten canal that once linked Luoyang with Nanjing, linking the Yellow River with the Yangtze. Meters below the modern farmland, they have found a quayside that once teemed with boats, and an entire sedimentary layer of Tang dynasty porcelain. The region remained a thriving trade hub throughout the Song, and among the display cases at the site, I saw a small, finger-sized clay figurine, glazed not with the brown, green and cream of Tang style, nor the all-over green of the Song, but with reds and blues that marked it out in the little-discussed fashions of the Khitan era. It fell over the side of a boat, or was thrown in the canal by a naughty child, late in the waterway's life, when dredgers came at increasingly wide intervals, traffic was down, and trade had moved on. Within a few decades, the canal had entirely silted up, closing centuries of life and activity as merchants migrated to the new north-south waterways serving the Mongol capital in what is now Beijing.

The author and poet Du Renjie (1201–82) grew up in Mongol-occupied north China, and twice declined an offer from Yelu Chucai to accept high government office—this may have been a genuine desire to occupy himself with poetry, or a polite refusal from serving the invaders. His surviving works are charming and wry portrayals of everyday life in the 13th century, such as *A Peasant Knows Not the Theater* (*Zhuangjia Bu Shi Goulan*). Set to the tune of a preexisting ballad, it outlines the experience of a country bumpkin's first experience of a play, its eight verses presenting a complete account of what we would now call his "customer journey."

> Blows the wind and falls the rain, and the people are content
> None so happy as we peasants
> When there's grain for us and mulberry for the silkworms
> And the officials are not pestering us.
> So I came to the city to pray for village matters
> Downtown, where I could buy some papers to burn
> Passing by the market, I see bright hanging banners
> And nowhere have I seen such a commotion, so many people!

A barker is holding the gate open with one hand, beckoning customers with other, proclaiming a late show with standing-room only, starting with a performance of Guan Hanqing's *The Moon and the Breeze*, but with later delights to come. Our hero pays his 200-coin admission, entering a hall for which his only previous comparison is a temple, with a towering stage, faced by a semicircle of seats in wood tiers. The crowd "like a whirlpool," and lady musicians at the side, it is like no religious ritual he has ever seen.

Our first-time theater-goer is dazzled by motley costumes, startled by the actions of the villain, entertained by a staged conversation between a grandfather and a barkeep as they discuss the bride price of a young girl. He is briefly confused by an actor's staged footwork and shocked when someone gets hit on the head with a mallet.

Surely they will go to prison for this!? No... wait, it was a fake; it was an act. The audience are laughing. He is desperate to see more, but nature calls.

> My bladder swells, I'm bursting for a piss
> I try to hold it in so I can see the next scene
> Hoping in vain these donkeys won't laugh themselves to death
> at me.

Far from living under the iron heel of barbaric invaders, Du's theater-goer is enjoying a night out. He enjoys the freedom to burn paper tokens to his ancestors. He has money in his pocket and is relatively free of cares, and he is dazzled by the entertainments on offer in town. These would only increase during the period of domination by foreigners, as would-be literati were excluded or recused themselves from public office, and instead found other outlets for their interests in the arts. One case in point was Guan Hanqing (1241–1320), the author of the play that our peasant saw, a Beijing playwright credited with some 65 works, of which only fourteen survive today. And although Du Renjie may not have realized it himself, the fact that he was not running a provincial town, but instead documenting the popular culture of his age, was itself part of the same phenomenon.

Nomad rules of succession being what they were, and Mongol conquests being so successful, the furthest frontiers of the Mongol advance were already far to the west. The grand Mongol empire, stretching from Hungary to Korea, was already creaking with its sheer mass, showing the first signs of fragmenting into smaller, more localized states—what would eventually become the Ilkhans in Persia, the Golden Horde nibbling at Eastern Europe, and the Chagatai Khanate in Central Asia. Regions were parceled out to Temujin's descendants along lines that pushed the eldest to the edges while the young remained at home. Eventually, this left Mongolia and north China in the hands of Temujin's grandson, Khubilai Khan (r. 1260–94).

Khubilai is remembered as a merciful and wise ruler, although some might say that anyone would look like a saint compared to his predecessors. He certainly enjoyed the dividends of his forefathers' achievements, not only inheriting an efficient infrastructure, but also a fearsome reputation that sped up his conquests—stories of his grandfather's atrocities often encouraged towns to surrender before he needed to commit any troops. However, he did not begin his career auspiciously. He mismanaged the first domain he was given to run, and, when sent on a military campaign in Yunnan, declared it over before the last stragglers of his enemies were mopped up. He spent much of his reign in a series of wasteful succession struggles with his cousins, and did not acquit himself all that well in battle. On one occasion, he gave up on a campaign and rode out of the desert in a tactical withdrawal, abandoning his poorly-supplied foot soldiers to die of thirst.

Temujin had lived to take the young Khubilai on his first hunt, but died before his grandson could grow up to be the prophecy fulfilled of a Mongol turned native, draped in fine robes, living in a palace and dining on delicacies. Later portraits of Khubilai show him to be morbidly obese—one tribute gift from his Korean subjects comprised soft sharkskin shoes to help him cope with gout. He did make a show of going hunting up at his summer residence in Shangdu, but travelled in a palace mounted on a platform borne by four elephants, and lived in a ridiculously opulent super-tent, a "sumptuous house of pleasures, which may be removed from place to place." It was later accounts of this, much muddled in transmission, which led the poet Samuel Taylor Coleridge to write: "*In Xanadu did Kubla Khan a stately pleasure dome decree.*"

Khubilai, however, proclaimed himself to be a Chinese emperor, writing the Mongols into the narrative of Chinese history. He selected the site of modern Beijing as his capital, refurbishing the Grand Canal in order to keep the city fed with grain. Announcing that the Song dynasty had lost the Mandate of Heaven, he preemptively declared the Yuan (Beginning)

China During the Yuan Dynasty

YUAN

Beijing

Guangzhou

China During the Yuan Dynasty
China's Modern-day Border

dynasty in 1271, initiating eight years of conflict as armies played catch-up to turn his announcement into a reality. A force led by Mongols, but heavily staffed with Chinese soldiers from the north, took the Southern Song capital in 1276, along with its five-year-old emperor. A small force of Song loyalists proclaimed his even younger brother as his successor, and stayed on the run until 1279, when they met their final defeat in a naval battle off the coast of Guangdong. Standing at the very edge of what had once been his domain, the eight-year-old last emperor of the Southern Song watched from the cliffs. His commander and guardian, Lu Xiufu, admonished him that they could not afford to be taken alive and paraded, like his elder brother, before Khubilai in his capital. Instead, he gathered the young emperor in his arms and leapt into the sea below.

The Mongols' short-lived Yuan dynasty (1271–1368) was the first of two culminations of China's "barbarian" problem. It, and the later Qing dynasty (1644–1912), mark points in history when far from being a nuisance to be dispelled, the barbarians actually won, sweeping over the entire country and, indeed, carrying their standards further afield, claiming new territories for what would eventually swing back into Chinese control.

Some histories of China give this "Mongol century" its own separate chapter. More recent books, like Timothy Brook's *The Troubled Empire*, choose to lump the Yuan dynasty in with the Ming dynasty that followed it, on the basis that both were symptoms of a long-term series of climatic slumps—the Nine Sloughs—which compromised any attempt by a ruling regime to hang onto power and maintain equilibrium. Three of these occurred during the Yuan era: 1295–97, 1324–30, and 1342–45.

I choose to combine the Yuan dynasty with the Song era because, in ethnic terms, the Mongols regarded themselves as the inheritors of centuries of established nomad rule in China. It was the Mongols who supervised the writing of the official histories of the Liao dynasty and the Jin dynasty, thereby incorporating the Khitans and Jurchens into an official narrative that had previously privileged only the experience of Han Chinese.

The flight to the south caused by the Mongols led to a little-observed demographic peak. By the year 1290, barely 10% of the population of China lived north of the Yangtze. The south was the lifeboat and cradle of Han civilization, but would never contain quite such a proportion of it again. By the end of the Yuan dynasty, the numbers were climbing back up again, towards a 50/50 parity in the late 20th century.

China had not been unified since the collapse of the Tang dynasty in 905. Now it was whole again within Khubilai's realm, which also encompassed the Western Regions (Xinjiang), alongside new additions like Tibet and Yunnan, and Khubilai's native Mongolia, swamping Chinese culture with new contacts and ideas. The south would spend the next century reeling from the culture shock. Yunnan stayed for a while under the rule of its defeated kings, but ended up in the hands of a Muslim governor. A Tibetan priest was commissioned to impose a new form of writing, which failed to catch on. Uyghur officials bickered with Turks and Khitans over new government policies. In terms of the newly evolving social system of Khubilai's empire, such men were the *semuren*, or "persons of the various categories," second in the hierarchy only to the Mongols themselves. The nation was divided along four ethnic groups: Mongols themselves, their non-Chinese *semuren* vassals, northern Chinese who had been under Mongol rule since 1234, and southern Chinese who had only been conquered in the 1270s. This latter category was referred to by the new administration, with deep and impertinent irony, by the Bronze Age designation *Manzi*, or Southern Barbarians.

The disconnection between north and south ran so deeply that foreign observers regarded them as two different countries—Cathay or Khitai in the north, deriving its name from the Khitans, and Manzi in the south. For Marco Polo (1254–1324), the Venetian merchant who worked as one of Khubilai's *semuren* for sixteen years, the land of the Southern Song was a conquered territory, its great buildings in ruins; its residents subjected to martial law; its customs and traditions garbled and occasionally impenetrable. Khubilai's China was an occupation regime, staffed by an officer caste so diverse that their default communications appear to have been not in Chinese or Mongol, but in Persian or Turkish. Marco Polo's account of China often seemed to misname things, and he remained oblivious of what went on behind closed doors in the south—tea-drinking, foot-binding and the use of chopsticks. Even his term for Khubilai's capital, the city we now call Beijing, uses language derived from the Central Asian Turks: *Khanbaliq*—the Khan's City.

A similar melting-pot confusion afflicted religions in Khubilai's domain. The wide spread of the Mongol conquests had assimilated an equally wide range of different religions. This had been obvious even in Temujin's day, when the Great Khan had held together his disparate tribes by proclaiming a position of religious tolerance. Khubilai kept to this policy, increasing his reputation as a wise and syncretic ruler, turning his court into a salon of contending traditions, as Daoists, Zoroastrians, several Buddhist sects, Muslims, Jews and Nestorian Christians competed to impress him and his family. Many of the visitors to Khubilai's court labored under the misapprehension that Khubilai was trying to make up his mind, and that the right performance or argument would cause him to permanently adopt one faith above the others. This was certainly how some of Khubilai's cousins behaved elsewhere—one became a Christian, another founded a dynasty of Muslim rulers—but it is likely that Khubilai was following Temujin's policy of keeping everybody guessing.

Despite an overt policy of tolerance, there were deadly tensions beneath the surface. Daoism was split into a "true" faction revering Laozi (of whom Khubilai was a fan) and a lesser sect of conjurors and trouble-makers, who were not above distributing forged scriptures claiming that Buddha had been a pupil of Laozi, or setting fire to Buddhist temples. Meanwhile, in Hangzhou, Khubilai's Tibetan head of reconstruction created a massive scandal by returning buildings to the state they had had before Hangzhou became a refugee capital. This included "desecrating" Song imperial temples that had once been Confucian shrines, much to the annoyance of locals.

An ongoing drama, first discussed at the time of Temujin, and breaking out in a palace feud in the 1280s, involved a ban on halal and kosher meat. Temujin had been appalled by what, to him, was a wasteful habit of bleeding butchered animals. He insisted that Muslims and Jews slaughter their animals in the Mongol manner, retaining the blood inside.

Unsurprisingly, the practice simply went underground, only to manifest once more when Khubilai, in a magnanimous gesture at a banquet, sent meat from his table to a group of visiting Muslim dignitaries, who refused to touch it. In the argument that followed, Khubilai reiterated Temujin's law, and the incident might have blown over, were it not for Jesus the Christian, a *semuren* official who decided that now was the ideal time to mention to Khubilai that the Muslims wanted to kill all non-believers.

Jesus pointed Khubilai at Quran IX: 5, an infamous passage in the Muslim holy book that calls for the deaths of anyone who worships more than one god. When an imam was dragged in to explain it, translation error or foolhardiness only made things worse, since he appears to have told Khubilai that the passage was indeed true, and the only reason that Khubilai and his people had not been murdered in their beds was that the Muslims had lacked the means and opportunity. With Khubilai on the verge of ordering reprisals against an entire faith, a second opinion was swiftly solicited from one Hamad al-Din, from Samarkand, who supplied Khubilai with plenty of quotes that mitigated the controversial phrase, and seemed to acknowledge him as a great and just ruler, and the Muslims as his loyal servants.

The strife was defused, at least for the moment, although Marco Polo's own observations on what he called "the accursed doctrines of the Saracens" made it clear that the trouble was not over. Reading between the lines, the problem was not religious in nature, but reflected the fact that "men with beards" (mainly Muslims but plenty of other Central Asians of other faiths) formed the bulk of the *semuren* class, which was charged with carrying out all the front-line tasks of managing China. Chief among these were the extraction of heavy taxes and corvée labor obligations, burdening the conquered Chinese people with the expense of the construction and renewal for which Khubilai usually takes the credit. If there was a tax to be collected, a house to be requisitioned, a sentence to be decreed or a punishment to be carried out, the Mongols were stretched far too thinly to do it. It was their *semuren* collaborators who were most likely to get the blame. Some, like Saiyid Ajall Shams al-Din (d. 1279), the Muslim governor of Yunnan, are remembered as great statesmen. But for many Chinese, in the decades that followed the Mongol conquest, it was the collaborator class that represented the face of foreign oppression and corruption.

Muslims, in fact, also formed a key market for Chinese goods, newly opened to them by cross-cultural contacts within the Mongol Empire. The increased proximity of the Arab world, and the mixture of Arab potters with the Chinese, introduced the Chinese to use cobalt blues in their pottery. The Islamic world favored patterned designs, leading the Chinese to add what they regarded as garish and barbaric images of flowers and trees to their ceramics—the widely popular blue-and-white porcelain.

Transporting Chinese porcelain and silks was now a sea-borne trade, out of teeming southern Chinese ports like Quanzhou (the Arabic name of which *Zaytun*, is the origin of our word *satin*), and Guangzhou. Friar Odoric of Pordenone wrote of Guangzhou in the 1320s: "And this city hath shipping so great and vast in amount that to some it would seem well nigh incredible. Indeed all Italy hath not the amount of craft that this one city hath."

A generation later in 1345, the Arab visitor ibn Battuta said of the city of Quanzhou that its harbor was "one of the greatest in the world—I am wrong, it is the greatest! I have seen there about one hundred first-class junks together; as for small ones they were past counting."

Khubilai might have conquered China, but he had pursued it to its geographical limits. Beyond the cliffs from which the last Song emperor had hurled himself, there was open water. Beyond his territory in Yunnan (literally "South of the Clouds") there were forbidding mountain passes that led down into tropical jungles. The "Mongol" military was now a third-hand inheritance, packed with south Chinese conscripts, Koreans and *semuren*. It was also substantially more maritime in outlook, as it needed to be in order to travel beyond China. Despite the acknowledged achievement of Khubilai's generals in conquering the Southern Song, further Mongol victories were in short supply. The rulers of what is now Vietnam gave Khubilai the runaround for years. Mongol armies toppled the

Pagan Empire in what is now Myanmar, but did not stay to enjoy the fruits of their victory. In Java, the same fleet that accompanied Marco Polo partway on his voyage back to Europe would land an army hoping to secure tribute from the local king. Meddling in local politics, they backed the king's rebellious son-in-law, but were double-crossed by their local ally. Most infamously of all, two Mongol fleets spectacularly failed to invade Japan, defeated on both occasions not only by fanatical samurai resistance on the beaches, but by the Divine Wind (*Kamikaze*) typhoons that sank their troop transports. Unsurprisingly, this is when Khubilai began promoting Mazu, the Goddess of the Sea, in the state's divine hierarchy.

Heavy weather would come to play an increasingly influential role in Yuan dynasty China. Global temperatures dropped significantly in the century after 1270, bringing an end to the Medieval Warm Period. Radiocarbon data from Tibetan glaciers shows them advancing in the first overtures of the Little Ice Age. The same downturn in climate that caused the European colony in distant Greenland to fail also created difficult conditions for the aging Khubilai and his successors. The Little Ice Age had two phases, both paralleling regime change in China. Its first peak came in 1368, the year that the Chinese would overthrow the Mongols. Its second, even colder peak came in the 1640s, amid events to be covered in the next chapter.

Smaller, more localized events within China nevertheless took a huge toll. In 1286, already a famine year, a full quarter of Beijing's vital grain supplies were lost at sea, causing the administration to speed up renovation work on the Grand Canal. Neglect of dams and levees could make even normal rains disastrous after a drought. In 1295, the year after Khubilai's death, there was massive flooding on the Yangtze. The following year, both the Yangtze and the Yellow River burst their banks. "The fields and houses," wrote the Mongol chroniclers, "disappeared under the waves." Just to round it off, 1297 saw a plague of locusts. In 1303, a series of earthquakes hit Shanxi, including a 8-Richter scale monster that killed hundreds of thousands, left many more homeless, and continued to shudder in aftershocks for two more years.

Floods became an annual affair after 1301 and a national emergency in the 1320s and 1330s. In an era of increasing paranoia, there was no space for trouble-makers. In distant Tibet, the 52-year-old abbot of the Sakya Monastery wrote a poem in which he wistfully remembered his childhood. It seemed almost like a dream, but there was a time as a child when he had been placed on a throne and feted as an Emperor. He remembered flights in the night, and storms on the sea, and the day his royal mother led him by the hand to the Mongol camp to surrender. He, it turned out, had been the penultimate child-emperor of the Song dynasty, granted ducal status by Khubilai, who had lived until his teens in Beijing, before being sent off to Tibet into monkish seclusion. There, he might have lived out his days, were it not for the inadvisable poem that recalled times past and a regime lost. The Mongols ordered his death in 1323.

Coastal communities suffered assault from both sides, with overflowing rivers from the hinterland and tidal waves from the sea. Khubilai's great-grandson, Yesün Temür tried to fight the damage in 1328 by ordering Tibetan monks to hurl hundreds of Buddhist statues into the sea, but this accomplished nothing. Since the money to pay for sea defense had to come from somewhere, the Mongols over-printed their paper money, which only increased inflation. Such desperation on the coasts reflected an increasingly bloody rivalry among the Mongols themselves, over who got to enjoy the dwindling fruits of their domain, even as the Grand Canal began to silt up through neglect. When Yesün Temür died that same year, his son Ragibagh was fatally plunged into a succession crisis known as the War of the Two Capitals. Outlying provinces such as Sichuan and Yunnan became the sites of anti-Mongol unrest, placing further pressure on the center.

One in three Chinese people died from famine in the 14th century—six million alone during the Great Famine of 1333–37. Although the climate troubles lessened somewhat by the 1340s, the subjects of the Mongol Emperors were already thinking the unthinkable: that the Mandate of Heaven had been revoked, and the era of Mongol rule would soon be over.

The fourth of the Nine Sloughs, in the 1340s, comprised a drought, then a flood, and epidemics arising. The changes in ecology are liable to have forced sudden changes in the population migration of rodents and the fleas they bore, liable to have had some bearing on the spread of the Black Death, a plague which claimed millions of lives throughout Eurasia. It, coupled with the massacres unleashed during the Mongol invasion, surely contributed to the drop in the Chinese population from a peak in the late Song of 120 million, to a mere 80 million by the time they left.

It was last truly major climate disaster to hit China for a century, but it was the final straw for Zhu Yuanzhang (1328–98). A farmer's son who had been forced to watch his starving parents give away several of his brothers and sisters, he was one of only two survivors of his nine-strong family to make it through the Great Famine and the plague that followed. He threw himself on the mercy of a Buddhist temple, where he learned to read and write, sometimes resorting to begging in order to secure food to eat. By the 1350s, his home region was the site of an anti-Mongol uprising, the Red Turbans. When his home temple was destroyed during Mongol policing operations, he threw in his lot with the rebels, becoming one of several factional leaders within the Red Turbans.

By 1356, Zhu's faction, which he called *Ming* (Brightness) had seized Nanjing. With the Mongols pulling back towards the north, south China became a battleground between several splinters of the Red Turbans. It took Zhu until 1368 to defeat his rivals, who had been swift to declare themselves kings. Now the master of all the land on both sides of the Yangtze, as well the teeming metropolis of Hangzhou on the coast, he led a united army north against the Mongol authorities.

Zhu would become the master of ruins and ashes, his army raising its standard in the cities of the north as the few locals who identified as Mongols fled before them. The last Mongol emperor of China, Toghon Temür, lacking the manpower to initiate a planned apocalyptic purge of his own population—amounting, in fact, to a restoration of Temujin's original policy of killing nearly everyone—fled for Mongolia. His descendants would call themselves the "Northern Yuan," wandering the steppes for the next three centuries, but the Mongol era in China was over. Behind them, they left an enduring genetic legacy—modern DNA analysis reveals that the multiple sons of Temujin, each of them siring children on dozens of women, combined to make him the ancestor of some sixteen million men today, from Hungary to Korea.

Meanwhile, Zhu Yuanzhang, the farmer's son from Anhui, had somehow become the founder of the Ming dynasty.

# CHAPTER 7

# MOURNING GLORY: THE MING DYNASTY

The palace rebels of 1542 had no weapons but hairpins and ribbons. Many of them were teenage girls who lived in fear for their lives, having seen so many of their fellow concubines beaten to death for real and imagined transgressions. Taken from their families and imprisoned in the palace, they had been subjected to humiliating procedures at the hands of Daoist alchemists. Raped by the Jiajing Emperor soon after their first menstruation, each palace concubine had then been treated like cattle, sequestered every month on a diet of nothing but mulberry leaves and rainwater, to provide higher quality menstrual discharges to feed the Emperor's thirst for "Heavenly Innate Cinnabar." Anyone who fell ill was cut from the herd and cast out. Some had been fed strange potions designed to alter their bodies, so that they might help the Emperor in his quest for immortality. Some of those potions—likely to have contained mercury—had been fatal.

The details of their plan are unclear—how can they ever have expected to get away with it? Perhaps they hoped there would be strength in numbers, not only in the execution of their deed, but in testifying to its necessity.

The Emperor spent the night with Consort Duan, the mother of his daughter and his concubine for over a decade. This in itself was rare—his constant craving for young flesh meant that most of his palace women were under sixteen years old.

The Emperor was done with Consort Duan. The pair dozed in her quarters as the conspirators approached in a rustle of silk skirts.

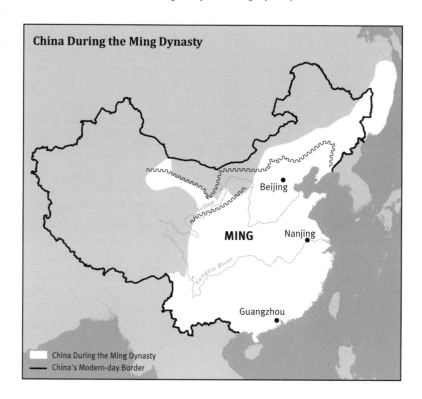

**China During the Ming Dynasty**

MING

Beijing

Nanjing

Guangzhou

Yellow River

Yangtze River

☐ China During the Ming Dynasty
— China's Modern-day Border

"Let's do it now," said Tranquillity. "This is better than waiting for him to kill us."

There were over a dozen of them, and they leapt on the bed to hold the Emperor down. The Emperor tried to yell, but one of the girls had him by the throat.

As he choked and gasped, they threw a silk cloth over his head (fittingly in imperial yellow) and a cord around his neck. Some say it was a ribbon from a girl's hair. Others that it was a sturdier rope used to hang one of the banners above the chamber.

"Don't let go!" hissed one of the girls, as the Emperor thrashed beneath them.

In earlier times, the commotion would have brought a eunuch or a guard, but the Jiajing Emperor had always liked his privacy, and none were nearby. His slight attackers held down his arms and legs, sitting astride his torso as their fellows pulled the strangling cord ever tighter.

The Emperor twisted, his legs kicking free.

Thinking fast, one of the girls pulled out her hairpin and stabbed him in the groin. There was a muffled shriek from below the silk, and he continued to struggle.

Still, the Emperor would not die. Unknown to his would-be killers, a pair of knots in the garrote had mashed against one another, preventing it from being tightened to the full. The Jiajing Emperor continued to thrash beneath them, and one of girls suddenly had a change of heart.

"This is wrong," stammered Golden Lotus. "He is not dying."

"Pull harder!" hissed Jade Fragrance. "Don't give up!"

"He is not dying because he is a dragon," whispered Golden Lotus. The immortality treatments had worked after all. Unpleasant though their ordeal had been, the Emperor was an immortal… how ironic they should discover this as they tried to kill him.

"He is fading!" said Tranquillity. "Just hang on. Don't let go of him! Come back!"

But Golden Lotus fled the bedchamber in panic, screaming for help.

Outside she could hear the rush of feet.

Empress Fang, still gathering her robes around her, gasped from the doorway at the chaos on the bed.

"Get her!" shouted Tranquillity.

"What is the meaning of th—?" sputtered the Empress, until she was silenced by a punch in the face. She staggered back beneath a fury of fists, as one of the girls tried in vain to wrestle her to the ground.

Guards arrived in twos and threes, towering over the tiny girls on the bed. The Jiajing Emperor had always liked his concubines thin and petite. They were easily overpowered, and the Empress, nursing scratches on her face, tore the cord from around his neck. The Emperor lay still, barely breathing, his face a mess of blacks and purples.

He would lay unconscious for several days, while his Daoist alchemists bickered and fretted over the correct treatment. Eventually, one of them won out with a special prepared tincture, which caused the Emperor to suddenly sit bolt upright, and vomit a bowl's worth of black, rancid blood.

Hoarse and weak, he thanked Empress Fang for saving his life, and listened with mounting anger as she recounted the events of the intervening days.

She had, she explained, wasted no time in having the traitors killed.

She had ordered a punishment suitable for those who betray their husbands and lords—*lingchi*, the death by slow slicing. Each of the girls had been tied to a wooden frame and publicly tortured to death, screaming as she watched her own breasts mutilated, her fingers mashed and torn, the flesh torn from her arms and legs. It was a punishment calculated not only to impress upon onlookers the severity of the crime, but to deny the victim a whole body in the afterlife.

"Whom did you kill…?" asked the Emperor slowly.

"Tranquillity, of course, she was the ringleader. Pure Orchid, Chrysanthemum Flower, Jade Fragrance—all of the girls I found on top of you. Three more who obviously knew of the scheme, even if they were not pulling the ropes themselves. Ten of their relatives. Another twenty enslaved and given to loyal officials to deal with as they pleased. If Your Majesty wishes, you can be carried in your litter to the walls, where their traitorous remains are hung in public. But today is not a good day. The whole city has been shrouded in thick fog. It fell on the day the executioners began their work, and has not yet let up. Perhaps now that Your Majesty has recovered–"

"At least tell me they did not harm the Consort Duan."

"Who didn't?"

"The girls."

"No, the girls did not harm Consort Duan. I did, when I ordered her torture and death."

"She did nothing."

"She did nothing to stop the attack! The conspirators struck in her bedchamber. She was clearly involved in some way."

"That cannot be so."

"She wanted Your Majesty dead."

"If that were true, she could have struck in so many ways. She could have just poisoned me."

"It is too late now," said Empress Fang in a small voice.

The Emperor would never forgive her. In the aftermath of the conspiracy, palace officials came to believe that Consort Duan, the Emperor's favorite, had indeed been innocent. What was left of her body was returned to her father, who erected an imperial-style gate, lacking any inscription, as a wordless, accusatory memorial to her wrongful death. The Jiajing Emperor became even more reclusive in his habits, replenishing his harem with a new intake of young victims.

Five years later, there was a fire at the palace. Empress Fang was trapped inside.

Eunuchs asked the Emperor if they should break down the doors and rescue her, but the Jiajing Emperor said nothing, and watched as the building burned.

⊙—⊙—⊙—⊙—⊙

The Ming dynasty is fondly regarded by many historians, in part for its rich cultural heritage. It was a period that saw more direct contacts between China and Europe, which advanced on it from both east and west—around Cape Horn from Africa, and across the Pacific from the Spanish Americas. The Ming dynasty saw the first stirrings of what would become a global fad for tea, but China itself would be altered forever by new arrivals—by changes in gun technology, by the spread of Christian missionaries, and by the arrival of new commodities, including tobacco, the chili, the sweet potato and opium.

In the days before the country's sense of self radically reoriented to include many former "barbarian" ethnicities, the Ming dynasty was also regarded as the last period before the modern era that China was ruled by the Chinese themselves. Throughout the centuries that followed it, it was seen as something of a Golden Age, a lost kingdom of glorious Han culture, when fleets of super-galleons carried Chinese embassies as far as the coast of Africa, where Buddhism and Daoism saw a great flowering of worship and philosophy, when China burst into a long summer of rich cultural pursuits: a pinnacle of poetry, publishing and art. After the sudden drop in numbers under the Yuan, China's population more than doubled during the Ming. This would become at least part of the Ming's problem, with the emperor's subjects increasing at an unprecedented rate, too fast for the bureaucracy to keep up. As new lands were opened up, and new crops developed that allowed even Fujianese hillsides to deliver bountiful harvests, there were not enough officials in place to adequately administer the empire. In good times, tax collection often failed to gather in profits; in bad times, budgets would not stretch to feed all the new hungry mouths and newly established townships.

The emperors' subjects were not the only population to increase. The first Ming emperor alone had over 40 children, few of whom stood any chance of participating in government. Indeed, attempting to do so might have been seen as a power-play against the chosen heir. Instead, princes and princesses, dukes and barons, their children and grandchildren formed an idle aristocracy dispersed throughout the empire. Culturally, the Ming imperial family would create a ready and enriching market for fine porcelain and decorative arts, books, plays and musical entertainment; financially, the descendants of some seventeen Ming emperors would become a constant drain on the imperial coffers, eventually costing more than the annual military budget.

Ming China was sandwiched between two occupation regimes, a fact which has influenced both its self-identity, and its historical memory. It was exuberantly ethnocentric, fulsome in proclamation of China for the Chinese, dedicated to stamping out the last remnants of the Mongols, while also clinging possessively to the new frontiers that the Mongols had conquered. Its people enjoyed a century of relatively peaceful weather, allowing for much of the giddy, halcyon development for which the Ming is remembered. However, it was then hit by the last six of the Nine Sloughs. Hardly a generation went by after the 1450s without the country facing some terrible climate crisis, famine or flood. One might even argue that the true achievement of the Ming did not arise during its gilded early days, but in the remarkably tenacious long decline, when disasters that would have easily destroyed many earlier regimes failed, at first, to bring it completely to its knees.

The Ming dynasty began unsteadily, the threat of a Mongol resurgence worrying its early rulers. Zhu Yuanzhang, the Hongwu Emperor (r. 1368–98) remained skittish and thin-skinned about his lowly upbringing, ever ready to take offense at imagined references to his youth as a wandering monk. Determined to kick away the ladder of rebellion by which he had come to power himself, he was eternally paranoid about conspiracies real and imagined, and pursued several witch-hunts against those he thought were plotting against him. In doing so, he refashioned the power structure of Chinese government so that emperors thereafter enjoyed substantially more direct influence.

When a powerful, assertive sovereign sat on the throne in the Ming and subsequent Qing dynasties, it could create long periods of dynamic, go-getting government. When, as often happened, the Emperor shirked his responsibilities or receded into his quarters for weeks or even months, there was no longer a top echelon of ministers to which he could delegate. Lower, less qualified, or even unsanctioned officials (including eunuchs or palace women) might step into the breach, which could serve to create uneasy, indecisive policies.

The Ming dynasty was seen, then and now, as a great reassertion of native Chinese values after a long period of rule by invaders, and Hongwu made his drive for purity clear in an edict that instructed his ministers to "refrain from evil." In it, he characterized the administration of the late Yuan dynasty as a parade of corruption, in which officials prized material treasures above virtue and their own families. He bragged that he had lived through such dark times, but that he clung onto his virtue. Well, almost.

In an odd aside, Hongwu confessed to a crime that had been troubling him—the rape of an enemy's concubine at the fall of the city of Wuchang. He pointed to it as his sole transgression in the fourteen years he had fought to free China, and mused about his motivation. In an attempt at penance, he claimed that he had "done away with music, beautiful girls and valuable objects," in an attempt to live an ascetic lifestyle. He was determined, he wrote, to be a better person, rather than "a success in the morning and a failure in the evening," and he demanded that his officials follow his example, avoiding corruption, adhering to the laws, being severe in punishments and fearless in doing what was right. He personally wrote the preface to *The August Ming Ancestral Instruction* (1373), a guidebook in thirteen chapters to managing his state, pushing for personal austerity, adherence to ritual, tips on managing the imperial household, and an I-Spy list of misdeeds, treachery and trouble-makers. These were all noble sentiments, but since Hongwu himself often changed his mind on matters of policy, many a loyal minister found himself on the Emperor's bad side.

If Hongwu had been hoping to wipe out Mongol influence, he missed a vital element within his own family. Predeceased by his eldest son, he nominated his grandson as his heir, much to the annoyance of his surviving sons. It was fitting, in native Chinese tradition, for the eldest son of the eldest son to carry on the line. But for a generation of nobles reared amid nomad-influenced fraternal competition, it was unacceptable.

Hongwu's short-lived successor, the Jianwen Emperor (r. 1398–1402) had just reached adulthood shortly before his coronation, inculcated with precisely the kind of gravitas that the Hongwu Emperor had hoped for.

Perhaps he even surpassed his grandfather in the spirit, rather than the letter of the law, since he began his reign by pardoning many subjects who had been caught up in Hongwu's vindictive campaigns. Taking the advice of Confucian ministers, he took steps to limit the power of the eunuchs in the palace, and made it clear to his uncles that he had the power to strip them of their titles and powers if they failed to obey him.

Jianwen may have been imitating the reforms of the early Han dynasty, when emperors with a shaky power-base had appointed relatives to far-flung provincial responsibilities, chipping away at their local autonomy once the coast was clear. But if that were Jianwen's intention, he moved too soon. His uncles were still smarting at being passed over in the succession, and one was particularly proactive, co-opting control of the army garrisoned in the north for the Mongol campaigns, and marching on the capital, Nanjing.

It was an embarrassing end to the grand plans of the Ming's founder. The rebel proclaimed that he had been a loyal subject, coming to rescue his nephew from an attempted coup, but that the youth had unfortunately burned to death in his own palace. Within four days of this unfortunate accident, the uncle proclaimed himself to be the new ruler, the Yongle Emperor (r. 1402–1424). He soon began tinkering with the official story, erasing the Jianwen Emperor from official chronicles as if his reign had never happened—for many years to come, the Yongle Emperor would be falsely described as the "second" ruler of the Ming dynasty, as if he had been the heir all along. Fearing reprisals and conspiracies, the Yongle Emperor also moved his capital in 1403, back to the northern frontier where he had been based for his skirmishes with the Mongols—it is for this reason, the ongoing Mongol threat and the aftermath of Yongle's coup, that the capital of China ended up in Beijing, far from the country's actual geographic or demographic center.

Foreign influences were quelled. The country's remaining Muslims and other non-Han were strongly urged to dress and act like the Chinese. Expats who knew what was good for them adopted Chinese names and kept their heads low. A century of *semuren* in power was swiftly eroded by the reinstatement of the old-fashioned civil service exams—the very nature of the Confucian classics, requiring intimate knowledge of old-time Chinese and poetic allusions, was sure to squeeze any non-Chinese out of the administration.

The rebellious beginning and fractious early days of the Ming dynasty ensured that it maintained a military footing. There were pockets of Yuan loyalists to be mopped up in the south, and Yuan acquisitions (Tibet, Yunnan, and Dai Viet, what is now northern Vietnam) that needed to be prevented from seceding. Of these three, Dai Viet successfully wriggled free—Yongle's occupation force overthrew an independence-minded usurper, and pursued a successful scorched-earth policy to wipe out non-Chinese books, printing blocks and inscriptions. But the local resistance was intractable, and the Ming dynasty would grudgingly recognize the independence of the region by the mid-1400s.

The threat of the Mongols' return *en masse* would steer much Ming foreign policy. The early Ming enjoyed a climate dividend, as desertification in Mongolia reversed between 1380 and 1450, making the Mongols less likely to push out of their homeland in search of better pastures. The Chinese weren't to know, however, and so the dynasty as a whole saw five major campaigns launched north against the enemy, and the strengthening of border defenses into that most iconic of Chinese creations, the Great Wall. There had been many walls before it, but it is the Ming version that stretches for the greatest distance, and is most often pictured today. Such a huge enterprise required substantial manpower, plunging Ming China not only into building works on the frontier, but the vast industrial operation required to make the bricks and mortar required, creating an entire line of secondary towns below the wall itself. Staffing the wall would also be a factor in encouraging the Ming to cast aside the former policy of hiring mercenary troops, and creating instead a permanent, *hereditary* army. Many of the watchtowers on the Wall are named for specific families after soldiers were permitted to move there with their wives.

Ming expansion moved elsewhere in a concerted effort by its early emperors to carry news of China's resurgence to faraway places. A series of missions along the rivers of Manchuria carried news of the Ming foundation to the remnants of the Jurchens and their fellow tribes, pushing the borders of China further north than they had ever been before, to the Siberian coast.

However, the most famous of the Ming's public-relations voyages were the seven expeditions across the Indian Ocean, chiefly led by the admiral Zheng He (1371–1433). The Mongol era had left the Chinese more aware of the extent of the world that was not under direct suzerainty, and Zheng's mission was to display Chinese pomp and military might as far afield as possible, inviting tribute and diplomatic submission from all the kingdoms of the West.

Zheng He has become the poster boy of the early Ming era—a descendant of the much-loved Muslim governor of Yunnan, his grandfather and father both appear to have made pilgrimages to Mecca. Captured at the fall of Yuan-era Yunnan, the 10-year-old boy was castrated and given as a slave to the prince who would become the Yongle Emperor. Growing to an imposing height, he ended up as one of Yongle's soldiers, and received the surname Zheng in imperial thanks after he led the defense of Beijing's Zhenglunba reservoir during Yongle's grab for power—his surname until then had been the common Chinese Muslim designation Ma, derived from the first syllable of Mohammed.

Zheng He's first voyage, from 1405–07, took his fleet from Fujian, along the coast of Indochina, past Java and into the Indian Ocean. Several further voyages, each of them commenced only a few months after the previous one, lasted two years apiece, a veritable bus service for tributary nations to send ambassadors, gifts and diplomatic communiqués, reports on their countries and requests for aid in local disputes or against pirates. On several occasions, Zheng's fleet undertook military action, although the main contribution of the missions was surely a regular, recurrent appearance in local waters by the Chinese fleet, either on its outward journey or on the way back. Although the voyages were not described in such terms, we might easily compare them to later Christian missionary endeavors heading the other way. By spreading Chinese culture far and wide, the Treasure Fleets were at least partly an exercise in what we might call Confucian outreach, offering foreign kingdoms the chance to become part of the Chinese world, theoretically starting the long process of acculturation that might let them become true subjects of the Emperor.

In 1414, Zheng He returned with a treasure prized more than any gemstone or gold ingot—a giraffe, originally sent to Bengal by the ruler of the African coastal state of Malindi, and brought aboard the fleet when one of its breakaway flotillas called in on the Indian coast.

It was an unprecedented sight in China, and celebrated by poets and minstrels for having "the body of a deer and the tail of an ox, boneless horns, with luminous spots like red clouds or a purple mist, its hooves do not tread on [living] beings and in its wanderings it carefully selects its ground." This strange, gentle creature, with its timid gait and towering height was surely a *qilin*—one of the fabled unicorn creatures last seen at the time of Confucius, and hence thought to herald the beginning of a Golden Age. Several more giraffes would be scooped up on Ming voyages, along with zebras that were lauded as "heavenly horses" and many other strange creatures to fill Yongle's menagerie. The construction work on Beijing was nearing completion; the city had been stocked with new residents and prepared with new public buildings and thoroughfares. The Grand Canal was back up and running. Safe in the knowledge that Heaven itself had blessed his regime, Yongle took up residence in the capital he had been awaiting for a decade, Beijing.

Unsurprisingly, the fifth voyage, undertaken in 1416, and the sixth in 1421 sent Zheng's fleet even further afield, to Africa itself, in search of the so-called *qilin*'s homeland in Hormuz, Mogadishu and Malindi. It would, however, be the last voyage for a while, as Yongle diverted expenses into his campaigns against the Mongols. Yongle died in 1424, and his son authorized only one further voyage, in 1431, once again as far as Hormuz, and with a breakaway flotilla putting men ashore at Jeddah, in order to travel inland to Mecca. Zheng He's seventh voyage arrived with envoys from eleven foreign countries, although the emissaries would need to make their own travel arrangements for the return trip, as there would be no more Treasure Fleets.

The Ming government did not suddenly identify the Treasure Fleets as a waste of money—Yongle had been winding them down even in his lifetime. Possibly, there were diminishing returns now that initial contacts were established, private traders could take up the slack, and the novelty of the exotic animals and artifacts had worn off. At least part of the original rationale for the voyages was to put on a show of looking for Yongle's "lost" nephew, supposedly burned in his palace in Nanjing, but still the subject of a pious performance from the man who had usurped his throne. If so, such a show was simply no longer necessary after the death of Yongle in 1424.

By the 1430s the Ming dynasty's heyday was at an end. Cash was running low after a generation of Mongol skirmishes and the failed invasion of Dai Viet. China could not expand indefinitely; Confucian officials in the capital counseled a more austere, inwardly-focused regime. It is likely that the recognition of Dai Viet's independence and the cancellation of further Treasure Fleet voyages were part of the same cutbacks.

The world was still in its Little Ice Age; 1433 saw the return of cold weather severe enough to cause crop failure, famine and diseases for two years. A second dip in temperatures in 1437 gave way to repeated floods until 1448. Timothy Brook describes the first half of the 1450s as a "full-blown ecological crisis"—the return of cold weather in 1450s Mongolia pushed the Mongols south, and increased the risk of frontier conflicts.

The collapse of the Ming government's interest in the maritime world has forever colored our understanding of maritime China. The great treasure ships of Zheng He's day were left to rot, their shipyards repurposed, even the know-how of their construction fading from general knowledge. While sea-borne trade went on, it became increasingly underhand and off-the-books. Maritime trade would continue in the shadows, but from the 1450s, it was not undertaken with government support or sanction. Instead, the Chinese empire retreated into a siege mentality, literally walling off its northern border, determined to cling to what it had, instead of striking out in search of more. We might even say that, in big-data terms, the whole Ming dynasty saw much of officialdom's attention misdirected—as in the days of the split of the Southern Song, China below the Yangtze continued to prosper, while its northern half shriveled. Yongle's relocation of the capital of China to Beijing would constantly pull the focus of Chinese government away from the south, where business was booming, and concentrate it on endless pushing and shoving across an arid frontier. Although many would become millionaires in the black economy of the south, the government's refusal to interfere in trade deprived the Ming of the kind of revenues that could have sustained the dynasty for centuries. "Rivers and lakes" (*jiang-hu*), originally a catch-all phrase for the trade routes of the Yangtze delta and hinterland, transformed into a term for the real, material world, as opposed to the misplaced interests of the authorities.

Both the northern borders and the maritime coasts would provide Ming China with its two lengthiest and irresolvable conflicts. The former reached its crisis point in 1449, when, heralding bad weather conditions that were only just starting to make themselves felt further south, Mongols under the leader Esen Taiyisi invaded China. Repudiating bribes from the Ming dynasty that had kept them at bay for a number of years, Esen's Mongols attacked at three separate points along the Chinese border. The young Zhengtong Emperor (r. 1435–49, 1457–64), Yongle's great-grandson, had only just reached the age of majority, and unwisely twisted free from the influence of the regents who had managed his state during his teenage years. Believing instead the counsel of new, eunuch advisers, Zhengtong decided that he would personally lead the Chinese army that went out to deal with the Mongol threat. Over-extended and over-exposed out in the steppes, Zhengtong's army began a tardy tactical withdrawal, only to be ambushed. It was one the most embarrassing defeats in Chinese history, not only because half a million Chinese soldiers had been outclassed by a mere 20,000 Mongol horsemen, but because Zhengtong was taken prisoner.

Timothy Brook notes that a nursery rhyme from the era neatly encapsulates the tense relationship between weather and politics. After over a decade of drought, it first seems like a simple prayer for rain, to the gods of the city and of the earth. However, a little punning leeway, and it suddenly becomes an arch commentary on the succession crisis caused by the loss of the Zhengtong Emperor, and the hasty appointment of his brother as an interim sovereign:

> Raindrop, Raindrop (or: *Gave his brother, Gave his brother*) […]
> If the rain comes back again (*If the emperor comes back again*)
> Thank Earth God for bringing rain (*He'll have to hand it back again*)

The appointment of a new emperor at least made it clear that China would not be negotiating over the return of the captured sovereign. Esen handed Zhengtong back after a year, plunging Beijing into a new crisis, because his brother was already installed on the throne. Consequently, Zhengtong spent several unhappy years under house arrest in the Forbidden City, while his brother struggled through the fourth of the Nine Sloughs, regarded by many of his subjects as signs of Heaven's displeasure. It was only in 1457, after more terrible weather, disease, and the enveloping of Beijing in a choking dust-storm, that a coalition of palace officials took action. With Zhengtong's brother too ill to attend the court ceremonies on the first day of the Chinese New Year, a pro-Zhengtong faction reinstalled him on the throne, under the new name of Tianshun (Obeying Heaven's Will). The brother died soon after, possibly murdered, and the restored Emperor added insult to injury by refusing to bury him with imperial honors with the rest of his ancestors.

The unpleasant story might have ended there, were it not for the Tianshun Emperor's own overwhelming shame at dragging his country into such a situation in the first place. He seems to have found it unbearable living among the ministers who had been prepared to consider overthrowing his brother, and soon hounded them all out of office in a series of putsches that, if anything, only ruined his reputation all the more.

Meanwhile, China's grain harvests and local mercantile transport remained safe on the rivers and canals, but the coasts could all too easily become vulnerable to predatory attacks by a different kind of wandering enemy. Shortly after the fifth of the Nine Sloughs—a carnival of disasters from 1516–19 including cold spells, epidemics of disease, famine and earthquakes—the coastal raids hit their peak. Throughout the Ming dynasty, the Chinese coast was subject to attacks by "Japanese pirates," fleeing unrest and deprivation on their native islands and turning to crime on a foreign shore.

That, at least, was the official story. While there are many cases of Japanese fishermen and traders turning to illegal means to sustain themselves in troubled times, the readiness of the Chinese to write them all off as "Japanese pirates" served other purposes. It was helpful to blame China's new coastal problems on foreigners, and not on, say, Chinese fisher-folk driven to desperation by the same bad conditions. And it was certainly helpful for the Chinese, as the severed head of a "Japanese pirate" brought a higher reward from the authorities than that of a mere Chinese one. Japanese pirates hence got the blame for a number of incidents that smarter observers might have suspected to be signs of more local problems. In 1551, the Ming government tried to make the problem go away by decree, not merely outlawing foreign trade, but even forbidding fishing boats from leaving port. By 1554, the "pirate" problem transformed again, with coastal raiders establishing fortified bases on Chinese shores, from which they advanced in concerted military operation, with soldiers, artillery and cavalry that advanced as far inland as Nanjing. Such hosts, not dissimilar from Viking war-bands in medieval England, were multiracial coalitions, including genuine Japanese, alongside other, unspecified foreign adventurers, out-of-work mercenaries, and local Chinese toughs.

The pirate problem would only truly subside in the 1560s, although in one final irony, the Chinese then had to deal with a new bandit problem in the area, after local paramilitaries, recruited to fight the pirates, turned

CHAPTER 7

to crime after they were disbanded in lean times. The last of the pirates drifted south into Fujian, where many of them were dispelled by the simple expedient of allowing them to become legal traders once more. Watchtowers on the coast maintained a better control not only on the pirate problem, but on the local population that might offer aid to them in times of strife. Meanwhile, the Chinese had acquired sufficient supplies of the matchlock guns that may have given the early pirates a technological advantage. Far to the south, a deal struck with the Portuguese allowing trade a southern port, also offered a legal outlet for those sea-faring Japanese visitors who wished to buy and sell Chinese goods—legalizing the activities of some sailors who had previously been written off as smugglers.

However, as any reader familiar with Japanese history might have already observed, the sudden cessation of the Japanese pirate problem masks the fact that Japan in the 16th century was plunged into decades of civil war. There was hence ample opportunity for plunder and privateering in Japan, reducing the number of sailors looking for trouble further afield. While China congratulated itself over dealing with the Japanese pirate problem in the 1570s, it returned, rebranded in 1592, when a Japan newly united under the warlord Hideyoshi would deal with its surfeit of samurai by ordering them all to invade Korea. Far from giving up on China, the Japanese returned in their thousands—the invasion of Korea had been intended by Hideyoshi as the first stage of a full-scale assault on China itself, although it never got that far, and the Japanese were gone by the turn of the century after Hideyoshi's death in 1598.

Although Ming China was left intact, the whole sorry affair was a firm challenge to the military might that had been projected far and wide by the dynasty in its earlier days. The rulers of the mid-Ming period did not help a whole lot. The Zhengde Emperor (r. 1505–21) lived an oddly profligate life, kept a massive harem but failed to sire any surviving children on his wives and concubines, and openly cavorted with male lovers. He was not the first Chinese emperor, by any means, to be homosexual or bisexual, but he was so hated by his successors that palace diaries that might have otherwise been more discreet made much of the male bedmates who "slept and rose with the emperor." Many odd stories accompany the reign of the Zhengde Emperor, including the allegation that he had a penchant for Muslim girls, to the extent that he once issued an edict against the use of pork, prompting palace gossip to briefly believe that he

*198*

had converted. He also developed a habit of disguising himself as a commoner, not only in elaborate palace games in which he forced his courtiers to dress up as townsfolk and re-enact marketplace life, but in expeditions out into his realm, where he would inevitably cause trouble by trying to kidnap someone's wife. His most prolonged excursion involved his adoption of the pseudonym Zhu Shou, quitting his imperial duties, and leading a Chinese army in a military campaign against the Mongols.

When he died in 1521, from an infection picked up from the Grand Canal, into which he had fallen during one of his drunken adventures, he left no heir, plunging the realm into a succession crisis.

To be fair, all that his young cousin, the Jiajing Emperor (r. 1521–67) had to do was agree that he had been "adopted" as the late Emperor's brother. Unfortunately, in a harbinger of a bloody-minded and difficult reign to come, the 14-year-old Jiajing Emperor did no such thing, immediately insisting that he wanted to elevate his deceased biological father to the rank of Emperor instead. That way, he argued, he would not be betraying his natural father, but he would also be legitimately inheriting the throne from a dead, uncrowned but backdated Emperor. It might sound like a minor issue of protocol, but it left the courtiers fumbling for excuses to deny it. Two of Zhengde's own relatives had mounted rebellions against him, and China could ill afford any further challenges by other cousins. The Jiajing Emperor's proposal risked making it easy for a usurper to legitimize himself after the fact by posthumously promoting his ancestors until they were suitably high-ranking.

The matter became known as the Great Ritual Controversy, and arguments about it would continue for years, until several hundred ministers tried to force Jiajing's hand by staging a mass protest in 1524. Jiajing used it as an excuse to purge the court of many of Zhengde's cronies and supporters, but by then he had new problems.

Jiajing was having trouble siring an heir of his own. He turned increasingly to Daoist remedies, relying on esoteric medicine men and sorcerers to help him find the right aphrodisiacs and fertility potions. Popular rumors of the time suggested that his palace was infested with Dark Afflictions (*heisheng*)—shadowy creatures that preyed on human beings, until they were believed to have been dispelled by a Daoist exorcist who spat amulet-water onto a ceremonial sword. Such priests stuck around to help Jiajing with his infertility problems, pushing him into a bed-hopping routine that paired him up with a succession of increasingly young girls.

A decade after he came to the throne, Jiajing's breeding program finally bore fruit, not with his empress, but with several of his concubines delivering children. Few of the offspring, however, survived to adulthood, accentuating an already tense situation within the palace that escalated in a sudden incident during a lecture about *The Book of Songs*. Jiajing's first wife, Empress Chen, had only been appointed to that role because of family connections (her aunt had been the previous emperor's mother), and lived in a state of simmering resentment and recriminations with her imperial husband. While two consorts prepared tea for the Jiajing Emperor, Empress Chen flew into a rage at the sight of her husband staring at their delicate hands. The couple had a monstrous fight, after which the pregnant Empress lost her child.

Both of the consorts present would replace the Empress in turn, the first for only a few years before she was demoted for unknown reasons. The second became Empress Fang, the woman who would rush to Jiajing's rescue in 1542, when sixteen of his concubines tried to murder him. Empress Fang's actions in the immediate aftermath ensured that none of the girls survived to tell their side of the story, and nor did Jiajing's favorite, Consort Duan, who was executed because the attack happened in her quarters.

The years that followed the concubines' revolt were widely interpreted as a sign of Heaven's displeasure. The sixth of the Nine Sloughs, three years of famine and disease, hit China from 1544–46. Asides in contemporary accounts suggest that Jiajing was often irascible and physically abusive. Two hundred of his palace women died during his reign, often in beatings dished out for displeasing him. One Ming chronicler could not resist alluding to the Great Ritual Controversy, making the unlikely claim that Jiajing's bad behavior was the result of simple exhaustion, caused by the doubled effort of having to pray to two separate groups of ancestors.

But Jiajing does not appear to have been swayed by weather or rebellion, and his early interest in fertility treatments also developed in later years into an obsession with the alchemy of immortality. He pursued a number of crazy schemes in that regard, including spending a time eating only from silverware, which was supposed to help prolong his life. Even his own courtiers regarded some of the practices as hokum, but none dared protest after a minister was executed for voicing his suspicions. Accordingly, there was nobody on hand to prevent his Daoist advisers prescribing a series of potentially dangerous elixirs that affected his health and sanity. There remains some confusion in the historical record about the precise ingredients. White arsenic (arsenic trioxide) and red lead (lead tetroxide) were two of the poisonous substances that hastened his end, although the latter has been garbled in some accounts with the magical substance "Heavenly Innate Cinnabar" (*xiantian dantian*), a supposedly magical essence that could only be procured from young girls after their first menstruation. In the 1550s, he would recruit almost 500 new preteen girls as his new consorts in waiting. As he grew older, and his desperation to hold off mortality with sex-magic increased, he ignored the elaborate protocols and registrations of his bedmates, and was known to force himself upon his palace women whenever the mood took him. Insomniac since 1560, and subject to violent mood-swings and diminished mental capacity by 1565, he wasted away for a year.

Only one of his officials dared to stand up to him—Hai Rui (1514–87), a junior revenue minister who submitted a memorial criticizing his failures. Legend has it that Hai Rui bought himself a coffin and said goodbye to his family before sending his report, which ridiculed Jiajing's immortality program as being no more helpful than "trying to stop the wind or catch a shadow." Hai Rui pleaded with his addled Emperor to wake up to his imperial duties, alluding to the possibility that Jiajing's seclusion had led to him being misinformed by his courtiers. "It has already been some time," he wrote, "since the people under Heaven started to regard Your Majesty as unworthy."

After months of waiting for an answer, Hai Rui was sentenced to death for his impertinence, although fate handed him a reprieve. The Jiajing Emperor died in early 1567, leading to a pardon for his loyal opposition. Eleven years later, a Chinese doctor would publish the *Compendium of Materia Medica* (*Bencao Gangmu*) identifying poisoning from immortality elixirs as a substantial contribution to the deaths of many emperors.

Jiajing's death transformed Hai Rui's reputation. For much of his career Hai Rui had been regarded as something of a stuffy eccentric, with unwelcome progressive ideas such as favoring the poor in cases against the rich. In an age when old-school Confucianism was something of a joke, Hai Rui had been its most notorious stickler, clinging unrealistically to the more naïve ideals of the ancient sages. Now, suddenly, he had become the daring minister who had risked his life by speaking truth to power.

The Jiajing Emperor's son, the Longqing Emperor (r. 1567–72) had little choice but to reinstate and promote the outspoken official, packing him off to Nanjing to keep him out of trouble. Inevitably, Hai Rui rocked the boat, protesting that he had been given a meaningless post with no real responsibility, and that he might as well be allowed to retire. Rattled personnel managers in Beijing gave him something to get his teeth into—a governorship in the merchant town of Suzhou, where Hai Rui soon annoyed the locals by imposing a harsh austerity drive and clamping down on interest rates. This put him into conflict with local loan sharks, who complained that his reforms, far from defending the poor and downtrodden, were actually encouraging legions of chancers to come out of the shadows and persecute the rich. Impeached for encouraging the very corruption he was fighting, and accused in a whispering campaign of murdering at least one of his wives, he would resign in defeat in 1570, declaring that the Beijing court were "a bunch of women."

The Longqing Emperor had inherited an empire suffering from years of neglect and mismanagement, ill-suited to cope with continuing pressures from nomad peoples to the north, and sea raiders on the coast. His own son, the Wanli Emperor (1572–1620) similarly struggled to deal with declining finances and a moribund administration. He even called the aging Hai Rui out of retirement to help clean things up, but China's most cantankerous official could not resist creating a fuss. Wryly observing that he doubted he could drag his imperial master away from women and horses for long enough to make a difference, he sent a memorial urging Wanli to reinstate the harsh death and torture penalties for corruption that had previously been in place during the reign of the first Ming Emperor. His enemies at the court were swift to discredit him, and Wanli himself concocted the ultimate punishment to silence the eternal critic. Hai Rui was side-lined into a powerless posting from which Wanli repeatedly refused to allow him to resign, which both kept him from making trouble and prevented the disastrous optics of the incorruptible minister leaving another administration. It was the ultimate bureaucratic exile, and Hai Rui would die in office in 1587, after seven unsuccessful attempts to quit.

For centuries, the vast distances of Central Asia had kept Chinese and European contacts to a bare minimum. The Ming dynasty arose at the dawn of Europe's "Age of Discovery," as explorers from Spain and Portugal ventured out into the seas in search of new conquests and opportunities.

By 1522, the year in which Ming dynasty officials first acquired and began copying Portuguese-designed cannons, Portuguese sailors completed the first circumnavigation of the globe. In 1543, during the aftermath of the concubines' assassination attempt against Jiajing, Portuguese sailors came ashore at Tanegashima in Japan, introducing the warring samurai clans to the matchlock gun. In 1557, two years after Jiajing's agents brought 160 prepubescent girls to his palace to serve in his immortality rituals, the Portuguese were granted the right to live and trade in Macau, a port settlement as far from the heart of China as it was possible to be. In 1573, two Spanish galleons, heavily laden with silk and porcelain from China, sailed from the Philippines to Acapulco, initiating a century of fruitful cross-Pacific trade with the New World. Commodities reaching China by return included Mexican silver, but also new crops—the chili, which would revolutionize Chinese cookery; tobacco, which created a whole new vice, and the sweet potato, a new staple that saved millions of lives in the famine-prone south. In 1570, shortly after Jiajing's death, the first Jesuit schools in Macau began training missionaries in the Chinese language, hoping to carry Christianity to the people of China.

The Ten Commandments were translated into Chinese in 1579, by a missionary who saw the potential for introducing Christianity as a moral philosophy like the teachings of Confucius. In 1584, a larger work introducing Christian themes was also published in Chinese, under the title *The True Record of the Lord of Heaven* (*Tianzhu Shiliao*). However, although these works found a small and growing group of converts among some of the Ming aristocracy, they had a lot of competition from other works to distract, inform and entertain the Chinese people. The sheer size of the Ming publishing industry helped ensure that more of its books survived, creating several of its enduring classics of literature. Although the books have stood the test of time, their authors are often difficult to wholly attribute—some of the men claimed as the authors of China's classics may have been collators, editors or amanuenses for other authors. Regardless, the Ming dynasty produced some of China's more famous works of fiction, including *Journey to the West* (*Xiyouji*, 1592), attributed to Wu Cheng-en, a struggling scholar from Jiangsu. A fictionalized account of the travels of the Tang-dynasty monk Tripitaka, it is most-loved in China for its supporting cast of Tripitaka's supernatural servants—Sandy the water spirit, Pigsy the bawdy pig-man, and Sun Wukong, the Monkey King. The tale is deeply invested in social satire and considerations of Buddhist belief, but has endured for so long because none of that matters if you are a seven-year-old child watching a puppet show, or in more modern times, a cartoon, in which a monkey with a stick beats up a gang of demons. *Journey to the West* is a perennial favorite not only with Chinese children, but with storytellers in multiple media who know it is well-known enough not to rock the boat with investors or censors.

An even older series of stories would form more adult reading in the Ming dynasty—Luo Guanzhong's retelling of and expansion upon multiple legends from the era of the collapsing Han dynasty, and the three-way civil war that ensued. His *Romance of the Three Kingdoms* (*San Guo Zhi*, 1522) was intended as something of a corrective to a growing body of spurious plays and apocrypha about the fall of the Han, and successfully made literary heroes of its scheming warlords.

Also very loosely based on true events in a previous dynasty was *The Water Margin* (*Shuihu Zhuan*, c. 1589). This book was attributed to the same Luo Guanzhong, although it was widely believed that he had merely refashioned preexisting tales more than a century old. A tale of rebellion and injustice safely situated in the Song-era past, it includes the life stories of 108 outlaws who hide in the titular wasteland—the marshes of Liang Mountain—to resist corruption in a failing dynasty. A lively, colorful cast of characters, each with a bunch of dramatic anecdotes to tell and vendettas to pursue, it similarly formed the inspiration for many subsequent plays and stories. The survivors are eventually pardoned by the Huizong Emperor, in time to lead a resistance against the invading Khitans from the north, a historical resonance that would lead it to be placed on a list of banned books 200 years later, when the Khitans' distant cousins became the rulers of China once more. But both of the books attributed to Luo were regarded as potentially dangerous—his stories of earnest young rebels were a bewitching distraction for idealistic youth, while his tales of warlord intrigues were thought to be catnip for bitter old officials. Luo's books became the source of many enduring Chinese proverbs, including one about the books themselves: "*Don't let the young read The Water Margin. Don't let the old read Romance of the Three Kingdoms.*"

Another of the enduring classics of Ming literature ostensibly began as *Water Margin* fan fiction, elaborating on the backstory of a minor adversary whose main role in the original is to be killed in revenge for murdering a hero's brother. In *The Plum in the Golden Vase* (*Jin Ping Mei*, 1610) a femme fatale kills off her husband and joins the household of her lover, where she is plunged into the elaborate intrigues, jealousies and spats one might expect in a world where a husband is obliged to juggle six bed-mates. With some 72 different sexual acts described in its pages, it became something of an erotic classic, and was often the subject of censorious crackdowns.

But these are only the most widely known of Ming publications. The era saw a booming industry in cookbooks, architecture manuals, guides to *feng shui* and martial arts, books on home improvement and management. Although the aforementioned classics are the ones that get the most attention by literary historians, the Ming dynasty also saw a remarkable flowering in writing by women, mainly in the Yangtze delta region, near the Suzhou-Hangzhou conurbation. The flood of Ming-era publishing had inundated the wealthy families of the Yangtze delta with biographies of exemplary women and guides to proper comportment, initially written by men. But the enthusiastic lady readers of the region continued to search for new books, becoming the market for a new boom in fiction, poetry and romance. Some of these works were written by women themselves, including the playwright Ye Xiaowan's garden musings on the death of her sisters: "The fragrant flowers stab the eyes under bright and sunny skies," she wrote. "This lovely scenery offers me nothing but sorrow for company."

Around the same time, merchant widow Gu Ruopu wrote a powerful, polemic essay about her own self-education, arguing that her maternal duties to raise her children well obliged her to learn the Confucian classics and *The Book of History*. In answer to conservative ridicule, she wrote a poetic rebuttal, defending her right to read, to help her turn her children into better people: "I am ashamed of my own ignorance... And yet, I feel pity for those of today / Who worry about their looks and pretty clothes... It is through study that children are molded."

The period affords us access to writings by women of other classes, not with words put in their mouths by men, but writing for themselves. Liang Xiaoyu, for example, was a courtesan who wrote plays and poetry about intimate elements of women's experience. "The flowing cinnabar is fully expressed," commented one critic, alluding to her visceral accounts of lust and love, including a poem about an ancient kingdom-wrecker, which pleaded for the male-run state to take the blame for its own failings, and not to lay them at the door of an unfortunate concubine.

Subjects of the Ming dynasty were aware that something was going wrong. Even in the prosperous south, among the Yangtze literati, writers alluded to Heaven's displeasure and a thinning of moral conduct. Zhang Yingyu's *A New Book for Foiling Swindlers: Based on Worldly Experience* (1617) gave 84 examples of scams and con-tricks run by the gangsters and crooks of the "rivers and lakes"—the poetic geography of the Yangtze mercantile region starting to take on a new meaning. "Worldly" experience now meant temptations and traps –Zhang's *jiang-hu* referred to the sights and smells of a vibrant merchant community, where kind-hearted visitors needed to keep their wits about them if they were not to have their pockets picked, inheritance snatched, or virtue vanished.

Philosophers tried to find a way for contemporary people to do the right thing. In his *Ledger of Merit and Demerit*, Yuan Huang (1533–1606) tried to codify good and bad behavior into a points-based system. Where previous Song-dynasty ledgers had been relatively tame, Yuan's version presented a veritable score card of gamified human living. One hundred points was still awarded for saving someone's life, although this now included preventing infanticide and halting an abortion, and also "ensuring the fidelity of a woman," albeit by indefinite means. There were fifty points for burying an unclaimed corpse or adopting an orphan; five points for dissuading a plaintiff from bringing a court case, and one point for saving the life of an insect.

Yuan's points-based system had good intentions. There were clear leanings in certain directions (vegetarians would score high, for example), but unlike its Daoist inspiration, *The Ledger of Merit and Demerit of the Taiwei Immortal* from the Song dynasty, it was not related to any single religion. In fact, the idea of keeping a ledger of when he was naughty or nice was, Yuan wrote, something recommended to him by a Buddhist priest. The proliferation of scoring demonstrated the diversification of occupations and conditions in an urban society, and new ways in which to define charitable or uncharitable behavior. Such moral books caught on, although their critics pointed out that as mathematical systems, they were open to abuse. The more craven ledger authors were prepared to put a literal price on charity, awarding points based on the estimable worth of donations to charity. A canny ledger-fiddler could, for example, theoretically murder someone on Monday, and then breeze through a marketplace on Tuesday buying and releasing all the caged animals until he made up his quota.

This was surely not in the spirit of good living that the author had intended. The fad for moral ledgers also showed a shift in religious attitudes, away from a concern about how one might be treated in the afterlife, and towards a more Confucian focus on the best way to behave in this one. The more advanced ledgers also began to distinguish between good deeds that cost money and those that did not, leading to a publishing sub-genre in books such as *Meritorious Deeds at No Cost.*

Despite such aspirations for good karma, the Ming dynasty's golden age could not last forever. The Wanli Emperor (r. 1567–1620) presided over renewed wars with the Mongols, the Japanese invasion of Korea, and a tribal rebellion in the south. He had the good luck of an able regent in his youth, and spent his early adulthood as a competent, active monarch, before giving up in the 1600s. Amid ministerial arguments and a prolonged spat about which of his concubines' sons should succeed him, Wanli retreated from palace business, leaving the state rudderless once more. He could not have picked a worse time.

Ming China would fall after over a century of stagnation and decline, its coffers exhausted by wars in Mongolia and Korea, its coast besieged by pirates, its people hammered down by several natural disasters. It fell to invaders from the north that had spent a decade preparing to take over. From a northern palace conceived as a mirror image of Beijing's Forbidden City, they had shadowed the last days of the Ming dynasty, and would arrive at its burning capital, ready to proclaim themselves as the new rulers of All Under Heaven.

In the northeast—*north*, in fact, of the Great Wall that marked the frontier, Chinese settlers in the Liaodong peninsula had run into the Jurchen people once more. United under a strong leader of their own despite officially being a Chinese vassal tribe, the Jurchens built a copy of Beijing's Forbidden City in Mukden (modern Shenyang), with additional outbuildings representing each of the eight "Banners" of their quasi-military state organization. They developed a written script, and in 1616, in the midst of wars against neighboring tribes, the Jurchen leader Nurhaci proclaimed the foundation of a rejuvenated Jin dynasty, recalling the distant past when his ancestors had ruled all of China north of the Yellow River. Two years later, Nurhaci published a list of seven grievances, outlining what he regarded as malicious actions against his people by the Ming dynasty, including territorial violations, political interference and the unjust seizure of lands that were rightfully his.

It would take another generation before the Jurchens would make their move. In the intervening time, they slowly assimilated much of the territory north of the Great Wall, conquering Mongol tribes and Korean vassals. The Chinese colonists north of the Great Wall also defected to the Jurchens, forming ethnically Chinese legions within the growing Banner system. By the 1630s, Nurhaci's son had renamed both his subjects and his dynasty, claiming that the peoples united under the Jurchens were now called the Manchus, and that he was the Emperor of the Qing (Clear/Pure) dynasty. "Manchu" is liable to have been intended to refer to some sort of unity of strength. "Qing," however, is a sign of the Jurchens' increasing understanding of Chinese protocols. If the Ming (Bright) dynasty was made up of the sun and moon, characters associated with the element of fire, then the state fated to replace it would have to be named for the element of water. The word Qing was composed of the characters for "water" and "blue," making it doubly watery, sufficient to quench the doubled fires of the Ming. Now all they needed was to persuade the Chinese in the south that their time had come.

The last legitimate emperor of the Ming dynasty, Chongzhen (r. 1627–44), presided over a period of severe weather fluctuation, interpreted by many as a sign that the Mandate of Heaven had been withdrawn. Matters were already bad in the years before his succession; in 1614–19, for example, the Ming chroniclers described a drought so severe that the land was "burned." The drought did not merely impact society as a whole with reduced crops, higher prices and a rise in starvation and poverty. It hit the country where it hurt, all along the arid expanses of the Great Wall, where the soldier-farmers were expected to grow their own provisions.

On the southern coast, government authority had already declined to the extent that the warlords were in charge. Zheng Zhilong (1604–61), a.k.a. Nicholas Iquan, had fought his way to the top of a maritime organization that eventually claimed some 800 ships. The extent to which the ships were "his" is a matter of interpretation—Iquan controlled enough craft to enforce levies on other traders in the region, license to whom was granted in the form of a Zheng family flag to fly from their ships. This inevitably enmeshed dozens of other captains into the Zheng family's interests and trade routes, obliging them to help in the policing and recruitment of rival sailors. The Zheng "family" in fact, included Iquan himself,

**THE TEMPLE OF HEAVEN** The Temple of Heaven in Beijing, built by the Yongle Emperor of the Ming dynasty (r. 1402–24), but most recently renovated during the reign of the Qianlong Emperor (r. 1735–96) in the Qing dynasty. It remained a site of the highest-level imperial weather and harvest ceremonies until the early twentieth century. *Photo: Kati Clements.*

**FIGHTING FOR THE MASSES** The Red Detachment of Women, one of Jiang Qing's model entertainments that dominated Chinese media during

the Cultural Revolution. It tells the story of guerrilla warfare on the southern island of Hainan. *Photo: National Ballet of China.*

**A WALK IN THE PARK** Soldiers from the People's Liberation Army, on an outing to the Temple of Heaven in Beijing, 2006. The PLA remains the world's largest military force, with over two million active personnel. *Photo: Kati Clements.*

**THE OLD OBSERVATORY** Some of the astronomical instruments at Beijing's Old Observatory, looted by German soldiers during the Boxer Uprising, and returned to China in 1919 as scant compensation for the loss of the entire province of Shandong. *Photo: Kati Clements.*

**EMPIRE OF LIES** The imperial seal of the Japanese puppet state of Manchukuo can still be found in scattered locations around its former capital in Changchun, Jilin. Here it is resplendent on the gates of Puyi's former home, now known as the Palace of the False Emperor. *Photo: Kati Clements.*

**THE MARBLE BOAT**  A marble lakeside pavilion in the shape of a steamboat, built in 1893 for Empress Dowager Cixi at the New Summer Palace to divert her from real-world issues, using money that might have been better spent on the Chinese navy. Cixi has become the scapegoat for the Manchu elite that refused to address threats to their power until it was too late. *Photo: Kati Clements.*

**CARVING CHINA UP**
"China, the cake of kings... and of emperors." An 1898 cartoon from *Le Petit Journal*, in which caricatures of Britain's Queen Victoria, Germany's Kaiser Wilhelm II, Tsar Nicholas II of Russia, "Marianne" the personification of France, and a samurai (presumably intended to represent Japan's Emperor Meiji) squabble over the partition of China. *Photo: Bibliothèque Nationale de France.*

**MAKING CHANGE?** Ghost money, intended to be burned in ceremonial respect for one's ancestors, endures today despite the opposition of the People's Republic of China to superstition. This 10-million yuan note from the "Bank of Hell" bears the face of Chairman Mao, just like real Chinese money. *Photo: Jonathan Clements.*

**TOOLS OF THE TRADE** (Above) Brushes on sale on the Street of Calligraphers, Xi'an, Shaanxi. Calligraphy and ink painting became integral to the Chinese arts in the Song dynasty, as exiled Han Chinese clung to new definitions of cultural expression. The stroke order for making a Chinese character with a brush remains a vital component of modern Chinese handwriting recognition software. *Photo: Kati Clements.*

**PRAYER WHEELS** (Left) Buddhist monks walk a corridor of prayer wheels at the Labrang Temple, Xiahe, Gansu. All religions were suppressed during the Cultural Revolution as part of the campaign against the "Four Olds." *Photo: Alicia Noel.*

## THE WEDDING MARCH
(Above) A traditional bridal procession, complete with red palanquin and bearers, navigates the streets of modern Beijing. In the year 2020, China is estimated to have 30 million more marriageable men than women, along with a population raised in the One-Child Policy era, now facing the double burden of supporting their four aging parents and two children. *Photo: Kati Clements.*

## FACING THE FUTURE (Left)
New Year's slogans, traditionally written in golden ink on red paper, lie drying in the sun in Xi'an, Shaanxi. *Photo: Kati Clements.*

**CAPITALISM AT WORK** Wangfujing, the main shopping area in modern Beijing, became the site of many new arrivals from the West during the Deng-era reforms, including China's first McDonald's. *Photo: Kati Clements.*

**THE CARNIVAL OF VALUE** A street performer poses outside the twin golden towers of the Sheraton International Business Center in Chongqing. *Photo: Kati Clements.*

**PILGRIMS AND TOURISTS** (Above) Contemporary visitors in the precincts of the Shaolin Temple, near Luoyang, Henan, famous as a historical center for Chan (Zen) Buddhism, but also as the home of Chinese martial arts. *Photo: Kati Clements.*

**ECHOES OF DIVERSITY** (Left) A replica Miao drum tower peeps above the trees in Beijing's Ethnic Culture Park, founded to celebrate China's 55 recognized ethnic minorities. More than a 100 million Chinese citizens are part of non-Han ethnic groups, such as Mongols, Manchus, Uyghurs and Koreans. *Photo: Kati Clements.*

**GOLDEN IDOLS**  Garish effigies of hippos and Greek gods festoon the staircases and environs of the Sheraton International Business Center in Chongqing—a far cry from Communist austerity and the hero-worship of Mao-era public artworks. *Photo: Kati Clements.*

**GLOBAL MEETS LOCAL**  A Kentucky Fried Chicken restaurant in Urumqi, Xinjiang, features the Uyghur language most prominently on its storefront, with Chinese and Roman lettering confined to the shadows. *Photo: Frederik L. Schodt.*

**SHANGHAI EXPRESS** A Harmony-series high-speed train pulls into a Shanghai station. Bullet trains have become one of the icons of 21st-century China, connecting almost every provincial capital, and forming the largest high-speed rail network in the world, spanning 29,000 kilometers by the end of 2018. *Photo: Kati Clements.*

**CITY OF THE FUTURE** Little more than farmland at the time of Deng Xiaoping's reforms, Shanghai's Pudong district has become a symbol of modern China's meteoric rise. *Photo: Kati Clements.*

**ON YOUR BIKE** Despite the rise in automobile ownership among affluent modern Chinese, rental bicycles from multiple companies are returning to Chinese cities as part of ecological initiatives. *Photo: Kati Clements.*

his biological brothers and cousins, and a bunch of adopted "brothers" as well—one surviving list of his high command includes 22 captains, 15 of whom are Zhengs with animal designations that may have been guild nicknames—Iquan, Zheng *Zhilong* himself, was Zheng *the Dragon*, but his "brothers" included the Panther, the Bear, the Leopard and the Phoenix.

As his Christian alternative name implies, Nicholas Iquan was intimately involved with the multicultural ferment of 17th century coasts. He was baptized as a Catholic in Portuguese Macao, and served his early days with a trading organization in Japan, smuggling goods along the Ryūkyū islands, via Taiwan and into and out of the Fujian coast. He worked as a fixer, agent and sometime interpreter for the Dutch traders, helping them in their rivalry with the Portuguese, and taking their money in a number of power-plays. It is likely that at least part of his rise to prominence in the region was as a puppet of the Dutch, although he happily entertained overtures from the Ming government.

Recognizing him as the de facto ruler of Fujian, a region which he seemed to own more than half of, and the lucrative trade of which was almost entirely under his control, he was "appointed" as an Admiral, turning on his former Dutch allies and chasing them out of Chinese waters. We can see in this the same sort of political brinkmanship that characterized other Chinese dynasties in decline, such as the "shepherds" appointed to run regions of the collapsing Han empire, often in tardy recognition that they were already local warlords.

North China was drought-ridden in the Ming dynasty almost twice as often as in previous eras, but the very worst came in 1641, where the Grand Canal itself ran dry in the summer. Tree-ring data suggests that it may have been the worst drought to hit China in 1,100 years. Storms whipped desert dust into the air, where it returned to earth by falling as red rain, and created eerie, dazzling sunsets. Unexpectedly for anyone following the rise of the Manchus in the north, it was the effect of the weather on conditions within China that would lead to the final collapse of the Ming.

On February 8, 1644, the first day of the Chinese New Year, officials in Beijing arrived at the Forbidden City for a traditional ceremony, only to find the Chongzhen Emperor weeping in his throne room. There was no money left—the Grand Canal had fallen into disrepair; the post rider system had been shut down; worst of all, there was barely enough money in the vaults to pay the soldiers on the Great Wall for another month.

Inspired, to a large extent by the foundation of the Ming dynasty itself, peasant uprisings in hard-hit famine regions coalesced into a challenge to the dynasty. Blaming the Ming administration for harsh taxes and poor disaster relief, several revolts eventually combined to form an army, the eventual leader of which, Li Zicheng (1606–45), an unemployed post rider, proclaimed himself to be the first emperor of yet another new dynasty. Announcing that the Ming dynasty had failed its people, Li's horde roamed over much of the Yellow River floodplain, growing to some 30,000 people, and benefiting, somewhat haphazardly, from the continued damage done to local military response by continued floods and famine.

In April 1644, Li Zicheng's men arrived in Beijing itself and proceeded to sack the impoverished city. The Ming heir apparent was smuggled to safety, but the Chongzhen Emperor fled from the north gate of the Forbidden City to the base of Prospect Hill, where he hanged himself from a tree.

In control of 40,000 troops at the strategic Shanhai Pass, general Wu Sangui (1612–78) was a remnant of the Ming regime stuck between two would-be successors—Li Zicheng's self-proclaimed new dynasty and the Manchus north of the wall. Except they were not necessarily "Manchus"— many of the soldiers Wu would have seen from the battlements were other Chinese, who had grown up in the Liaodong region and accepted the Manchus as the curators of the new Mandate of Heaven. He had remained faithful to the Ming administration, even after it had demoted him in 1641 for losing a battle. Now news drifted in that the Ming dynasty had fallen, and that a glorified postman not only sat on the throne in Beijing, but had raped Wu's own concubine and executed his father.

Wu could march south to retake Beijing, but risk losing the Great Wall frontier to the Manchus. He could pledge allegiance to the rebels, and hence declare the Ming dynasty dead. Instead, he chose a third option. Since he was still loyal to the idea of the Ming dynasty, and Li Zicheng had managed to kill people who were dear to him, Wu Sangui chose to open the gates of the Shanhai Pass and let the Manchu army in.

The Great Wall ceased to function as the Chinese frontier. Wu and his former enemies hounded Li Zicheng's forces out of Beijing and beyond, taking all the cities north of the Yellow River, and heading ever further to the south. The rebels, they proclaimed, were defeated, but the Ming dynasty was dead.

A Manchu child-emperor, Nurhaci's grandson, was proclaimed as the new Son of Heaven amid the ruins of the Forbidden City. The army continued to roll southward. Some battles were won without casualty, as local Chinese accepted the regime change—in such cases, local hierarchies were often left untouched, with just a small garrison of Manchu soldiers left to keep order. Soldiers in such instances were co-opted into the multi-racial Manchu army, and sent on ahead to demand the submission of the next town along.

Some, inevitably, resisted.

# CHAPTER 8

# GREAT ENTERPRISE: THE QING DYNASTY IN ASCENT

**N**obody had to be a hero. That was the message that the Manchus sent ahead of their armies as they marched south. The Ming dynasty had lost the Mandate of Heaven, but the newly declared Qing dynasty was here to fix things. In concert with good soldiers of the old regime, like Wu Sangui, they had come through the Great Wall and chased the rebel usurpers out of Beijing. But the Chongzhen Emperor was dead and there was no point in restoring his ruined regime. Instead, the Qing dynasty would be taking over, and all who acknowledged it would be safe.

Such proclamations made the Qing advance southward remarkably swift. Many of the heralds who rode up to each town were themselves Chinese, former colonists from Liaodong, full of enthusiastic tales about the glorious Manchu regime, or defectors ready to sing the praises of their new masters. At Huai'an, midway between the Yellow and Yangtze rivers, the defending general was offered the choice of fighting to the death or accepting the rank of viscount in the new administration. He took the easy path, and his men switched their flags for the new Qing banners.

The problems started in Yangzhou, a major trading junction on the Grand Canal, center of thriving trades in salt, silk and rice, one-time home of Marco Polo. The garrisons on both approach roads had already switched sides to the Manchus, but that still left the incorruptible Shi Kefa (1601–45) in charge in the town itself. Shi was an officer *and* a gentleman, a Confucian scholar who had served as the Grand Secretary in the Min-

**China During the Qing Dynasty**

Shenyang

Beijing

*Yellow River*

**QING**

*Yangtze River*

Guangzhou

☐ China During the Qing Dynasty
— China's Modern-day Border

istry of War in Nanjing, as well as in canal administration and fiscal policy. He had a habit of speaking unwelcome truths, and wrote to his wife of eighteen years of public service in which he had "tasted every bitterness." He was even in trouble with the Ming resistance, having reprimanded the pretender to the throne about military matters.

Even so, Shi Kefa would not surrender. Letters arrived promising him rich rewards for acknowledging the Qing dynasty. Shi Kefa firmly but politely refused. Fully aware of his arguments with the pretender, Manchu scribes suggested that he surely already knew he was serving a lost, depraved master? Surely it would be better to join forces with the new Manchu order and pursue the true enemy: the rebels. Even now they were fleeing to the west and south; Shi should join the Manchus to chase them.

Eventually, a Chinese turncoat came as close to the battlements as he could and yelled that a name and reward awaited Shi Kefa, only to scurry back under cover as Shi shot at him with an arrow.

The invaders attacked. Yangzhou was well-supplied with small-scale artillery, which killed the attackers in their thousands. Before long, the mound of corpses at the foot of the wall was high enough that the attackers no longer needed siege ladders. With attackers mounting the walls at multiple points, the defenders did not have time to retreat by the stairwells. They leapt from the battlements onto nearby rooftops and their rickety gun platforms, creating a cacophonic clatter as their feet dislodged the tiles.

She Kefa tried to kill himself as the city fell, but was dragged bleeding before the Manchu Prince Dodo, who offered him a noble rank. Still Shi Kefa refused, saying: "I offer you no favor except death." It took three days for Prince Dodo to ascertain that Shi Kefa was not holding out for a better deal, but truly remaining loyal to the lost Ming.

Angrily, Prince Dodo beheaded him, and ordered his troops to make an example of Yangzhou.

The diarist Wang Xiuchu reported multiple fires turning the sky red "like lightning." After locals went into hiding following the first round of atrocities, Chinese and Manchu soldiers lured them out with false promises that anyone who surrendered peacefully would be spared. The women were rounded up and enslaved. The men were killed.

> Babies lay everywhere on the ground. The organs of those trampled like turf under horses' hooves or people's feet were smeared in the dirt, and the crying of those still alive filled the whole outdoors. Every gutter or pond that we passed was filled with corpses, pillowing each other's arms and legs.

Yangzhou's people ceased to exist. The handful of residents who survived the ten days of atrocities that ensued were sold and deported deep into Central Asia. Years later, travellers in Manchuria and Mongolia would report sightings of old slave-women with scarred faces and Yangzhou accents.

$$\odot - \odot - \odot - \odot - \odot$$

The Manchu Prince Dodo, architect of the Yangzhou Massacre, had his reasons. After his troops effortlessly took the city of Nanjing, which surrendered without a fight, he would observe that the Manchus had initially modest ambitions, intending to halt their advance at the Yangtze, reoccupying the same political limits as their Jurchen ancestors in the time of the Southern Song. They had been plotting the invasion of China for a decade, but even they had been surprised by how easily it had fallen.

According to Dodo, there were so few *actual* Manchus in his army, that its advance might have been halted by a single Ming victory in the field. Just one unified response north of the Yangtze, a single sign of true resolve on a battlefield, and the Manchu army might have stumbled, its turncoats deserting, its assertion of the Mandate of Heaven suddenly revoked and handed back to a resurgent Ming. Shi Kefa's resistance had spooked him, and the specter of Ming revival had to be expelled before a counter-attack could come. Yangzhou, he said, had been a necessary evil, a terrorist atrocity to cow the southern cities into submission. It certainly worked at the Yangtze, where the defensive line crumbled, and where Nanjing opened its gates to the Manchus.

It was not, in fact, as easy as all that—it just seemed that way to the Manchus because they were not the ones doing the heavy lifting. What did it matter to the Manchus if their Chinese slave-soldiers died fighting other Chinese? With relatively little risk, and the Ming often putting up a mere token resistance, the Manchu advance continued. But the Manchu conquest of China comes draped with hundreds of stories of noble and ultimately futile Ming loyalty. Round-ups and purges saw multiple beheadings of loyalists and possible candidates for restoration.

As in the last days of the Song, the interests and resources of the retreating dynasty became increasingly maritime in outlook, with the Zheng family, led by Nicholas Iquan, leaping ahead in a series of power vacuums and promotions. Amid a domino-effect of multiple surrenders and defections, the Ming loyalists were soon crammed in Fujian, the mountainous coastal province that was effectively Nicholas Iquan's personal fief. The Manchus in Beijing had proclaimed the Ming dynasty over, and they its worthy successors, but this did not stop the southern resistance from crowning their own Ming pretenders. Their Longwu Emperor (r. 1645–46) enthroned in Fujian by power-brokers who had only recently been outlaws and smugglers, swiftly conferred titles and court positions on anyone who remained prominent in the resistance.

Iquan's nephews and brothers were ennobled, and in a crowd-pleasing move, his 21-year-old son Zheng Chenggong (1624–62), an upstanding, Confucian scholar whose expensive education had made him a stranger to his father, was conferred with the Ming imperial family surname, Zhu. Thereafter, the boy was often known by the title "Knight of the National Name," *Guoxingye*, swiftly garbled in the local dialect to something that sounded more like Koxinga. It amounted, at least in the eyes of a resistance desperate for Iquan's support, to a symbolic adoption, from a ruler whose only biological son had died in infancy.

The Ming pretender was hoping to curry favor with his last loyalists, and to offer hope and inspiration for a counter-attack against the Manchu invaders. However, he had an impossible struggle to cobble together enough resources and manpower to fight the enemy, the frontline troops of whom largely comprised recently defected Ming soldiers. As for the Manchus themselves, they were, and would remain, identifiably different from the Chinese they ruled.

The Italian Jesuit Martino Martini, who encountered Manchus not long after the conquest, observed:

> …their faces are comely, and commonly broad as those of China also have; their color is white, but their nose is not so flat, nor their eyes so little, as the Chineses [*sic*] are; they speak little, and ride pensively. In the rest of their manners they resemble our Tartars of Europe, though they may be nothing so barbarous. They rejoice to see Strangers; they no way like the grimness and sourness of the Chines [*sic*] gravity, and therefore… they appear more human.

Their sleeves, he noted, were drawn together at the forearm and then flared out above the hands, creating an effect not unlike that of a horse's hoof. Horses were hugely important to the nomad conquerors, whose mandated hairstyle involved the shaving of the front of the head, and the gathering of the hair behind in a long plaited, ponytail. This was nothing new; indeed it had been the Jurchen hairstyle for hundreds of years, but the Jurchens had previously backed away from imposing it upon the conquered Chinese. In April 1645, the Manchu regent Prince Dorgon suddenly announced that all Han Chinese men were to shave their heads and plait their queues in the Manchu manner within the next ten days, or face execution for treason.

It may sound callous, so soon after the 80,000 or more deaths at Yangzhou, to describe *this* as the single greatest threat to the Manchu conquest, but the uproar caused by a humble haircut threatened to reignite the Ming resistance. Chinese complained that the Manchu queue was a symbol of enslavement, and a betrayal of the natural hair that all filial Chinese accepted as a gift from their parents. For a number of collaborators in search of an easy life, the haircut directive was a rude awakening.

*"Heaven is high,"* goes the Chinese proverb, *"and the Emperor is far away."* Many had seriously believed that the regime change would amount to little more than a few changes in signage and uniforms, and that life in China would go on much as before. Instead, no Chinese man would be able to do much as look in a mirror without being reminded that they had been subjugated. China was under new management, and the very appearance of the Emperor's subjects would now be altered. Ever after, long and natural hair would be regarded as a symbol of Ming resistance; the shaved head and long plait a signifier of subjection to the Manchus.

But for those who shrugged and decided it was only a haircut, the Manchus proved an irresistible temptation. Nicholas Iquan stalled in Fujian for several months, attempting to persuade the Ming pretender that he should lean on overseas trade and military assistance to bolster his failing regime. When the Manchu army inevitably arrived at the Fujian mountain passes, Iquan switched sides, turning himself in to the Manchus, who promptly made him a Count in the new political order. Iquan, along with his new masters, expected the rest of his family to withdraw their support from the Ming resistance, depriving the Longwu pretender of his army, navy and primary financial support.

However, his son Koxinga fought on. Burning his Confucian scholar's robes in a ritual of preparation for war, the youth wrote a poem outlining his position:

> Though men's hearts may be blind
> The Way of Heaven rewards the true of heart
> If my life must be a game of chess
> I am not afraid of the final move
> Let the people say what they will
> It is not easy to be a dishonest man
> In a distressed and wicked time.

Prominent among the last Ming loyalists, Koxinga is one of the great heroes of Chinese history, claiming to be the chosen one of Mazu, Goddess of the Sea. Charismatic and intensely (some might say naïvely) loyal to the Ming regime, he was the leader of the resistance at 22, and was promoted to prince by the age of 31. Letters arrived from Nicholas Iquan, begging Koxinga to give up on the Ming dynasty, but they reckoned without the youth's passionate sense of justice, and the fact that Iquan's defection was at least partly responsible for the Manchu assault on the Zheng family stronghold, which caused the death of Koxinga's Japanese mother. Drawing on his father's powerful maritime presence, the height of Koxinga's power came in 1659, when he lead a huge ship-borne advance up the River Yangtze, against a Manchu-constructed series of barrages and floating forts called the Boiling River Dragon. He made it as far as Nanjing before he was turned back, fleeing for an offshore stronghold on Taiwan. In order to wipe out his power-base and support network on the mainland, the Manchus depopulated the entire Fujian coast to a distance of nearly 50 kilometers (31.07 miles).

Koxinga's retreat is itself famous for a different reason. Defeated by the Manchus, he nevertheless scored one of China's most important historical victories by ousting the Dutch occupiers of his new redoubt. In defeating the Dutch and banishing them from Taiwan, Koxinga became the first Chinese military leader to defeat a modern European army. His victory has been a matter of some debate ever since—did he defeat the Dutch through clever tactics and bold strategies, or did he simply overwhelm them with superior numbers?

Pockets of resistance, claiming allegiance to the "Southern Ming," held out for two generations. Rather than conquer the far south themselves, the Manchus handed it over to their most prominent turncoats—Wu Sangui himself becoming the overlord of Yunnan, in the name of the Manchus. Other defectors served as the governors of Guangdong and Fujian, the last provinces to fall. It was Wu Sangui, in 1662, who arrested and executed the last Ming pretender in 1662 in Myanmar. The unfortunate man's wife, a Catholic convert, had written in vain to the Pope in Rome, begging for a crusade in China that, she promised, would place her son Zixuan Constantine on the throne as China's first Christian emperor.

Koxinga did not long survive the news of the last pretender's death. He died of malaria at his Taiwanese retreat, although his descendants would cling to the island for two more decades. Ming resistance enjoyed a brief resurgence in 1673 when Wu Sangui and his fellow turncoat warlords began to see that their own days were numbered. Ordered to retire and move to Manchuria, they rose up in revolt to protect their local power-bases, leading Koxinga's son to land an army in Fujian as reinforcements. However, this "Rebellion of the Three Feudatories" was put down, and with it, the last embers of the Ming dynasty. It was the strategic need to wipe out the House of Koxinga that led the Manchus to attack Taiwan in 1683, and hence to incorporate the island for the first time within the political frontiers of China. Shi Lang, the admiral who led the landings on Taiwan, would claim in his reports that he had seen a vision of the Goddess of the Sea, Mazu herself, standing hip-deep in the water, fighting on his side. In thanks to her for conferring blessings on the Manchus, and not the Ming resistance, the Manchu emperor upgraded Mazu to the title she enjoys in many overseas Chinese temples to this day: *Tian Hou*—the Queen of Heaven.

The fall of Taiwan removed the threat of a sea-borne resistance, causing the Manchus to relax maritime prohibitions. In 1684, the Kangxi Emperor (r. 1661–1722) issued an edict lifting the restrictions the Manchus had placed on Chinese overseas:

> Now the whole country is unified, everywhere there is peace and quiet, Manchu-Han relations are fully integrated so I command you to go abroad and trade to show the populous and affluent nature of our rule. By imperial decree, I open the seas to trade.

Kangxi's proclamation put an official seal on preexisting Chinese communities overseas, in the harbors of southeast Asia and the Philippines. Ryūkyū islanders, who by a quirk of diplomacy paid tribute to the emperors of both China and Japan, formed a stealthy trade route between the two countries, even though Japan was supposedly closed to outsiders.

Kangxi's edict freed his subjects to sail further afield—fishing off the Spratly Islands; harvesting sea cucumbers off the coast of Australia; trading with Vietnam and the Philippines; establishing plantations and overseas Chinese communities in Indonesia. What it specifically did not do was open China to foreign traders in return. Despite attempts by several European powers to gain a foothold, the Manchus clung to the arm's-length policy of their predecessors, corralling all foreign traders into a small containment area at the estuary of the Pearl River. The Portuguese traded in Macau; other foreign powers were grudgingly permitted to dock in Guangzhou (Canton) a little upriver.

However, the Manchus were ill-prepared for the arrival of a different group of foreign traders, not in the south, but in the north, on the banks of the Amur River at the edge of Manchuria itself. Russian explorers, settlers and traders had been walking east for decades, and were now investigating the rivers, forest and tundra of Siberia, the frontier of which with Manchuria was undefined.

Trying their luck, the Russians tried to define it themselves, building a fort at Albazin on the banks of the Amur river. Now free of worries about the Ming, the Manchus sent an army to chase the settlers out of Chinese territory—true to their usual policy, putting recently acquired turncoat troops in the front line. Marines evacuated from Taiwan were hence made to prove their loyalty to their new Manchu masters by fighting the Russians in Albazin in 1685. Practically naked, with their large rattan shields on their heads and swords in hands, the soldiers were called "big-capped Tartars" by the Russian defenders, and managed the remarkable feat of defeating the Russians without suffering a single casualty.

Albazin was demolished in 1686, and the Manchus signed the Treaty of Nerchinsk in 1689, defining the border between Manchuria and Siberia. Negotiated in Latin by Jesuit missionaries, the treaty avoided many of the put-downs and epithets directed at "barbarians" by previous Chinese communiqués. Instead, it expressed a hope for further dealings without recourse to violence. The Chinese empire would continue to look down on foreign dealings for another century or more, but in the Treaty of Nerchinsk there are the first whispers of dealing with Europeans on different terms.

It was a victory of sorts for the Chinese—another European nuisance sent packing, although the Russians had other interests further to the east that would occupy them for a century. Eventually, they would colonize Alaska, and the profitable fur trade between "Russia" and China would find a new, even more profitable route by sea, between North America and Guangzhou.

The Manchus, meanwhile, had other interests, to the west. Owing to the escalating and ultimately cataclysmic contacts with Europeans, the history of the Qing dynasty is often told as one of the sea—the Manchus' lack of interest in their own coastal issues and frontiers, and the maritime zone as one of increasing contacts with foreign technology, trade, ideas and corruptions. But the Qing dynasty was also the era that carried China's frontiers to their broadest-ever limits, reaching as far as the Siberian Pacific coast in the east, and encompassing Outer Mongolia, and parts of what is now Russia, Kyrgyzstan and Kazakhstan as far west as Lake Balkash and Lake Baikal. The Manchu policy of turning around their newly surrendered enemy troops and pushing them onto a new frontier war continued long after the conquest of China. Just as troops evacuated from Taiwan fought at Albazin, multi-ethnic bannermen carried Qing rule to Mongolia. Mongols helped the Manchus regain control of the oases of Xinjiang, and a combined Mongol-Uyghur army under a Manchu flag wiped out the Dzungar people at China's western frontier. The Dzungars were the closest that the 17th century came to inheritors of the old nomad empires, a horde of Mongol-Oirat horsemen who extracted tribute from the oases of the Xinjiang desert, and had the unerring habit of supporting anti-Manchu agitators in Tibet. The Manchus were so set on exterminating the Dzungars, over these and many other slights and insults, that the Kangxi Emperor would eventually order their leader killed by slow slicing, and for his bones to then be pulverized and scattered—in other words, denying him not only life, but also afterlife. To be fair, the Manchu massacres only accounted for a third of the Dzungar deaths. Substantially more were killed off by smallpox, while the rest were removed by either fleeing as refugees or being kidnapped as Manchu slaves. The empty space left in western China was refilled through a Manchu migration scheme, moving Han, Uyghur and other minority settlers into the region.

The genocide against the Dzungars was matched by a similarly harsh suppression of the Jinchuan hill peoples, a Tibetan subgroup in Sichuan. In their first century as rulers of China, the Manchus also fought less successful frontier wars with Nepal, Vietnam and Myanmar. The early Qing, however, is remembered for almost doubling the territorial area of its Ming predecessor, restoring China's dimensions up to and even beyond the previous extents of the Han and Tang dynasty. By reaching such epic proportions, Qing China removed many of the old "border" issues—although the Russians were a harbinger of a new kind of foreign threat, the Manchus themselves had removed the need for the Great Wall by incorporating the old nomad regions within China itself. China, meanwhile, had reached an appreciably "natural" geographical limit—walled off by mountains to the south and west, and the sea to the east, with only the Manchuria-Siberia border on the north open to question and contest.

The organization of the Manchu empire rested to some extent on a system that would have been familiar to earlier dynasties, and even to the Bronze Age. Local headmen were responsible for every "ten houses"—the classical term for a village, repurposed in a more modern age to encompass ten families, a city block or urban enclave. In echoes of the system introduced by the First Emperor, the village headman was responsible for the crimes and misdeeds of his charges, encouraging a form of local accountability and neighborhood watchfulness.

As outsiders themselves, the Manchus had a better appreciation of how multicultural their domain was. They were eager to acknowledge those who, unlike the people of Yangzhou or the Dzungar tribes, accepted Qing rule—rather than writing them off as barbarians, as earlier Chinese dynasties might have done, the Manchus took a ready interest in Tibetan Buddhist iconography, Mongol leatherwork, or Uyghur dances. The Qing era saw a palpable variation in the style of Chinese arts and crafts, as imperial porcelain and court dress incorporated Manchu themes, but also ideas and imagery from the many other ethnic communities. The Han ethnic group were still in the majority, but no longer had any claim on the political or cultural high ground.

Although they adopted many of the accoutrements of Chinese emperors, the Manchus remained aloof from their Chinese subjects. Intermarriage was discouraged, and the Manchus never adopted the Han custom of foot-binding. As in the Mongol era, the Han Chinese were forced to accommodate themselves as being just one of several ethnic groups within a larger polity—while their masters were keen to behave in as "Chinese" a fashion as possible, they had many points of similarity with their Mongol subjects, and were careful to show respect to their Muslim Uyghur and Tibetan Buddhist subjects, as well as tribal headmen in the multi-racial south. In Yunnan, for example, where the rarefied air made Manchus reluctant to linger, the Qing dynasty chose to leave the dominant Mu clan in charge, maintaining a social order that had endured throughout the Yuan and Ming dynasties. The Mu overlords ran Yunnan as their personal domain for decades, first as princes, and then as hereditary governors until they were suddenly replaced by an outside political appointee in 1729.

The Qing Emperors had substantially more trouble interfering in Tibet, where local religious beliefs held that the ruling Dalai Lama did not die, but was merely reincarnated in a new body. It was hence much more difficult to establish who his "heir" would be, particularly when, as happened in 1682, the Tibetans kept the 5th Dalai Lama's death secret, so the Manchus could not interfere with the selection of his successor. Their caution proved wise, as when the Kangxi Emperor finally found out about the deception in 1700, he soon arranged for the kidnap and execution of the 6th Dalai Lama, who was denounced as an imposter in 1706.

Christianity presented Kangxi with fewer problems than Tibetan Buddhism, at least initially. Early in his reign, he ruled that Christian missionaries were harmless and often useful foreign visitors, decreeing that: "The Europeans are very quiet; they do not excite any disturbances in the provinces… it may be permitted to all who worship this God to enter these temples, offer him incense and perform the ceremonies practiced by according to ancient custom by the Christians." Essentially admitting the presence of Christian churches as merely more temples to yet another foreign god, such a policy of live-and-let-live helped foster an increased presence of European missionaries. However, as the Chinese had already noticed, the Europeans were constantly arguing amongst themselves about the nature of their God, and had even gone to war over it, repeatedly, in their home countries. A matter of constant debate, for decades, concerned the habit of Chinese people of venerating their ancestors in the afterlife. Some missionaries regarded it as a harmless tradition, others as tantamount to the worship of graven idols. This argument came to be known as the Rites Controversy (not to be confused with the Great Ritual Controversy of the Ming dynasty), and it reached its height in 1715, when Pope Clement XI decreed that no Chinese Catholic was permitted to worship ancestors, or even to watch someone else doing so.

Clement's decree also took missionaries to task for fudging the translation of "God" in Chinese by using terms like Heaven and Shangdi that misleadingly recalled Daoist spirituality. The aging Kangxi, who had already had several arguments in court with pushy papal legates, retaliated in 1721 by revoking his mild policy on missionaries, ordering them out of the country unless they could demonstrate some secondary usefulness such as medical skills, astronomical knowledge or some other form of learning.

Westerners are petty indeed. It is impossible to reason with them because they do not understand larger issues as we understand them in China. There is not a single Westerner versed in Chinese works, and their remarks are often incredible and ridiculous.

Dismissing the Christians as no better than some of the crazier Buddhist or Daoist sects, he ordered them to cease preaching in China. Some missionaries, such as the Jesuits who had long argued, in the Confucian mode, that ancestor worship was a social tradition, not a "religious" belief, got to stay if they could prove themselves useful.

The Kangxi Emperor's words hid a greater suspicion—that there was no place in the Manchu world order for a belief system that offered allegiance to authorities outside China. The Chinese Emperor was, by rights, the high priest of Chinese traditional religion, charged with conducting the fertility and harvest rituals that kept China prosperous and, hopefully, kept natural disasters at bay. There was no place in Chinese life for a Christianity that recognized the authority of a foreign Pope, or an Islam that focused on Mecca rather than Beijing. The Qing dynasty celebrated its multiculturalism, but subordinate to the grand authority of the Manchus themselves, who would accept no dissidence or whispers of revolution.

For the three centuries of Manchu rule, the specter of the Ming dynasty remained a constant threat. Severe censorship restrictions prevented writers, singers and poets from alluding to the Ming, even obliquely with mentions of its signature flowers or colors. One poet was executed for writing that red peonies were the best, and all others mere foreign imports. Government officials even frowned at too resonant a poetic reference to "the sun and the moon"—the two elements that, when combined on paper, formed the character for *Ming*. It was safer, to be sure, not to write about the Ming dynasty at all, a directive that would help preserve many older forms of Chinese narrative. Plays of the Yuan dynasty, often alluding even further back to the Song and Han, thrived in the Ming-dynasty repertoire. The big literary smashes of the Ming era all took place in bygone days— *The Romance of the Three Kingdoms* was about the aftermath of the collapse of the Han dynasty; *The Journey to the West* was a heavily fictionalized and magical account of Tripitaka's Tang-era wanderings; *The Water Margin* was a tale of rebels in the Song dynasty. All three remain staples of modern Chinese literature, at least in part because more up-to-date competition in the early Qing era was a risky proposition.

From 1772 onwards, the Qianlong Emperor (r. 1735–96) initiated a series of purges and campaigns against sedition in China. In the guise of inspecting private libraries in the compilation of an ultimate catalogue of all the books in China, Manchu agents confiscated and burned thousands of literary works perceived as attacking the Qing dynasty's legitimacy, or supporting anti-Manchu actions. Books were burned for using the reign titles of Ming pretenders, and thereby implying that they were real emperors, or for faithfully quoting Ming-era sources that happened to describe the Manchus as barbarians. Chinese publishing and the arts began to rely increasingly on obfuscation and misdirection—authors were reluctant to use their true names and many martial arts schools gained entire fictionalized "founders," in order to avoid associating living teachers and their relatives from the consequences of charges of treason.

Qing China would encounter many modern innovations—from the clocks and textiles donated by Western envoys, to goods and medicines brought in by Chinese traders. But the sheer size of the Chinese population, which trebled once more during the Qing, brought little incentive for labor-saving devices. To put it bluntly, labor was the one thing that the Chinese had in abundance, and it did not need to be "saved," causing many of the developments of the early industrial revolution to languish unknown or unappreciated in China. Chinese workers, in fact, became one of the country's most recognizable exports, showing up as diggers, porters and plantation workers in the Philippines, Indonesia, Hawaii and points beyond. By 1807, the British were using indentured Chinese laborers as far away as Trinidad, signing them up for several years of hard work that relied on their "bitter strength" (*kuli*)—one of several possible origins for the word coolie.

Coolies also formed a vital part of the trade in tea, expanding beyond its original frontiers in southern China into an export enterprise. Picked and processed in China into powders, dried leaves or hard cakes, tea had been traded for horses for centuries across the Himalayas and into the Indian subcontinent. However, it was now finding a ready market much further afield, with an unexpectedly insatiable demand.

The words in foreign languages for tea are often rooted in the way it reached the end user. Countries that first encountered tea shipped overland, tended to derive their local word for it from the Mandarin pronunciation: *chá*—leading to the Persian *chai*, Russian *chay* and Hindi *chāy*.

But for those countries whose first encounter with the dried leaves came by sea, shipped at first by Dutch merchants from the coasts of Fujian, the pronunciation sounded more like the word in the Hokkien dialect: *teh*—leading to the Dutch *thee*, the German *tee*, and the English *tea*.

In Europe, particularly in Britain, tea was taking over. For Thomas Short, author of the *Dissertation upon Tea* (1730), it was immensely prized by men of "sprightly Genius," for its "...remarkable Force against Drowsiness and Dul-ness, Damps and Clouds on Brain and intellectual Faculties." He did, however, advise against more than four cups in an afternoon, in order to prevent "frightful Dreams." The meteoric success of tea in Britain was the best possible news for the East India Company, which had previously been failing to draw any significant profit from its China activities. Its merchants, like those of other countries, were confined to a single quayside ghetto in Guangzhou, forbidden from bringing their own families, nor interacting in any meaningful way with the Chinese, nor even from choosing their stock. Instead, they went through the convoluted process of having each ship assigned to a local guarantor, who would then charge a fee to arrange for their cargoes to be taken ashore and for suitable bartering. A monopoly of Qing officials would periodically arrive and tell them that their tribute had been received by the Emperor, and that he in turn would be granting them some gifts—porcelain, silks or the all-important tea. Should they wish to make another "gift" to the Emperor, they would return with more. The Emperor mainly liked "gifts" of gold or silver. Whenever emissaries arrived from the Emperor, in accordance with Confucian protocol, the merchant was obliged to behave as if the Emperor himself was present. This meant dropping to one's knees and literally knocking one's head (*kou tou*) to the floor—the origin of the English loanword *kowtow*.

Despite this humiliating position, in which everybody was obliged to pretend that the British King accepted the Emperor as his superior, the tea trade was worth a fortune. The East India Company, however, was subject to high taxation in Britain and heavy competition from smugglers. The British government, which benefited greatly from the company's management of India, threw it a number of waivers and loopholes in an attempt to help its finances, the most consequential of which was the chance to ship its tea directly to Britain's American colonies, without passing through the usual red-tape and taxes required by a stop in Britain. The reaction in the American colonies, where tax-paying locals feared that their own businesses would be undercut by the East India Company, led in 1773 to protestors in Boston throwing cases of East India Company tea into the harbor. The "Boston Tea Party," as it would be known, was part of escalating local resistance to taxation without representation, although its aftermath is a matter for a different book.

The East India Company's trade in China began to bear fruits in the 1780s, when a relaxation of the tea tax in Britain helped to destroy the competition from smugglers. A growing middle class, enriched by the Industrial Revolution, had turned into an eager market not only for tea, but for silks, porcelain and other goods from the burgeoning East Asian marketing, creating a fashion for *Chinoiserie* visible all over Europe. Mock pagodas sprang up everywhere from St Petersburg to Portugal, along with "Chinese" gardens that imitated the orientalist scenes on the porcelain tableware that itself came to be known as "china." But the East India Company's profits were not merely bolstered by the growing fad for Chinoiserie—its officers had found a commodity that they could sell *to* the Chinese, thereby allowing them to stop transporting costly silver. Instead, EIC ships could load up with their wonder-cargo in India, sell it in China, and then sail home with holds full of tea. There was one problem—it was illegal.

The East India Company's magic new cargo, allowing its captains to double-dip their profits on a single trip, was "tears of the poppy," better known as opium—a resin formed from an extract of the flower *Papaver somniferum*. The Chinese had known about the drug's powerful pain-killing properties for centuries, but it had formerly been in short supply. Recreational use, when mixed with tobacco from the 17th century onwards, had alerted some Chinese officials to its addictive and debilitating effects. The opium derivative *madak* was banned in China in 1729, leaving a brief loophole that still allowed for the import of pure opium for medicinal purposes.

By the 1780s, opium was forming an increasingly important secret element of Britain's China trade. East India Company ships were stopping short of the Pearl River estuary for clandestine rendezvouses with local smugglers and dealers—their favorite anchorage being the waters near a nondescript fishing village called Hong Kong. Their Chinese underground contacts would pay for the opium with silver, which the ships would then take a few miles upstream to the Guangzhou quayside to exchange for everyday goods like tea and porcelain. Even as the legal trade continued, the new, illegal exchange in Chinese silver and Bengal opium was making millionaires of Chinese smugglers, while also boosting the profits for the East India Company. Like any other illegal drug, it was also creating a rapidly growing underclass of addicts, draining southern China of resources and manpower.

However, other countries were muscling in on the China trade. The United States of America sent its first trader, the *Empress of China*, to Guangzhou in 1784, laden with silver and Appalachian ginseng. Unsure of how these arrivals from a previously unknown country were related to the Europeans, the Chinese termed them "the New People." While loading his vessel up with *nankeen* cloth, tea and porcelain, the *Empress of China's* young supercargo Samuel Shaw began preparing his report for the US Secretary of Foreign Affairs, in which he complained about the restrictions of trading with, and even seeing the sights of China.

> In a country where the jealousy of the government confines all intercourse between its subjects and the foreigners who visit it to very narrow limits, in the suburbs of a single city, the opportunities of gaining information... can be neither frequent nor extensive. Therefore, the few observations that can be made at Canton cannot furnish us with sufficient data from which to form an accurate judgment....

These restrictions frustrated all foreign traders in China—crammed into a single quayside in Guangzhou at the very edge of the empire, at the mercy of a tiny monopoly of local bigwigs, without direct access to the millions of potential customers further afield.

The Macartney Embassy of 1793 was an attempt by Great Britain to persuade the Chinese that King George III deserved special treatment. The trading system in Guangzhou was unnecessarily complex and outmoded, and surely it would be smarter to let British ships trade at a thousand other points north along the coast? In fact, there were so many British merchantmen keen to buy tea, porcelain and silk that George Macartney rather hoped to be granted a new docking station near the mouth of the River Yangtze. He also wanted the Chinese to enter the world of international diplomacy, inviting Qianlong to send an emissary to London, and offering himself as Britain's first ambassador to Beijing.

Macartney's entourage landed at Guangzhou and traversed the whole of China on its long journey to the north, leaving a priceless record of daily life in the middle of the Qing dynasty. This, however, was of little consolation to its backers at the East India Company, who had to foot most of the bill for a year-long journey, and a cargo of gifts and trade samples that filled 85 wagons. Sure in his own mind that Britain was the greatest empire in the world, Macartney was convinced that he was paying the Chinese a compliment by addressing the Qianlong Emperor as an equal, and by offering a unique opportunity to become Britain's greatest ally. He laid on the most ostentatious and impressive diplomatic event possible, arriving at the Qianlong Emperor's residence in Jehol in a ludicrous cape of swirling pink satin, studded with diamonds and a gold chain dripping with medallions. He was thus rather surprised to find that his months of travel and fruity fineries had earned him nothing more than one of three embassies paying "tribute" to Qianlong on that day, having to share the festivities with delegations from the Kalmuk nomads and the Burmese.

Qianlong received the letter that Macartney brought from King George, and graciously invited him to sit in the place of honor at the ensuing banquet. Macartney, however, fumed throughout at the acrobats and plate-spinners, sourly observing in his diary that he had seen a better circus in London, and that the fireworks were better in Java. As he began his long journey back to England, he commented that the gifts from the Emperor were frankly unremarkable samples of tea and porcelain.

The feeling was mutual. Qianlong wrote a response to King George III, who, if he wasn't already mad, was sure to be soon after reading it. It thanked the King of Britain for his "humble desire to partake of the benefits of our civilization" and pointed out that the emperor had allowed for the bearers of King George's tribute to be admitted into his presence. He would, however, not be granting any of their requests. They already had the right to trade in Guangzhou, which was more than enough for everybody's sake, and Qianlong was hardly prepared to offer special concessions to the British, when he was getting similarly unwelcome requests from the Italians and the Portuguese. There was no need for a permanent embassy in Beijing, and besides, even if there were, he doubted very much that even the greatest ambassador in the world would internalize Chinese ways to the extent required to become Chinese. As far as Qianlong was concerned, he had done Macartney a great favor by even agreeing to see him, and there was no need for trade, embassy, or concessions to Christian missionaries. His response carried with it the weight of centuries of Chinese empire, treating the British like a subset of Central Asian barbarians, without even useful horses or jade to offer, and so hopelessly alien as to stand no chance of ever learning how to be truly Chinese.

> Swaying the wide world, I have but one aim in view, namely, to maintain a perfect governance and to fulfill the duties of the State: strange and costly objects do not interest me. If I have commanded that the tribute offerings sent by you, O King, are to be accepted, this was solely in consideration for the spirit which prompted you to dispatch them from afar. Our dynasty's majestic virtue has penetrated unto every country under Heaven, and Kings of all nations have offered their costly tribute by land and sea. As your Ambassador can see for himself, we possess all things. I set no value on objects strange or ingenious, and have no use for your country's manufactures.

Macartney had envisioned his mission as a fantastic opportunity that the Chinese had failed to understand—the chance to initiate a golden age of widespread trade with Great Britain, opening the hidebound empire to a flood of technology, education and business opportunities. Instead, he had been condescended to like a precocious child—Qianlong had taken the greatest interest in a young boy with the delegation who had picked up a few words of Chinese, as if the entire embassy was little more than a school outing.

What Macartney had not mentioned to the Qianlong Emperor was that the British were coming whether the Chinese liked it or not. Although the costly expedition achieved no immediate results, it had permitted Macartney and his military escorts ample opportunity to observe the Manchu realm from top to bottom, from the countryside beyond the ports, to the commerce on the Grand Canal. While the Chinese had been looking the other way, they had even drafted reports on the fortifications of the Great Wall. Far from being dumbfounded by the pomp and power of Qianlong's empire, Macartney reported on it as a rotting hulk, likening it to a warship that had seen better days, staffed by an incompetent crew, and impossible to fix up to any sailable standard. If China were a ship, Macartney wrote, it was drifting, rudderless towards the rocks.

> The breaking-up of the power of China (no very improbable event) would occasion a complete subversion of the commerce, not only of Asia, but a very sensible change in the other quarters of the world. The industry and the ingenuity of the Chinese would be checked and enfeebled, but they would not be annihilated. Her ports would no longer be barricaded; they would be attempted by all the adventurers of all trading nations, who would search every channel, creek, and cranny of China for a market, and for some time be the cause of much rivalry and disorder.

Macartney foresaw a day in the near future when the authorities of the Manchus would crumble, leaving its teeming millions vulnerable to any outside traders, conmen or raiders who could get there first.

> Nevertheless, as Great Britain, from the weight of her riches and the genius and spirits of her people, is become the first political, marine, and commercial Power on the globe, it is reasonable to think that she would prove the greatest gainer by such a revolution as I have alluded to, and rise superior over every competitor.

Macartney was careful not to encourage an open challenge to Manchu authority—he would take no joy in watching China fall apart, not the least because of the damage it would do to trade for a generation. Although he believed that a handful of British warships could easily trash the fortifications of Guangzhou and lay waste to China's entire coastal defenses, he had rather hoped that the British could have wormed their way into the Manchus' government as helpers and providers of advice and upgrades in military technology. As far as he was concerned, his mission had been China's last great hope to avoid oncoming disaster.

# CHAPTER 9

# CENTURY OF HUMILIATION: FROM THE OPIUM WAR TO THE LONG MARCH

I t took them five days to come for her.

At first there was the uproar at the Anhui Police College on July 6, 1907, where the lone gunman Xu Xilin shot at the chief of police during the new recruits' graduation ceremony. He was dead by the next day—his heart cut out and his head cut off, supposedly after supplying the authorities with a list of his accomplices. They were plotting a rebellion on the 19th, and Xu had only acted alone because he thought he had been betrayed.

It is widely believed that Xu gave up nothing. Guifu, the Manchu provincial prefect, had his suspicions and circumstantial evidence, and he was sure that something was going on at the school that Xu had set up in Shaoxing.

Some of the local people had already been deeply suspicious of activities at the Datong School for Girls, where the pupils studied Japanese and English, and conducted military drills in the yard with real rifles. And there were plenty of whispers about Xu's cousin, Qiu Jin (1875–1907), the hard-drinking poetess who was the school's principal. Recently returned from studies in Japan, where she had edited a progressive magazine and delivered stirring speeches about democracy and women's rights, she cut a remarkable dash in the streets of Shaoxing, dressed in man's clothes without cosmetics, riding on a horse, a Japanese sword at her hip.

The Datong School for Girls was a front for revolutionary activities—a training camp for terrorist cells, where Qiu Jin had been expecting to participate in a coordinated uprising later that July. She had, in fact, already injured her hand while making bombs the previous month. But when the news arrived of her cousin's suicidal gun attack on the police school, Qiu Jin seemed strangely unmoved.

A music teacher from the nearby middle school called on Qiu Jin, warning her that Guifu had arrived with two groups of soldiers, intent on searching the home of Xu Xilin, and then the Datong School. Later that morning, the school cook arrived from town and said that she ought to leave, because word in the teahouses was that she was going to be arrested.

Qiu Jin refused, saying that even though Xu Xilin had founded the school she worked at, he did not work there anymore. "I am a pure and spotless woman, and haven't committed the slightest crime," she said, "so why should I run away and provide people with an excuse to accuse me of fleeing like a coward?"

Qiu Jin's staff pleaded with her to run, but she refused, dismissing the Manchu authorities as "barbarian officials," and pointing out that the rifles on the school grounds had been legally obtained and licensed. There was nothing for a search party to find.

This, however, did not stop the troops from treating the school with extreme prejudice. With Qiu Jin calmly playing her zither inside, 400 soldiers surrounded the school, shooting and killing students who tried to flee. Qiu Jin was arrested and roughly pushed along the road, while the soldiers looted the school finances. One trooper threw two pistols to the ground and claimed that they had fallen from Qiu Jin's clothes.

At the Shanyin district office, Qiu Jin was interrogated. When she refused to cooperate, she was tortured on the rack. Eventually, a confession was written for her, and she was told to sign it.

She wrote *Qiu* (autumn), the first syllable of her name, and then paused in thought. Then she continued writing, not with her name, but with the poem that was fated to be her last: "*Autumn rains and autumn storms kill me with their sorrow.*"

She was sentenced to death by the evening, despite any real proof. Unmoved, she continued to act in a matter-of-fact manner, demanding that the authorities return the five hundred silver dollars looted from the school. She was told that none of her requests would be granted, and merely sighed in reply.

At dawn, she was led out in shackles, escorted by a platoon of soldiers. She was beheaded at Xuanting Crossing.

Qiu Jin had been executed without evidence or any meaningful trial. Under torture, her colleagues refused to confess any information that would justify her execution after the fact. Her body, unclaimed for some time, was eventually collected by colleagues, and buried in Hangzhou, close to the tomb of the famous Song dynasty rebel Yue Fei. When the Manchu authorities heard of this, they demanded it be removed to somewhere less obvious.

When the Qing dynasty fell, a mere four years later, Qiu Jin's body was returned to its rightful resting place, as a martyr of the new Republic.

$$\odot - \odot - \odot - \odot - \odot$$

Historians talk of a "mode of emplotment"—the desire to impose a story on historical events, so they have clear beginnings and endings, highs and lows, chapter headings and messages. Such a process is only natural in popular history, and is certainly at work in the book you are reading, but it's important to note just how much of it is subject to objections and revisions.

The chapter divisions in this book reflect those of traditional scholarship in both China and the West, which identifies the 1840s as a critical turning point, when foreign predations began to escalate, a chain of events that would end with the empire crashing down, rotten to the core within, and damaged beyond repair by outsiders.

Western scholarship saw the 1840s as a series of influences dragging China into the modern world, confronting it with global economics and the transformations of science and democracy. Chinese scholars saw similar factors at work, but emphasized the "Century of Humiliation" (*Bainian Guochi*)—a term still prominent in school textbooks in the People's Republic. The modern world, for these scholars, amounted to a constant assault of double-crosses and betrayals, hypocrisies and corruption, until China broke free of both imperialism and capitalism with the creation of the People's Republic.

Lord Macartney's description of China as a shipwreck waiting to happen might have sounded persuasive, but Chinese historians insist the ship still had a crew—the Manchus were overthrown by *Chinese* rebels; the imperial system would be replaced by a Republic of *China*; that Republic was toppled by *Chinese* rebellion, and when the civil war was done, it was the *Chinese* who proclaimed the People's Republic. Foreign powers certainly meddled, but the Chinese themselves were complicit in both good and bad developments. The "foreign mud" of the opium trade was often grown by Chinese natives or plantation workers, smuggled in by Chinese sailors, and in later years, grown in China itself. The rebellions of the 19th century might be couched in the record as "Christian" or "Muslim" movements, but were chiefly the work of starving Chinese subjects. More appositely, the supposedly foreign institutions and forces that preyed upon China did so with a large support staff of Chinese people.

Some scholars have argued that far from clinging to the past until they were overwhelmed, the Qing *created* modern China in 1644, by establishing a previously unseen level of centralized control, and by wiping out the northern border problem. The Qing dynasty is hence, in the words of William T. Rowe, "a constantly moving target," only passing from living memory in the last decade.

We might equally argue that the period of "humiliation" began not in the 1840s, but two hundred years earlier, in 1644, when the first and most successful foreign element, the Manchus themselves, swept in from the northeast to form a lasting, exploitative aristocracy. Or, if we accept, as all modern Chinese books do, that the Manchus were simply another sector of the Chinese world, and that they were hence not really foreign, then surely their regime, with its wars of conquest in Central Asia, its self-assurance of its racial and cultural superiority, and a military mission that doubled the size of Chinese territory in the space of 150 years, was an immensely successful imperialist power, not all that different in attitude from the outsiders that would bring it down.

Just as the ancient Zhou dynasty sat on the cusp between the Bronze and Iron Ages, the Qing dynasty was confronted with technological changes that disrupted the old order forever. The Kangxi Emperor regarded 18th century China as a *mission accomplished*. Order was restored; borders were firm; society was thriving. However one wanted to define the Manchus, as local innovators or foreign interlopers, their state was booming. Despite the dizzying growth in numbers, the Grand Canal did its job in moving supplies of grain to the hungry north. Meanwhile, the first signs of urbanization were visible around the mouth of the Yangtze, where the silk industry and its various processes—spinning, weaving, dyeing, tailoring—had taken over much of the farmland that would have allowed several cities a self-sufficient food supply. There is a definite sense in the proclamations of Kangxi, his son Yongzheng (r. 1722–35) and grandson Qianlong (1735–96) that they have inherited and fixed up a national machine that is now running smoothly. Within its own, expanded borders, Qing China was doing very well. The early Qing dynasty had ample infrastructure in place to deal with food shortages and disaster relief. If it stumbled in its efforts to deal with such issues in later years, the blame might be laid not at the elements, but at the constant damage done to the Qing by human forces. Communist historiography, in search of forerunners of China's revolutions, often treats these uprisings as manifestations of a more modern China, as the common people kicked against centuries of oppression.

There was money to be made in the China trade, but the temptations of the illegal opium run were too great. Merchants racked up great fortunes by selling furs, sealskins and sandalwood from the American northwest, but none of these commodities offered the same return as opium, which American traders could pick up in Turkey. The Turkish variety lacked the quality of the Burmese, but this merely drove down the price in China, and made opium more affordable for everyone, creating a wave of new addicts.

In 1833, under pressure to allow freer trade for British merchants, the British government ended the East India Company's long-standing monopoly on the China trade. This was intended to increase the amount of tax-paying freelancers docking in London, but it also obliged the Royal Navy to fill the gap left by the East India Company's armed merchantmen. It was this that would ultimately bring Macartney's prediction to pass, as military vessels flying the British flag started to police the activities of a trading community that was, itself, illegal.

Commissioner Lin Zexu (1785–1850) arrived in south China in 1839, tasked with ending the opium problem. As he had done in previous anti-drug campaigns in the north, he set about attacking the issue at every stage of the process. He targeted the addicts themselves, confiscating 70,000 opium pipes, and their local suppliers, arresting over 1,700 drug dealers.

In an attempt to shut down medium-term supplies, Lin offered to swap tea for all the opium that he knew to be in foreign traders' local warehouses. When the merchants resisted, he went all-in, confiscating the supplies of illegal opium and destroying it all.

The destruction took 500 laborers more than three weeks of burning, diluting, and dumping in the sea. For this, Commissioner Lin would be remembered as a hero of the war on drugs—today's UN International Day against Drug Abuse and Illicit Trafficking is on June 26, marking the completion of his grand confiscation in Guangzhou. However, Lin and ultimately his boss, the Daoguang Emperor (r. 1820–50), were defeated by their naivety regarding the power of law and the rules of propriety. Lin genuinely seems to have believed that the foreign smugglers would be cowed by a stern talking-to and a punitive confiscation. Opium was, after all, illegal in China, and as a good Confucian scholar, he believed firmly in the rules of moral behavior. To make his position clear, he even wrote a chiding letter to Queen Victoria, which she never received, although it would eventually be published in a British newspaper.

In his letter, Lin reiterated that the opium trade was illegal, and that Chinese subjects involved in it were subject to capital punishment. He had confiscated 20,283 chests of opium from the traders in Guangzhou, and frankly considered that the smugglers "who, by selling it for many years have induced dreadful calamity and robbed us of enormous wealth," were getting away rather lightly. Next time, he warned, he would treat the foreigners like he treated the Chinese, with the full force of the law, and he was sure that Queen Victoria, as a noble and just sovereign, would see why this was necessary.

> Your foreign ships come hither, striving the one with the other for our trade, and for the simple reason of their strong desire to reap a profit.... By what principle of reason, then, should these foreigners send in return a poisonous drug, which involves in destruction those very natives of China?

Lin did not stop at threatening the death penalty for drug dealers. He hinted that further infringements would see a suspension of trade in all those harmless commodities that the Chinese sold to the foreigners—no more porcelain, no more satins... and worst of all, no more tea!

Lin demanded that the merchants sign an agreement not to trade in opium. Several captains agreed—not every foreign trader was a drug dealer. Charles Elliot, however, superintendent of the British in Guangzhou refused on the grounds that it was an infringement of his right to free trade. A former naval officer turned diplomat, Elliot was soon at odds with Lin again, when two drunken British sailors killed a Chinese local, and Elliot refused to hand the men over to the Chinese, claiming instead that they would be disciplined aboard a British ship. Angry at the rejection of his authority, Commissioner Lin forbade the sale of food to the British, leading to a tense blockade and sea battles between Chinese and British ships.

Elliot was not above firing on his own countrymen, either. A Quaker-owned British vessel, refusing to trade in opium on religious grounds, was permitted to dock at Guangzhou, leading Elliot to fret about the precedent for an opium-free trading environment. Accordingly, he started to blockade *his own country's ships*, ordering the British to fire on any vessel that did not follow his "free-trade" line. The opportunity soon arose when the opium-free *Royal Saxon*, another British vessel, headed for Guangzhou, and the Royal Navy ships that were supposed to be protecting trade in the area opened fire on it. To add to the insanity, Chinese ships fired on the Royal Navy, to protect the *Royal Saxon*.

"The men of Britain desire nothing but peace," lied Elliott in a circular to the foreign community. "To deprive men of food is the act only of the unfriendly and hostile." And there was none so hostile as the furious Daoguang Emperor, who ordered that nobody, foreigner or Chinese, should sell supplies to the British. It was tantamount to an order exiling the British from Chinese territory, and implied that any foreigners who disobeyed would be similarly banished.

Demanding "satisfaction for the past and security for the future," the British Foreign Secretary Lord Palmerston dispatched a naval squadron to chastise the Chinese. Elliot was given a wish-list of demands, buzzing with earnest terms like respect, justice and recompense, and calling for an end to the restriction of British traders in a single southern port.

The resulting Opium War (1839–42) involved the whole coast of China from Guangzhou in the south to the Dagu forts that protected Tianjin in the north, as well as an advance up the Yangtze as far as Nanjing. The subsequent Treaty of Nanjing, signed in 1842, granted the British a swathe of concessions, including the access to new docking and trading facilities ("treaty ports") in Amoy, Fuzhou, Ningbo and Shanghai, fixed tariffs instead of the fiddly liaison system, and the granting, in perpetuity, of a small island at the mouth of the Pearl River Estuary, which the British could use thereafter as a base. Its name in Chinese meant "Fragrant Harbor," in the local dialect: *Hong Kong*.

Alongside financial reparations, amounting to charging the Chinese a fee for losing a war, there were two other critical points. One was *extraterritoriality* for British subjects, conceding that the Chinese could not be trusted to administer their own justice system, and that any Briton accused of a crime would be tried and sentenced by his own people. The other was *Most Favored Nation Status*, which allowed for the British to be included automatically in any agreements struck between the Chinese and other powers.

And so, when the United States of America concluded a similar deal in 1844 in the Treaty of Wanghia, it, too insisted on Most Favored Nation Status, snagging the same concessions as Britain, but also allowing the British to benefit from one of the new riders, which was the right for foreigners to learn Chinese, previously illegal. The US treaty, in fact, was a little kinder to the Chinese, allowing that opium traders were not covered by its protections, but nevertheless was another "Unequal Treaty" in the eyes of the Chinese, signed not as an amicable agreement between equal powers, but under duress.

Similar Unequal Treaties followed with France, Sweden and Norway, Russia and Portugal, setting them up as a cartel untouchable by Chinese law, each piggy-backing on the other's concessions, gaining ever greater rights to exploit Chinese markets, continually undermining the authority of the Qing emperors in their own country. From 1854 onwards, the foreigners even took over the collection of trade tariffs. Pronouncing the Qing dynasty incompetent at collecting its own taxes, and demanding greater efficiency in order to collect all those reparations the Chinese kept incurring, the foreign powers started up an Imperial Maritime Customs Service, staffed chiefly by Britons, but also by other members of the foreign powers. China got its cut only after all the deductions had been made by this new bureaucracy, which would remain operational in some form until 1950.

A Second Opium War (1856–60) only made matters worse. The British went into battle after Chinese law enforcement had boarded a suspected pirate vessel that was actually Chinese, but flew a British flag. The French joined in after a French missionary was executed for illegally preaching the Gospel in Guizhou. The Treaty of Tianjin, concluded partway through in 1858, granted Britain and France (and thanks to Most Favored Nation Status, everybody else) eleven more treaty ports and the right to create a diplomatic enclave (the Legation Quarter) in Beijing itself, within site of the Emperor's Forbidden City. One of the new treaty ports was Hankou, which was not on the coast at all, but 800 kilometers (497.1 miles) inland. Getting there required another concession: freedom of foreign shipping (including military vessels) to navigate the River Yangtze. Foreigners, in fact, were now permitted to roam anywhere they wanted within China, and in a devious touch, Christians in China were afforded religious liberty. In other words, the Qing-era ban on missionaries was wiped out—since foreign priests were free to take their message wherever they wanted, and anyone who accepted their faith was now legally protected from harm if they did so.

A final clause in the Treaty of Tianjin, without a shred of irony, insists that the Chinese to stop calling foreigners "barbarians" (*Yi*) in their official correspondence.

It should not have surprised anyone that the youthful Xianfeng Emperor (r. 1850–61), his authority so thoroughly undermined, should have trouble making his treaty stick. When a British naval force arrived at Tianjin to drop off the first British and French ambassadors, Xianfeng sent a Mongol general, Sengge Rinchen, with orders to refuse passage to their military escorts. Determined to accompany the envoys all the way to Beijing, the convoy started shelling the Dagu Forts. The captain of a US vessel, supposedly only there as an observer, felt obliged to join in.

A simple delivery having turned into a military action, the multinational force took Tianjin and advanced on Beijing. Attempts to negotiate were thwarted when a British ambassador insulted his Chinese host, and worsened when over a dozen British expedition members were tortured to death by Chinese captors who had seized them under a flag of truce.

Lord Elgin, leader of the British forces, proclaiming that he only wanted to hurt the Chinese aristocracy, not their blameless subjects, he ordered the destruction of the Manchus' Old Summer Palace, the Garden of Perfect Brightness (*Yuan Ming Yuan*) to the north of the city. Garnett Joseph Wolseley, who wrote an account of the whole war, observed that

"...the light was so subdued by the overhanging clouds of smoke, that it seemed as if the sun was undergoing a lengthened eclipse. The world around looked dark with shadow."

The destruction of the Summer Palace remains a landmark event in the Century of Humiliation. Wolseley and his colleagues regarded it as a necessary punishment to show the Chinese that they meant business—a warning of the fate that would befall the Forbidden City itself unless the Emperor gave in. He also made a point of mentioning that many of the buildings were practically empty when set ablaze. Lest anyone think it was a "Gothlike act of barbarism" he noted, the French allies had helpfully "shorn the place of all its beauty and ornament by the removal or reckless destruction of everything that was valuable." A century and a half later, the Garden of Perfect Brightness is left pointedly in ruins as a symbol of China's suffering at the hands of the foreign imperialists. An entire museum in modern Beijing is filled with repatriated artifacts, bought back on the international antiques market from a boggling array of unexpected places. Bronze statues have been found adorning a Californian swimming pool; intricate roof tiles on display in a Paris hotel foyer. An entire book, *Who Collects the Yuan Ming Yuan?*, reconstructs the fragments of the palace from their known locations all over the world today.

The subsequent Convention of Beijing piled on further Unequal Treaties, including the opening of Tianjin as a treaty port perilously close to Beijing itself, blanket "religious freedom" in China, and the legalization of the opium trade. Kowloon peninsula, across the water from Hong Kong Island, was handed to the British. A supplement, signed just a couple of weeks later, ceded the entire Siberian coast to the Russians, costing the Chinese thousands of square kilometers of what had once been Outer Manchuria.

Such was the external pressure that beset the Xianfeng Emperor and his successor, exacerbating local problems in China that would have been more than enough to keep any Emperor busy. Climate, of course, played a part. In the Qing dynasty, we are out of the torment of the "Nine Sloughs" that hounded the Yuan and Ming, but the weather continued to exert an influence. Much like the Ming dynasty before it, the Qing could be said to have enjoyed a century of more of relative equilibrium, before trouble struck once more.

Catastrophic Yellow River flooding in 1851 and 1855 played its part in destabilizing the Qing's ability to manage further crises, and in inciting two internal uprisings. The Nian Rebellion (1851–64) consumed much of the Yellow River basin, and was motivated by simple deprivation; one of the rebels' main slogans was "*Kill the rich and aid the poor.*" Tensions between Muslims and Han settlers flared in Yunnan in the Panthay Rebellion (1856–73), which led to a million deaths, and the brief declaration of a separatist sultanate.

A modern theory adds gender to the mix—many of the regions that suffered unrest also had a high surplus population of unattached males, itself the result of a decade of more of female infanticide. It is estimated that in the century after 1774, 20–25% of Chinese girls were killed as children. The continuing tradition of polygamy among the rich ensured that marriageable women were in short supply, creating an underclass of single youths, or "bare branches." In the region of the Nian Rebellion, for example, one in four men was unable to find a wife, undermining the rural traditions of family and homestead, and creating a prime recruiting ground for bandits and rebels.

The Taiping Rebellion (1850–64), on the other hand, was couched in pseudo-Christian rhetoric—an uprising consuming the Yangtze and points further south, led by Hong Xiuquan (1814–64), a failed intellectual who declared himself to be the Son of God, brother of Jesus Christ, and earthly emissary of a new Kingdom of Heavenly Peace (*Taiping Guo*). Despite such shaky philosophical foundations, the Taiping rebels are regarded by the modern People's Republic as noble precursors of the revolutionary tradition. A collection of marginalized peoples (Hakka, Zhuang and the Cantonese-speaking Han of the south), they were not only anti-Manchu, but opposed to footbinding and private enterprise, and occasional promoters of women's rights. The use of the term "Rebellion" to describe their movement has been rejected in some circles as a euphemism for what it really was: a civil war in which several regions of China attempted to overthrow the Qing dynasty. Fearing for their own possessions and investments along the Yangtze, foreign powers actively intervened on the side of the Emperor, leading to one of the era's strangest sights, the Ever Victorious Army. Comprising European officers, Chinese soldiers trained in modern Western warfare, and in its later years, an increasingly suspect lower echelon of European mercenaries, deserters, ship-jumpers and escaped convicts, it was instrumental in saving the Qing to fight another day.

The use of the Ever Victorious Army was part of a belated Chinese effort to embrace reforms. This "Self-Strengthening Movement" was doomed from the outset by its refusal to allow foreign-owned industries, foreign investment or changes to the law, alongside heavy grass-roots resistance to mechanization and industrialization which, the peasants feared would "break their rice bowls" by taking away their jobs. Out in the hinterland, there were complaints that the foreigners' new churches were sharp-edged buildings damaging the local *feng shui*. Catholic missionaries arrived in scattered towns, inconveniently asking for the return of church real estate abandoned two centuries earlier when they were cast out. In 1870, Nuns running a Tianjin orphanage and offering money for foundlings were accused of harvesting Chinese children for sacrificial rituals. In the ensuing argument, the French consul drew his pistol and shot at the Chinese investigator. A riot broke out, in which ten nuns, four priests and three innocent Russian bystanders were killed. It was one of hundreds of incidents, many of them based on religious misunderstandings that invited repeated reprisals from the foreign powers.

Ironically, the worse things got, the more certain powers tried to shore up the Chinese government. Britain and the United States, in particular, had trade interests all over China, which meant they stood to lose out if the country was partitioned between competing foreign interests. Such concerns propelled Britain and the US into proposing an "Open Door" policy that sought to discourage fellow foreign powers from seizing any more Chinese territory.

It was too little, too late. Russia was already pushing into Manchuria; Germany had designs on Shandong. An unexpected latecomer to the raiding party, Japan, was also pushing for its own share. Japan claimed the Ryūkyū Islands as its own in 1872, and sent a punitive expedition to Taiwan in 1874 to avenge the murder of shipwrecked Ryūkyūan sailors by Taiwanese aborigines. Having successfully modernized at a breakneck pace, Japan intended to join the imperialist powers exploiting China, although sometimes this desire manifested itself more as a form of benign pan-Asianism, offering to help the Chinese shake off the foreign oppressors.

Drought in the 1870s, now understood to be a factor of the *El Niño* weather cycle in the Pacific, was markedly severe, leading to a famine in the north that spanned 1877–79. Shanxi province suffered more than others, in part because the access roads were so poorly maintained, preventing relief from getting through. However one wanted to assign blame, the disaster is believed to have caused up to 13 million deaths.

Unsurprisingly, people sought to escape—in opium, in denial and in dreams. The popular stories of the Qing dynasty, forced to survive in a hostile, censorious environment, had turned away from the present day. When any comment on evil officialdom was sure to be taken as an attack on the government, when the depiction of any criminal act might be taken as a glorification or incitement of that act, and when any reference to the Ming dynasty might be taken as a call to revolution, it was far easier for storytellers to drift towards a nebulous, unspecified dreamtime. *Jiang-hu*, the "rivers and lakes," once a term for the material world of the prosperous Yangtze delta, transformed into a more fantastic concept—the Chinese equivalent of "days of yore" or "the Wild West." The rivers and lakes became the site of wandering heroes and sword-wielding damsels; powerful Daoist sorcerers and demon infestations. Outcast knights stood their ground against predatory bandits, in a fantasy genre that favored martial arts and heroic romance.

In 1889, a fire at one of the gates of the Forbidden City cast a bad omen over the wedding of the young Guangxu Emperor (r. 1875–1908). In 1898, Japan chased Chinese influence from Korea and turned the entire island of Taiwan into a Japanese colony. For Guangxu, it seems, this was the final straw, propelling him into proclaiming a sweeping series of reforms, to drag China out of the mire and save it further humiliation.

Guangxu had been frustrated for much of his life. Enthroned at the age of four, he had endured the long regency of his aunt, the Empress Dowager Cixi (1835–1908), only gaining active control at the time of his wedding, aged eighteen. Finally believing himself in a position to get something done, he initiated a series of reforms inspired by the Self-Strengthening Movement. Guangxu decreed that it was time to abolish the traditional examination system—it might have been sufficient for screening officials in the Han dynasty, but it was no use in staffing a forward-thinking, modern bureaucracy. Guangxu wanted to cancel all the time-wasting, cash-draining sinecure positions that kept the palace over-stuffed with hangers-on. He wanted a modern university in Beijing, a school system that emphasized math and science, industrialization, a bureau of railways and mines. He was ready for a constitutional monarchy, and wanted members of the imperial family to study abroad.

None of that was going to happen. Guangxu's well-intentioned decrees were slapped down by conservatives among the Qing imperial family. The Hundred Days' Reform, as they would be known, came to a sudden end in September 1898, with the Empress Dowager planning a coup, while a hastily organized counter-coup failed to ignite. The reformists who had encouraged the teenage Emperor were executed or fled into exile in Japan, while Guangxu himself spent the rest of his reign under house arrest.

The Empress Dowager was back in power at the center of a clique of anti-foreign, anti-reform Manchu princes, still clinging to the glory days of the Qing dynasty. If Guangxu was tragically naïve in thinking he could transform China by decree, Cixi was ruthlessly self-interested and pragmatic in closing her eyes to its problems. She spent much of her time in the New Summer Palace—not the ruined Garden of Perfect Brightness, but the nearby Garden of Perfect Harmony—while her entourage continued to enjoy the pomp and luxury of the Manchu elite. With China's regions collapsing into warlord provinces or foreign enclaves, Cixi ate 120-course banquets and played with her 20 dogs, who themselves had four dedicated human servants. Holding out for a miracle, she may have believed one arrived in 1900.

The Society of Righteous Harmony (*Yihe-tuan*), also known as the Boxers, had been harrying Christian missionaries for several years in Shandong. A community of toughs, outlaws and unemployed youths, the Boxers were implicated in numerous lynchings, murders, and arson attacks. Fearing that Christian missionaries were the vanguard for further Unequal Treaties and concessions, their battle-cries included, tellingly for an unbearably hot summer: "When the foreigners are wiped out, the rains will fall."

"The whole country," wrote the American Minister Edwin H. Conger in a cable to Washington, "is swarming with hungry, discontented, hopeless idlers." After the Empress Dowager had controversially issued an edict in support of the Boxers, they began to advance on Beijing. There, they were joined by the Gansu Braves, a 7,000-strong division of Muslim troops loyal to the Emperor, who declared Chinese Christians to be "secondary devils" deserving of death.

The 900 foreign residents of Beijing's 5km square Legation Quarter—mainly Europeans, Americans and Japanese—abandoned the outer buildings and barricaded themselves within a city block between the Russian,

French and British legation buildings, bordered on the south side by the towering Tartar Wall that separated Beijing's inner and outer cities. Some 2,200 Chinese Christians fled burning churches to form a shanty-town in a nearby park.

Some sources refer to these events as the Boxer Rebellion, but to do so is to repeat the assertions of the Manchus, that the Boxers acted also against them, and that they were somehow powerless to control them, rather than offering tacit support. Modern scholars prefer the term Boxer Uprising, to reflect the fact that the Boxers' slogan was one of "supporting the Qing and expelling the foreigners"—which is to say that they did not regard the Manchus as foreigners themselves, and indeed enjoyed secret backing from the authorities. It surprises me that more is not made in modern times of the role of the Gansu Braves, who were more obviously servants of the Qing regime, but also apparently starting their own jihad.

Cixi's hope that the Boxers would remove the foreigners for her would backfire terribly. While the world's press held its breath (some reporting the Foreign Legation residents as already dead in a massacre) an Eight-Nation Alliance landed 20,000 soldiers at Tianjin and marched on the Chinese capital, bringing relief to the besieged legations after 55 days. The Eight-Nation Alliance was billed as a humanitarian intervention, coming to the aid of missionaries and Christian believers under attack from savage cultists, but amounted to a multinational invasion of Beijing. The Manchu imperial family fled in disgrace, guarded by the Gansu Braves, while foreign troops ransacked the Forbidden City.

From hiding, Cixi sent emissaries to negotiate, resulting in the signing of the Boxer Protocol in 1901. Foreign countries gained the right to station their troops within Beijing itself and the Boxer Indemnity, 450 million taels in silver, was to be paid out to the aggrieved nations over the next 39 years. Membership of an anti-foreign society in China was henceforth decreed to be a capital crime. Chinese were no longer allowed to live in the Legation Quarter, the Manchus were forced to create a more "modern" foreign ministry to deal with international issues, and in a stinging rebuke, civil service exams in areas of Boxer crimes were suspended for five years. This last clause was intended to sting the young students who might have offered support to anti-foreign movements in their home towns, although its effect was reduced by the general decline of the exam system—the ancient examinations designed to test the mettle of Confucian officials were abolished anyway in 1905. Other demands were similarly softened in their execution—heads did roll among certain government officials, but others were "exiled" to cushy postings in their home provinces or simply out of sight of foreigners. Cixi herself, regarded by many as the Boxers' secret mastermind, escaped censure.

This was the environment that created Qiu Jin (1875–1907) and others like her—Chinese subjects determined to overthrow the Qing dynasty and establish a Republic. In her early twenties, Qiu Jin had been a poet writing about flowers and gardens. Moving to Beijing with her husband in 1902, she became increasingly disillusioned with her life. The city was a wreck, still reeling from the double impact of the Boxer Uprising and the foreign military response. Her husband was a cad, pawning her jewelry and demanding a concubine. She read forbidden pamphlets, printed by the revolutionary overseas Chinese organizations in distant Japan, and she wrote *The Song of the Precious Sword*, in which she accused China of being in a coma. China, she wrote needed to wake up and remember its great past. It needed to listen to the tolling of the bell signified by the "white devils" who occupied Beijing. It needed people like her to risk their lives, pick up swords, shining brighter than jewels "in the light of the sun and moon."

There! There it was, a sun-moon reference to the lost Ming dynasty—a clarion call to rebels. And if that were not clear enough, the song included a call for suicidal resistance, recalling the infamous assassination attempt on the man who would become the First Emperor.

> Don't you recall Jing Ke's visit to the court of Qin?
> When the map was unrolled, the dagger appeared!
> Although he failed to stab him there in the palace,
> He still managed to rob the evil tyrant of his soul!

Qiu Jin sometimes liked to use a pen-name meaning the Woman Warrior of Mirror Lake, likening herself to a wandering heroine from a fantasy novel. Her writings obsess constantly over swords, using terminology lifted from heroic romances. She idolized the Song dynasty hero Yue Fei, writing at least two songs of her own to the tune of his *The River All in Red*:

> My body will not allow me
> To mingle with the men

But my heart is far braver
Than that of a man.

It was in Beijing that Qiu Jin stopped wearing make-up and started attending protests in men's clothes. Arguing with her wastrel, abusive husband, who wanted to take a concubine for himself, she walked out on him and their two children. "I have pawned my hairpins and my rings," she wrote, "to travel across the ocean."

The author Lu Xun, then a young medical student in Japan, witnessed her brandishing a knife before a crowd of Chinese ex-pats and telling them they could stab her with it if she bowed to the Manchus. Qiu Jin published several short-lived magazines and polemic articles in Japan, working towards a theory of revolution that argued that China's men had failed, and that the country could only become strong again through the education and liberation of its women. Alluding to the medieval feminism of Empress Wu, she wrote that women in ancient times were fully the equals of men. Referring to *Uncle Tom's Cabin*, then a hit in translation among Chinese literati, she compared the status of women in China to that of Negro slaves in America.

Women, she said, had to stand up, and that involved unbinding their feet from centuries of oppression. "These... shoes," she wrote, "condemn us to inaction. This must change!"

In Japan, Qiu Jin began work on an epic poem, *Stones of the Jingwei Bird*, a reference to a drowned princess, reincarnated as a bird, who drops pebbles one by one into the sea in a vain attempt to fill it. A powerful, on-the-nose allegory of China, it was set in a fantasy realm, whose ancient Yellow kings had once been great men, but whose descendants were increasingly somnolent and distracted, and whose modern successors were in a state of permanent slumber. Their ministers were befuddled and myopic, prepared to bow to the throne even when a foreigner sat on it, looking only to their own self-interest, and pointing at "primitive books" that justified "keeping women in fetters and ensure that they remained stupid."

Foot-binding, she wrote, was merely the most obvious, painful, pointless hobbling of women in Chinese society, and Chinese society could not see that by holding back its womenfolk—from education and liberation—it was holding back its own ability to resist foreign oppression. And in her fictional allegory, the Queen Mother of the West, ancient Daoist deity, sent a divine squadron of "golden lads and jade maidens" to study in Japan and return to China to save it from itself.

She returned to China, travelling third-class, dressed as a man and wearing a sword for protection. She was fulsome in her praise for Japan, which had proven the power of modernization by winning the Russo-Japanese War of 1904–5. Back among her friends in Shanghai and Shaoxing, she encouraged them to get drunk and perform sword-dances. In 1907, she accepted the post of principal of the Datong School for Girls, where her students would sing lyrics like her *Lament for China*:

> So why do we find it impossible to surpass these white men?
> It is because we are locked in a prison of darkness...

Qiu Jin blamed white men for China's troubles, but she also blamed men in general for ruining women's potential. In particular, she blamed the Manchus—the symbol of her rebel organization was the character *Han*, asserting a desire for return of Chinese rule to the Chinese.

Qiu Jin's later writings had an oddly suicidal tone, as if she knew her days were numbered, and was expecting, like Jing Ke the assassin, to die without seeing if her mission was a success. Her refusal to run after several warnings that the authorities were on to her was either an act of misplaced confidence, or the resignation of woman ready for martyrdom. She had, in fact, been given up by two of Xu Xilin's associates who had cracked under pressure and named her as an accomplice in his intended uprising.

The story of Qiu Jin's arrest and execution may itself be a compromised source—a propaganda story circulated in Shanghai soon after her execution. Since she was already dead, it may be that the rebels deliberately played up her innocence and nonchalance, in order to sow discord and doubt about the Manchu authorities. Regardless of the evidence the Manchus may or may not have had, Qiu Jin most definitely was part of a terrorist cell, and was planning on participating in the abortive uprising. She was even nursing an injured hand, from where she had hurt herself while making bombs the previous month. There would be thousands more like her, and soon they would prevail.

The Empress Dowager Cixi would not live to see it fall apart. As she lay dying in 1908, she ordered a meeting with Guangxu, the nephew whose reforms she had shut down so many years earlier. Guangxu was also seriously ill, and so the two adversaries merely stared balefully at each other from their couches. Soon afterwards, they both died. Forensic tests made on Guangxu's remains in 2008 revealed that his body contained 2,000 times the acceptable level of arsenic. Cixi had poisoned him, to ensure he would not have the last word.

On her own death-bed, she chose a successor who was not even three years old, the Xuantong Emperor (r. 1908–12). The baffled infant burst into tears at his coronation, leading his father and regent, Prince Chun, to soothe him with ominous words of comfort: "Don't worry. Soon this will all be over."

Qiu Jin and thousands like her formed an undercurrent in the last decade of the Qing dynasty, the catalysts of dozens of acts of social dissent, protests and outright uprisings. The Manchus' hold on China was slipping, not only in the provinces, but even within the Forbidden City itself, where the conservative and modernist factions at the court were split on largely racial lines, between Manchus and Han Chinese. Qiu Jin's false plot was one of many false starts, although as the years went by, the level of organization and success grew palpably. An uprising in Guangzhou in 1895 had fizzled before it could start; its instigators went into exile. 20,000 men in nearby Huizhou fought for a fortnight in 1900, before dispersing at the order of their shadowy leader. In 1903, an aging veteran of the Taiping Rebellion tried to proclaim a restoration of the Ming dynasty. In 1907, the year of Qiu Jin's execution, three separate uprisings broke out; another three in 1908. Like an automobile's starter motor straining to catch, the attacks on the Qing increased in momentum and magnitude. News of them spread, and with it, a confidence that a national revolution was approaching.

The ever-faster rise of anti-Qing activities owed something to the amalgamation of multiple revolutionary groups. Literary societies, martial arts schools, factions in military academies, concerned teacher associations, even criminal gangs were slowly unifying.

Sun Yat-sen (1866–1925) had been born into a poor family in Guangdong, but had made good abroad, receiving a modern education in Hawaii. Returning to Hong Kong and planning to study to be a doctor, Sun first courted controversy aged just 17, when he smashed a statue of a Daoist healer-god, reprimanding the locals for having no faith in modern medicine. Sun Yat-sen had been one of the architects of the failed Guangzhou Uprising, and fled to Japan, where he received strong support... at least until he tried to whip up revolution among the Chinese residents of Japan's Taiwan colony. Instrumental in at least ten abortive rebellions, he became a leading figure in an alliance of overseas revolutionaries, calling for the ousting of the Manchus and the modernization of China. By 1905, this had transformed into his Three Principles of the People. Taking a leaf from Abraham Lincoln's "Government of the people, by the people, for the people," Sun proposed *"Minzu, Minquan, Minsheng"*—a people's nation, a people's franchise, and a people's life, usually translated as a call for nationalism, democracy and social welfare. The Three Principles amounted to a call for an inclusive government of all Chinese people, a republican democracy, and a new path that avoided the traps of capitalism and colonialism.

It was to Sun Yat-sen that the republican movement turned in 1911 when one of the uprisings finally caught on. He was, briefly, the provisional president of a new Chinese republic, before he was obliged to step down. Yuan Shikai, the warlord who held Beijing, was the man with his own army, leaving Sun little choice but to relinquish his. Proclaimed as the leader of the Republic of China on January 1, 1912, Sun gave way to Yuan on March 10. He would fail to oust him in another revolt the following year, and spent the rest of his life trying to steer the Republic away from a collapse into warlordism.

One of the icons of Sun's quest for a new alternative was his clothing. Rejecting both traditional Chinese costume and European garb, he instead favored the "Yat-sen Suit." Modeled on Japanese cadet uniforms, it would be loaded with extra symbolism in the years after his death—four pockets in honor of the Four Virtues, five buttons in honor of the five branches of Republican government, and three buttons on each cuff to represent the Three Principles of the People.

Similar symbolism was at work with the original Republican flag, which barely flew for a decade before it was supplanted by something more partisan. Its simple design comprised five colored stripes, evocative of the five elements of Daoist alchemy. Imperial dynasties had associated themselves with a particular element, usually invoking it as proof that they were the rightful heirs to their predecessors, just as the water of Qing quenched the fire of the Ming. The Republican flag, however, manifested an idea that had been brewing since the time of the Mongol conquest, that the colors represented the separate peoples that combined to form the Chinese state.

Republic of China

RUSSIAN EMPIRE

MONGOLIA

MANCHURIA

Tarim

REPUBLIC OF CHINA   Beijing

Yellow River

TIBET

Nanjing

NEPAL

BHUTAN

Yangtze River

BRITISH INDIA

TAIWAN

FRENCH INDO-CHINA

SIAM

Republic of China
China's Modern-day Border
Taiwan, returned to China in 1945

Whereas ancient attitudes once assumed that the Han people were Chinese and that everybody else was barbaric to a varying degree, the Republic of China asserted that there were five flavors to the Chinese melting pot: the Han (red), the Manchus (yellow), the Mongols (blue), the Muslims (white) and the Tibetans (black). This was, of course, a gross oversimplification: it ignored some groups, like ethnic Koreans, that outnumbered some of the races included in the stripes, and created classification headaches for others. The "Muslims" (*Hui*), after all, were not a race, and the word used to describe them could either refer to ethnic Uyghurs, who were not necessarily of the Islamic faith, or Chinese people who happened to be Muslims. At other times, the word *Hui* had been used to refer to all foreigners in China, which might make the white stripe the most inclusive of all, except then it would include people only by defining them as outsiders!

Much as the Guangxu Emperor had failed to reform by decree, the early days of the Republic of China were troubled by the continued presence of all the problems that had brought down the empire. Xuantong, the "Last Emperor," was persuaded to abdicate in 1912, Sun Yat-sen's revolutionary alliance was refashioned as the Nationalist Party (*Guomin Dang*), but the Manchus were still an idle aristocracy, swiftly turning vagrant after their imperial stipends were shut off. Large stretches of China were still lawless or practically independent, foreigners from the Imperial Maritime Customs still held the purse-strings for much of the national budget, and the coast was still riddled with treaty ports. Nor was Yuan Shikai much of a democrat, presiding over a revolving door of prime ministers and a conservative faction spoiling for a counter-coup. In 1915, Yuan went so far as to proclaim himself Emperor, in a move that impressed absolutely nobody. His coronation ceremony repeatedly postponed, the ailing President gave up on the idea in 1916 and died soon afterwards.

Much of Yuan's term as President was troubled by the First World War, in which Japan "liberated" Shandong province from Germany. Unable to provide military assistance, but determined to be at the table during the postwar drawing-up of treaties, China contributed 140,000 laborers in place of soldiers, shipping trench-diggers, laborers and laundrymen to Europe to free up able-bodied white men for the war effort. It was the sinking of a ship transporting some of these laborers that propelled China to officially join the war against Germany in 1916, thereby securing China a place at the Paris Peace Conference that followed the armistice.

There, China's hopes were dashed. Shandong, the birthplace of Confucius and a territory the size of a European country, was handed, not to the Chinese, but to the Japanese who had fought for it, swapping one colonial master for another. "Now the policeman comes along," commented one observer, "rebukes the robber, but allows him to keep the stolen property." All China got in the Treaty of Versailles was the return to Beijing of some antique astronomical instruments, looted by Germans during the Boxer Uprising.

China's envoy refused to sign the Treaty of Versailles on May 4, 1919, and protests broke out all over China at its betrayal by the Western world. The most prominent was in front of the Tiananmen gate, at the front of the Forbidden City in Beijing. Modernization, it seemed, was an empty promise if the foreign powers still dealt China back and forward to each other like a pack of cards. The protests, and the subsequent May Fourth Movement that they engendered, led to a new modernization drive that called for the welcoming of the symbolic figures "Mr. Science" and "Mr. Democracy." It rejected not only the traditional values of imperial China, but many of the claims and promises of western capitalism, earnestly calling for some sort of alternative.

The newly formed Soviet Union was swift to offer one.

"If the Chinese nation desires to become free like the Russian people," wrote the prominent Soviet Commissar Lev Karakhan, "and to escape the destiny prescribed for it as Versailles in order to transform it into a second Korea or a second India, it should understand that its only allies and brothers in the struggle for liberty are the Russian worker and peasant and the Red Army of Russia."

Within the year, China had gained a Socialist Youth League, and Soviet agents were encouraging the formation of a Chinese Communist Party, ready to challenge the incomplete, stumbling Republican revolution with a second uprising—a true movement of the masses, to overthrow the old order and create a Marxist-Leninist state.

China's early Communists enjoyed an uneasy truce with the government of the Republic of China. Soon they were at each other's throats, each accusing the other of pandering to foreign interference and plotting to topple the new order from within. Open hostilities broke out in 1927, when Sun Yat-sen's successor General Chiang Kai-shek (1887–1975) launched the round-up and execution of known Communists. His action would split the Nationalist Party between those who supported his actions, and those who thought they betrayed the principles of Sun Yat-sen.

With China splintering once more, an attempt was made in Jiangxi and Fujian provinces to establish a Chinese Soviet Republic in 1931. This short-lived enclave held out for three years, before it was crushed. Its last defenders commenced a prolonged retreat across the Chinese countryside, hounded by the Nationalists. It would take them 370 days to walk 9,000 kilometers (5,592.3 miles)—west as far as Yunnan, then north through Sichuan, Gansu and east through Ningxia—a journey riddled with hazards and dead-ends, until barely one in ten of them made it to safety, uniting with Communist sympathizers in the Shaanxi wastelands.

The Long March, as it has come to be known, is one the enduring mythologies of the Communist Party. Historians quibble with every element of its narrative, from the number of marchers that left Jiangxi, to the number that joined them en route, to the length of their journey, to the nature of their multiple battles, to the degree to which they enjoyed support from the local peasantry. This is not the place to argue any of these points—suffice to say that despite terrifying deprivation and deadly resistance, they made it, and by the time they did, they had been honed into a fighting force both physically and ideologically prepared to re-engage with the Nationalists. One might also speculate about the kind of posttraumatic stress that might arise in anyone if they were forced to abandon their children, starve on the march, fight off bandits and enemy soldiers, and periodically learn of the execution of one's loved ones and desecration of family graves in distant hometowns. Those that the Long March did not kill, it arguably made stronger, but also meaner, a possibility that would return to haunt the Communist Party in decades to come.

The Long March was certainly a crucible of future political leaders, with military action and internal in-fighting killing off many of the potential rivals for the leading position. Shortly after it reached its terminus, in Yan-an, Shaanxi, one Mao Zedong (1893–1975), the former leader of the Jiangxi Soviet, was named Chairman of the Military Commission.

Chairman Mao was an accomplished survivor. A former librarian and trainee teacher, he was an ardent Communist who swiftly turned his hand to treatises on the nature of the Revolution and Party ideology. He soon was leading the Party both directly, in person, and remotely, through the publication and dissemination of his many speeches and articles. One of his most influential early works was *On Guerilla Warfare* (1937), in which he outlined the need for the Communists to pursue an asymmetric strategy against the enemies that outnumbered them, making surgical strikes against men and materiel, but also ensuring that they won the support of nearby non-combatants.

He would not, however, sanction open conflict with the Nationalists for another seven years. Despite his hatred for Chiang Kai-shek, he accepted that both Communists and Nationalists needed to unite to hold off a greater threat. The Empire of Japan had annexed northeast China, proclaiming the breakaway state of Manchukuo in the old Manchu homelands, and seizing a wide strip of territory stretching from Inner Mongolia to Shanghai. From 1937–45, the mortal enemies of the Nationalists and Communists would form a united front against the Japanese, only turning against each other once more after the defeat of the Japanese in 1945.

Then, however, the Chinese Civil War reignited. Since no peace treaty or armistice has ever been signed, it is technically still ongoing. It would cost China another six million lives between 1946 and 1949, before Chiang Kai-shek, his currency in freefall, his local power-bases destroyed, would flee mainland China. The last of the Nationalists, some two million people, bolted for Taiwan, which had been restored to the Republic of China only four years earlier after 50 years as a Japanese colony. There, they continued to claim sovereignty over the whole of China, even though the Republic of China now amounted to little more than Taiwan itself and a few outlying islands. The Communists had every intention of taking Taiwan. The Nationalists had every intention of taking back the rest of China. The stand-off between them, however, has endured ever since, as both sides have been distracted by other concerns. For the next two decades, the United Nations continued to recognize the Republic of China, now on Taiwan, as the rightful government of the entire country, as if expecting the Communists to fade away.

Chairman Mao had other ideas. On October 1, 1949, he climbed the steps to the balcony of Tiananmen, the Gate of Heavenly Peace, from which imperial decrees had traditionally been read out to the Emperors' waiting subjects. He did so alongside a gaggle of Communist Party officials, who had approved proposals for Beijing to be the capital of new "People's" Republic, and for Mao to be its new head of state. Below them, the area in front of the gate had been enlarged to make space for a larger crowd—parkland cleared and relaid with flagstones. The portrait of Chiang Kai-shek, which once graced the front of the gate, had been torn down and replaced by one of Mao himself.

Mao cleared his throat and addressed the crowd below.

"We, the 475 million Chinese people, have stood up," he proclaimed, "and our future is infinitely bright."

# CHAPTER 10

# THE EAST IS RED: THE PEOPLE'S REPUBLIC

T here is plenty of drama on show, to be sure. Wu Qinghua, the poor peasant's daughter, somehow wrests herself free from her bonds in the evil landlord's dungeon, shortly before he could sell her into slavery to pay off her family debts. She flees into the coconut palm forest of her native Hainan, but is recaptured and whipped by the landlord's lackeys. Rescued by scouts from the Red Army, she tells them of the landlord's crimes against the masses, and is co-opted into the Red Detachment of Women. It's a steep learning curve for the inexperienced Qinghua. She almost blows a mission when she fires her gun in haste, but she accepts the criticism of her colleagues, and embarks on training in marksmanship and grenade throwing.

The soldiers of the Red Army befriend the local people, the Li aborigines, who are keen to join the Revolution. But the battle against the oppressors is hard, and the commissar Qinghua idolizes sacrifices himself to cover a strategic withdrawal.

As battle joins with the enemy a seemingly unending line of Red Army soldiers leaps and bounds across the stage. It seems to go on forever. They must be scurrying around the back and getting on the end again.

Watching in the audience, US President Richard Nixon smiles wryly. His day has been long enough already, including a four-hour meeting with President Zhou Enlai, in which they'd tried to come up with some kind of answer for the Vietnam War. Now this… He resists the temptation to look at his watch. Outside, there are flurries of snow in the Beijing air, but the theater feels stuffy.

He realizes that his neighbor is looking intently at his expression, and

he has to say something or she will think he is mocking the performance.

"Amazing!" he whispers, as the interpreter behind him hisses a translation. "Such an amazing... musical."

Jiang Qing, the wife of Chairman Mao, frowns at the last word.

"Musical?" she asks, in a normal tone of voice, sure that nobody will reprimand her for talking during the show.

"Well, musical, ballet, acrobatic display, it really has everything!" he says, and she nods as if he has come up with a more correct response. "And that girl in the lead, such a mover!"

"Ah yes," says Jiang Qing, smiling thinly. "Comrade Xue plays the role with such grace and intensity. She was in the film version, too. I picked her out from many contenders. She reminds me of myself when I was younger."

Nixon nods, smiling uneasily, trying to think of something to say. He looks to his left, hoping for some aid from his wife, Pat, but Mrs. Nixon is staring fixedly at the stage as *The Red Detachment of Women* clocks up its second hour.

"Who wrote this?" Nixon asks. "I mean, who is responsible for it? I heard it was all you."

Jiang Qing thinks for a while as the music continues to play. Onstage, the evil landlord character, who looks uncannily like Henry Kissinger in the right light, is arguing with his flunkies. The captured commissar is dancing in a torn uniform.

Jiang Qing wants to tell Nixon that yes, it was all her. Every single element of this performance is hers. Forget the writer, forget the dancers, forget the choreographers and the set designers, the director. *It was all her.* Without her, it wouldn't have even gone into production in the first place.

But then she swallows, takes a deep breath and carefully replies.

"It was created," she says, "by the masses."

$\odot-\odot-\odot-\odot-\odot$

"Chairman" Mao derived his title from multiple positions—leader of the Military Commission, leader of the People's Republic of China (PRC), but also of the Chinese Communist Party. This helps to explain, and indeed predict, much of the fluctuations in his policy and outlook in the three decades that followed. His authority could wane within the government, but he still held the reins of the Party, giving him an unassailable position as the curator of Party ideology. And there was always the People's Liberation Army to lean on if things got rough. He remains an unassailable icon of Chinese Communism—his portrait still hangs before the Tiananmen gate in Beijing, and his image can be found in statues and posters all around the country. Ironically for a man who once wanted to ban money, his face is to be found on all Chinese banknotes of one yuan or above. Lower denominations contained diverse images of China's ethnic minorities, but inflation has almost entirely removed these notes from circulation, leaving only the higher-value banknotes bearing Mao's image.

Party policy wonks would be swift to quell any comment that likened Mao to an emperor or a god, but he has achieved a quasi-religious status in modern China. He was the last man standing of the original, chaotic interest groups that opposed the old order, a leader and a thinker who had endured incredible hardships to drag China up by its bootstraps, resisting not only the Qing dynasty, but also the foreign imperialists and the Nationalist regime that had promised change but failed to deliver. He had rallied the Chinese people against enemies from both within and without, and lived to proclaim the People's Republic of China. If only, his supporters might be heard to utter, he had stopped there.

Tang Xiaoju's *Concise History of the Communist Party* (2012), published by the Party's own press, glosses over the period from 1956–76 by pleading that "some mistakes were inevitably made," admitting that the Party "rushed things through in economic construction after 1957," and committed the "overall and long-term mistake" that was the Cultural Revolution of 1966–76. Such comments reflect the assessment of Party grandees in more recent years, prepared to admit that Mao was a vital spur for resistance and revolution, but that after coming to power, he was a toxic decision-maker. Battlefield justice and permanent revolution might have propelled him to victory in the wars against the Japanese and the Nationalists, but left him ill-suited to consider the effectiveness of wide-ranging, game-changing national policies.

General histories only have room for a few major players—a book such as this lacks the space to chronicle the nuances of ideological argument that created factions and power-brokers within the government. Mao was ousted from his presidential role by 1959, causing him to cling ever more tightly to his more title as the chairman of the Party itself. In his later years, this position, which we might reasonably call one of power without responsibility, allowed him to meddle in state matters to an unprecedented degree.

Party grandees were swift to take the credit for early successes—kind weather, better planning and logistics certainly helped, but China enjoyed something of a honeymoon period in the early 1950s, its social engineers unaware of how much they owed to the climate itself. But when matters took a turn for the worst again, it was no longer possible to discuss the possibility that an imperial Mandate of Heaven had been withdrawn. Communist China was supposed to be a final escape from the fluctuations of the past, a literal end to history, which meant even the idea of backsliding on productivity was a sign of counter-revolution. Even when the good harvests declined, Party officials were fearful of reporting the truth, while Mao continued to push for the realization of his utopian dreams. Communism, at least as far as Mao defined it, was an earnest promise to make during wartime struggles. But now the Communists had won, their supporters were faced with the prospect of continued, fundamental changes to their lives and world.

"For many years," Mao had said, "we Communists have struggled for a cultural revolution as well as for a political and economic revolution, and our aim is to build a new society and a new state for the Chinese nation. That new society and new state will have not only a new politics and a new economy but a new culture."

Maoism would take the May Fourth Movement to extremes, openly proclaiming that China in the past had been "kept ignorant and backward under the sway of the old culture." Much as the First Emperor had established a year zero for his new state, Mao's China aimed to discard old laws, land allocations and even customs. Some were more easily discarded than others.

Communist China did not exist in a vacuum. Within a year of the proclamation of the People's Republic, China was dragged into the Korean War, losing a million men in the fighting, including Mao's own son. By the end of the conflict in 1951, the US was patrolling the Taiwan Strait, keenly bolstering Chiang Kai-shek's rump regime on Taiwan. The PRC had ended the 1940s convinced that it was only a matter of time before its last wayward province could be won over. Now, with whispers on the mainland that "Chiang Kai-shek would be back in time to eat his moon cakes" (that is, that he would conquer the mainland by the Autumn Festival), the Communist Party turned more paranoid.

The first casualty was the planned land reform. Party policy had wavered in severity throughout the 1940s, and remained undetermined. There were times when the Communists had planned only to confiscate large land-holdings and the possessions of Japanese collaborators; others when the Party position was the confiscation of all land before it was redistributed to the peasants. Mao himself supported a supposedly moderate process, in which only the holdings of the richest were taken. This backfired terribly, as the poorest Chinese with literally nothing to lose interpreted his ruling as a license to steal everything that was not nailed down. Honest farmers in Henan, for example, many of them supporters of the Party, were reclassified as "rich" by local gangs simply for owning a single surplus chicken or similar such arbitrary distinctions. They were not merely deprived of their land, but all their possessions (something expressly forbidden in the reform rules), while industrial premises (similarly ring-fenced in the reforms) were ransacked by mobs.

Mao's answer to this growing chaos was to rip power away from the peasants until they had learned how it was supposed to be used. Every village was put under the control of a peasant militia, at first to police possible Nationalist insurgence, but then to classify the landlords. Only then was the militia authorized to move on capitalist exploitation, "encouraging" landlords to cancel debts and reduce rents, before enforcing the redistribution of land through an elected village council.

The Party's reforms also targeted the industrial sector, much of it in areas that had been formerly held by the Japanese. Campaigns in Manchuria rooted out bribery, the theft of state property (either literally or through tax evasion), cheating on government contracts and the theft of state economic information. Private businesses came under intense scrutiny, with workers incentivized to report any potential wrong-doing by their employers—as in the farms, this inevitably turned into a purge against former beneficiaries of the capitalist system.

In understanding the exuberance and the extremes of the early Communist era, we need to consider just what that generation had been through. Someone like Mao himself, had been born in the imperial era—indeed, Mao had been one of the last candidates to prepare for the old civil service examinations, dating back to the Han dynasty. His generation had seen the end of two thousand years of imperial rule, fifteen years in a war against Japan, and four years of civil war against the Nationalists. The Chinese people, as Mao announced in 1949 in his speech from the Tiananmen gate, "had stood up," although now they found themselves in a new and unsure world, in an increasingly tense relationship with their fellow Communists in the Soviet Union, and confronted by political maneuverings from the colonial powers ousted from China. Even as China proclaimed itself free of the Unequal Treaties and predatory foreign powers, it found itself sharing frontiers with American-supported and American-influenced regimes in Southeast Asia, South Korea, Japan and Taiwan.

Mao idolized the First Emperor. The founder of China's first, short-lived imperial dynasty had been vilified throughout Chinese history as a tyrant, but Mao saw in him a hard-pressed ruler with an impossible job to do, determined to demolish the old order and build a better world on the rubble. Like many a dynasty before it, Communist China enjoyed a regime-change dividend. While not quite as extreme as the slave labor legions that built the roads, walls and tomb of the First Emperor, there were entire battalions of demobilized Nationalist soldiers, vagrants, prostitutes and beggars that could be resettled on the western frontiers, creating a military-industrial cabal in the wastes of Xinjiang, and swamping the local population with Han colonists.

Like the First Emperor's grand schemes for China, Mao's modernization required a central control, in order to ensure that widespread, specialized areas were able to support each other. His grand schemes for farm collectivization, road-building, industrial streamlining and irrigation works all have echoes of the large-scale state enterprises from the ancient state of Qin, but also of the optimistic science-centered modernism of Soviet government planning.

In imitation of Soviet Russia's Five-Year Plans, Mao turned to a series of state-wide targets and reforms—China's First Five-Year Plan spanned 1953–58, its Thirteenth matures in 2020. For the First, Mao called in Soviet advisers on 694 construction projects, while moving more than half of China's surviving private enterprises into state ownership. Farming and handicraft cooperatives turned former cottage industries into increasingly large-scale enterprises controlled by the state. Income for participants in these new collectives was originally assessed on the amount of *land* someone brought to the enterprise; before long, that was changed to the amount of *labor* they brought, equalizing everybody to the level of a single, productive worker.

Again, in an echo of the First Emperor's reforms, the language itself was simplified, with many of the more complex components of Chinese writing reduced to more manageable graphics. The scheme boosted literacy in schools, at least in part by making literacy in Mandarin more easily achievable, although it had the side-effect of rendering any pre-1950s Chinese document harder to read without specialist training. Books from Nationalist-held Taiwan, or Japan, or Hong Kong, all of which used older-form Chinese characters, also became less intelligible to mainland readers.

The same period also saw a reform in the way Chinese was Romanized. Deriding the old spelling system as a colonial imposition, the People's Republic introduced its own set of approved spellings for Chinese words. Older spellings were born from the 19th century or earlier, when many a foreigner down south was struggling to make sense of Chinese with a pronounced Cantonese or Shanghai accent. The new spelling reforms favored the northern accent, but also a certain preference for Russian orthography—a few too many "zh" and "x" sounds for some. Peking was now Bei-jing—the words are intended to be pronounced the same, which tells you all you need to know about the unsuitability of the old system. Nanking was now Nanjing. As with the writing reforms, these changes made life easier for the younger generation (including late 20th century learners of Chinese, like myself), but also forced many a reader into cross-eyed con-centration over conflicting spellings. This book has used Pinyin Roman-ization throughout, but works published a hundred years ago spell most nouns distractingly differently.

Communist China inherited a concept, from both the Republic of China and the Qing Dynasty that preceded it, that there was more to China than the Han people. At least according to the law, all ethnic minorities were recognized as equal. Not all minorities, however, were even aware that there was no longer an Emperor, and several outreach teams were dispatched into the hinterland in the early 1950s to register, report, and administer basic healthcare to China's scattered tribes. The 1953 national census recognized some 400 groups of "self-reported" ethnic minorities, although teams of linguists, geographers and ethnographers subsequently whittled that number down to a more manageable fifty-five. They did so in something of a hurry, forcing them to rely to on some categories derived from the era of the Republic, as well as inadequate blanket categories, fudges and guesswork. There are still, occasionally, grumbles from the minorities about formerly separate tribes being grouped under the same catch-all umbrella, merely because a Soviet-trained phonologist thought they had a similar word for "dog."

Racism was counter-revolutionary—the very idea that there were su-perior and inferior races was a creation of the foreign imperialists, leading Party rhetoric of the 1950s into a series of acrobatic claims that both im-plied the superiority of the majority Han, while also deconstructing the "chauvinism" that Han privilege brought with it. Some ethnic groups were awarded autonomous homelands to quell separatist tendencies, repeating many of the arrangements of ancient "loose rein" policies. Xinjiang be-came the Uyghur Autonomous Region, alongside similar autonomous areas for Tibetans, Mongols and sundry other tribes. While it might have looked good on paper, in practice the ethnic enclaves were carefully bal-anced. Autonomous regions were under the control of local boys who had made good by joining the Communist Party; local bigwigs were often the products of urban education in the Han heartland. As for the regions themselves, their ethnic make-up was often diluted or compromised—a "Kazakh" prefecture with a heavy Uyghur population; a Miao county comprising practically unmanageable hillside farms, requiring close connections with its Han-majority neighbors to survive. The rhetoric of racism might have been discouraged, but it was replaced by a new snobbery that favored Party affiliation. If you talked like a peasant and displayed a healthy mistrust of intellectuals; if you were a long-standing Party member and best of all, came from a family of workers, you were part of the new elite. If you had Manchu blood or were the child of former landlords, you were a second-class citizen in Mao's New China. A new aristocracy developed of Party dignitaries—"princelings" whose fathers and mothers had been present at the Long March or in battles against the Japanese.

Many intellectuals, victimized by the Nationalist government, had embraced the Communist Party as a better alternative. Social scientists, especially, found a ready home among the national experiments of the PRC, but so, too did many humanities scholars and authors, lured by Mao's early promises of intellectual freedom.

One of Mao's early victims was Liang Shuming, an author who had often written about the contradictions between a traditional Confucian society, the concerns of the individualist, capitalist West, and Marxist class struggle. Mao turned on Liang for even suggesting that there were alternatives to Marxism—the future would be a socialist utopia, and all previous systems were wrong.

Nor did Mao spare the arts in his search for enemies of the Party, drilling down to matters of interpretation and attitude. He directed the full force of his anger at *The Life of Wu Xun*, a film about an orphan who campaigned for rural educational reform. Mao, however, was furious that its protagonist was shown seeking *charity*, when a true revolutionary should have just taken what was theirs by right. Anonymously, he attacked it in a vicious editorial in the *People's Daily*—the first nationwide criticism of a work of art in the short history of the People's Republic. It would not be the last, as Mao pushed against a "black line" of unacceptable cultural products that were not to be tolerated in China.

Party members were not safe. In 1954, the writer Hu Feng published the *Report on the Practice and State of Art and Literature in Recent Years*, intended as an audit of early Communist cultural policy. In it, he warned of the "Five Daggers" pointed at creativity in China. There was, he wrote, too great a concentration on Marxism, which should not be allowed to impinge on the arts. There was too much about reforming thought, which risked turning every artwork into a hectoring moral message; too much about peasants, soldiers and the working class, as if everybody else had ceased to matter. There was a bullish refusal to embrace any new ideas (many of which inevitably came from the discredited west), and an obvious trend towards endlessly "sunny subjects" from authors and artists afraid of being censured for negative attitudes towards the new government.

Hu Feng had been a leading figure in the May Fourth Movement and a powerful presence in the Party, but his opinion was deemed unwelcome and counter-revolutionary. He was thrown in prison in 1955 and would only be released in 1979, long after the Five Daggers he foresaw had ruined a generation of Chinese culture.

Mao's 1957 speech "On the Correct Handling of Contradictions Among the People" attempted to wrestle with the fact that the first Five-Year Plan had not been perfect, and that the Soviet Union itself kept changing its mind about Marxist policies that everybody had expected to be right forever.

Arguing, Mao had decided, was a good thing. It was a good idea to let people come up with alternative views and self-criticisms designed to fine-tune the perfect state. In a classical reference that alluded to the clashes of rival philosophies in the Warring States period, Mao decreed: "Let a hundred flowers bloom; let a hundred schools of thought contend."

It is likely that Mao regarded this as the ideal chance to whip his own faction into action, and that any criticisms arising would be directed at his rivals. If so, he was taken by surprise by a growing fervor for attacking his own policies. He swiftly changed his tune, and would later claim that the entire campaign calling for honest criticism had been a ruse to lure his opponents into the open. "How can we catch the snakes if we don't let them out of their lairs?" he said to his colleagues. "We wanted those [bastards] to wriggle and sing and fart... that way we can catch them."

The friendship between China and the Soviet Union obscured the last of the great land-grabs. Nikita Khrushchev, the Russian premier, made a great show of coming to China to hand back the treaty port of Lushun, but neglected to mention that huge areas of "Russian" Siberia had been Chinese until 1858. Whereas Mao and his inheritors would lobby for the return of Hong Kong and Macau from the British and Portuguese, the Russian ownership of the Siberian coast remained uncontested.

But the Russian love-in was soon over. In 1956, Khrushchev signaled a change in attitudes in the Soviet Union by openly criticizing the late dictator Josef Stalin and his personality cult. The speech had explosive consequences in China, since it admitted that a Communist state could still make mistakes that required correction. Since Mao and his colleagues had been diligently following Stalin's economic and social models for years, it also implied that they had been getting something wrong. Concerned that Soviet reforms would allow capitalism to sneak back in, Mao began to speak again of permanent revolution, warning his people to be on constant guard to prevent a slide back into the old ways.

A decade after the proclamation of the People's Republic of China, Mao demanded a Great Leap Forward, a concerted national effort and sacrifice that would drag China out of its agrarian roots and turn it into an industrial, socialist economy. Still aping the Russians, Mao observed that Khrushchev had promised to overtake the U.S. economy within 15 years. "I can also say, 15 years later, we may catch up with or exceed the UK," he boasted. His plans for doing so involved further social experiments. Private land ownership was to be supplanted by publicly owned communes, in which relentless time and resource management was designed to squeeze the maximum productivity from human beings and their labor. Crops were planted closer together or within deeper furrows in misguided attempts to increase yields. Citizens were encouraged to increase steel production by constructing backyard furnaces, although these rarely produced anything of value. Instead, villagers desperate to show acceptable levels of productivity were reduced to melting down their own metal tools in order to have something to show for it. Grain yields similarly failed to live up to expectations, although few cadres dared to report the true figures. Mao had already made it clear that failure to live up to his expectations was a tacit criticism of his policies, after all.

The climate initially appeared to bend to Mao's will. The harvest in 1958 was bountiful beyond all expectations, although ironically many crops were left to rot in the fields, because peasants had been reassigned to fruitless smelting duties. Heedless, Mao doubled his productivity requirements, expecting an "explosion" of energy among the Chinese as they found themselves free to run their lives without foreign interference. Party cadres passed their unrealistic projections down the chain of command, until peasants on the ground found themselves facing impossible demands for up to six times the previous level of productivity. Falsified reports may have saved them from immediate danger, but would return to bite them as poor harvests returned and official records showed them having such a high grain surplus that they would require no food aid.

The Great Leap Forward from 1958–61 turned from optimism to disaster, as Mao's unquestionable authority caused hare-brained schemes to be applied on a national level. The backyard furnaces generated little useful metal, but required so much fuel that hillsides were stripped of trees, and vital coal supplies were wasted. Productivity requirements infected all areas of public life—archaeologists began "excavating" sites with bulldozers in order to find more artifacts to meet their quotas, while families were encouraged to have as many children as possible, to create a generation of future workers. Everything would be fine—the grain reports showed that there was plenty of food to go around, after all... right? His most infamous was a campaign against pests, exhorting the peasants to hunt down every sparrow in the country, in order to preserve more grain for human consumption. The loss of the birds had an unexpected cascade effect, wiping out the leading predator that had kept bed-bugs and locusts under control, and leading to new plagues.

Mao realized that his projections were woefully over-the-top, and he dropped his quotas by 30%, not realizing that this was still far above reasonable levels. It was too late, the climate in 1959 turned to drought, leading to famine and political unrest. A revolt in Tibet, suppressed by the People's Liberation Army, led to the flight of the Dalai Lama into exile, and Mao resigned as national leader—not as an act of contrition, but as a political gambit in order to allow his successor to carry the blame for escalating problems. Making a show of self-criticism, he piously advised his fellow Party members to learn from the example of the Ming dynasty official Hai Rui, who had fearlessly cautioned the Jiajing Emperor when he disapproved of his actions.

By the time the Chinese were able to take stock of the situation, China had suffered through drought, famine, a plague of locusts, floods after the Yellow River had burst its banks, creating a further cycle of famine and disaster. Conservative estimates place the number of deaths—not only from starvation, but from unrest and in the later stages in some places, even cannibalism—at thirty million people. It also cost Mao his role as head of state, thereby forcing him to cling to his power and privileges by enforcing ideological policies instead.

A 1962 war with India supposedly erupted over frontier disputes, but truly owed much of its motivation to the two countries' influence over Tibet. India had offered asylum to the exiled Dalai Lama, leading Mao to suspect that India had designs on Tibet itself. Witch-hunts were conducted against suspected Indian agitators in Tibet, and the conflict itself broke out over areas which would have had strategic value in a future Indian invasion of Chinese territory. Mao had counted on the Soviets to support him; when Soviet sanctions and actions against India were not forthcoming, he began to suspect that Russia, too, coveted Chinese territory—perhaps grasslands of north Xinjiang.

Resolving not to make the same errors as the Qing dynasty, Mao embraced modern military technology. China tested its first nuclear weapon in 1964, detonating a 22-kiloton device at Lop Nur, the salt pan in Xinjiang that had once been a brackish ancient sea at the edge of the Taklamakan Desert. The device, codenamed "Project 596" was named for the date, June 1959, when the Soviet Union had withdrawn support for a Chinese nuclear program. Of equivalent power to the bomb dropped by the U.S. on Nagasaki in 1945, it announced China's entry into the club of nuclear powers.

Foreign enemies suitably warned off, Mao turned to enemies within, complaining that the younger generation in China had grown up complacent, without enduring the sacrifices and hardships of the parents who had made the revolution happen. The revolution, as Mao tirelessly reminded people, was not a single one-off event, but an ongoing, evolving program of deep, invasive social change that would not be over for decades. It was necessary to carry it forward, not only in the forms of laws and social reforms, but in terms of attitudes and expectations. His weapon in this campaign was more destructive than any of the bombs being tested in the Taklamakan Desert, ultimately costing hundreds of thousands of lives—the "Little Red Book" of quotations from his articles and speeches, compiled by editors at the *People's Liberation Army Daily*.

*Quotations from Chairman Mao Tse-Tung*, to give it its full title, unreformed spelling and all, not only pushily asserted his unspecified chairmanship (you might be forgiven for forgetting that he was now Chairman of the Party, not the country), but also condensed his decades of revolu-

CHAPTER 10

tionary work into a collection of pithy sayings and aphorisms. His faction within the Party ensured that it swamped Chinese publishing—print runs went into the millions, even in the early stages, crowding out more established theorists like Marx and Engels from bookshelves and conversations. But then again, as Mao was sure to argue, they had been foreigners without any appreciation of the unique conditions and requirements of Chinese socialism. It was time to stop slavishly following the playbook of foreign troublemakers (including, it was implied, the Soviets), and to interpret the facts from a Chinese perspective.

Mao's words made their way onto propaganda posters and badges, often stripped from context and rearranged. "Let the past serve the present," asserted one Mao badge. "Let foreign things serve China, let one hundred flowers bloom, drive out the old and promote the new."

One of his new developments was "The East is Red" (*Dong Fang Hong*), an old Shaanxi folksong retooled in a revolutionary age. It had originally been a ditty about a love-sick girl making dinner, but had gained new lyrics in the 1940s celebrating Communist heroes. It had been a popular singalong in the revolutionary days, but fell out of favor after 1949 when Party opinion-formers objected to its hero-worshiping tone. By 1966, however, Mao's faction had reintroduced it, to the extent that it was heard all over China, and even sung in place of the country's official national anthem.

The east is red, the sun is rising
From China comes Mao Zedong
He strives for the people's happiness
Hurrah, he is the people's savior.

Chairman Mao loves the people
He is our guide
In the building of a new China
Hurrah, lead us forward!

The Communist Party is like the sun
Wherever it shines, it is bright
Wherever the Communist Party is
Hurrah, the people are liberated!

Songs were not the only battleground. Mao used any means necessary to go for his enemies. In an era when open criticism could lead to censure and arrest, Mao became justifiably paranoid about allusions and allegories in works of supposed fiction. He realized that the Party official and some-time author Wu Han had played him for a fool, facetiously taking him at his word to be "more like Hai Rui," and writing a series of articles and a play about the famous Ming minister, investigating what that might really mean. Hai Rui, after all, had been ridiculed by his contemporaries for his refusal to compromise, and attacked by corrupt ministers for being an in-ept hypocrite. But Hai Rui had been a true champion of the downtrodden, a fearless official who had refused to bend to corruption, who had been sentenced to death by a crazy, misinformed tyrant. The final straw came when Wu wrote an opera on the subject, *Hai Rui Dismissed from Office* (*Hai Rui Ba Guan*) which was widely acknowledged as a retelling of Mao's purging of his most honest critics in 1959, with the drugged, deluded, ranting Jiajing Emperor standing in for Mao himself.

Mao struck back in the newspapers, arranging for a Shanghai critic to denounce *Hai Rui Dismissed from Office* as an attack on Mao himself. In an attempt at damage control, Wu's superiors tried to suppress the ar-ticle, giving Mao the excuse to proclaim a nest of enemies—rightists and counter-revolutionaries—in Beijing itself. He mobilized his own forces against them.

The Little Red Book found enthusiastic support among the youth Mao wanted to cultivate, a generation of young Chinese who had grown up with the personality cult of Mao as the supreme leader. When, in 1966, Mao proclaimed that the state had been infiltrated by revisionists intent on walking the country back to capitalism, his supporters took to the streets in his name, proclaiming themselves to be Red Guards, defenders of the revolution.

The Red Guards appointed themselves as judges of revolutionary spirit, taking to heart Mao's dangerous exhortation that rot had set in at the heart of the government, and the only way to preserve the revolution was to "bombard the headquarters." Mobs turned on teachers for claiming to know more than their students; on engineers for using dangerous foreign knowledge. Intellectuals were hated, as were ethnic minorities who failed to support the revolution—old-style Han chauvinism now manifesting itself as an assault on those who race or religious beliefs did not conform.

Wreckers attacked the "Four Olds"—Old Customs, Old Habits, Old Customs and Old Ideas. As one might expect when fervent teenagers were put in charge of cultural policy and told to destroy anything old, this amounted to almost anything that predated their own birth. Museums and libraries were wrecked, artworks destroyed, streets and shops hastily renamed with earnest revolutionary titles. At the Ming Tombs outside Beijing, Red Guards destroyed the statue of the Yongle Emperor. They dragged the remains of the Wanli Emperor and his two concubines from their tomb, denounced them and set them on fire. In Shandong, Red Guards set about the tomb of Confucius with pickaxes, eventually speeding along the process by destroying his grave with dynamite.

The Red Guards were stopped by the People's Liberation Army at the gates of the Forbidden City itself—Mao's colleague Zhou Enlai having decided that enough was enough. The chaos had cost untold lives and ruined many cultural artifacts, no to mention disrupting the education of an entire generation. The aging Mao, already in his seventies, had purged some of his rivals and accusers in the Party, and continued his program with a demand for "re-education," in which anyone with insufficient revolutionary credentials would be sent to the countryside to work on farms and learn first-hand about the realities of peasant life.

Those in need of such re-education included anyone regarded by Mao or his faction as "capitalist roaders" intent on returning to the old ways, which inevitably meant anyone who seemed in any way opposed to any Communist ideas: intellectuals, people with relatives overseas, and anyone with connections to religion or tribalism that might be seen as opposed to Communist principles.

The Cultural Revolution led to a population in fear, the men all dressing alike in Yat-sen suits in order to avoid sticking out or betraying Communist principles—the ubiquity of the uniform tunic in the period has led to the Yat-sen suit being widely known outside China as the "Mao suit." Meanwhile, Mao's wife Jiang Qing (1914–91), one of the anonymous authors of the attacks on *Hai Rui Dismissed from Office*, became Mao's most enthusiastic ally in the world of the arts. A former actress and notorious hypochondriac, Jiang Qing had had little to do in the postrevolutionary world until she found her true profession as Mao's cultural hatchet-woman. Taking to heart Mao's attacks on unwelcome "feudal and bourgeois" elements in so much contemporary entertainment, she was appointed as deputy director of the Central Cultural Revolution Group, in which role she purged the media of anything that could be seen to promote privilege, old ways, or forbidden ideas. Mao had already said "Culture a peasant cannot understand is not culture;" Jiang Qing took his pronouncement to outrageous extremes, with no foreign text, imperial theme, or proscribed historical figure permitted in the public eye. Jiang became the arbiter of all taste in entertainment, and with few creatives prepared to risk angering her, soon became the impresario behind almost the entire artistic repertoire of the Cultural Revolution era.

Her pride and joy were the Eight Model Plays, each deemed to reach the correct levels of education and worthiness. Although none of them was the work of Jiang Qing herself, she was so invasive in their selection, rehearsal, staging and casting that they were often regarded as "her" plays. *The Legend of the Red Lantern*, for example, told the story of girl living in China under Japanese occupation, who discovers that she is merely the latest generation in her family to take on revolutionary struggle for the freedom of her people. *Taking Tiger Mountain by Strategy*, on the other hand, focuses on the struggle between the Communists and the Nationalists in 1946, based on a true story about a scout who disguises himself as a bandit in order to infiltrate an enemy installation. Best known of all, however, was *The Red Detachment of Women*, loosely based on another true story, about a female Red Army group that fought against landlord oppressors on the southern island of Hainan. Mixing Party political messages with balletic re-enactments of military operations and dances inspired by the island's aboriginal people, it had everything—tropical scenery, noble sacrifice, a feminist message and stirring set-pieces.

> March on, march on
> As soldiers we face duty, as women we face oppression
> In ancient times, Hua Mulan enlisted for her father's sake
> The Women's Detachment fights for the masses.

If you wanted to argue, you could point out that Mulan was a fictional character, and a heroine of the discredited traditional operas that Jiang Qing and her cronies had banned. The ballet sections, while incorporating Chinese themes and movements, nevertheless had an awful lot of bourgeois European ballet going on in them. Regardless, the Cultural

Revolution successfully shrank the Chinese theatrical repertoire to a tiny handful of approved works. In later years, some have been praised for their technical merits, but during peak Revolution, pure "entertainment" was looked down upon. There was plenty of time for scenes that played more like homework, including an inevitable pause in the action for someone to sing about the usefulness of Chairman Mao's thoughts on education.

Mao was ailing. Not even the greatest emperor could live forever, and even though his Red Guards had been calling for him to live for "Ten Thousand Years," the official imperial greeting, he would not live to see his revolution concluded. The machinations over his successor, and the direction of Chinese policy after his inevitable death, similarly took on the tone of many an imperial succession crisis.

The cooling relationship with the Soviet Union broke out into open conflict over a tiny islet in the Ussuri River on the Russo-Chinese border in 1969. Unsure of his old friends' loyalties, Mao sought alliances elsewhere, a plan helped greatly by the tardy admission of the United Nations that the People's Republic was the true government of China. Until the adoption of UN Resolution 2758 in 1971, China's seat on the UN Security Council had been occupied by the *Republic* of China. The Republic continued to claim sovereignty over all of China (including Outer Mongolia and Tibet), even though its representatives had been in exile on Taiwan since 1949.

Amid protests from the Republic of China's representatives, and hefty dissenting votes from 35 member states, the United Nations voted to acknowledge the People's Republic as the government of China, plunging the Republic of China into international limbo. As the ancient Chinese saying goes, there could not be "two suns in the sky"—both factions acknowledged that Taiwan was part of China, but for as long as the Republic claimed sovereignty over the entire country, it was relegated to the status of a rogue province, neither able to call itself the Chinese government, nor admit to its de facto status as an independent island.

The reversal was a cause for scandal among many overseas Chinese, including in the USA, where President Richard Nixon had been elected to power with the support of a powerful lobby of Chinese-Americans with strong ties to Taiwan. Nixon, however, wasted no time in cementing relations with the People's Republic, rushing to Beijing in 1972 for the first visit to the People's Republic by a U.S. president.

Nixon's visit to China marked the beginning of the normalization of relations between China and the United States—before long, there would be ambassadorial appointments, trade deals and diplomatic deals. For both sides, it amounted to a message delivered to the Soviet Union that there was no such thing as Communist "bloc"—not all Communist countries followed the Kremlin's party line, and China could make deals elsewhere.

Nixon's visit to China was celebrated in postage stamps, in commemorative plates and posters, and in a minimalist opera by John Adams. It is remembered most for Nixon's presidential comment on seeing the Great Wall—"*It sure is a great wall.*"—and for the Shanghai Communiqué, a joint declaration that has steered Sino-U.S. relations ever since. As well as promising that neither country would seek political dominance in the Asia-Pacific region, it asserted that there was only "One China"—this overtly innocent statement has served over the ensuing four decades to exclude representatives of the Republic of China from attending any international summit, conference or even sporting events attended by representatives from the People's Republic of China.

As Mao neared death, his would-be successors were divided into two factions, both only known by the names used by their enemies. His wife Jiang Qing and her allies (the "Gang of Four") hoped to cling to power and continue his counter-revolutionary policies. Their oft-repeated soundbite was to live true to the "principles laid down" by Mao in his later decrees. Ranged against them was another group, which we might tentatively call the "capitalist roaders," using the term of abuse coined by Mao for his enemies, coalesced around Zhou Enlai and Deng Xiaoping. They similarly argued that they were inheritors of Mao's wishes, but as would only later become apparent, were prepared to twist his words in unexpected directions. The phrase they chose to cling to in Mao's works was itself a quote from the ancient *Book of Han*: "Seek the truth from facts." In other words, they would argue, Mao himself would change his policies if faced with overwhelming evidence. The Cultural Revolution has been a "mistake," and it was time to find a new way forward. In asking what Chairman Mao would have done, how would he have adapted to fit modern conditions, the reformists hoped to do just what Mao had warned against—to dismantle the revolution in the guise of continuing it.

For a while, it seemed like the Gang of Four had the upper hand. Zhou Enlai died in January 1976, depriving the reformists of their most powerful figurehead. Then again, anyone in an obvious position was too easy a target. The tussle over the succession to Mao would be won by Deng Xiaoping, a former Finance Minister and chairman of several minor commissions, who would never hold the highest offices in China. Neither president, nor prime minister, nor even ceremonial head of state, Deng Xiaoping was able to cling to power from the shadows while his higher-profile rivals fought in public.

Mao died in September 1976. Jiang Qing, a well-known fan of Empress Wu, argued that she should inherit her husband's chairmanship and carry on his good works. But economic power-brokers and military factions were allied with the reformists, and the Gang of Four were soon arrested.

Only Jiang Qing tried to defend herself during the ensuing show-trial.

"I was Mao's dog," she shouted. "When he said '*Bite!*' I bit!"

Her death sentence was commuted to life imprisonment. A decade later, in 1991, she hanged herself at the hospital where she was being treated for throat cancer. She left a suicide note that was the last word on the Mao era: "Today the revolution has been stolen by a revisionist clique... unending evils have been unleashed upon the Chinese people and nation."

# CHAPTER 11

# INTERESTING TIMES: THE CHINA DREAM

N anjing, 2010. It's another episode of the new game show *If You Are the One*, in which suitors line up to fire questions at aspiring celebrities. You might call it car-crash television—the press and the TV censors repeatedly criticize it for its dubious morals and materialist message, but 50 million people keep tuning in anyway. Outside it is winter, but the contestants are dolled up for a cocktail party, and Zhao Chen, our eager bachelor in an ill-fitting jacket, has winnowed the field of twenty-four down to three perky girls.

First question: Why did they break up with their ex-boyfriends? A series of vague complaints soon arises—he was too stubborn; he wanted me to quit my job; he was irresponsible. Zhao Chen asks for clarification, but it's not clear who he's asking, because his eyes keep drifting away from the girl he is facing, to the busty, red-clad Ma Nuo, an aspiring underwear model draped with jewelry and diaphanous silk.

This, it seems, is cause for funny boinging noises on the soundtrack, as the producers desperately try to wring some entertainment from this conversation. But one of the girls says that she's seen the bachelor bicycling on social media, and she would happily pedal around on a bike with him if they were poor.

He's got one more question, so it's a simple one. Would the other girls like to laugh with him on the back of a bike?

"I'd rather cry in the back of a BMW!" giggles Ma Nuo.

The moment passes in an instant. She finds it more funny than anyone else, and it could have easily evaporated, unnoticed, into the ether. But when we're back from the commercial break, the bachelor inexplicably chooses her, reciting a trite, rehearsed homily about how she is beautiful on the inside as well as the outside, and how he will move to Beijing, where she lives, and look for a job soon.

Even Ma Nuo stares at him in disbelief, and when pressed, she gingerly says: no, he is plainly not the man for her.

"Right then," says the host. "On your bike!"

"I don't think she understood me," stammers Zhao Chen in his exit interview, before the show rolls on with 24 girls and one new hopeful bachelor.

The incident turned Ma Nuo into one of the icons of contemporary China, for good or ill. Detractors were swift to call her a shallow gold-digger, impressed only by wealth—the Chinese term for a BMW is, coincidentally "Treasure Horse" (baoma), which only made her comment seem all the more money-minded. Linguists debated if she had actually said "A BMW would be cooler," which made her sound a little less soulless. Sociologists observed how times had changed, from when the bicycle was once a ubiquitous mode of Chinese transport, to modern times when every city was clogged with cars.

Defenders, including some of her fellow contestants, protested that she was only stating an unwelcome truth: that the youth of the 21st century were under immense pressure to succeed. So many parents, with an eye on retirement, were leaning heavily on their sole child to find riches and marry well. There was simply no space in modern life for airy, Western-influenced romantic notions. Ma Nuo, like every other girl of her generation, needed to grab enough wealth with both hands to support her parents and protect her future, so… no. She was not going to ride off with a jobless guy on a bike.

Steely and pragmatic, Ma Nuo initially protested that she was merely flailing around for something funny to say—a suitable sound bite that played on the vehicular theme that had arisen. But even that explanation incited media ire, as it only served to remind everyone that *If You Are the One* was nothing but pointless noise and filler in between the adverts.

The BMW controversy would run and run. A month later, a smarmy rich kid bragged on the show that he had a personal fortune of six million yuan and owned three racing cars. Maybe, he suggested cheekily, Ma Nuo would like to come and cry in the back of one of them.

And then, that April, Ma Nuo faced a self-appointed spokesman for the people of the Internet, a bachelor from Shanghai called Luo Lei, who laid into her about her "picky demands" and for wasting a slot on a program that could better serve someone who was genuinely looking for love. She would be better off in a beauty pageant for millionaires, he sneered, causing his target to bolt from the stage in tears.

The show's blatant grandstanding and manipulation was a matter of some annoyance for the State Administration for Film, Radio and Television, which chided it that June for promoting "immoral people and unhealthy ideas." A Chinese retread of the foreign dating show *Take Me Out*, the program only survived by radically toning down its calculated provocation. In the meantime, *If You Are the One* inadvertently served as a barometer of modern Chinese demographics, as a large, fickle population of women gets to set an ever higher bar for the suitors who outnumber them. China has an "army of bachelors"—by the year 2020, an estimated 30 million more men than women.

$$\odot - \odot - \odot - \odot - \odot$$

The 1979 One-Child Policy was one of the last great Communist exercises in social engineering, one of the more obvious reversals of Mao's own policies, which had encouraged the rapid growth of the Chinese population. It bore all the hallmarks of earnest Communist policy—on paper, a brutally efficient means of streamlining the population and controlling resources. In reality, an initiative that created huge new demographic issues for China, and wreaking havoc on families that will play out for generations.

It was officially known as the Family Planning Policy, since only normal Han-majority families were restricted to single children. Ethnic minorities and families with a disabled child or parent in "special circumstances" were permitted to have more, as was anyone with the wherewithal to beat the system—enough money to pay the escalating punitive fines, for example, or a foreign home where they could have non-Chinese children across the border. In theory, it was a generation-long limit on population growth to prevent the drain on resources caused by 400 million extra births. In practice, it played havoc with the Chinese traditions that Communism claimed to have eradicated. Boys were still worth more than girls—not merely on the farm, but in the marriage market. If a family's lone child was a daughter, destined to marry out, who would care for her parents and grandparents in their old age? Policy-makers in most provinces started to fudge the system by the mid-1980s, allowing even Han Chinese the leeway to have a second child if the first turned out to be a daughter.

The effect on the position of women was mixed. At a medical, physical level, there were many forced abortions and sterilizations—promotion within certain government offices and in certain professions was sometimes contingent on it. There was also the implication that despite the claims of the state that women and men were entirely equal, that female children were second-class. "A girl is just as good as a boy," government slogans proclaimed from walls and signposts.

For many families, a lone female child became the focus and fulcrum of several generations' ambition and hopes. China experienced a huge surge in female university graduates, as families that might have once invested more heavily in their male offspring had nowhere else to turn. But there was also a surge in unwanted girls, dumped on orphanages, unregistered, by rural parents who hoped to try again for a boy. Many such girls were adopted abroad, while the treasured boys stayed behind, eventually outnumbering Chinese women. If Ma Nuo seemed picky and demanding, that's because she, and an entire generation of Chinese women like her, could afford to be.

They were created by a generation of economic growth unprecedented in Chinese history, as the survivors of the Cultural Revolution stood on the ruins and implemented a carefully-worded retraction of many of Mao's policies. The Communist Party remained the governing body of the People's Republic, but in the 1980s and 1990s, China increasingly adopted a system best described as "state-capitalism." The Party remained instrumental in organization, management and even ownership of many enterprises; it was often impossible to get things done without Party sanction. But the Party now approved of private enterprise for the betterment of the state. "It does not matter," said Vice-premier Deng Xiaoping (1904–97), "if a cat is black or white, so long as it catches mice."

The last man standing after the death of Mao and the downfall of the Gang of Four, Deng never officially held a paramount office in China—he was never the ceremonial head of state or even Party secretary. He was, however, widely acknowledged as the man who held the true reins of power throughout the 1980s, letting others seize the limelight and, if necessary, take the fall. He put into action the long-mooted plans of his late mentor, Zhou Enlai, for Four Modernizations—improvements in Agriculture, Industry, National Defense and Science/Technology. Deng had seen first-hand on foreign trips just how far China lagged behind, not only the capitalist west, but also revisionist Communist regimes like Yugoslavia. "Recently our comrades had a look abroad," he said in 1978. "The more we see, the more we realize how backward we are."

Deng kept up appearances by phrasing everything in terms of Mao's political cult. Even as he dismantled much of the apparatus of the previous generation, Deng Xiaoping was keen to stress it was business as usual. Refusing to do to Mao what the Soviets were doing to Stalin, he offered a compromise: Mao was 70% good and 30% bad. He made some mistakes, to be sure, but he was still the sun in our hearts. The percentages were a nice touch—they made it sound less like a dismissive shrug at the expense of millions dead, and more like a statistically verified, scientific opinion, as if Santa's elves had been totting up all the evidence as to who had been naughty or nice.

Deng's take on Mao was of a leader who achieved great things when he had the right information at hand, who would have radically changed his position under contemporary conditions. This was not actually true— Mao had repeatedly stuck to his guns even when it was sure to cost millions of lives, and he had even bragged that the sacrifice was worth it. But Deng was speaking to a population that was ready to hear him out if he had found a way.

Deng wanted to use the money of the capitalist world to bolster China's economy. The booming Japanese miracle was his touchstone, although he was careful not to allude too often to China's old enemy. Instead, he fixated on Hong Kong, the prosperous colony just across the border, where an ethnic Chinese population was thriving under capitalism. Deng met Hong Kong head-on by establishing the Shenzhen Special Economic Zone, a strip of factories and industrial plants right along the border, offering cheap Chinese labor to foreign entrepreneurs. The Japanese, in fact, were the single largest source of investment in China for much of the 1980s, although the optics looked better if the "foreigners" rebuilding local businesses were overseas Chinese from Singapore or the United States.

By 1982, Deng had reversed the mass collectivization on Chinese farms, encouraging agricultural laborers to return to private enterprise.

Early incentives for the chemicals industry brought cheap access to fertilizers, helping to generate a grain harvest in 1984 that was 25% higher than the year before. Instead of buying all rice at a fixed rate, the Chinese government let the market run free, causing a boom in market gardens, crop substitutions and cash crops.

His greatest coup was Hong Kong itself, the return of which to Chinese sovereignty he successfully negotiated with Britain in the mid-1980s. Chairman Mao had previously acted as if all treaties made before the declaration of the People's Republic were void, suggesting that Chinese territory remained within the borders it had in 1949—the Siberian coast now part of Russia, Outer Mongolia now independent. Portugal itself had offered to return Macau (a transfer eventually arranged in 1999).

But Hong Kong was a special case, since while the island itself had been ceded to Britain in perpetuity in 1842, the nearby New Territories had only been leased in 1898, for 99 years. Realtors and mortgage lenders wanted to know if this was still in effect, because it seemed impossible to extricate Hong Kong Island, a British possession, from the larger area to its north that held most of its water and power stations.

The Joint Sino-British Declaration of 1984 agreed that all of Hong Kong would be returned to China in 1997, but that the area would be a "Special Administrative Region," with special laws and concessions until 2049. For the British, this was a reasonable fudge, since as times had already shown, a lot could happen in 50 years. The Chinese were also pleased with the result, although many of the people of Hong Kong complained over their own marginalization from negotiations concerning their own future. Since many of them were denied British passports, the handover amounted to swapping one set of unelected masters for another—concessions were made in the newly drafted Hong Kong Basic Law for some level of local autonomy, although its implementation and practice has been a matter of some controversy ever since.

For Deng, the deal over Hong Kong was a message to the Republic of China on Taiwan, which he had sincerely hoped would reach a similar deal with the People's Republic in his own lifetime. Chiang Kai-shek's intractable son, Chiang Ching-kuo had bolstered his position in 1979 with the Three No's—proclaiming that there would be No Contact, No Compromise and No Negotiation with the People's Republic. Martial law on Taiwan was only lifted in 1987, the year before Chiang Ching-kuo's death, and Deng may have hoped that the subsequent opening of Taiwan to opposition party democracy might encourage a local faction to push against the Nationalists' position. Instead, Taiwanese politics drifted closer to an assertion of the island's de facto independence, causing both Nationalists and Communists to reiterate that there was only One China. Taiwan's position in political limbo, a prosperous Chinese province somehow disconnected from the rest of China, continues to this day.

"We shall try our best to achieve the peaceful reunification of China since Chinese should not fight Chinese," said Deng's successor, Jiang Zemin in 1995. "We do not promise not to use force. If used, force will not be directed against our compatriots in Taiwan, but against the foreign forces who intervene in China's reunification and go in for 'the independence of Taiwan.'" Despite being radically opposed to one another, both the Nationalists and Communists could apparently agree on that.

Deng's reforms were roughly contemporary with those of Mikhail Gorbachev in the Soviet Union, although as far as he was concerned Gorbachev had gone too far by pushing for political as well as economic change. Communist Party hard-liners complained that Deng's underhand capitalism might well be creating short-term benefits for those prepared to "jump into the sea" (*xia hai*—contemporary slang for taking a leap of faith away from the old ways), but surely capitalism was the enemy that had almost ruined China in the 19th century? Already there were signs of rural populations moving to towns in search of more opportunity, and rising crime rates. Deng pleaded with his critics to give it a few years and see what happened, emphasizing at all times the success stories, and not the accompanying tales of bankruptcies and inflation.

There were plenty of reversals and about-faces. Like Mao before him, Deng called for the people to offer constructive criticism when it suited him to solicit grass-roots support for dealing with political rivals. A patch of wall near a central Beijing bus stop soon transformed into a "Democracy Wall" of dissenting pamphlets and posters, but was shut down in 1979 when its lively subculture began to turn into active protests. Where, asked Deng's most prominent critics, was democracy itself, the unspoken Fifth Modernization that they had been promised since the May Fourth Movement?

The closure of the Democracy Wall was clarified by Deng in a statement designed to appease the hardliners. However strange his reforms might appear to be, they were not to be met with media criticisms of the

Communist Party, Chairman Mao or the Communist Party itself. Even if they looked like capitalism, Deng's reforms were firmly intended in the service of the Communist state.

"You have to use a two-fisted approach," Deng said. "With one hand, you grab reform and opening. With the other, you grab every kind of criminal behavior. You have to have a firm grip with both hands." Much of the argument in the ensuing decades of Chinese society has been about the nature of such criminality.

Deng's reforms created a multi-headed hydra of dissenters, assembling in Tiananmen Square on May 4, 1989, under the guise of mourning a recently departed Party dignitary, but refusing to leave and camping out for a month. Many of the protesters were students who felt that Deng's reforms had not gone far enough, either in policing corrupt officialdom or in implementing democracy—an always-difficult issue in the People's Republic, where the rule of the Communist Party was regarded as the ultimate and final implementation of the will of the people. It was this faction that erected the hastily constructed effigy of a "Goddess of Democracy," holding a torch aloft, defiantly facing the portrait of Mao himself on the front of the Tiananmen gate. But others in the Square were laid-off workers protesting that Deng's reforms had gone too far, and demanding greater state controls.

Some of the protesters in the square sung "The Internationale," a Communist anthem establishing them firmly as inheritors and supporters of the ideals of the People's Republic, but insinuating that perhaps Deng had lost his way:

> Stand up all victims of oppression
> For the tyrants fear your might
> Don't cling so hard to your possessions
> For you have nothing if you have no rights.

Others, however, found a touchstone in a much more recent song, 'Nothing to My Name' (*Yi Wu Suoyou*) by the pop star Cui Jian, who came to the Square to sing to the crowds, leading to a ban on him performing in Beijing for much of the following decade. Framed as an unrequited love poem, sung by a boy to a girl who spurns his advances, the song evokes a sense of loss and marginalization.

I have asked you endlessly, will you go with me?
But you always laugh at me
I have nothing to my name.

I want to give you my dreams and my freedom
But you always laugh at me
I have nothing to my name.

Its proverbial title contains a double meaning. "*Yi Wu Suoyou*" contains no subject; it could be a lament that boy is poor, but it could equally be a comment that both of the couple are missing out—on money, on success, on opportunity. He could be complaining that he has nothing to his name, or he could be commenting on their shared situation—*neither* of them has anything. Both are being swindled by powers beyond their control.

Beijing was not the only site of protests, but it was the location most likely to be covered by foreign journalists when the People's Liberation Army arrived to restore order with tanks and tear gas. The mayor of Shanghai, Jiang Zemin, managed not only to shut down protests in his city, but also to keep a lid on media coverage. Beijing supplied most of the iconic imagery of the incident, as the Goddess of Democracy was torn down, wounded civilians were rushed to hospitals and morgues, and one unknown man was filmed, shopping bags in hand, playing chicken with a column of tanks.

But the Tiananmen Square Incident of 1989 is remarkable by its absence from Chinese media ever since. It has been scrubbed from newspapers and the Internet, and even mentioning the date on social media leads to swift censorship. This reflects the iron hand of Jiang Zemin, who would serve as President of China from 1993–2003, although he had other roles to play.

The post of Chairman of the Communist Party was abolished in 1982, but subsequent political leaders have usually amassed several appointments at once, in order to achieve paramount leadership. The People's Republic has four high-level offices—the President is the notional head of state, but intended as something of a ceremonial figurehead. The Premier of the State Council holds an executive role more like that of a Prime Minister. The General Secretary of the Communist Party is more powerful than either, since there is only one Party worth speaking of in Communist China. But the Chairman of the Military Commission, in controlling the

People's Liberation Army, is also a powerful role.

It was with Jiang Zemin that this careful separation of powers came to be thwarted, with one man taking on multiple roles, much as Mao had done in his heyday. Jiang Zemin was the President but also the Chairman of the Central Military Commission. His successor Hu Jintao served as President from 2003–13, but was *also* General Secretary of the Communist Party and Chairman of the Central Military Commission.

Hu Jintao's era saw the fruition of many of his predecessors' schemes. China joined the World Trade Organization in 2001, and hosted the Olympics in 2008, marking its integration further into the international community. The buzz-word for Hu's period in office was *hexie* (harmony), in recognition of his constant return in his speeches to a concept of a "Socialist Harmonious Society."

Hu's focus on harmony was in part a return to traditional values, recalling the pronouncements of Confucius on duty and social conscience, but also contained more sinister echoes of the Mao era—if harmony was the goal, then any form of dissent risked ruining it. A citizen of Hu's China needed to learn not to rock the boat, to play along with whatever changes such harmony would require. Taken to extremes, Hu's definition of harmony might include, say, censoring news reports of a dangerous new disease, as happened when Severe Acute Respiratory Syndrome (SARS) broke out in 2002.

China's increased interaction with the outside world, and the onward march of technology also brought the country into contact with the Internet, which risked exposing Chinese citizens to uncensored dissent, pornography, fake news and, who knows, maybe even real news. China's response to the threat presented by social media has been the so-called Great Firewall, a series of Internet censorship initiatives included automated bots searching for proscribed topics (Dalai Lama, the date of Tiananmen, Voice of America…), the Golden Shield organization which uses tens of thousands of human monitors to police online content, and Green Dam Youth Escort, which was an attempt to create a nanny software program that would come preloaded on Chinese computers, ready to shut down a list of forbidden sites and stop surfers from seeing photographs with too much pink in them. This came unstuck when it proved to block not only Western pornography, but also pictures of pigs. Hu Jintao himself called for concerted efforts to reinforce "ideological and public opinion," resulting in the hiring of legions of online Party stooges, charged with cor-recting counter-revolutionary statements on online forums, calling out disharmonious activities, and spreading a more pro-Party message. Based on an apocryphal belief that they received 50 *fen* per posting (about 7 U.S. cents), they became popularly known as the 50-centers, although they are also termed the Net Critical Monkeys (*wang ping yuan*), or the Net Navy (*wang haijun*), tasked with "flooding" social media with approved mes-sages. Reflecting the capacity of the Internet, even in its limited Chinese reach, for endless invention, such satire has become the nexus of a whole subculture, mythologizing the monkey-wrenching tactics of dissident "al-pacas" (the term in Chinese, *cao ni ma*, is a pun in Chinese on motherf*ckers), versus the pious, conservative censorate of the "river crabs" (in Chinese, a pun on *hexie*, harmony itself).

But such wrangles do not reflect a fear of the Internet—instead, they demonstrate how much the Communist Party appreciates its worth. The Internet, after all, helped create China's wealthiest man, Jack Ma, whose Alibaba Group became an e-commerce powerhouse. It also affords im-mediate contact between the Party and the "mass line" of public opinion, when flame-wars and online allegations against public figures or corporate malfeasance, can manifest with sudden real-world consequences. Far from being out of touch, the Communist Party seems to be at the cutting edge of social media engagement, which is why it takes memes so seriously. In 2010, it was dragged into a war of words with the U.S. Embassy in Beijing, which ran a Twitter account posting regular updates on levels of air pol-lution. In 2011, it even clamped down on the traditional Chinese song "Jasmine Flower," after overseas dissidents began encouraging pro-democ-racy campaigners to adopt it as a ringtone in homage to the Jasmine Rev-olution that had struck Tunisia that same January.

Technically, however, China is not a "one-party state." Today's Com-munist Party occupies 2,119 of the 2,980 seats on the National People's Congress, but there are still eight legally recognized minor parties, such as the China Party for Public Interest, founded in San Francisco in 1925, which represents the interests of returned overseas Chinese. The Taiwan Democratic Self-Government League, formed of Communist exiles from Taiwan, still sends 29 members to the National Party Congress. The Jiusan Society, formerly the Democracy and Science Forum, similar has just over a hundred representatives on the council, but all these groups are political minnows compared to the Communist Party. With its own army, a national membership of more than 89 million people, and 71% of the congress seats, the Communist Party holds all the cards, and allows the smaller interest groups to remain as long as they approve all its policies.

We can actually learn a lot more from the parties that are *banned* in modern China, which include the Democracy Party (founded 1978) that called for truly free elections, the Union of Chinese Nationalists (founded 2004) that favored a return to the Republic of China, and most telling of all, the anti-revisionist Maoist Communist Party (founded 2008), that wanted to dismantle all the reforms since 1979. China has undoubtedly transformed radically since the days of Mao's "Permanent Revolution," which is why it is all the more surprising that more recent Party rhetoric has so strongly reasserted its Marxist-socialist credentials.

President Xi Jinping (b.1953) came to power in 2012 through the same method as his recent predecessors, by acquiring the triple basket of political positions—head of the state, the Party and the armed forces. He also refused to anoint an obvious successor among his deputies, thereby establishing that he was just about to break with the new protocols of power. Although he should have expected to resign in 2022 after serving two five-year terms, the Party agreed in 2018 to suspend the term limits imposed after the disaster of the Mao era. For better or worse, Xi is now, like Mao before him, the public face of an entire era and attitude, no longer obligated to step down. Health and power politics permitting, he will not only see the centenary of the Chinese Communist Party in 2021, but perhaps even the 100th birthday of the People's Republic in 2049, a few months after his 96th birthday. Whether or not he lives to see that day, President Xi has characterized this as the China Dream (*Zhongguo Meng*)—the glorious emergence of China as a fully developed modern nation, a century of achievement sufficient to wipe out the century of humiliation that preceded it.

The first Chinese paramount leader to be born *after* the Revolution, Xi came with impeccable credentials, the son of the Party official who had welcomed the survivors of the Long March to their Yan-an base. More recent Party propaganda has emphasized the role of Xi's father in supporting Deng Xiaoping's economic reforms, even to the extent of a portrait of Deng listening with pleasure while his "mentor" points at a map of the Pearl River delta.

Xi Jinping Thought, a 14-point policy outline designed to steer China through the 2020s, has been enshrined in the ideology of the Party and the People's Liberation Army, is an intriguing amalgam of the PRC's foundational principles, the touchstones of Maoist rhetoric, and the pragmatic reforms of Deng and his successors. It restates outright the centrality of the Communist Party to the Chinese state, and its rulership over the People's Liberation Army. It promises a continued "comprehensive deepening of reforms" and the rule of law, and clings to Deng Xiaoping's idea of "socialism with Chinese characteristics"—always a handy bit of boiler-plate to slap on any complaints. Xi Jinping Thought also nods to the idea of a China reunified through peaceful means (a little hello there to the people on Taiwan), but also China's further integration into a "peaceful international environment."

Although Xi began by talking of a China Dream, he soon came up with a new concept intended to make that dream happen. The Belt and Road Initiative was a scheme designed to generate new markets and opportunities for Chinese goods and services, through Central Asia to Europe, but also across the Indian Ocean to Africa. Infrastructure investment alone amounted to up to US$4 trillion, creating road and rail links along a new "Silk Road." China was by no means the only country in the 21st century to attempt to influence Central Asian economics, but it certainly invested more than anyone else, and more productively. The Belt and Road Initiative allowed China's construction industry to find new markets outside China, with soft-power spin-offs such as the likelihood that Vietnam's high-speed rail track gauge, and Myanmar's new power station, and Kazakhstan's phone network, would follow Chinese standards.

The Belt and Road Initiative is a staggering outreach policy, comparable in some minds to the U.S.'s postwar Marshall Plan. It creates jobs for Chinese companies, and markets for Chinese products, but also sets up routes for raw materials back into China. It is so wide-ranging that it often seems to come attached to any new development at all—a Great Bay project designed to link the infrastructures of Macau, Hong Kong and Canton, is somehow part of the Belt and Road, as is the construction of a new railway freight terminal in Xi'an. Attach yourself to the Belt and Road, the belief seems to be, and you're climbing onboard for the China Dream. End points include everywhere from London's Docklands, where a new business hub will cater to Xi's China Dreamers, to East Africa, a vital supplier of ores, oil and other commodities. This in turn creates other spin-offs in dozens of unexpected places. China is investing, for example, US$50 billion in Pakistan alone, more than the U.S. has spent there in the last thirteen years. At least part of the money is to be spent on a highway linking the Indian Ocean seaport of Gwadar with the Khunjerab Pass that leads to China's western border, a route that could slash up to 5,000 kilometers (3,106.9 miles) from the distance that cargo (including oil) has to travel from Africa and the Persian Gulf to Chinese cities.

The Belt and Road Initiative is the subject of enthusiastic back-slapping and optimistic product launches in China proper, where the local media shields the population from any considerations of its possible ill effects. Parallels with the sudden overseas escalations of the British East India Company in the 19th century seem to elude the Chinese, whose own policy documents repeatedly stress that all this is in the interests of peaceful internationalism and mutual benefit.

But let us take Gwadar as a case in point—a simple sea port, the redevelopment of which has been 80% funded with Chinese money. It is painted locally as a success story (the extent of Chinese investment played down by Pakistan's own politicians), but it is in a region contested by a Baluchistan independence movement, and the road to China goes perilously close to Kashmir, claimed by India. China's simple interest in Indian Ocean trade has exposed it to the possible need for policing or even military actions in the Persian Gulf and Pakistan, and risks angering the Indians, who are already jumpy about the "string of pearls"—their word for the chain of China-friendly, China-funded ports that now stretches across the Indian Ocean. Such local issues are repeated in dozens of different ways along the Belt and Road countries, leading some observers to question what action China is liable to consider in order to protect its investments in these areas.

Such talk is frowned upon in China. It is regarded as negative or nihilist to offer doomsday scenarios, even though they are often paramount considerations in the countries in question. It is particularly unpopular in China's border regions where ethnic minorities might have more in common with their cousins across the frontier. The People's Republic has long been fretful about possible Islamic insurgence in Xinjiang, or anti-Chinese protest in Tibet. Its pursuit of a China Dream occasionally pays lip service to ethnic diversity, but would prefer it to be restricted to cultural entertainments and foods, not anything that might be construed as a challenge to the authority of the Party. In the 2020s, social media may come to serve the Party in a way that may transform the nation once more.

Originally outlined as a move to bolster the levels of trust in China's economy, trial runs of various social credit systems (*shehui xinyong tixi*) began in 2015. The ultimate in customer and business feedback, they rate the abilities of citizens to pay their bills and fulfill contractual obligations. Data is also collected on social media, including the sort of posts that an individual "likes," the kind of hobbies they follow, and the kind of company they keep. Barring a sudden reversal of the policy, after 2020, all Chinese citizens could be digitally rated, rewarded or punished, based on these systems. You might think this is no different from getting penalty points on a driving license, but mooted consequences include flight bans on airlines, reduction of Internet speeds, hotel blacklists and exclusion of one's children from the best schools. While some of the scores seem obvious, such as having a criminal record, which is sufficient to exclude an individual from certain activities in many other countries, others seem more arbitrary and politicized. Is it really of any concern to the Chinese government if someone is seen to buy imported Japanese cartoons, cheat at online games, or forget to pay their electricity bill? Apparently, it is. And, of course, there are benefits for those who play along, including queue-jumping for hospital treatment, waivers on rental car deposits and VIP access to exclusive dating sites. When purchasing decisions are apt to influence one's score, does this effectively criminalize smoking or drinking? Will there be new and exploitable loopholes, such as buying diapers or making charity donations to trigger "responsible" flags in mitigation?

In the proposed social credit system, we can see something that is both a return of Confucian rectitude, but also a chilling magnification of the medieval *Ledgers of Merit and Demerit*. Whereas the original ledgers were a kind of moral game, undertaken at the player's discretion, like a points-based diet or a loyalty scheme, the social credit system offers increasingly fewer opportunities to opt out. The government constantly trots out "harmony" as its buzzword, but with increasing pushiness, such that the word *hexie* is transforming in modern Chinese from a noun to a verb. "Oh no," some joker will comment on social media, "I've been *harmonized*." The company you keep, the things you say and do, are subject to approval ratings.

Under ever increasing scrutiny, citizens of the People's Republic are complicit in their own monitoring, as purchases become increasingly logged within digital finance systems, someone's location becomes easier to spot, and even applying for a visa now requires a photo optimized for facial recognition software. In this regard, as in so many other 21st century issues, it would be a gross error of judgment to see the Chinese as somehow backward or remiss—they are, in fact, experiencing a possible future that awaits other societies. Social credit systems have been billed as the pinnacle of the Confucian aspiration for a truly harmonious society, but they are just as readily seen as the culmination of Legalist control, a country that is not only entirely under surveillance, but also with citizens incentivized to monitor each other's behavior, report on deviations from the norm, and put on a constant performance of compliance.

No wonder the ethnic minorities are under increasingly heavy pressure to conform. It is difficult to be defined by one's otherness in an environment that demands everybody be of one heart and mind. China's own sense of its ethnic minorities was codified and fixed in the 20th century, mainly recognizing the divisions of the late Qing Empire—today's ID cards still distinguish between the likes of Han and Manchu, Tibetan and Mongol, but not those Han families who carry genes from Dark-Age Xiongnu or medieval Tabgatch nomads. Today, the Party would prefer ethnicity to evaporate in a shared unity—one nation prepared to dream the China Dream—which has led to occasional attempts to abolish any concept of ethnicity at all.

This has caused some odd about-faces in the way that Chinese history is written. Qiu Jin, the self-styled woman warrior who plotted a terror campaign against the Manchus, remains a heroine in today's China, although modern versions of her story play down her hatred for the people she described as "foreign" invaders. Yue Fei, the national hero who fought to save China from the Jurchens during the Song dynasty, was officially stripped of this designation in 2002, when Chinese school teachers were instructed to stop using it—he could be a people's hero, but not a national one. The problem, of course, was that he had been defending the *Han* Chinese of the Southern Song from the *Manchu* Chinese of the Jurchen tribes. Although the Jurchens would have doubtless approved, that is certainly not how Yue Fei would have seen it, as the words of *The River All in Red*, make all too clear.

Similarly, Koxinga, the "Knight of the National Name" and leader of the 17th century Ming resistance, is now remembered not as a national hero, but as a people's hero, celebrated not for fighting the Manchus (who are now "Chinese"), but for throwing the Dutch out of Taiwan.

Ethnic diversity is a double-edged sword among the Chinese. The Han majority has done what any other elite would do—it has cherry-picked the inventions and cultures of its subject peoples, taken ownership of their womenfolk and songs, and swiftly forgotten that these things were ever considered alien. The Chinese language rolls over everything, knocking the edges off foreign names and words, until Persian refugees and Uyghur Muslims, Russian émigrés and Manchu invaders are all indistinguishable from the rest.

Every now and then, you'll catch a glimpse of China's ancient divisions, in such innocuous places as car number plates, where each province is denoted by a single character. Beijing, of course, bears the character for "Capital," but cars from Shandong province are marked *Lu*, the name of the ancient homeland of Confucius. Plates from Shanxi are marked *Jin*, named for the country whose collapse signified the beginning of the Warring States period some 2,400 years ago. Plates from the modern megacity of Chongqing are marked *Yu*, its name in the short-lived Sui Dynasty in the 6th century CE.

Starbucks and Kentucky Fried Chicken, iPhones and "Treasure Horses" are now part of Chinese history, too. The Family Planning Policy, relaxed in 2016 and liable to soon be reversed in a drive to create more consumers, will echo for decades, not merely in the sudden contraction of families, but in the sudden, exultant releasing of restrictions, and the burden that will place on the country's millennials—the only generation in human history, perhaps, whose members will be obliged to support two children and four grandparents.

We are, say the Marxists, approaching the end of history—the culmination of the long series of conflicts and transformations by which humanity climbs up into perfection. China escaped from the slave society of ancient times, and made it through the feudal era of history, and the capitalist era that preceded socialism. It has its bourgeois revolution in 1911, and then in 1949, its Communist revolution. But much as ancient historians sought to see the growth and decay of dynasties like living organisms, modern Marxists really want to see modern China as a step on the road to utopia. You might think that much of the evidence points to slide back out of socialism and into capitalism, but that would be the wrong thing to say.

Archaeology that supports the approved story, like the military achievements of the First Emperor, is welcome. Discoveries that challenge it, like red-haired mummies in the Taklamakan desert, less so. Even though historians live to confront old presuppositions and challenge pre-existing paradigms, the modern Chinese establishment prefers that history stays locked within the traces that have been put on it, obediently following the path that leads to the present and to the predicted future. There can be no alternative ideas that once flourished and might flourish again, no suggestions that a cherished political icon might have made a fatal error that cost millions of lives. The leaders are the best men for the job. Everything is going according to plan. Everything is equal.

But the ethnic minorities are not equal. Like similar groups all over the world, many of them were starting with the deck stacked toweringly against them—living in the most deprived regions of China, often because that was where their ancestors had been forced to relocate. They, too, want a part of President Xi's China Dream. Many rural residents, Han and ethnic minority alike, have been lured to the big cities since Deng's reforms. The result has been the largest population movement in human history, dwarfing the migrations of the Mongols or the invasions of the Xiongnu, with an estimated 120 million undocumented migrants leaving their home towns in search of work elsewhere. The Chinese population register forbids unsanctioned movement between country and town, depriving these workers of legal residence, social security or education for their children, many of whom are left behind with grandparents. They are officially invisible, although their presence shows at the edges in shanty towns and junk markets, or inexplicable drains on urban water and electricity supplies. The Belt and Road Initiative is intended, too, to improve their lot in life. One might consider that an impoverished area like Kashgar or Urumqi might benefit from a road to Pakistan increasing local opportunities. But so, too, would distant Shanghai, if the increased opportunities in such faraway places reduced the number of desperate migrants coming to town and forming the beginnings of a criminal economy.

Sheer weight of numbers, of course, is not merely an issue within China itself. The size of modern China's cinema audience began to influence world cinema in the 2010s, steering decisions in casting, production and

Contested Areas in the South China Sea

content from film-makers hoping to reach what would become the world's largest film market in 2018. A Chinese middle class, estimated to reach 630 million members by 2022, has exerted a noticeable effect on global consumption, tourism and travel, but also on overseas investments, with real-estate prices sky-rocketing in favorable locations from Wellington, New Zealand to Vancouver, Canada. Venture capitalists of the Deng era spoke excitably of the trade potential of a billion Chinese people all opening a can of Coca Cola every day. Contemporary ecologists are more worried about disposing of a billion empty cans.

Whereas refrigerators, televisions and washing machines were rare sights in 1985, they are commonplace in most Chinese homes. Between 1995 and 2004, the proportion of Chinese homes with air conditioning rose from 8% to 70%. Such signs of affluence make life easier for dwellers in the new suburbs (often reached by one of China's 200 million motor cars), but they also place increasing strain on the power grid. Unsurprisingly for the country with the world's largest population, China is also the world's largest emitter of carbon—the power to run even a Tesla electric car has to come from somewhere, and in China, that still usually means coal. In many cases, China's pollution is generated on behalf of foreign countries—Europe can boast of reduced carbon emissions, but only because it has outsourced so many factories. Unchecked, global warming will wipe out all China's mountain glaciers by the year 2100. Xinjiang, where once there was an inland sea, will get no water at all.

Green initiatives, however, are prominent in Xi Jinping Thought, with energy conservation and environmental protection forming Principles #4 and #9 of his statement of core values. Ironically, a country with an authoritarian government may find it easier to impose blanket ecological initiatives, but one wonders how Xi and his successors will square that with Principle #10, which asserts a strengthened national security. So far, Xi's requirements for national security have included the occupation and militarization of the South China Seas, extending Chinese territorial claims into disputed waters 1,000 kilometers (621.4 miles) south of Hainan, towards resource-rich atolls off the coast of Brunei, pushing it into new disputes with Indonesia, Vietnam and the Philippines.

Xi Jinping's era has every opportunity to usher China into a sustainable, future-conscious golden age, becoming a world leader in renewable energy and sustainable waste management. Unlike a paltry 54% of U.S. respondents in a 2014 survey, 93% of those questioned in Xi's China accepted that global warming was the product of human activity. The next decade of Chinese history will determine if they are able to do anything about it.

The infrastructure investments of the Belt and Road Initiative might bring prosperity to millions of their neighbors and new business opportunities to far-flung markets. Or... China's increased exposure on the global stage might provoke increasingly bitter contests over resources in an increasingly unstable world. Despite its earnest claims to have universal interest at heart, the Belt and Road Initiative might usher in a new era of colonial exploitation, as China clings to its new economic model for consumer-led growth, making many of the same mistakes as the capitalist West it hoped to outwit.

Modern science has given us a radical new perspective on the rise and fall of ancient dynasties, allowing us to see with unprecedented detail the degree to which the cycles of Chinese imperial power correlated with changes in the weather. Volcanic winters, cold spells, mini-Ice Ages and warm periods have all played their parts in events seen by chroniclers of the past as barbarian incursions, crop failures, famines and plagues. Tree-ring data, pollen counts, and ice cores have provided us with compelling data. We translate the term *tian ming* as "the Mandate of Heaven," but in old Chinese it might just as easily be rendered as "Climatic Fate." The best Chinese dynasties prepared for the worst, and tried to shield themselves from fluctuations in fortune, but no wall could ever stop a storm. In an era where humanity itself has inadvertently transformed the weather, we risk a return to the concerns of the most ancient of kings, on our knees before the gods, praying for gentle rain.

# Further Reading

T he opening vignettes in each chapter are sourced from or inspired by books in the bibliography. Cavils with the popular story of the discovery of the Wastes of Yin, as found in the Introduction, derive from the alternate versions in Wilkinson's *Chinese History: A New Manual.* The story of the Beauty of Loulan from Chapter One draws on the archaeology in Barber's *The Mummies of Ürümchi,* and the historiography in Hu and Zhong's *Mysteries of Xinjiang.* The story of the Battle of Muye and the fall of the last Shang king is taken from Sima Qian's *Grand Scribe's Records,* in the Nienhauser translation, and Liu Xian's *Exemplary Women of Early China,* in which both Daji and Baosi, the girl born of dragon spit, are included among "the depraved and favored."

The story of Duke Mu of Qin, whose funeral opens Chapter Two, is told in the *Grand Scribe's Records* and in several sections of the *Annals of Lü Buwei*; the story of his wife pleading for the life of her brother is in *Exemplary Women of Early China,* among the "worthy and enlightened." The importance of Duke Mu's funeral to Warring States authors is discussed in Durrant et al's *Zuo Tradition,* which notes that the author's habit of coming up with prophecies after the fact make it unlikely that predictions of Qin's ensuing slump could have been written after 360 BCE, when it began its unstoppable rise to the top once more.

The brides traded with the nomads, whose stories begin Chapter Three, are featured in Idema and Grant's *The Red Brush.* Transcriptions of Xiongnu names and the scandalous life of Liu Xijun's father are taken from Loewe's *Biographical Dictionary,* with the caveat that some of the facts about him may have been concocted after his attempted rebellion in an attempt to demonize him.

The story of the short-lived Liang dynasty's long-lived Emperor Wu, is taken from Tian's *Beacon Fire and Shooting Star.* His disastrous meeting with Bodhidharma, which opens Chapter Four, can be found in Sekida's

*Two Zen Classics*, and his entry in the Buswell and Lopez *Princeton Dictionary of Buddhism*.

The strange relationship between Yang Guifei, the Precious Consort, the Xuanzong Emperor and An Lushan (Roxshan), which opens Chapter Five, is from Levy's *Harem Favorites of an Illustrious Celestial*.

The strange life and afterlife of Lin Moniang, a.k.a. the goddess Mazu who first appears in Chapter Six, has many versions and contradictions. I have used the accounts in Clark's "Religious Culture of Southern Fujian" and Pregadio's *Encyclopedia of Taoism*.

The story in Chapter Seven of the Renyin Plot, named for the year in which sixteen of the Jiajing Emperor's concubines tried to murder him, is richly detailed in the chronicles of the Ming dynasty but remarkably under-reported in English-language sources—it is, for example, too lurid a handmaids' tale for the *Cambridge History*, despite four pages devoted to Jiajing's Daoist obsessions. The full story can be found in McMahon's *Celestial Women* and Shang's *Tales of Empresses and Consorts*, both of which quote directly from the Chinese chronicles.

The Massacre of Yangzhou, which begins Chapter Eight, is taken from a number of sources collated in my own *Coxinga and the Fall of the Ming Dynasty*, along with direct reportage taken from Shi Kefa's last letters, and the eye-witness account of the scholar Wang Xiuchu, both of which can be found in Struve's *Voices from the Ming-Qing Cataclysm*.

An eyewitness account of the last days of Qiu Jin, which begins Chapter Nine, can be found in Idema and Grant's *The Red Brush*, and Edwards' *Women Warriors and Wartime Spies of China*. Edwards sets Qiu in context as the last form of traditional heroine, and the first of a new kind of female role model—she outlines the fluctuating fortunes of Qiu as an icon *after* her death.

Chapter Ten's opening performance of *The Red Detachment of Women* on February 22, 1972, attended by Richard Nixon, is mentioned in multiple sources, including the President's memoirs and those of his entourage, as well as an interview given by Jiang Qing to Roxane Witke six months after the event, and Harris's article "Re-makes/Re-models."

Ma Nuo's demand for a BMW, which opens Chapter Eleven, is readily found on the Internet, but a blow-by-blow account with nuanced analysis is in Kong's *Popular Media, Social Emotion and Public Discourse in Contemporary China*.

This work is intended for the general reader, and omits detailed specialist discussions or foreign-language citations. When the subjects of mere paragraphs can be expanded by academic authors not only into books, but into specialties that can engulf a whole life's career, it can be useful to make a few recommendations, not just for those who want to know more, but also anyone who has been sputtering in indignation about the omission of entire decades and major historical figures.

Lieberman and Gordon's *Climate Change in Human History* is necessarily brief on the specifics of Chinese weather, but its bibliography is packed with specialist papers such as Su, et al., Wang, et al., and Zhang, et al., which have provided much of my gossip on weather conditions and dynastic collapse. The last-mentioned paper is perhaps the most striking, reviewing the last 1,810 years through the drip-drip-drip effects of monsoon rains on a single stalagmite in a cave in Qinghai. For a more focused study on anthropogenic environmental change in China, see Elvin's *The Retreat of the Elephants*. My comments in the preface about the relative values of a barrel of oil and the requirements in human labor for maintaining a relatively comfortable lifestyle are based on Nikiforuk's *The Energy of Slaves*.

The ever-changing contentions of Chinese prehistory are beyond the scope of this book, but readers who wish to get to grips with its multipolar world will find plenty to enjoy in Underhill's *Companion to Chinese Archaeology*. The genetic data alluded to within the Chinese population is to be found in Feng, et al.'s article, cited in my bibliography. As for the legendary Xia, both denied and affirmed by scholars, these two extremes are best summarized in Allan's *The Shape of the Turtle* and Nivison's *Riddle of the Bamboo Annals*. Quotes from the Xia dynasty are from the Legge translation of *The Book of Documents*.

As legend, archaeology and history finally comingle with the Shang, I recommend Li's *Early China* and Thorp's *China in the Early Bronze Age*. The *Cambridge History of Ancient China* is the go-to source for the time before Qin, after which the Harvard *History of Imperial China* series by Brook, Kuhn, Lewis and Rowe, spans much of the most recent 21st-century scholarship in six accessible volumes. I have had the multi-volume *Cambridge History of China* at my side continuously throughout the writing of this book, but the Harvard series is not only more recent, but also more concise and affordable. The case for Central Asian societies making a substantially greater contribution to China than the records admit, even down to the possible transmission of bronze and chariots, is made most persuasively by Beckwith in *Empires of the Silk Road*.

The Chinese historiographical tradition is rich and multi-layered. Entire books have been filled with footnotes to the *Spring and Autumn Annals* and the *Grand Scribe's Records*. Miller's mind-blowing *Gongyang Commentary on the Spring and Autumn Annals* shows just how much can be implied by single words and simple phrases within the dour reportage of Chinese chronicles. As for a one-stop shop for China's most famous philosopher, Chin's *Confucius* is the best place to start.

To offer a counterpoint to the dry and distanced commentary from the official chronicles, I have chosen to include songs and ballads from some eras. I find these to offer sharp glints of insight into everyday life, and into the lives of women, marginalized in the official histories. Some might scoff that this is about as useful as trying to extrapolate life in the 1970s from the lyrics of "You're So Vain" and "I've Never Been to Me," but I could probably do that, and I invite you to try it, too.

I have made my own translations from the Zhou-era *Book of Songs*, but readers interested in delving deeper into these fascinating snapshots of archaic China are directed to Ha Poon Kim's *Joy and Sorrow: Songs of Ancient China*, which translates the first quarter of the canon. It is recommended not only for its clarity, but for the skepticism with which Kim treats many of the over-wrought attempts by Confucian commentators to read some sort of deeper meaning into simple love songs. Birrell's *Popular Songs and Ballads of Han China* does something similar for the early imperial era, showing us the fake news, gossip and fashions of people who lived more than two thousand years ago. I think it's a worthwhile experiment in a history for the general reader.

Readers interested in delving deeper into the historicity of the Qin are directed to my own *First Emperor of China*, which examines some of the other legends that have accreted around it. As for the Han dynasty, if you like the style of narrative used in Tuttle Publishing's *Brief Histories*, do check out Loewe's *Bing: From Farmer's Son to Magistrate in Han China*, an entirely fictionalized but thoroughly grounded account of everyday life around 70 BCE, as seen through the life of an imaginary everyman.

Lewis's *China Between Empires* inspired me to give the period between Han and Sui a chapter of its own, and his arguments over even such a simple matter as nomenclature are recommended for any reader who wants to investigate further. My two main sources for the period's local color are Yan's *Admonitions for the Yan Clan*, a guide for the southern gentleman, and Yang's *Record of Buddhist Monasteries in Luoyang*, a memoir of the ruined capital of the Northern Wei. The dramatic events of the fall of the Northern Zhou, and the maniacal qualities of its teenage Caligula, are covered in the final chapter of Pearce's "Yü-wen Regime." For more granular detail of life in the Southern and Northern Dynasties, including David Knechtges discussing Shu Xi's *Rhapsody on Pasta*, see Swartz, et al.'s *Early Medieval China: A Sourcebook*.

For the opulence of the Tang dynasty, nothing can quite beat Schafer's *Golden Peaches of Samarkand*. The term "Silk Road" was not coined until the 19th century, but the Tang was unquestionably its height—Tripitaka's adventures in non-fictional form are most readily found in Wriggins' *Great Silk Road Journey*. Beckwith's *Tibetan Empire* is a startlingly original book about the Tang era's mirror counterpart to its southwest, discussion of which is often muted in modern Chinese sources that don't know how to bring up the subject before its conquest by the Mongols in 1244. Wang, et al's *Tibet*, for example, carefully begins then, with Tibet officially becoming part of China, rather than discussed as a separate culture. For the treatment of Li Bai, see Wu's *Four Seasons of Tang Poetry*. For Theophylactus Simocatta's wonderfully evocative account of Tang China, see Yule's *Cathay and the Way Thither*, volume one. My own book on the controversial Empress Wu has been roundly drubbed by many critics for being way too feminist and forgiving of her. I hence recommend it to you wholeheartedly.

Zhang Ruyu's economic appraisal is taken from Shiba's *Diversity of the Socio-Economy in Song China*, which is also my source for Wang Mai's comments on sumptuary laws. As for the rise of nomad power within China, presented within the context of nomad power within Central Asia as a whole, Grousset's *Empire of the Steppes* tells a story that begins and ends outside China, including that marvelous quote from Temujin, which in the 20th century would be stolen and put, almost word-for-word, into the mouth of Conan the Barbarian. For the period specific to the Mongols' activities within China, Rossabi's *Khubilai Khan* and Lane's *Daily Life in the Mongol Empire* are excellent starting points. Regarding Khubilai's most famous acquaintance, Haw's *Marco Polo's China* deals ably with the debates surrounding him. There are those who are prepared to claim that he never went to China; while that was certainly a question worth asking in the 1990s, it has since been well answered, not only by Haw, but also by Larner in *Marco Polo and the Discovery of the World*. I have made my own translation of Du Renjie's evocative *A Peasant Knows Not the Theater*, but you can read the work in full in Xu's *300 Yuan Songs*.

Brook's *Troubled Empire* was a major framework for my coverage of the Ming dynasty—indeed, its focus on the repercussions of downturns in the weather formed a key inspiration for this book as a whole. For an extract from the first Ming emperor's *August Ming Ancestral Instruction*, see de Bary and Bloom's *Sources of Chinese Tradition*. The story of the voyages of Zheng He is told in Levathes' *When China Ruled the Seas*. Further detail on China's maritime technology can be found in Kimura's *Archaeology of East Asian Shipbuilding*. The comments of both Odoric and ibn Battuta are from Yule's *Cathay*, volumes II and IV. For the full story of the Japanese pirates, see So's *Japanese Piracy in Ming China*; as for the Dark Afflictions and previous scares about vampiric creatures in Chinese history, see ter Haar's *Telling Stories*. I feel slightly guilty presenting such a downbeat assessment of the magnificent Ming dynasty, but my conclusions reflect Huang's *1587: A Year of No Significance*, which points out that many of the issues of corruption, decadence and mismanagement that brought the dynasty down were already apparent a century before its collapse. That's not to discount the amazing flourishing of culture in the Yangtze delta; a more detailed summary of the "First High Tide of Women's Literature" in the Ming dynasty, can be found in Idema and Grant's *The Red Brush*.

Struve's *Southern Ming* is a wonderful source on the twenty years of the early Qing dynasty in which loyalists to the previous regime mounted a doomed resistance. Wakeman's two-volume *Great Enterprise* remains the most comprehensive source on the upheavals of the early Qing, which is why I've lifted its title for Chapter Eight. My accounts of modern Qing historiography are from Rowe's *China's Last Empire*, a deliberately revisionist account of China's last imperial dynasty. Space prevents me from commenting on the East India Company except where it touches on Chinese history—for the incredible full story, see Keay's *The Honourable Company*. For the frankly under-appreciated story of Qing successes in Central Asia, see Perdue's *China Marches West*, and for the rise and fall of 19th-century jihad, see Kim's *Holy War in China*. Hudson and den Boer's *Bare Branches* summarizes recent research in the surplus of adult males in

China, liable to have been a contributing factor to the uprisings of the mid- to late-19th century.

Amid thousands of books about the Qing dynasty and China in the 20th century, it is difficult to pin down a shortlist of the truly illuminating. The reader can rarely go wrong with the works of Jonathan Spence, whose achievement is in rendering complex issues readable without compromising his scholarship. To pick just one liable to appeal to someone who has read this far in *A Brief History of China,* his *China Helpers* is an intriguing introduction to the many foreign visitors who came to the Middle Kingdom with noble intentions. Lovell's *The Opium War* is as good a place as any to delve into the incredible story of Qing China's demise, although Stephen Platt's books form a narrative line from the Opium War to the Taiping Rebellion and beyond. For greater insight into extraterritoriality, Clark's *Gunboat Justice* chronicles the whole sorry tale of a century of British and American criminal cases involving the Chinese.

Tang's *Concise History of the Communist Party in China* makes Beijing's case for the incredible achievements of turning China from a balkanized, failed imperial state into a modern superpower, and pleads for mitigation in consideration of 1950s and 1960s "mistakes." But modern Chinese publications are deeply reluctant to engage with the awful human cost of those mistakes. Dikötter's *Tragedy of Liberation* and *Mao's Great Famine* make for sobering reading. Clark's *The Chinese Cultural Revolution: A History* provocatively considers the drab, joyless performances of the era as works of art no less deserving of consideration than any other.

As for the major players in the People's Republic, I recommend Short's *Mao: A Life*, Han's *Eldest Son: Zhou Enlai and the Making of Modern China*, and Terrell's *Madame Mao: The White-Boned Demon*. For an unexpected perspective on the end of the Mao years, see the oddly entertaining *China Diary of George H.W. Bush*. As for the little man who overturned it all and ushered in the 21st century, see Vogel's *Deng Xiaoping and the Transformation of China*. As we move into more recent times, the historian becomes all too aware that events he has witnessed in real time, be it in person or in the media, are difficult to cram into a work of this nature. Louisa Lim's *The People's Republic of Amnesia* is recommended as a greater investigation not only of what happened at Tiananmen Square in 1989, but how the story has evolved in the two decades since. For more granular account of the 1990s and 2000s, glossed over in my haste to close on the most conspicuous transformations of the Xi Jinping era, see Fewsmith's *China Since Tiananmen.*

Since many overseas readers may be interested in seeing what happened to their own beliefs in China, I recommend Charbonnier's *Christians in China*, Pan's *The Jews in China*, and for Islam, Aldrich and Nikol's *The Perfumed Palace.* In a world overwhelmed with first-hand impressions of today's China, I recommend the intimacy of Meyer's *Last Days of Old Beijing*, and the non-Western perspective of Aiyar's *Smoke and Mirrors.*

Chinese historiography (the history of history itself) moves fast. I've alluded to some of the recent spats between academics in this book, and some of the ideological issues underlying certain choices in wording and nuance. Frederic J. Wakeman Jr can be lauded, essentially as the creator of 20th century American Qing studies, and yet also subjected to constant scholarly assault from his students and *their* students in subsequent generations, as they question his assumptions and hold him to account using technologies and methods unimagined in his own lifetime. This is how academic discourse works, but it plays havoc with a "brief history" that needs to tie everything up with a bow. When it comes to modern scholarship on the last 150 years, I hence recommend the most up-to-date, but also most readable textbook I could find, Zheng's *Ten Lessons in Modern Chinese History* (2018), which ably incorporates what she calls "post-Mao hindsight," and takes the story of modern China right up to Xi Jinping. For a glimpse of the policy-making and long-term planning that influences Xi and his government, and a sense of what is likely to be in the next Five-Year Plan and the one after that, Chi's *The Road to China's Prosperity in the Next Three Decades* is a truly fascinating window into the China Dream. As for what happens the day after tomorrow, you'll need the newspapers, and the *SupChina* website (http://www.supchina.com), as well as the *Little Red Podcast* (https://omny.fm/shows/the-little-red-podcast) and the *Sinica Podcast* (https://supchina.com/series/sinica/), which will keep you at the cutting edge of Chinese studies in the 2020s.

# Bibliography

O n the assumption that a reader with a working knowledge of classical sources and modern Mandarin scholarship is unlikely to be reading an introduction to Chinese history, this list of sources keeps to works in the English language that I have consulted or allude to directly in writing this book.

Aldrich, M.A., and Lukas Nikol. *The Perfumed Palace: Islam's Journey from Mecca to Peking*. Reading, UK: Garnet Publishing, 2002.

Allan, Sarah. *The Shape of the Turtle: Myth, Art and Cosmos in Early China*. Albany: State University of New York Press, 1991.

_____. *The Heir and the Sage: Dynastic Legend in Early China*. Revised and Expanded Edition. Albany: State University of New York Press, 2013.

Barber, Elizabeth Wayland. *The Mummies of Ürümchi*. London: Macmillan, 1999.

Beckwith, Christopher. *The Tibetan Empire in Central Asia*. Princeton, NJ: Princeton University Press, 1993.

_____. *Empires of the Silk Road: A History of Central Eurasia from the Bronze Age to the Present*. Princeton, NJ: Princeton University Press, 2009.

Benn, Charles. *China's Golden Age: Everyday Life in the Tang Dynasty*. Oxford, UK: Oxford University Press, 2002.

Birrell, Anne. *Popular Songs and Ballads of Han China*. London: Unwin Hyman, 1988.

_____. *Chinese Mythology: An Introduction*. Baltimore, MD: Johns Hopkins University Press 1993.

Blunden, Caroline, and Mark Elvin. *Cultural Atlas of China*. Revised Edition. New York: Checkmark Books, 1998.

Bush, George. *China Diary of George H.W. Bush: The Making of a Global President*. Edited by Jeffrey A. Engel. Princeton, NJ: Princeton University Press, 2008.

Buswell, Robert, and Donald Lopez. *The Princeton Dictionary of Buddhism*. Princeton, NJ: Princeton University Press, 2014.

Charbonnier, Jean-Pierre. *Christians in China: AD 600 to 2000*. San Francisco: Ignatius Press, 2002.

Chi Fulin. *The Road to China's Prosperity in the Next Three Decades*. Beijing: China Intercontinental Press, 2010.

Chin Annping. *Confucius: A Life of Thought and Politics*. New Haven, CT: Yale University Press, 2008.

Clark, Douglas. *Gunboat Justice: British and American Law Courts in China and Japan (1842–1943)*. 3 volumes. Hong Kong: Earnshaw Books, 2015.

Clark, Duncan. *Alibaba: The House that Jack Ma Built*. New York: HarperCollins, 2016.

Clark, Hugh. "The Religious Culture of Southern Fujian, 750–1450: Preliminary Reflections on Contacts across a Maritime Frontier" in *Asia Major* Vol. XIX, part 1 (2006), pp. 211–40.

Clark, Paul. *The Chinese Cultural Revolution: A History*. Cambridge, UK: Cambridge University Press, 2008.

Clements, Jonathan. *Coxinga and the Fall of the Ming Dynasty*. Stroud, UK: Sutton Publishing, 2005.

———. *Wu: The Chinese Empress Who Schemed, Seduced and Murdered Her Way to Become a Living God*. 2nd Edition. London: Albert Bridge, 2014.

———. *The First Emperor of China*. 2nd Edition. London: Albert Bridge, 2015.

———. *A Brief History of Japan*. Rutland, VT: Tuttle, 2017.

———. *Confucius: A Biography*. 2nd Edition. London: Albert Bridge, 2017.

Cook, Constance, and John S. Major (eds). *Defining Chu: Image and Reality in Ancient China*. Honolulu: University of Hawaii Press, 1999.

Cranmer-Byng, J.L. (ed). *An Embassy to China, Being the Journal Kept by Lord Macartney during his Embassy to the Emperor Ch'ien-lung 1793–1794*. London: Folio Society, 2004.

Danby, Hope. *The Garden of Perfect Brightness: The History of the Yuan Ming Yuan and the Emperors Who Lived There*. London: Regnery, 1950.

De Bary, W. Theodore, and Irene Bloom. *Sources of Chinese Tradition: From Earliest Times to 1600*. Second Edition. New York: Columbia University Press, 1999.

De Crespigny, Rafe. *Fire Over Luoyang: A History of the Later Han Dynasty 23–220 AD*. Leiden, NL: Brill, 2017.

Di Cosmo, Nicola. *Ancient China and Its Enemies: The Rise of Nomadic Power in East Asian History*. Cambridge, UK: Cambridge University Press, 2002.

Dikötter, Frank. *Mao's Great Famine: The History of China's Most Devastating Catastrophe, 1958–62*. London: Bloomsbury Publishing, 2010.

———. *The Tragedy of Liberation: A History of the Chinese Revolution, 1949–57*. London: Bloomsbury Publishing, 2013.

———. *The Discourse of Race in Modern China*. Revised and Expanded Edition. New York: Oxford University Press, 2015.

Durrant, Stephen, et al. *Zuo Tradition / Zuozhuan: Commentary on the "Spring and Autumn Annals."* Seattle: University of Washington Press, 2016.

Edwards, Louise. *Women Warriors and Wartime Spies of China*. Cambridge, UK: Cambridge University Press, 2016.

Elvin, Mark. *The Retreat of the Elephants: An Environmental History of China*. New Haven, CT: Yale University Press, 2004.

Fairbank, John K., and Merle Goldman. *China: A New History*. 2nd Edition. Cambridge, MA: Harvard University Press, 2006.

Fan Ka-wai. "Climate Change and Chinese History: A Review of Trends Topics and Methods," in *WIREs Climate Change*, 2014.

Feng Zhang, et al. "Genetic Studies of Human Diversity in East Asia," in *Philosophical Transactions of the Royal Society B: Biological Sciences*. June 29, 2007; 362(1482): 987–996.

Fewsmith, Joseph. *China Since Tiananmen: From Deng Xiaoping to Hu Jintao*. Second Ed. Cambridge, UK: Cambridge University Press, 2008.

Fish, Isaac. "Why Michelle Obama Shouldn't Meet with Peng Liyuan," in *Foreign Studies*, July 2013.

Geary, Norman, et al. *The Kam People of China: Turning Nineteen*. London: Routledge Curzon, 2003.

Goodrich, Luther. *The Literary Inquisition of Ch'ien-Lung*. Baltimore, MD: Waverly Press, 1935.

Gray, Jack. *Rebellions and Revolutions: China from the 1800s to the 1980s*. Oxford, UK: Oxford University Press, 1990.

Greenhalgh, Susan. *Just One Child: Science and Policy in Deng's China*. Berkeley: University of California Press, 2008.

Grousset, René. *The Empire of the Steppes: A History of Central Asia*. Translated by Naomi Walford. New Brunswick, NJ: Rutgers University Press, 2008.

Han Suyin. *Eldest Son: Zhou Enlai and the Making of Modern China 1898–1976*. London: Pimlico, 1995.

Harris, Kristine. "Re-makes/Re-models: *The Red Detachment of Women* between Stage and Screen," in *The Opera Quarterly*, Vol. 26, Nos. 2–3, pp. 316 –42.

Haw, Stephen. *Marco Polo's China: A Venetian in the Realm of Khubilai Khan*. London: Routledge, 2006.

He-Yin Zhen. *The Birth of Chinese Feminism: Essential Texts in Transnational Theory*. Edited by Lydia H. Liu, Rebecca E. Karl and Dorothy Ko. New York: Columbia University Press, 2013.

Hill, John. *Through the Jade Gate to Rome: A Study of the Silk Routes During the Later Han Dynasty 1st to 2nd Centuries CE*. Cooktown, AU: John E. Hill, 2009.

Hsieh Bao Hua. *Concubinage and Servitude in Late Imperial China*. Lanham, MD: Lexington Books, 2014.

Huang, Ray. *1587: A Year of No Significance—The Ming Dynasty in Decline*. New Haven, CT: Yale University Press, 1981.

Hu Jia and Zhong Xizheng. *Mysteries of Xinjiang*. Beijing: China Intercontinental Press, 2010.

Huang Xinya. *The Urban Life of the Tang Dynasty*. Translated by Tu Guoyuan and Yan Hongfu. Reading, UK: Paths International Ltd., 2014.

Hudson, Valerie, and Andrea M. den Boer. *Bare Branches: The Security Implications of Asia's Surplus Male Population*. Cambridge, MA: MIT Press, 2005.

Idema, Wilt, and Beata Grant. *The Red Brush: Writing Women of Imperial China*. Cambridge, MA: Harvard University Press, 2004.

Johnson, Robert. *Far China Station: the U.S. Navy in Asian Waters 1800–1898*. Annapolis, MD: Naval Institute Press, 1979.

Keay, John. *The Honourable Company: A History of the English East India Company*. London: HarperCollins, 1993.

_____. *China: A History*. London: HarperCollins, 2008.

Keightley, David. *These Bones Shall Rise Again: Selected Writings on Early China*. Albany: State University of New York Press, 2014.

Kim, Ha Poon. *Joy and Sorrow: Songs of Ancient China—A New Translation of Shi Jing Guo Feng*. Eastbourne, UK: Sussex Academic Press, 2016.

Kim Hodong. *Holy War in China: The Muslim Rebellion and State in Chinese Central Asia 1864–77*. Stanford, CA: Stanford University Press, 2004.

Kimura, Jun. *Archaeology of East Asian Shipbuilding*. Gainesville: University Press of Florida, 2016.

Knoblock, John, and Jeffrey Riegel. *The Annals of Lü Buwei: A Complete Translation and Study*. Stanford, CA: Stanford University Press, 2000.

Kong Shuyu. *Popular Media, Social Emotion and Public Discourse in Contemporary China*. London: Routledge, 2014.

Kuhn, Dieter. *The Age of Confucian Rule: The Song Transformation of China*. Cambridge, MA: Harvard University Press, 2009.

Lane, George. *Daily Life in the Mongol Empire*. Westport, CT: Greenwood Press, 2006.

Larner, John. *Marco Polo and the Discovery of the World*. New Haven, CT: Yale University Press, 1999.

Legge, James. *The Book of Documents*. Reprint edition. Los Angeles: Lionshare Media, 2015.

Levathes, Louise. *When China Ruled the Seas: The Treasure Fleet of the Dragon Throne 1407–33*. New York: Oxford University Press, 1997.

Levy, Howard S. *Harem Favorites of an Illustrious Celestial*. Taichung, CN: Chung-T'ai, 1958.

Lewis, Mark. *The Early Chinese Empires: Qin and Han*. Cambridge, MA: Harvard University Press, 2007.

_____. *China Between Empires: The Northern and Southern Dynasties*. Cambridge, MA: Harvard University Press, 2009.

Li, Dun J. *China in Transition 1517–1911*. New York: Van Nostrand Reinhold, 1970.

Lieberman, Benjamin and Elizabeth Gordon. *Climate Change in Human History: Prehistory to the Present.* London: Bloomsbury, 2018.

Lim, Louisa. *The People's Republic of Amnesia: Tiananmen Revisited.* New York: Oxford University Press, 2014.

Liu Xiang. *Exemplary Women of Early China: The* Lienü Zhuan *of Liu Xiang.* Translated by Anne Behnke Kinney. New York: Columbia University Press, 2014.

Loewe, Michael. *A Biographical Dictionary of the Qin, Former Han & Xin Periods (221 BC–AD 24).* Leiden, NL: Brill, 2000.

_____. *Bing: From Farmer's Son to Magistrate in Han China.* Indianapolis, IN: Hackett, 2011.

_____ and Edward L. Shaughnessy (eds.). *The Cambridge History of Ancient China: From the Origins of Civilization to 221 BC.* Cambridge, UK: Cambridge University Press, 1999.

Lovell, Julia. *The Opium War: Drugs, Dreams and the Making of China.* London: Picador, 2011.

McMahon, Keith. *Women Shall Not Rule: Imperial Wives and Concubines from Han to Liao.* Lanham, MD: Rowman & Littlefield, 2013.

_____. *Celestial Women: Imperial Wives and Concubines in China from Song to Qing.* Lanham, MD: Rowman & Littlefield, 2016.

Meyer, Michael. *The Last Days of Old Beijing: Life in the Vanishing Backstreets of a City Transformed.* New York: Walker & Company, 2008.

Miller, Harry. *The Gongyang Commentary on the Spring and Autumn Annals: A Full Translation.* New York: Palgrave Macmillan, 2015.

Mote, Frederick. *Imperial China 900–1800.* Cambridge, MA: Harvard University Press, 2003.

Mullaney, Thomas. "Ethnic Classification Writ Large: The 1954 Yunnan Province Ethnic Classification Project and Its Foundations in Republican Era Taxonomic Thought," in *China Information*, Vol. XVIII (2), pp. 207–41.

Nienhauser, William, et al. *The Grand Scribe's Records.* Bloomington: Indiana University Press, 1994–. Six volumes.

Nikiforuk, Andrew. *The Energy of Slaves: Oil and the New Servitude.* Vancouver: Greystone Books, 2012.

Nivison, David. *The Riddle of the Bamboo Annals.* Taipei: Airiti Press, 2009.

Ouyang Xiu. *Historical Records of the Five Dynasties.* Translated by Richard L. Davis. New York: Columbia University Press, 2004.

Paludan, Ann. *Chronicle of the Chinese Emperors: The Reign-by-Reign Record of the Rulers of Imperial China.* London: Thames & Hudson, 1998.

Pan Guang. *The Jews in China.* Second Edition. Beijing: China Intercontinental Press, 2015.

Pearce, Scott. "The Yü-wen Regime in Sixth-Century China." Princeton University PhD dissertation, 1987.

Peterson, Barbara (ed). *Notable Women of China: Shang Dynasty to the Early Twentieth Century.* London: Routledge: 2015.

Pillsbury, Michael. *The Hundred-Year Marathon: China's Secret Strategy to Replace America as the Global Superpower.* New York: Henry Holt & Co., 2015.

Platt, Stephen. *Autumn in the Heavenly Kingdom: China, the West, and the Epic Story of the Taiping Civil War.* New York: Viking, 2012.

_____. *Imperial Twilight: The Opium War and the End of China's Last Golden Age.* London: Atlantic Books, 2018.

Porter, David. *The Chinese Taste in Eighteenth-Century England.* Cambridge, UK: Cambridge University Press, 2010.

Rossabi, Morris. *Khubilai Khan: His Life and Times.* Berkeley: University of California Press, 1988.

Rowe, William. *China's Last Empire: The Great Qing.* New Haven, CT: Yale University Press, 2009.

Pregadio, Fabrizio (ed). *The Routledge Encyclopedia of Taoism.* London: Routledge, 2011.

Sage, Steven. *Ancient Sichuan and the Unification of China.* Albany: State University of New York Press, 1992.

Schafer, Edward H. *The Golden Peaches of Samarkand: A Study of T'ang Exotics.* Berkeley: University of California Press, 1963.

Schuessler, Axel. *ABC Etymological Dictionary of Old Chinese.* Honolulu: University of Hawaii Press, 2007.

Sekida Katsuki. *Two Zen Classics—The Gateless Gate and the Blue Cliff Records.* Boston: Shambhala, 2005.

Shang Yang. *The Book of Lord Shang: Apologetics of State Power in Early China.* Translated by Yuri Pines. New York: Columbia University Press, 2017.

Shang Xizhi. *Tales of Empresses and Imperial Consorts in China.* Translated by Liang Liangxing. Hong Kong: Hai Feng Publishing, 1994.

Shaughnessy, Edward. *I Ching: the Classic of Changes—the first English translation of the newly discovered second-century B.C. Mawangdui texts.* New York: Ballantine Books, 1996.

Shiba Yoshinobu. *The Diversity of the Socio-economy in Song China 960–1279.* Tokyo: Tokyo Bunko, 2011.

Short, Philip. *Mao: A Life.* London: Hodder & Stoughton, 1999.

So Kwan-wai. *Japanese Piracy in Ming China During the 16th Century.* East Lansing: Michigan State University Press, 1975.

So, Sherman, and J. Christopher Westland. *Red Wired: China's Internet Revolution.* London: Marshall Cavendish, 2010.

Spence, Jonathan. *The China Helpers: Western Advisers in China 1620–1960.* London: Bodley Head, 1969.

_____. *God's Chinese Son: The Taiping Heavenly Kingdom of Hong Xiuquan.* New York: W.W. Norton, 1996.

Stein, Aurel. *Sand-Buried Ruins of Khotan: Personal Narrative of a Journey of Archaeological and Geographical Exploration on Chinese Turkestan.* London: Hurst and Blackett, 1904.

Steinke, Kyle with Dora Ching (eds.). *Art and Archaeology of the Erligang Civilization.* Princeton, NJ: Princeton University Press, 2014.

Struve, Lynn. *The Southern Ming 1644–1662.* New Haven, CT: Yale University Press, 1984.

_____. *Voices from the Ming-Qing Cataclysm: China in Tigers' Jaws.* New Haven, CT: Yale University Press, 1993.

Su Y., et al. "The Relationship between Climate Change and Wars waged between Nomadic and Farming Groups from the Western Han Dynasty to the Tang Dynasty" in *Climate of the Past*, 12: 137–150, 2016.

Subramaniam, Arjun. *India's Wars: A Military History 1947–1971.* Noida, India: HarperCollins India, 2016.

Sun Tzu. *The Art of War: A New Translation.* Translated by Jonathan Clements. London: Constable, 2012.

Swartz, Wendy, et al. *Early Medieval China: A Sourcebook.* New York: Columbia University Press, 2014.

Tan Ye. *The Historical Dictionary of Chinese Theater.* Lanham, MD: Scarecrow Press, 2008.

Taenzer, Gertraud. *The Dunhuang Region during Tibetan Rule (787–848): A Study of the Secular Manuscripts Discovered in the Mogao Caves.* Wiesbaden, Germany: Harrassowitz Verlag, 2012.

Tang Xiaoju. *Concise History of the Communist Party of China.* Beijing: Central Party Literature Press/China Intercontinental Press, 2012.

ter Haar, Barend. *Telling Stories: Witchcraft and Scapegoating in Chinese History.* Leyden, NL: Brill, 2006.

Terrell, Ross. *Madame Mao: The White-Boned Demon.* Revised Edition. Stanford, CA: Stanford University Press, 2000.

Tian Jiyun. *Time-honored Brands in Beijing.* Beijing: People's Daily Press, 2009.

Tian Xiaofei. *Beacon Fire and Shooting Star: The Literary Culture of the Liang (502–557).* Cambridge, MA: Harvard University Press, 2007.

Tinios, Ellis. "Loose Rein" in *Han Relations with Foreign Peoples.* Leeds, UK: Leeds East Asia Papers, 2000.

Tudda, Chris. *A Cold War Turning Point: Nixon and China 1969–1972.* Baton Rouge: Louisiana State University Press, 2012.

Underhill, Ann. *A Companion to Chinese Archaeology.* Chichester, UK: Wiley-Blackwell, 2013.

Vermeer, E.B. (ed). *Development and Decline of Fukien Province in the 17th and 18th Centuries*. Leyden, NL: Brill, 1990.

Vogel, Ezra. *Deng Xiaoping and the Transformation of China*. Cambridge, MA: Belknap Press of Harvard University Press, 2011.

Wakeman, Frederic. *The Great Enterprise: The Manchu Reconstruction of Imperial Order in Seventeeth-Century China*. Berkeley: University of California Press, 1985.

Wang Guochen, et al. *Tibet: 700 Years of History*. Beijing: China Interncontinental Press, 2009.

Wang Xunming, et al. "Climate, Desertification and the Rise and Collapse of China's Historical Dynasties," in *Human Ecology* (2010), 38: 157–172.

Wilkinson, Endymion. *Chinese History: A New Manual*. Cambridge, MA: Harvard University Press, 2012.

Wolseley, Garnet. *Narrative of the War with China in 1860; To Which is Added the Account of a Short Residence with the Tai-ping Rebels at Nankin and a Voyage from Thence to Hankow*. London: Longman, Green, Longman and Roberts, 1862.

Wriggins, Sally Hovey. *The Great Silk Road Journey with Xuanzang*. Revised and Updated. Boulder, CO: Westview Press, 2004.

Wu, John C.W. *The Four Seasons of Tang Poetry*. Rutland, VT: Tuttle, 1972.

Wu Weixi and Zhu Zhaorong. *The Sanxingdui Site: Mystical Mask on Ancient Shu Kingdom*. Translated by Zhao Baohua. Beijing: China Intercontinental Press, 2005.

Xiao, Lily, and A.D. Stefanowska (eds.) *Biographical Dictionary of Chinese Women: Antiquity through Sui, 1600 BCE–618 CE*. Armonk, New York: M.E. Sharpe, 2007.

Xu Yuanchong. *300 Yuan Songs*. Beijing: China Intercontinental Press, 2012.

Xu Zhonglin. *Creation of the Gods [Fengshen Yanyi]*, in two vols. Translated by Gu Zhizhong. Beijing: New World Press, 1992.

Yan Zhitui. *Admonitions for the Yan Clan—A Chinese Classic on Household Management*. Translated by Zong Fuchang. Beijing: Foreign Languages Press, 2004.

Yang Xuanzhi. *A Record of Buddhist Monasteries in Luo-yang*. Translated by Wang Yitong. Beijing: Foreign Languages Press, 2007.

Yule, Henry, with Henri Cordier. *Cathay and the Way Thither: Being a Collection of Medieval Notices of China*. London: Hakluyt Society, 1916. In 4 volumes.

Zhang Pingzhong, et al. "A Test of Climate, Sun, and Culture Relationships from an 1810-Year Chinese Cave Record" in *Science* 322, no. 5903 (2008): 940–942.

Zhang Yingyu. *The Book of Swindles: Selections from a Late Ming Collection*. Translated by Christopher Rea and Bruce Rusk. New York: Columbia University Press, 2017.

Zheng Yangwen. *Ten Lessons in Modern Chinese History*. Manchester, UK: Manchester University Press, 2018.

# Index